Preparing to Teach in Secondary Schools

Preparing to Teach in Secondary Schools

A STUDENT TEACHER'S GUIDE TO PROFESSIONAL ISSUES IN SECONDARY EDUCATION

Second edition

Edited by Val Brooks, Ian Abbott and Liz Bills

Open University Press

Open University Press
McGraw-Hill Education
McGraw-Hill House
Shoppenhangers Road
Maidenhead
Berkshire
England
SL6 2QL

email: enquiries@openup.co.uk
world wide web: www.openup.co.uk

and Two Penn Plaza, New York, NY 10121-2289, USA

First edition published 2004
This edition published 2007

Copyright © Val Brooks, Ian Abbott and Liz Bills 2007

A catalogue record of this book is available from the British Library

ISBN10: 0 335 22534 9 (pb)
ISBN13: 978 0 335 22534 7 (pb)

Library of Congress Cataloging-in-Publication Data
CIP data applied for

Typeset by RefineCatch Limited, Bungay, Suffolk
Printed in Poland by OZ Graf. S.A.
www.polskabook.pl

Contents

Notes on contributors

Ian Abbott is Deputy Director of the Institute of Education at the University of Warwick. Formerly he was the coordinator of the PGCE Economics and Business Studies course and he has taught on a number of teacher education programmes. He has substantial teaching experience in a number of schools and colleges. His research interests include 14–19 education, vocational education and training, education business links and initial teacher education.

Chris Bills was a secondary school mathematics teacher and has worked as a KS3 mathematics consultant in two local authorities as well as spending two years at the University of Central England in Birmingham, as Secondary Mathematics Course Coordinator. His PhD research focused on young children's language and imagery related to mental calculation. He has followed this with research into children's language of explanation and proof. He co-authored *Thinkers*, an ATM publication of activities to stimulate mathematical thinking.

Liz Bills taught mathematics in secondary schools for ten years before moving to posts in higher education. She has been a tutor for secondary mathematics PGCE students for 12 years. More recently she has also taught and coordinated the Core Professional Studies element of the secondary PGCE course as well as being Director of secondary PGCE at the University of Warwick. She has a particular interest in innovative approaches to initial teacher education and has been active in promoting flexible and alternative routes into teaching. Her research interests are mainly in mathematics education and in classroom discourse. She is now a lecturer at the University of Oxford.

Val Brooks taught English in secondary schools and a sixth form college before she became a lecturer in the Institute of Education at Warwick University where she is Deputy Director of Graduate Studies. Formerly, she coordinated the Flexible Postgraduate Initial Teacher Training programme. Her research interests include assessment and initial teacher education.

Jo Crozier was a tutor on the PGCE programme at the University of Warwick from 1993 to 2006 where she ran and taught on teacher education programmes. Her research has focused on the experience of disaffected pupils, including a study of gender issues in relation to school disaffection and disruption with a focus on girls' perspectives of their school experience. Her teaching experience extends from primary to adult education, and includes working with young people excluded or at risk of exclusion from school, both in a community-based unit and in local authority behaviour support provision.

Paul Elliott is Professor of Science Education in the School of Education and Professional Learning at Trent University in Ontario. He formerly coordinated the secondary science PGCE course at the University of Warwick. His early research was in insect ecology after which he taught for several years at an 11–18 comprehensive school in Wiltshire. Recently he has contributed to the international debate on the nature of scientific literacy and is particularly interested in the contribution that news articles can make to science teaching. He has also worked in the UK and elsewhere developing curriculum materials for use in biodiversity education and takes every opportunity to promote the conservation of bats.

Judith Everington began her career as a teacher and coordinator of religious education in Coventry secondary schools. She has been a lecturer and teacher trainer for 14 years and is currently associate professor and course leader of the Secondary PGCE in Religious Education at the Institute of Education, University of Warwick. She has written several RE textbooks and is co-editor of the Warwick RE Project books for Key Stage 1–3 pupils and their teachers. Her research is concerned with the relationship between beginning teachers' personal and professional lives.

John Gordon taught English and media studies in Norfolk and Suffolk secondary schools before becoming a lecturer and course leader for the Secondary PGCE in English at the University of East Anglia, Norwich. His current research interests include pupil responses to heard poetry, aspects of pupil behaviour and initial teacher education.

Michael Hammond has taught in secondary schools both in the UK and overseas. He has worked on several curriculum development projects and carried out evaluations on the use of ICT. He lectures in ICT at the University of Warwick where he has responsibility for a specialist ICT PGCE course and coordinates a teacher research programme. He has written widely on early teacher development, including the book *Next Steps in Teaching* (Routledge/Falmer). He has contributed to debates on the use of ICT in numerous articles for academic and professional journals.

Professor Alma Harris is Director of the Institute of Education, University of Warwick, England and Associate Director of the Specialist Schools and Academies Trust. Her most recent research work has focused upon leadership and organizational change. She is internationally known for her work on school leadership focusing particularly on ways in which distributed leadership can contribute to school development and improvement. Her most recent publications are: A. Harris and J. Chrispeels (eds) *International Perspectives on School Improvement* (Routledge Falmer 2006); A. Harris, P. Clarke, S. James, B. Harris and J. Gunraj *Improving Schools in Difficulty* (Continuum Press 2006).

Dimitra Hartas is a lecturer in special educational needs at the Institute of Education, University of Warwick, and a member of the Psychology and Special Needs Research Unit. She has undertaken research into the collaborative workings between teachers and speech and language therapists, and has evaluated gifted education programmes and government initiatives on tackling youth disaffection and school absenteeism. She has written on children's language and communication difficulties and their impact on social/emotional development, particularly in children with dyslexia.

Terry Haydn is a reader in education at the School of Education and Lifelong Learning at the University of East Anglia. He was a head of history at an inner city school in Manchester for many years before moving to the Institute of Education, University of London, to work in initial teacher education. For several years he was the Director of the Secondary PGCE course at UEA. His research interests are in the history curriculum, the use of ICT in schools, and the working atmosphere in the classroom.

Sandra Howard has taught pupils from minority ethnic backgrounds both in England and abroad over a period of many years. She is currently a programme coordinator for Race Equality and Ethnic Minority Achievement with Coventry Local Authority. In this role she provides advice and support to schools on all aspects of minority ethnic pupil achievement and delivers in-service training on inclusion, race equality and English as an additional language.

Alan Howe is a senior director with the Secondary National Strategy, the UK government's major school improvement strategy in England, where he leads on the Strategy's work on teaching and learning, with a particular focus on support for underachieving groups of pupils. He was National Director for English from 2002–2004, and before that was a regional director for the primary National Literacy Strategy. He has worked as an adviser in Wiltshire and a secondary teacher in Wiltshire, Kent and Australia, and has a particular interest in the development of children's oral language, having been involved in the National Oracy Project in the late 1980s.

Prue Huddleston is Professorial Fellow and Director of the Centre for Education and Industry, University of Warwick. She has a particular interest in the 14–19 curriculum focusing on vocational qualifications, work-related learning and the use of alternative approaches to schooling for those identified as underachieving. Before joining the University of Warwick, she worked for many years within the FE sector and on community and outreach programmes. She is involved in postgraduate teacher training, in addition to which she has been involved in assignments for the DfES, DTI, European Commission, British Council, Soros Foundation, companies, colleges, schools and local authorities. Recent publications include:

P. Huddleston and S.-A. Oh (2004) 'The magic roundabout': work-related learning in the 14–19 curriculum' in *Oxford Review of Education*, 30(1) March: 81–100; P. Huddleston and L. Unwin *Teaching and Learning in Further Education: Diversity and Change*, 2nd edn (RoutledgeFalmer 2002).

Chris Husbands is Professor of Education and Dean of the Faculty of Culture and Pedagogy at the Institute of Education, University of London and a board member of the Training and Development Agency for Schools. He taught in secondary comprehensive schools before working in higher education, and his teaching experience spans three continents. His research interests include curriculum issues, particularly in the teaching and learning of history, and education policy issues; he co-directed the national evaluation of Children's Trusts Pathfinders for the Department for Education and Skills between 2004 and 2007.

Alison Kitson worked in three secondary comprehensive schools for eight years before moving into higher education. She was Lecturer in History Education at the University of Warwick between 2000 and 2005 where she coordinated the history PGCE and undertook research in history education, including the teaching of history in divided societies. She has written widely on history education and was deputy editor of the journal *Teaching History* for three years. She is currently a programme leader in CPD at the Training and Development Agency for Schools where she leads a number of projects, including the revised professional standards for teachers, postgraduate professional development and CPD leadership.

Peter Lang is an associate fellow of the Institute of Education at the University of Warwick (where until 2002 he was a senior lecturer). He has taught, written and researched the areas of pastoral care and affective education in the UK and internationally for many years. He was one of the founders of the National Association for Pastoral Care in Education as well as its journal, *Pastoral Care in Education*, of which he was an editor until 2003. He has co-edited two series of books on pastoral care, personal and social education and affective education. In recent years, his research has included work on affective education in China and Taiwan and circle time in England, Portugal, Italy and Romania.

Daniel Muijs is Professor of Pedagogy and Teacher Development at the University of Manchester. He has conducted a number of large-scale research projects and programme evaluations and has published widely in the areas of school effectiveness and school improvement, effective teaching and learning and school leadership. With David Reynolds, he is author of the bestselling *Effective Teaching, Evidence and Practice*. He is editor of the journals *School Effectiveness and School Improvement* and *Educational Management Abstracts*.

Susan Orlik took a degree in history at the University of London and after graduating she taught in West Africa on Voluntary Service Overseas. She then taught in four different LEAs and for ten years was Deputy Head of a large comprehensive school in Bracknell New Town. On moving to Birmingham in 1990 she worked as a schools' adviser to the City of Birmingham. In 1993 she became for eight years head of a comprehensive school on the borders of Birmingham and Solihull. For the last five years she has worked for Sandwell as a headteacher consultant and for the University of Warwick where she was the tutor for Fast Track postgraduates and now mentor for MA students. She is a School Improvement Partner in two local authorities. In 1983 she was Schoolmistress Fellow at Clare College, Cambridge where she studied post-16 educational provision in Sweden and Norway. She is the co-author of two books.

Kate Shilvock is an associate professor at the Institute of Education at the University of Warwick where she is course leader for the Secondary PGCE in English with

Drama and also leads the Core Professional Studies course. A former Head of English in Warwickshire, she has had substantial experience of teaching in secondary schools across the country. She has also acted as both subject and professional mentor for ITE students in school. She is co-author of *Cross-curricular Literacy 11–14*.

Emma Westcott is a policy adviser to the General Teaching Council for England, where her policy responsibilities include standards, professionalism and the *Every Child Matters* agenda. She has previously held education policy posts with the Local Government Association and the Association of University Teachers. She is a school and further education college governor in the London Borough of Waltham Forest, where she lives.

Acronyms and abbreviations

A level	Advanced level
ADHD	Attention Deficit Hyperactivity Disorder
AFL	assessment for learning
ALIS	A Level Information System
AS level	Advanced Subsidiary level
Becta	British Educational Communications and Technology Agency
BICS	Basic Interpersonal Communication Skills
CALP	Cognitive Academic Language Proficiency
CASE	Cognitive Acceleration in Science Education
CAT	Cognitive Abilities Test
CEDP	Career Entry and Development Profile
CEM	(Centre for) Curriculum, Evaluation and Management
CPD	continuing professional development
CRE	Commission for Racial Equality
CVA	contextual value added
CYPU	Children and Young People's Unit
DDP	Diploma Development Partnership
DfEE	Department for Education and Employment
DfES	Department for Education and Skills
EAL	English as an additional language
EiC	Excellence in Cities
EMA	Educational Maintenance Allowance
EMAG	Ethnic Minority Achievement Grant
EPD	Early professional development
ESW	education social worker
EWB	electronic whiteboard
EWO	education welfare officer
FE	further education
FHEQ	Framework for Higher Education Qualifications
GCE	General Certificate of Education
GCSE	General Certificate of Secondary Education

GNVQ	General National Vocational Qualification
GTCE	General Teaching Council for England
HLTA	higher level teaching assistant
ICT	Information and Communications Technology
IEP	individual education plan
IQ	Intelligence Quotient
ITT	initial teacher training
KS	Key Stage
LAC	Literacy Across the Curriculum
LAL	literacy and learning
LEA/LA	Local Education Authorities are the predecessors of Local Authorities which were introduced in 2004 and 2005
LiL	leading in learning
LSA	learning support assistant
LSC	Learning and Skills Council
MI	multiple intelligences
MidYIS	Middle Years Information System
MS	Mathematics Strategy
NAC	Numeracy Across the Curriculum
NC	National Curriculum
NFER	National Foundation for Educational Research
NLS	National Literacy Strategy
NNP	National Numeracy Project
NNS	National Numeracy Strategy
NQF	National Qualifications Framework
NQT	newly qualified teacher
NVQ	national vocational qualification
OECD	Organisation for Economic Co-operation and Development
OHP	overhead projector
PE	Physical Education
PGCE	Post Graduate Certificate in Education
P-I-P	Private – Intimate – Public
PPA	planning, preparation and assessment
PSHE	Personal, Social and Health Education
PTA	Parent–Teacher Association
QCA	Qualifications and Curriculum Authority
QCF	Qualifications and Credit Framework
QTS	qualified teacher status
RAISE	Reporting and Analysis for Improvement through School self-Evaluation
RE	religious education
SCAA	Schools Curriculum and Assessment Authority
SEN	special educational needs
SENCo	Special Educational Needs Coordinator
SIP	School Improvement Partner
SMART	specific, measurable, achievable, realistic and time-related

SMCD	spiritual, moral and cultural development
SNS	Secondary National Strategy
SoW	scheme of work
SSC	Sector Skills Council
TA	teaching assistant
TDA	Training and Development Agency
WSI	Whole School Initiative
www	World Wide Web
YELLIS	Year Eleven Information System
ZPD	zone of proximal development

Introduction

1 Content and organization

This book has been written for those who are preparing to teach in secondary schools. It is intended to complement your subject studies by covering a range of core professional topics with which all teachers need to be familiar irrespective of their subject specialism. The teaching profession is at a point of considerable transformation: shifting relationships with para-professionals and other adults in the classroom; new ways of relating to other children's services; fresh opportunities created by technological advances; novel approaches to teaching in the light of brain-based research; new thinking on teachers' professionalism and teacher leadership; data-rich approaches to managing school and pupil performance; initiatives designed to personalise learning and ground-breaking research into the potential of formative assessment to enhance teaching and learning. The origins of some of these developments are to be found in academic research. The impetus for others is policy initiative at government level – part of an ongoing drive to raise standards of education nationally. Taken together, these developments have greatly expanded the core curriculum for initial teacher training (ITT). Their implications for those about to enter the profession – the opportunities and challenges they present – are an important feature of this book.

The book is divided into four sections:

Section 1: Becoming a Teacher

Section 2: Core Professional Competences

Section 3: Secondary Schools and the Curriculum

Section 4: Making Schooling Work for All: *Every Child Matters* and the Inclusion Agenda.

Those new to teaching may be most familiar with teaching as a classroom activity. The three chapters in Section 1 seek to broaden your perspective, placing teaching in its wider professional context and drawing attention to issues and challenges that student teachers will face. Chapter 1 addresses your most immediate challenge – that of learning to teach! It draws on research into teachers' early professional development to elucidate this process. Chapter 2 widens the context by exploring the legal and professional framework for teaching, and professional values and practice. Chapter 3 looks beyond your period of initial training, to highlight the range of opportunities, issues and challenges that new teachers will encounter as they embark on their early professional development. A key theme in Section 1 is the importance of regarding ITT not as an end in itself but as the opening phase in a teacher's ongoing professional development.

Having set the scene in Section 1, the nine chapters in Section 2 adopt a classroom focus. They examine some of the core professional competences – the knowledge, skills and understanding – that newly qualified teachers (NQTs) need to acquire. Chapter 4 opens by exploring the fundamental question of how learning takes place. Remaining chapters consider how different aspects of teaching – planning and differentiation, for instance – can be used to support learning.

In Section 3, the focus shifts to the secondary school curriculum. The opening chapter, What should we teach? Understanding the secondary curriculum (Chapter 13), provides a conceptual framework for the following chapters by discussing some of the basic concepts of curriculum thinking. Remaining chapters consider government initiatives across all three key stages of the secondary curriculum (ages 11–19). Ways in which schools provide for pupils' spiritual, moral and cultural development are also explored (Chapter 14).

Section 4 concludes the book by considering major components of recent government policy, *Every Child Matters* (Department for Education and Skills [DfES] 2003e) and the inclusion agenda, under the heading 'Making Schooling Work for All'. As well as examining some of the more enduring aspects of the inclusion agenda such as pastoral care (Chapter 24) and provision for pupils with special educational needs (SEN) (Chapter 21), this section discusses the impact of recent national initiatives, including *Every Child Matters* (Chapter 20), and concludes with an examination of the policy framework within which NQTs will teach (Chapter 26).

2 Ways of using this book

This book can be read in more than one way. It is possible to read it in its entirety, for instance as an introductory text at the start of your training. However, it is really intended for repeated reference throughout a course of study. To this end, each chapter is a self-contained entity, focusing on a specific topic and designed to be read as and when appropriate. For instance, you may read the chapter on 'Planning for learning' when you first attempt to construct lesson plans, whereas you may consult the chapter on 'Using assessment data to support pupil achievement' as part of your preparation for a written assignment on this topic. Chapters are cross-referenced to related material elsewhere in the text to help you to pursue specific interests.

This book is intended primarily for postgraduate students who are preparing to teach in secondary schools. It assumes an educated but non-expert audience. Therefore, imparting basic factual information about topics with which readers may be unfamiliar is an important feature of the book. However, this is not a text designed simply to be read to gain information. Reading is meant to be an active rather than a passive process so readers are invited to engage with the text and respond to it. Various stylistic features are designed to encourage you to do this. For instance, each chapter opens with a set of objectives to be achieved by the end of the chapter. Where we hope to challenge you to think about complex, sensitive or contentious issues, we may ask questions or provide case studies for consideration. Where we want to help you to further your knowledge or skills, we may set tasks or direct you to websites. At a time when professional information is increasingly available online, you need to be able to access web-based information and resources and to deploy a range of new technologies so, as well as making recommendations for further reading, there are references to relevant websites. Practical examples are used throughout to make abstract or unfamiliar ideas concrete and meaningful. Where appropriate, chapters provide a brief historical context or an outline of government policy to help make sense of a subject.

The text contains a mix of tasks, case studies and scenarios designed to help you to address issues that are raised and the practical application of ideas. Occasionally, chapters open with a question or a task, requiring you to engage directly with a topic from the outset. The majority of tasks are designed to be *self-contained* to enable you to complete them there and then, without obtaining additional resources. For instance, if a task requires you to analyze pupil performance data or to evaluate a school policy, a suitable example will be provided for that purpose. You are, of course, welcome to use your own materials if you have some to hand but being able to complete a task will not depend on this in most instances. Some of the tasks do, however, require access to a computer with internet access and several are school-based.

3 A note on terminology

Like all other professional activities, education has its own 'shorthand', which can appear as jargon to those who are unfamiliar with it. Terms which have a specialised meaning in education, separate from their everyday use, are explained at their first mention. Education also has its fair share of acronyms for the uninitiated to become acquainted with! When a commonly used acronym is introduced, it is spelt out in full on the first occasion, with the abbreviation used thereafter. Acronyms and abbreviations are also listed at the front of the book.

Many schools refer to their pupils as students. Trainee teachers are also sometimes described as students. To avoid confusing the two, we use the term 'student' to denote only those who are learning to teach. The young people who student teachers will teach are described as 'pupils' or 'children'.

The aim of this book is to promote a reflective approach to initial training amongst those who read it. We hope you find it a useful aid to your early professional development.

SECTION 1

Becoming a teacher

1

Learning to teach and learning about teaching

Val Brooks

1.1 Learning to teach: the challenge

Learning to teach may turn out to be the greatest challenge you have ever undertaken! This is the conclusion reached by many student teachers when they reflect on their experiences at the end of training. Fortunately, most of them also describe it as one of the most rewarding things they have ever done! The effort required to achieve an ambition is usually in proportion to the personal satisfaction it brings. Goals that are easily achieved rarely bring a sense of real satisfaction whereas hard-won successes are often deeply gratifying. An Ofsted overview report on *Quality and Standards in Secondary Initial Teacher Training* declared that: 'today's newly qualified teachers are the best trained that we have ever had' (2003b: 4) claiming that both the quality of their training and the standards student teachers had achieved by the end of training were higher than ever before. This chapter explores the process of learning to teach, examining some of the reasons why it is demanding and identifying some approaches to teacher development which are enabling the latest generation of new teachers to succeed.

By the end of this chapter, you should:

- be more aware of some of the challenges you are likely to face during training;
- know about approaches which you and those responsible for your training can use to support your professional development.

Many beginning teachers believe that behaviour management will pose their biggest challenge. Will they be able to command an adolescent audience? Get them to listen? Engage their interest? Obtain their compliance? Although the importance of learning to manage classrooms and pupil behaviour should not be underestimated, in reality the challenges are more subtle and wide-ranging than managing the behaviour of wayward adolescents! Indeed, poor standards of behaviour are often a symptom of an underlying problem and improve once the problem is tackled. The following two sections examine some less obvious reasons why learning to teach is challenging.

1.2 The personal challenge

Identifying tacit influences on the way you think and behave

One of the more subtle challenges in learning to teach is that it may force you to examine your own values, beliefs, prejudices and assumptions. This sometimes involves the unwelcome discovery that cherished beliefs or long-held assumptions do not stand up to scrutiny. Becoming an effective teacher may involve changing your personal theories about teaching and learning. Unlearning established ideas can be a difficult, even painful, business especially if you have thought something for a long time or have developed a theory based on personal experience. As Claxton (1984: 169) observed:

> All students when they arrive at a teacher-training course have a personal theory about education, schools, children, teaching and learning; what is important and what is not . . . They have their own intuitive, largely tacit, largely unexamined set of beliefs, attitudes and values that are variously idiosyncratic, partial, simplistic, archaic and rigid.

As Claxton notes, some of the ideas new teachers hold about teaching may be tacit. By this, he means that underlying values, prejudices and beliefs are sometimes so completely internalized that they are no longer part of our conscious thinking on a subject. This is especially true of long-held views or attitudes that have never been questioned. Although these ideas may be submerged, they have nevertheless been found to exercise a powerful influence on the way new teachers think and behave (e.g. Wubbels 1992). Section 1.4 describes two approaches to training which can help new teachers to examine their own tacit influences.

CASE STUDY 1.1

Alan was on his first teaching placement and his mentors had become concerned about the lack of variety in his teaching. Most of Alan's lessons followed the same format: a lengthy introduction which involved Alan standing at the front and lecturing classes followed by a written task which pupils were expected to complete independently, working in silence. Denied opportunities to interact with their teacher or each other, Alan's classes became restive. Alan agreed that his professional development targets should include experimenting with a wider range of teaching and learning styles. Nevertheless, in the classroom he continued to display a preference for whole-class, didactic teaching and written tasks designed to be completed independently and in silence.

What do you deduce about Alan's educational beliefs and preconceptions from this account?

Teaching and one's sense of self

Another reason why learning to teach is challenging is that it involves giving of oneself in a way that entering many other occupations does not entail. This is how Smith and Alred (1994: 106) put it:

> . . . learning to teach is also a process in which people's whole sense of themselves is involved. We are not denying that that there are classroom skills that can be learned . . . the point we are concerned to stress is that the experience of teaching . . . is one in which our feelings, our sense of our identity, our vulnerability as human beings are all involved . . . This, essentially, is what makes the business of learning to teach different from learning to be a gardener or a carpenter or a welder.

This is one reason why ITT is a period of heightened emotional sensitivity for many student teachers. Indeed, it is possible to leave a lesson feeling elated when a pupil remarks: 'That was really interesting, Sir', only to be plunged into gloom by the adverse reaction of the next class to a carefully prepared lesson. Rapid fluctuations in mood can make learning to teach seem like riding an emotional roller-coaster!

There is also an important moral dimension to teachers' work (see Chapters 2 and 14). During training, you are likely to encounter moral dilemmas that force you to wrestle with the rights and wrongs of situations. For instance, during a form group period you might overhear a child complaining to her neighbour about the behaviour of one of her teachers. Realizing that you have heard her, she tries to draw you into the conversation asking your opinion of the behaviour. She has described something that you regard as unprofessional conduct. How would you respond? Alternatively, you may find that you disagree with your department's marking policy which is inconsistent with recommendations you have read in books on this topic and with what you have learnt during university training sessions. Will you mark pupils' work in a way you believe to be correct or adhere to the department policy on this matter? Learning how to handle moral dilemmas will form an important part of your professional development. Chapter 2 explores the topic of professional ethics further.

I have started by identifying some personal challenges in learning to teach but the cognitive demands are equally rigorous.

1.3 The cognitive/intellectual challenge

Subject knowledge and understanding

A sound knowledge and understanding of the subject you are planning to teach is a prerequisite for teaching it competently and confidently (Shulman 1986; Bennett and Carré 1993). Most student teachers devote considerable time and energy to developing or consolidating their subject knowledge during training. Although good subject knowledge is the cornerstone of effective teaching, it is not enough on its own. You will need to develop what has been described as pedagogic content knowledge (Shulman 1986) by learning how to apply your knowledge to make the subject interesting and accessible to children. You will need to understand what secondary pupils like about the subject, what makes it difficult for them and what their common mis-conceptions are.

There are also many generic topics about which all teachers need to know irrespective of their subject specialism – core professional skills like the ability to plan and national policy initiatives which affect all teachers, such as the Secondary National Strategy (SNS).

Core professional skills

The ability to plan, to assess, to differentiate, to communicate effectively, to use questions skilfully and to manage behaviour are but some of the core professional skills required by all teachers. Research into the acquisition of skill has identified several phases through which learners typically pass. Tomlinson (1995: 44–5) argues that they can be summarized, albeit crudely, as follows:

- Phase 1: unconscious incompetence (learners start by not knowing what they don't know)
- Phase 2: conscious incompetence (learners come to recognize that they don't know how)
- Phase 3: conscious competence (at this stage, learners know in theory but apply only with difficulty)
- Phase 4: unconscious competence (involves knowing how to but not being fully aware of what you're doing).

You will certainly experience the first three phases during training although you are less likely to reach the stage of unconscious competence in any of the skills that are new to you. However, there are many other areas of your life where you already display unconscious competence. These are things that you can do without thinking about them but which you would find difficult to explain to someone else.

Task 1.1

Can you identify skills where you display unconscious competence? (This may involve something like programming a piece of equipment where there is a complicated sequence of actions to perform which you can do without thinking because you have done it so frequently before.)

Another challenge that you face is to your ability to make connections between the different learning experiences you have during training. You need, for instance, to be able to see the links between your work on planning and that on assessment or to appreciate the implications of taught sessions in your training institution for prac-tical experience in the classroom. Emerging teaching skills need to be melded in the classroom. Classrooms are busy places, full of lively, young people, where lots of things happen simultaneously. In some respects, a teacher is like the conductor of an orchestra; they orchestrate a lesson, attending to the multifarious elements that need to be managed so that everyone starts together and proceeds harmoniously to a satisfactory end point. The way in which concepts are presented, timing and the pace of progression, who talks and for how long, use of resources, the emotional climate in the room, seating arrangements and noise levels are but some of the elements of a lesson that a teacher needs to manage. Doyle (1986: 394–5) identified six attributes which make teaching a complex, dynamic activity:

- **Multidimensionality** (the sheer number of people gathered in one place who participate in a large number of events and tasks; one event can have multiple consequences)
- **Simultaneity** (Doyle [1986: 394] illustrates the number of things that could be happening at once thus: 'During a discussion a teacher must listen to student answers, watch other students for signs of comprehension or confusion, formulate the next question, and scan the class for possible misbehavior.')
- **Immediacy** (order in classrooms depends in part upon the maintenance of momentum and the flow of events; the pace of events is rapid, giving teachers little time to reflect before acting)
- **Unpredictability** (classroom events take unexpected turns and distractions and interruptions occur frequently; because events are jointly produced, it is difficult to anticipate how an activity will go on a particular day with a particular group)
- **Publicness** ('Teachers act in fish bowls' [Lortie in Doyle 1986: 395]; events, especially those involving the teacher, are often witnessed by a large proportion of the pupils who will use them to make judgements about the teacher based on their handling of specific events)
- **History** (a class that meets regularly accumulates a set of common experiences, routines and norms which form the foundation for classroom conduct; early meetings often shape events for the rest of the term or year.)

These characteristics are one of the reasons why learning to teach is not simply a matter of mastering a set of teaching 'recipes', formulae or rules which can be applied in all circumstances to enable you to succeed. On the contrary, teaching involves making numerous decisions about how to proceed where the choices are not straightforward and obvious. As well as the deliberate decisions that can be made at the planning stage, there are on-the-spot decisions that have to be made as a lesson unfolds. All decisions have to be context-sensitive – sensitive to school policy and procedures, the ability of the group, your previous relationship with a group or individual, a child's personal circumstances, what has happened earlier in the day and so on. It is this complexity, and the centrality of the professional judgement of teachers, which makes teaching both challenging and stimulating.

One of the keys to managing complexity is good advance planning which is the subject of Chapter 5. Although planning is only one aspect of a teacher's job, it has been described as being as: 'complex and cognitively demanding as the practice of medicine, law or architecture' (Clark 1989: 312).

> **Task 1.2**
>
> Take a topic that is taught in your subject at Key Stage (KS) 3 or 4. What factors can you think of that are likely to influence your planning of a scheme of work (SoW) for this topic?

Your list is likely to be a long one! However, it is one that you could undoubtedly extend as your training progresses and you become increasingly aware of factors that influence planning.

Clearly, the demands of learning to teach are multifarious: cognitive, intellectual, personal, moral and emotional. So what types of training will help you to develop on so many different fronts?

1.4 Some of the ways in which teachers develop professionally

Reflection

Reflection is regarded as a very important means of professional development and explains many of the activities you will be asked to take part in during training. A written assignment which requires you to give a critical account of some aspect of your teaching; taking part in seminar group discussions; producing written evaluations of lessons; one-to-one tutorials with mentors following lesson observations: at the heart of all these activities is the ability to reflect upon experience and learn from this reflection. The value of reflection is illustrated by a proverb which compares two fishermen; one has had 20 years' experience and the other has had one year's experience 20 times over. Although both men have been fishing for the same amount of time, one has the accumulated wisdom of 20 years' experience whereas the other still fishes in the same way that he did as a novice because he has failed to learn from experience.

A lot has been written about the role of reflection in teachers' professional development. One of the most influential figures in this field is Schön (1983) who developed his ideas about the 'reflective practitioner' as a result of studying the thinking and practices of different professional groups. Schön's findings led him to challenge a traditional model of professional practice which involves applying knowledge and practising skills acquired during a period of initial training. He found that reflective practitioners continued to develop as they accumulated a store of relevant previous experiences which acted as reference points, guiding their thinking and practices. They also acquired detailed contextual knowledge, becoming increasingly sensitive to the importance of context. He developed two models of reflective practice: reflection-in-action (i.e. during the event) and reflection-on-action (i.e. after the event). These ideas have been very influential in shaping approaches to teachers' professional development. As was noted above, many of your training activities will be based on the importance of providing you with opportunities for reflection-on-action. Reflection-in-action may not be feasible for the reasons identified by Doyle (see p. 11). Simply doing the job will probably demand all of your mental energy at the outset, leaving little mental 'space' for reflection-in-action. However, as you gain experience and start to develop unconscious competence, you will find yourself increasingly capable of reflection-in-action. This opens up the possibility of working on aspects of your teaching which can only be honed by focusing on them as you do them, for instance, allowing increased 'wait time' after you have asked a question (see Chapters 8 and 9).

Challenge and support

In some respects student teachers are like plants, needing appropriate growing conditions to thrive. Plenty of light but not enough water will not produce a sturdy plant any more than being kept in the dark but with plenty of water will help a plant to grow. Similarly, research into teacher development has focused on the importance of achieving an appropriate balance between challenging a student teacher and supporting them. Elliott and Calderhead's (1993: 172) two-dimensional model of the relationship between challenge and support (see Figure 1.1) shows how:

> In the quadrant where challenge and support are both low the *status quo* is likely to be maintained but when challenge is increased without comparative changes in support there is likely to be no growth. In this case the student is likely to withdraw physically from the development programme or, at best, resort to using previously formed ideas . . . There is evidence to suggest that challenge is a necessary component for professional growth to occur.
>
> (1993: 171–2)

Many people will play a part in your professional development. Some, such as mentors and tutors, will have a designated responsibility and others, such as fellow students and other teachers working in a school, will play a more informal role. The notion of a 'critical friend' is useful for thinking about the contribution of others to your professional development. As the name implies, a critical friend offers warmth, support and encouragement but is also prepared to question and criticize constructively. For all those involved in your development, the principle of balancing challenge with support remains an important one. A mentor, for instance, who provides only challenge, thereby obliging students to seek support elsewhere, will not create optimum conditions for growth. You are, however, unlikely to require challenge and support in equal measures at all stages in your training. Research by Furlong and Maynard (1995) illustrates why this might be. Furlong and Maynard studied a group of primary student teachers and identified five broad stages in their development while on school placement.

- Stage 1: Early idealism

  This was characterized by: 'clear, if idealistic, ideas about the sort of teachers they wanted to be, the kind of relationships that they would develop with their pupils, the physical appearance of their classrooms and the classroom atmosphere that they would create' (1995: 74).

- Stage 2: Personal survival

  'Once student teachers began their school experience, their idealism appeared

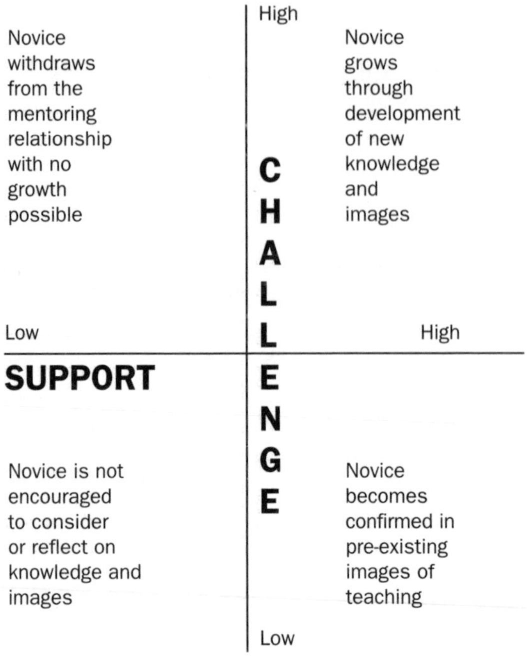

```
                              High
  Novice                              Novice
  withdraws                           grows
  from the                            through
  mentoring                           development
  relationship               C        of new
  with no                             knowledge
  growth                     H        and
  possible                   A        images
                             L
  Low                        L                High
  _____   L   _____
  SUPPORT                    E
                             N
  Novice is not             G        Novice
  encouraged                E        becomes
  to consider                        confirmed in
  or reflect on                      pre-existing
  knowledge and                      images of
  images                             teaching
                             Low
```

Figure 1.1 Elliott and Calderhead's two-dimensional model of the relationship between challenge and support
(Adapted from Daloz 1986)

rapidly to fade in the face of the realities of the classroom, and they became obsessed with their own personal survival. Personal survival meant detecting and "fitting in" with the teacher's routines and expectations, being "seen" as a teacher and, in particular, achieving some form of classroom control' (1995: 76).

- Stage 3: Dealing with difficulties

  At this stage, students learnt to make personal sense of what was happening in the classroom, identified some of the difficulties they faced and gained some measure of classroom control.

- Stage 4: Hitting a plateau

  'Having gained basic competence and confidence in management and organisation . . . there was a noted tendency for student teachers to "relax" a little; their learning seemed to "hit a plateau" . . . Having found one way of organising their teaching that worked for them – they were going to stick with it!' (1995: 89).

- Stage 5: Moving on

  Students were most successful at this stage when they worked with trainers who helped them to understand the need for change. For many students, moving on represented an enormous challenge that was met with varying degrees of resistance.

Findings such as these suggest that student teachers who are at different stages in their development will need varying measures of challenge and support. A student at the survival stage, for instance, will be in most need of support whereas someone who is deemed to have 'plateaued' will benefit most from being challenged. At Stage 5 (moving on), challenge and support may need to be carefully balanced.

The role of reading in professional development

The ITT curriculum has expanded greatly in recent years but the length of courses has remained broadly the same. Consequently, courses have become increasingly intensive and incapable of covering topics in the depth or detail that would be desirable if the curriculum were not so heavily loaded. Independent study is essential to supplement what is covered by taught courses. However, reading is much more than a default mechanism, making good the detail a taught course is unable to supply. Reading gives access to a wealth of information, ideas and alternative perspectives on a topic. Most important of all, it gives access to the wisdom of others, making it the ideal aid to reflection and professional development. In preparation for writing this chapter, I undertook a small survey of some student teachers to enquire into their reading habits. They reported that reading had played an important part at all stages in their training: before the course started; during university-based phases in preparation for seminars and written assignments; and while they were on school placements. They had used reading to deepen their knowledge and understanding; to suggest practical ideas for use in the classroom; to broaden their repertoire of teaching strategies; to seek solutions to problems; to meet targets for professional development; and to develop expertise in areas of special interest to them.

Having identified several approaches to professional development, the next question to consider is how all of this reading, reflection, challenge and support is to be managed so that it makes a genuine contribution to your development. It is possible to end up feeling overwhelmed by possible courses of action, not knowing where or how to start.

Adopting a systematic approach to professional development

One recommended approach to professional development is needs-led (DfES 2002a). It starts with a thorough audit of students' prior experiences, knowledge and skills against the requirements they are training to meet. These requirements include the statutory requirements for ITT that are specified in *Professional Standards for Teachers* (TDA 2007) plus any additional requirements of a particular training course. Initial audits create learner profiles, highlighting strengths and achievements which individuals can build on during training as well as identifying gaps and weaknesses that need to be addressed. This type of baseline assessment allows training to be tailored to an individual's needs and aspirations, and establishes the priorities for immediate development. However, it is essential to go beyond general aims (Black and Wiliam 1998a) to develop specific targets and an action plan for achieving them. The notion of 'SMART targets' is useful because it emphasizes attributes which make target-setting practicable and meaningful (see Figure 1.2).

S	Specific	Specific targets relate to a defined area of competence – perhaps related to one of the standards for QTS
M	Measurable	Measurable targets are couched in terms which allow you to point to evidence that they have been achieved
A	Achievable	Achievable targets are do-able rather than vague aspirations
R	Realistic	Realistic targets are defined in relation to the context in which you are working and the standards to be achieved
T	Time-related	Time-related targets have clear dates for review and monitoring in relation to the timescale available

Figure 1.2 SMART Targets
(Adapted from DfEE 1997b: 10)

It is helpful to distinguish between short-term targets (e.g. learning how to use a piece of software) and long-term goals (e.g. improving your subject knowledge in a 'multiple' subject such as science) which will, themselves, need to be broken down into a series of short-term targets. It is also important to work with a manageable number of targets at any given point in time. Regular, timetabled reviews where you can evaluate your progress with a mentor or tutor and decide on next steps are also part of a systematic approach to professional development. In fact, target-setting is one phase in a cyclical process which involves target-setting and action planning for the next phase, implementation of the plan followed by a period of reflection and review to complete the cycle. This cyclical process should be ongoing so that the end of one cycle also forms the opening stage of the next cycle with a review signalling new priorities for target-setting.

This process does not end when training is completed. As Chapter 3 explains in more detail, continuing professional development (CPD) has become a priority for the teaching profession. The transition from ITT to induction is managed using a bridging document, the Career Entry and Development Profile (CEDP). Each NQT enters their first teaching post equipped with a CEDP which provides the basis for planning early professional development during induction, a period normally lasting one year. ITT is, therefore, best viewed not as an end in itself but as the initial stage in a career-long process of CPD.

1.5 Conclusion

During a radio interview, I heard some primary school children talking enthusiastically about learning the 3 Rs! Further questioning revealed that the 3 Rs were resilience (refusing to be daunted by difficulties or to give up easily), resourcefulness (making best use of what is available to you) and reflection (identifying the lessons implicit in personal experience). This modern version of the 3 Rs is surely an excellent watchword for all learners!

1.6 Recommendations for further reading and webliography

The educational press is useful for keeping abreast of developments, for instance, the *Times Educational Supplement* (Friday) and the *Guardian* (Tuesday).

You could also join a circulation list for one of the email alerting services which perform a similar role. *Schools Research News* is a monthly newsletter, supported by the DfES, which is intended to keep practitioners up to date with newly published research, forthcoming events and research for practice. It provides a concise summary of items plus links to associated documents. To receive a copy, email victoria1.white@dfes.gsi.gov.uk

TeacherNet FirstBite is another newsletter, developed by the DfES, which adopts a similar format of a précis linked to a fuller account (www.teachernet.gov.uk/). It focuses on policy developments and school management.

Teachers is a magazine issued by the DfES, with primary and secondary variants. It is available online (www.teachernet.gov.uk/teachers/). Alternatively, you can arrange for a free copy to be delivered to your home.

www.gtce.org.uk is another useful website.

2

The professional framework and professional values and practice

Susan Orlik

2.1 Introduction

When you become a teacher, you do not just take up a new job; you acquire professional responsibilities and therefore need to understand the professional framework within which teachers work. There are two interlocking elements to this: the legal requirements and responsibilities laid on you as a teacher by the state; and ethical responsibilities to uphold and to exemplify certain professional values. During your preparation to become a teacher, you need to find out about these legal and professional requirements and to consider how your personal values fit with the common values espoused by the profession.

This chapter is divided into three sections:

- professional values and practice;
- teachers' legal responsibilities;
- the role of school governors.

These areas are inextricably linked to each other and form the statutory framework within which you will work in school. By the end of the chapter, you will have:

- an understanding of the purposes and issues raised by the introduction of a statement of professional values for teachers;
- an understanding of the ways the legislative framework in which you work is evolving;
- an understanding of the duty of care that teachers have;
- an understanding of the developing roles and responsibilities of governors and how these might affect your early professional life.

2.2 Professional values and practice

Values underpin everything that a school does – the teaching of the formal curriculum and the messages implicit in the hidden curriculum (see Chapter 13); provision for teaching and learning and extra-curricular activities; the kind of relationships that are formed between individuals. Nothing in schools, therefore, is value free. However, teachers and schools cannot afford to leave unexamined questions about what values underlie their practices and how widely those values are espoused by the school community.

New teachers face some difficult issues in relation to values. The first is to do with understanding the values which underpin teachers' and schools' responsibilities in the light of current legislative and policy frameworks. The second is to do with understanding how those values relate to the values – formally expressed or informally understood – of individual schools. The third is to do with examining the relationship between these elements and your own values, and developing strategies to resolve tensions and difficulties.

This section does not have any pretensions to explore general issues in the philosophy of education nor to engage in an exploration of moral education upon which other chapters focus (see Chapter 14). What it does, rather, is to encourage you to consider how your own values relate to those set down by the profession. The meaning of values has also been debated in many arenas: here it is used in the sense of the definition in the Oxford English Dictionary: 'one's judgement of what is valuable or important in life'. In this case, we mean what is important and valuable in the teaching profession. In considering this, we cannot detach ourselves from schools and pupils.

It is unwise to embark on the profession of teaching without having reflected on the question, 'What is the purpose of a school?' In answering that, you will progress in answering the lifelong question, 'What are my values as a teacher?'

Task 2.1

Make a note of what you consider to be the three most important purposes of secondary schools in the UK today. In each case, identify one or two values that are implied by that purpose.

In February 2002, the General Teaching Council for England (GTCE) agreed on a Code of Professional Values and Practice which was the result of a widespread consultation. This was the first time that a statutory body had attempted such a task in England. The code, now called a 'Statement of Professional Values' to distinguish it from the Code of Conduct, was revised in March 2006 and this new version is now available on the GTCE website at www.gtce.org.uk. The 2006 revisions took into account some of the changed responsibilities and relationships for teachers which arise from *Every Child Matters* (see Chapter 20).

The GTCE Statement may sound deceptively easy to implement but you will already know that pupils, parents and colleagues can deduce the values which guide your work as a professional teacher by observing you. All that you do and say is visible in the school. Because the values that you demonstrate in your actions are visible to pupils, there is a strong link to be made between the values you espouse as a teacher and the values that you promote to pupils.

You do not exist in a vacuum, nor do the professional values you hold. Indeed, the Statement states that you must work within the statutory framework. The 1988 Education Reform Act requires schools to provide a curriculum that pays attention to: 'the spiritual, moral and cultural . . . development of pupils at school and in society' in order that they may be prepared for the 'opportunities, responsibilities and experiences of adult life' (DES 1988: I(2)a, b).

The Revised National Curriculum (NC; QCA/DfEE 1999) explicitly laid out the values it wished to promote in education:

> Foremost is a belief in education, at home and at school, as a route to the spiritual, moral, social, cultural, physical and mental development, and thus the well-being, of the individual . . . Education is also a route to equality of opportunity for all, a healthy and just democracy, a productive economy and sustainable development. Education should reflect the enduring values that contribute to these ends. These include valuing ourselves, our families and other relationships, the wider groups to which we belong, the diversity in our society and the environment in which we live. Education should also affirm our commitment to the virtues of truth, justice, honesty, trust and a sense of duty.
>
> (from *Values, Aims and Purposes*, QCA/DfEE 1999: 10)

The National Forum for Values in Education and the Community has gone beyond this to develop in addition a more detailed statement of values (which you can find at www.nc.uk.net). The Forum claims that 'Schools and teachers can have confidence that there is general agreement in society upon these values' (QCA/DfEE 1999: 11) but also makes the point that agreement on values does not presuppose agreement as to the source of these values or on the practical application of these values. For example, 'support for the institution of marriage' is seen as a point of consensus, but the moral and religious grounds for that support and the behaviours that flow from it vary widely. This is an example of an area in which there is strong debate over whether teachers should impose their views on what is right and wrong. There are dangers in expressing your values in the fields of human relationships, politics and the social order, but arguably there are equal or greater dangers in not expressing them.

How will you as a teacher develop a coherent approach to professional values when the values of pupils, parents, employers and the wider community may or may not match the codified statements of the statutory bodies' approach to professional values? The GTCE Statement is a starting point. You will also already know that values are inherent in choices, and may be clear-cut in some situations but conflicting in others. One way of understanding your own values is to consider how you would react in situations in which different values make conflicting demands.

Task 2.2

Consider each of the five scenarios given below and think about how you would respond in each situation. What are the values that might drive you to act in a particular way? In each case identify which areas of the Statement you think are relevant to your decision and consider how the values expressed there may be in conflict with each other in these situations.

Scenario 1

Your patience and tolerance have been tested for some months by a child in a challenging Year 9 class that you teach. His behaviour has been linked to a very dislocated home life and he is a fairly recent arrival in the locality. The Special Educational Needs Coordinator (SENCo) has established an Individual Behaviour Plan but you know that an external assessment of his needs will not happen for months. His behaviour continues to be so disruptive to the class that parents of other children have complained that their children's education is being adversely affected by his presence in your class.

Scenario 2

In a tutorial, one of the Year 9 girls in your tutor group tells you that she is planning to leave school at the end of Year 11 because her parents think that further education is not appropriate for girls.

Scenario 3

One of your Year 11 tutor group asks to speak to you in private and complains to you that the class is, as she puts it, being bullied by another teacher. She says that they have been intimidated into staying at lunchtimes and after school to work on their coursework assignments, and that some pupils have been 'forced' to choose the subject for A level.

Scenario 4

Three Year 9 pupils have just been admitted to the school having recently arrived in the country as asylum seekers. Their education in their home country has been severely disrupted by conflict for many years and these pupils, as well as speaking very little English, are barely literate in their first language. In order for them to make any progress, they need a teacher to work exclusively with them full time. The funding received by the school to support these pupils does not cover this expense.

Scenario 5

You are working as a support teacher in a colleague's mixed ability class. Part of your role is to support differentiation in the lesson and you spend time with the highest and lowest attainers in the group. At the end of the lesson, the class teacher asks you if you will spend more time in the next lesson with a particular boy who is one of the highest attainers in the class because 'after all, he's the one who will be contributing most to my pension in a few years' time'.

Depending on your view of the purpose of schools, you may have professional values additional to those in the Statement and you will certainly place more emphasis on some than on others. You will want to work in schools that generally have values that match your own. How will you know? Nothing in a school is value free. You can get some sense of a school's collective values by reading what they say about themselves – the school's aims as laid out in their prospectus, for example. But you will also want to look, for example, at how resources are allocated, how decisions are made, how pupils and staff are valued and rewarded, and how pupils and staff relate to each other outside lessons.

So when you work in a school you will want to achieve a match. Student teachers often express a desire to work in a 'good school'. But how will you define a good school? You may want to work in a faith school or a selective school. You may want to work in a comprehensive school with strong expertise in SEN. You will want to work in a school where the teaching methods, content and organization most fit your own professional views about achieving your aims (why are you becoming a teacher?). Your aims will be the result of your values. While you might want to work in a school where the way you dress, speak and relate to pupils inside and outside the classroom matches the values of that school, this is not always possible.

Schools, by their nature, are places where individuals' exploration, development and expression of their own values need to be tested against and tempered by their membership of a structured community. And this is as much true of the teachers as it is of the pupils. Becoming a teacher may mean setting aside some of your personal values in favour of those of the community. How will you react if the school does things which conflict with your values? Even if you were to see yourself as just an employee, nothing you do or say as a teacher is value free.

So the last question is: What is not for sale in your professional life? If you were to be, in Tim Brighouse's exhortation (*Times Educational Supplement*, 21 February 2003), 'lovingly disobedient', on what matters would you be prepared to disobey 'lovingly'?

2.3 Teachers' legal responsibilities

The Standards for the Recommendation of Qualified Teacher Status (QTS) (TDA 2007: Q3a) require that those recommended for the award of QTS should 'Be aware of the professional duties of teachers and the statutory framework within which they work.'

There is a great deal of legislation relating to teachers' work and it changes constantly. There were more Acts of Parliament between 1990 and 2007 than in the previous 50 years. Legislation reflects changing government policy. The autonomous nature of schools, their need to compete in a quasi-market and the new bodies to heighten the professionalism of teachers are all reflected in the legislative framework. The most recent changes have resulted from the introduction of federated schools (which have created new kinds of partnerships between schools, reflected in new legal arrangements), and the new working arrangements outlined in the remodelling of the workforce proposals (see Chapter 3) as well as the all pervasive influence of the Children Act 2004, *Every Child Matters*.

With such a vast amount of legislation affecting your work as a teacher, you cannot be expected to know all the details of the laws which apply to you. There are areas that you need to know about, there are areas that you need to have an overview of, and there are areas where you will need to know where to get some advice from. What this section does is to explain the types of documents related to legal requirements that are published by the Government, to outline the main areas of legislation that affect teachers specifically and to discuss some of the issues involved in the interpretation of the law.

First you need to understand the difference between primary legislation, secondary legislation, guidance (or circulars), codes of practice and case law:

- **Primary legislation** comprises Acts of Parliament.
- **Secondary legislation** includes regulations, statutory instruments and orders made by the Secretary of State under powers invested in him or her by primary legislation. (The Education Reform Act in 1988, for example, gave the Secretary of State no less than 200 powers to make statutory regulations and orders.)
- **Departmental guidance** and circulars come from the DfES. (Until 2001 the name for these documents was 'circulars' and they were numbered and dated. For example, Circular 4/98 – which set out arrangements for teacher training – was the fourth circular issued by the DfEE in 1998. This numbering system was dropped by the department in 2002.) These circulars, now called guidance, give advice on the meaning and implementation of specific Acts. They do not have the force of law and occasionally the courts find that the department has given incorrect advice on an Act.
- **Codes of practice** are also issued for guidance. Although they do not have the force of law, they are similar to the Highway Code in that, while breach of a code is not in itself an offence, it may be used as evidence of negligence in a civil action, for example, if good practice advice in a code on a health and safety issue has been ignored and there has been an accident. The Secretary of State often has a duty to consult widely with the appropriate bodies such as local education authorities (LEAs/LAs) and the teachers' professional associations before promulgating a code of practice.
- **Common law** is the interpretation of the law through cases in the courts.

In most areas, the primary and secondary legislation gives only the barest outline of what teachers and schools need to do and what you will be most interested in are the codes of practice and guidance that help you to make decisions and put the law into practice in your own situation. However, you need to be aware of some of the most important Acts that govern aspects of your work.

The School Teachers' Pay and Conditions Act 1991 sets out the conditions of your employment as a teacher, including how your pay will be determined, what you can be asked to do and how many hours you can be expected to work. Annual updates to this Act are published in the School Teachers' Pay and Conditions Document. An amendment to this Act in 2001 set out the arrangements for the induction period, and recent Requirements have established procedures for Performance Management.

The Children Act 1989 sets out teachers' responsibilities to protect children from harm. This is a very wide-ranging piece of legislation and it is supported by a great deal of guidance. Amongst the most important topics in this guidance is the recognition of child abuse. Schools are required to designate a member of staff who will liaise between the school and other agencies in cases of suspected child abuse. Before you begin work in a school, you will need to prioritize finding out who this member of staff is and what systems operate within the school for the communication of concerns.

The Health and Safety at Work Act 1974 sets the basic framework for health and safety both of pupils and staff. You will need to familiarize yourself with the requirements both of the Act itself and of the particular policy of the school in which you work.

A number of pieces of primary legislation govern a school's and teachers' responsibilities in terms of inclusion. The Race Relations Act 1976 and Race Relations (Amendment) Act 2000, the Sex Discrimination Act 1975, the Disability and Discrimination Act 1995 and the Special Educational Needs and Disability Act 2001 all cover very complex areas of provision which are discussed in the appropriate chapters in Section 4 of this book.

An area of law which frequently concerns new teachers is that which relates to pupil behaviour and discipline, in particular the physical restraint of pupils. There are a number of relevant pieces of legislation. The School Standards and Framework Act 1998 requires schools to have a behaviour policy and individual teachers need to work within that policy. The Human Rights Act 1998 requires that treatment of pupils should not be inhuman or degrading. The Education Act 1997 gives more detailed information about the legality of keeping pupils in detention after school and of the use of physical restraint. It gives guidance on what is meant by the use of 'reasonable force' and in what kind of situations this might be deemed necessary.

You will find more detail about the law in each of these areas from the Bristol Guide listed under Further Reading and from the teaching unions which publish regularly updated guides to teachers' legal responsibilities. These are available direct from the unions or from their websites, listed in the webliography.

One area of the law which is especially open to legal interpretation is the teacher's 'duty of care'. Teachers have a common law duty of care towards their pupils resulting from their position *in loco parentis*, that is, in the place of the parent. This means that they are required to care for their pupils as a 'reasonable parent' would. There is no legal interpretation of this and judgements are based on the large amount of case law that has built up over time.

It is impossible to lay down hard and fast rules for every situation. A teacher must take the same degree of care that a reasonably careful parent would of their own children, taking account of the number of children in the class and the nature of those children. Regard must be paid to the likelihood of accidents in particular situations, for example, in science experiments. Older children can be allowed more freedom and discretion providing that the pupils are in a well-ordered environment.

Task 2.3

Here are two contrasting examples in recent leading cases. In each case, try to decide whether you think the school would be considered liable and what aspects of the situation might have been taken into consideration in coming to these judgements.

During a lesson, an 8-year-old boy is excused to go to the toilet. He slides down the banisters and falls onto the floor below, injuring himself. Discipline in the school was good and there had been no similar accident (*Gough v Upshire Primary School*, 2001).

A 15-year-old boy is in the playground five minutes before school and is struck in the face by a heavy leather football. There had been similar incidents before. Heavy leather footballs had been banned but no steps were taken to enforce the ban. There were 30 or 40 members of staff in the staffroom but nobody patrolling the playground (*Kearn-Price v Kent County Council*, 2002).

The decisions made by the courts were that, in the second case, the school was liable, but in the first it was not. In coming to these decisions they would have considered first whether the danger was reasonably foreseeable. In the primary school there had been no previous instances of pupils sliding down the banisters and, even at 8 years old, the pupil could reasonably be trusted to walk through the school building unsupervised. At the secondary school, though, there had already been similar incidents and so the danger was foreseeable. The second key question is whether the school had taken preventive action that was reasonably practicable. It was thought impracticable to insist that a pupil be accompanied each time they leave the classroom, but not impracticable for staff to be on duty in the playground before school.

As a professional teacher, you will:

- work within the legislative framework;
- know that acting 'reasonably' is the legal cornerstone of all you do;
- know that your school will have guidelines and policies lodged within the legislative framework;
- know that you can gain advice within your school on general and specific matters;
- know that you can gain advice from your professional association. These associations are experts in the application of the law to teaching. They produce general guidelines on the law and specific publications on certain issues and can offer, in cases where it is necessary, specific and specialised legal advice.

The law covers every aspect of schools. It changes frequently and, at this stage in your professional life, you do not need to know all the details but you do need to know those areas which affect your daily working life. Most of all, you need to understand and carry out the school policies.

When you take up your first post there are some fundamental preparatory things you can do:

- read the staff handbook; if it is not clear on areas of concern – detention, confiscating property, confidentiality, health and safety, off-site visits – then ask to see the policy concerned which has to be available to staff and parents;
- study the departmental handbook for the same reason;
- study the SoW and the assessment and reporting procedures;
- make sure you are a member of a professional association and receive their legal publication for new teachers;
- find out at an early stage who the people are, apart from your head of department

and head of year, who can give advice. For example, who is the expert in the school on copyright, Information and Communications Technology (ICT), classroom assistants, health and safety, learning mentors, child protection and SEN?

2.4 The role of school governors

Since the mid-1990s, the development of the roles and responsibilities of governors has quickened relentlessly. Since the 1988 Education Act, which gave governing bodies additional representation and unprecedented freedoms, and the advent of Local Management of Schools, governors' responsibilities and powers have been radically strengthened, largely at the expense of LAs. These changes have brought us to a position where it is the governors who strategically manage the central legislative framework for their school. The growth in governor training and support, and the number of national and local governor publications, indicate the burden on 350,000 governors nationally. An increase in central direction over the last 20 years, as reflected in the increase in primary and secondary legislation, for example in areas such as the curriculum and intervention in schools causing concern, has required governors to become involved in considerable detail previously left to head teachers.

The key responsibility of governing bodies is to provide a strategic overview for the school's development, albeit within the framework of national policy and guidelines. They have overall responsibility for the budgetary, staffing, curriculum and disciplinary frameworks within which staff work. Although their powers are wide, they are obviously constrained by legislative and policy frameworks; governors cannot, for example, derogate from the NC or national pay guidelines. Nonetheless, their responsibilities are extensive and most governing bodies will have constructed an elaborate committee structure to discharge their formal responsibilities. Governing bodies typically work through curriculum sub-committees, which have responsibility for the development, quality, coherence and assessment of the curriculum, a finance sub-committee which sets budget parameters and monitors spending, a personnel sub-committee which oversees the school's staffing plan and appointments and a premises committee which will oversee the school's site development plan. Other committees deal with exclusions, disciplinary hearings and appeals. It should be clear from this list that governors often have to deal with sensitive, contentious and difficult issues, such as grievance, discipline and, occasionally, dismissal. Effective governing bodies depend on the commitment of their members to discharge their responsibilities and undergo continuing training to update themselves on legislative changes.

Governors are unpaid volunteers drawn as widely as possible from all sections of the community. The current regulations require a school to have between 9 and 20 governors. Governors themselves are drawn from the following different categories:

- parent governors – who must make up at least one third of the governing body;
- staff governors – of whom there must be at least two, but no more than one third of the governing body as a whole;
- LA governors – who must be represented on all governing bodies, but in different numbers depending on the type of school;

- community governors – on all governing bodies except those of voluntary aided schools;
- foundation and partnership governors (in church schools, schools established by voluntary bodies or in foundation schools);
- sponsor governors – who may be appointed at the discretion of the governing body to represent those who give substantial support to the school financially or in kind;
- additional governors (the 1998 Act gave LAs the new power to appoint additional governors where the school is in a formal Ofsted category, such as special measures, or has failed to respond to a formal warning notice).

Parent and staff governors are elected and others are appointed or co-opted. A head teacher can choose to be a governor or not. He or she has the right in any event to attend and advise all meetings of the governors. The Nolan Committee principles on standards in public life, set out in 1996, apply to governing bodies as to any other public body, so that governors are required to work on the basis of objectivity, openness and accountability in all their proceedings.

In September 2003, there was a raft of procedural changes, changes to governing bodies' powers of delegation and new freedoms to innovate and create 'local learning communities', to federate and to increase the role of private and not for profit organizations in schools. The 'Extended School' initiative has allowed schools to provide services and activities such as childcare, adult and family learning, co-located health and social services, parenting support and other facilities of benefit to the local community such as credit unions or ICT access on the school premises. Governing bodies have been responsible for decisions to make these new forms of provision. The remodelling of the workforce (see Chapter 3) has required schools to make changes to staffing patterns to reflect the reduction in teachers' involvement in administrative tasks and governors have been involved in setting up new staffing structures in all secondary schools.

Each change brings an update or a complete revision in the Government's 'A Guide to the Law for School Governors' (DfES 2006c). This guide is produced in a number of different versions because there are differences in governance in Voluntary Aided and Voluntary Controlled Schools, City Academies and City Technology Colleges and some differences too for those in Foundation Schools as opposed to Community Schools. Some of the issues covered in this guide are:

- admissions;
- the school budget;
- premises;
- fund raising;
- relations between LAs and schools;
- school organization.

Schools depend on their governors and good governors can be effective sources of support and expertise for their schools – many governors bring their own experience in business, industry, public service or the voluntary sector to bear on their role. Nonetheless, governors do not have day-to-day responsibility for the management of the school, or of individual staff or curriculum areas: these responsibilities rest with the head teacher and senior staff. Governors' roles are strategic rather than directly managerial. Whether governors have the time or the capacity for the detailed work now required of them is an issue which has not been seriously addressed by successive governments. Recruitment and retention of governors is a major focus of the work of LAs. In some areas of the country they are very hard to recruit. Recruitment of governors from minority communities is a particular issue.

Task 2.4

What do you think governors can do? Where do you think power and responsibility lie? Work through the statements recording whether you think each of them is true or false.

1 Head teachers are responsible for deciding the policies for the school.
2 LAs have complete freedom to decide how much money to give to governing bodies of schools.
3 Governors should rely on head teachers to achieve best value.
4 The governing body is responsible for the sound management of all monies generated by the school.
5 The governing body decides the number of staff in a school.
6 The full governing body must set up a selection panel for the appointment of heads and deputies.
7 Governors must be involved in the appointment of all staff.
8 Governing bodies do not have to make reasonable arrangements to support the appointment of a disabled person as a teacher or as a member of the support staff.
9 No member of staff can be dismissed unless the whole governing body agrees.
10 The governing body must set and publish targets for pupils' performance in national tests at KS3 and KS4.
11 A governing body does not have to have any committees unless it chooses.
12 Part-time teachers may not be elected to serve on the governing body.
13 Parent, teacher and staff governors can be removed from the governing body by the head teacher.
14 Any governor can be elected to chair the governing body.

You can find the answers to these questions on pp. 29–30.

(Adapted from DfES 2005)

As a new teacher you will have a different perspective on the governing body. You may see the big picture of their roles as removed from the reality of your life. They do, however, have formal and informal connections, some of them only potential connections, with you. For example:

- they have responsibilities to you as an NQT. They are required to satisfy themselves that your induction year is being conducted properly so that you are being given every opportunity to succeed;

- at least one governor will almost certainly be involved with your appointment;
- they will establish policies and procedures that will have implications for you as a member of staff;
- one of the governors will be identified as a 'link governor' for your department and may be quite closely involved in the department's strategic development.

When you go into school, find out what type of school you are in and ask for a list of the governors with the category of governor. Ask to see agendas and minutes of the governing body. Also ask to talk to one of the teacher governors about the work of the governors in your school and how you are represented at meetings.

Most governors are very supportive of the school they serve and act fairly to the school and the staff. They show a genuine interest in the workings of the school and are keen for it to succeed. New teachers can feel vulnerable if they are teaching the child of a governor, or if a governor comes to spend time in their department, but you should remember that in the vast majority of cases the governors are there to play a positive, supporting role.

2.5 Recommendations for further reading and webliography

Department for Education and Skills (DfES) (2006) *A Guide to the Law for School Governors*. London: DfES Publications.
Document Summary Service (2005) *Teachers' Legal Liabilities and Responsibilities: The Bristol Guide*. Bristol: University of Bristol Graduate School of Education.

Teaching Union websites:

www.atl.org.uk (for the Association of Teachers and Lecturers)
www.nasuwt.org.uk (for National Association of Schoolmasters and Union of Women Teachers)
www.pat.org.uk (for the Professional Association of Teachers)
www.teachers.org.uk (for National Union of Teachers)

Websites for and about school governors:

www.governornet.co.uk
www.ngc.org.uk

Note

Answers to Task 2.4:

1   False
2   False
3   False
4   True
5   True
6   True

7   False
8   False. For prospective employees they must consider whether a reasonable adjustment could be made that would enable that person, if appointed, to work at the school.
9   False. The decision would have to be made by a committee. An appeal committee would hear any appeal.
10 True
11 True
12 False
13 False. Neither the head nor the governing body has a right to remove these governors from office once elected. Governors may be suspended from duty by the governing body in a limited number of circumstances.
14 False. Governors who are employed at the school may not be elected as chair or vice chair.

Acknowledgements

I wish to acknowledge the generous assistance of Keith Smith, Principal Officer Governance, Sandwell Education and Lifelong Learning Department, who read and advised me on the section on governors. Thanks are also due to my solicitor husband, Michael Orlik, who read and advised me on the legal section.

3
Key issues, opportunities and challenges for new teachers

Emma Westcott and Alma Harris

3.1 Introduction

Teaching is once again in vogue. Across many Western countries, there has been a renewed emphasis on improving teaching in the drive towards ever higher standards. Governments around the world are involved in the business of major educational reform focused primarily on expanding and improving the teaching profession. Even though there are few certainties about the ability of educational policy to secure higher performance from the educational system, the arguments for investment in teachers and teaching remain powerful and compelling. While the educational challenges are considerable and the route to reform is complex, the potential of individual teachers to influence pupil and school performance remains unquestionable. It has been consistently shown that the motivation of teachers and the quality of teaching which takes place in classrooms directly impacts on school and pupil performance (Muijs and Reynolds 2002). In short, whatever else is disputed, teachers continue to make a significant difference to the life chances of young people.

Although the work of teachers is acknowledged to be socially and economically important, it is also intellectually and ethically complex. Teaching is fundamentally about upholding certain key values: what to teach; how to deploy resources; what constitutes success; how to engage and to relate to young people. Teaching is not just about teaching a subject, having good classroom control or obtaining good examination results. There are wider moral and social purposes. As Day (1999: 11) notes: 'Teachers cannot limit their work to the classroom only, leaving the larger setting and purposes of schooling to be determined by others. They must take active responsibility for the goals to which they are committed, and for the social setting in which these goals may prosper.'

In summary, as you learn to teach you will be engaged in thinking about the moral, ethical, political and instrumental issues that will impact on your everyday practice, on your processes of decision making and on the pupils you teach. Reflection of this kind is important to all professionals in order to exercise responsibility and accountability for the decisions that they make. Being a teacher is more than demonstrating a narrow set of classroom skills or competences. It is about engaging more broadly with the many issues that impact on pupils' attainment and learning. As you get to know your pupils and the community in which they live, you will inevitably be aware of a range of social, political and economic influences that affect them and their potential to learn. Schools do not exist in isolation from the community they serve; neither do teachers. Consequently, as a teacher, you will need to engage with that wider community and the issues that influence it either directly or indirectly.

This chapter attempts to explore some of the opportunities and challenges facing new teachers today. It is not possible to talk about what teaching is like, when the experience of teaching varies so widely between schools, localities, and across careers. Moreover, the pace of educational change is such that it is always dangerous to try to capture a contemporary picture of teaching. By the time you read this book there will inevitably be new initiatives, strategies and expectations that are not reflected in these pages. Moreover, any change in education may prove to be an opportunity or a challenge, depending on how it is implemented, funded, supported and evaluated. It is perhaps wiser to think about the opportunities and challenges inherent in some of the facets of teaching today that look set to endure.

As a qualified teacher you will be part of an increasingly diverse school workforce. You will be working alongside a wide range of others professionals who support children's welfare and learning. Along with other agencies of support for young people, teaching is currently being restructured or remodelled (see Chapters 7 and 20). Most importantly, this will include para-professional support in the shape of teaching or classroom assistants. It is undoubtedly the case that teachers in the twenty-first century will be supported by a new layer of professionals who, although not qualified to teach, will take an increasing role in supporting classroom teaching.

There are also new expectations of teachers to take responsibility for their own continuous learning, and, increasingly, to contribute to the learning of colleagues. Teachers today are subject to multiple accountabilities, as individuals, as staff of their employing institutions, and as members of a profession subject to its own professional body, the GTCE. Some of the opportunities and challenges of these dimensions of teaching today are explored in this chapter following an initial discussion of what is meant by teacher professionalism. By the end of this chapter, you should:

- know about the work of the professional body that represents teachers, the GTCE;
- recognize that ITT represents the opening phase in a process of continuing professional development;
- understand how and why the teaching profession is being remodelled.

3.2 Teaching as a new professionalism?

Historically, specific characteristics have distinguished 'professions' from other occupational sectors. These frequently included: registration with a self-governing professional body; the definition of entry standards and standards of accomplishment; the specification of expectations regarding competence and conduct; and a commitment to use and develop a body of complex specialist knowledge in the client interest.

Teaching shares many but not all of the characteristics of established 'professions' and would make a strong claim to 'professionalism' in the broader sense of undertaking work in a manner that is demonstrably competent and diligent. However, it might be argued that teaching should forge a new, fit for purpose definition of professionalism, to avoid the allegations of self-interest and elitism that have been levelled at some established 'professions', and to articulate values that place the learner at the heart of professional practice. Teaching also needs to define 'professionalism' in a way that takes account of the wide range of people involved in teaching, not all of whom will be qualified, registered teachers.

This is one of the challenges facing the GTCE. Teachers had campaigned for over a century for the establishment of an independent body to represent their profession. The GTCE finally started work in 2000 as the independent professional body for teaching in England. Decisions are made by a 64-member Council. Most members of the Council are serving teachers, and other Council members represent those with an interest in teaching, including parents, governors, teacher educators and employers. Registration with the Council is compulsory for those employed as qualified teachers in maintained schools. Others with qualified teacher status (QTS), including those teaching in independent schools, are invited to register. The GTCE can hear cases relating to competence and conduct and has the power to remove teachers from the register if they are not meeting professional standards of practice. It also has the power to advise the Secretary of State on a range of matters including teacher training, teaching standards and the role of the teaching profession.

You will have your first contact with the GTCE while you work towards QTS. The Council contacts students to collect information that will enable it to award QTS to those who successfully complete their training. Students also work towards meeting standards for QTS that are based on the GTCE's Code of Professional Practice (the GTCE website is at www.gtce.org.uk). The code was the result of an extensive national consultation with teachers, and represents teachers' ideas about the characteristics of good professional practice (see Chapter 2). The *Professional Standards for Teachers* have been revised, including those for ITT. The revised framework of professional and occupational standards for classroom teachers took effect from September 2007 (TDA 2007).

Task 3.1

Note down your ideas about the characteristics of good professional practice. Now try to organize them into categories with sub-headings. Compare your own list with the Standards for QTS (www.tda.gov.uk/teachers/professional standards). To what extent are they similar? How do they differ?

The advent of the GTCE presents an opportunity for new teachers to get involved in professional networks and policy development. As a qualified teacher, you will be eligible to stand for election or seek nomination as a member of the Council, and to play a direct role in decision and policy making on behalf of your profession.

3.3 An increasingly diverse workforce

As is noted above, the current climate is one where the idea of teaching and who teaches is evolving and changing, with a particular emphasis on the role of adults other than teachers within schools. It could be argued that there has always been a range of people involved in the processes of teaching and learning in schools who do not have QTS. These include unqualified instructors, often meeting a particular curricular need, such as language assistants or dance tutors. In addition, schools have employed staff to support the learning of particular groups of pupils, such as those with special needs or English as an additional language (EAL), and staff such as technicians and librarians may play an indirect role in learning in some schools, but a very direct role in others. The role of the teaching assistant has developed considerably in the last few years from performing lower order practical tasks in the classroom to undertaking unmistakably pedagogical work with individuals or groups of pupils. Yet, in the current educational context the emphasis is on further changing and expanding the role of teaching assistants in schools. There is also a recognition that training must address the needs of both teachers and their assistants, and there is now a coherent career and qualifications structure for teaching assistants and other school support staff.

If there have always been people without QTS involved in teaching, legislation has made more radical changes in the composition of the school workforce possible. Historically, legislation has defined activities that can only be undertaken by a qualified teacher. Regulations following from the 2002 Education Act set out circumstances under which staff without QTS can carry out specified work relating to teaching and learning under the supervision of a qualified teacher (DfES 2002a). It is too soon to say what the impact of these new freedoms might be; some innovations may now be permissible but that does not necessarily make them desirable. For instance, a head teacher could lead a school employing no other staff with QTS but it is unlikely that they would opt to do so. At the time of writing, there are several factors driving the greater use of people without QTS in teaching. The first is recruitment difficulties, which are having a particular impact in some parts of the country and certain subject areas. This may diminish as a factor in the future with falling school rolls dampening demand for teachers and any economic downturn increasing supply. The second is a concern to tackle teacher workload. The Government recently signed an agreement with most of the teaching unions which identifies tasks that teachers should not routinely be required to undertake and guarantees a minimum entitlement to time for planning, preparation and assessment (PPA time). The agreement was predicated on the understanding that staff without QTS would be deployed in new ways in order to ease teacher workload. In 2006, secondary schools were required to redefine their staffing structures in such a way that responsibility allowances for qualified teachers were awarded only for work related closely to teaching and learning and not for administrative tasks, for example, supervising external examination entries. These tasks will now be undertaken by administrators rather than teachers. In addition, higher level teaching assistants (HLTAs) now receive training in areas of the 'QTS curriculum' and are able, for example, to cover classes under the supervision of a qualified teacher.

Task 3.2

Compile a list of the other adults who work in schools.

Look at these school staff lists to get a sense of the range of other adults employed:
www.castlemanor.suffolk.sch.uk/info/stafflist.php
www.banbury.oxon.sch.uk/wholeschool/contacting_us/staff_list.htm
www.stjosephs.s-tyneside.sch.uk/governors.html

Changing aspirations for schooling are the third factor that suggests a need for new configurations of staff. Parents arriving at the gates of their child's school in the middle of the previous century may have been greeted with a notice declaring 'No parents beyond this point'! The message of exclusion contained within such notices contrasts starkly with the current policy of extended schools. Extended schools are open between 8 a.m. and 6 p.m. and provide a core offer of extended services including wraparound childcare (in primary schools); parenting and family support; a variety of out-of-school activities such as breakfast clubs, after-school clubs and sporting and musical activities; and community use of adult and family learning plus ICT. These schools are also expected to make an important contribution to the protection and support of children at risk of harm, disaffection and underachievement, in conjunction with other professions that play a role in the lives of young people (see Chapter 20). Swift and easy referrals to specialist services are expected. Some schools have responded by increasing provision from the fields of social work, counselling and psychology, perhaps having an enhanced presence of other professionals on the school site. A multi-agency approach to supporting young people could include family services co-located on school premises.

Task 3.3

Use the Teachernet website (www.teachernet.gov.uk/wholeschool/extendedschools/) to produce a list of the different professional groups that may be encountered by teachers working in extended schools.

Secondary schools are also being affected by changes in the 14–19 curriculum (see Chapter 19). The Government wishes to institute reforms that will address our national underperformance in staying on rates at 17+ and comparative weakness in vocational skills. The school curriculum may (re)introduce subjects for which there are few or no teachers with QTS, or there may be an increase in the trend for provision to be made in further education (FE) settings for some school age pupils. Greater numbers of FE staff may be imported into schools; some of those staff have QTS while others have other teaching qualifications or relevant professional qualifications.

As a new teacher you are entering the profession at a time when the boundaries between teachers and non-teachers are less clear than ever. New teachers have every right to feel that their professional status is hard won, and that they are uniquely qualified to undertake certain teaching tasks. Conversely, they may feel that the role requires them to undertake too many activities that do not require the time of a qualified teacher, and that they could deploy their growing expertise more effectively if more support was available from other sorts of staff.

New teachers may be better prepared than their experienced colleagues for working with other adults within and beyond the classroom, as standards relating to workforce diversification are included in the Standards for Qualified Teacher Status (2007). While you may feel better prepared for this aspect of your work than other colleagues in your school, you may find the business of deploying older or more experienced staff challenging. Moreover, research (e.g. Clegg and McNulty 2002; Milbourne et al. 2003 and Tett et al. 2003) suggests that whilst the opportunity to collaborate with other children's services has the potential to improve the lot of children, working with other professional groups may prove to be a tricky business. Other groups may operate within an unfamiliar professional culture which has priorities that differ from those in schools. Their management systems and working practices may also be incompatible. The challenges it seems are no less great than the potential benefits.

Diversification of the school workforce may turn out to be an opportunity for new teachers only if certain conditions are met. Clarity about where teaching responsibilities lie will be important, as will the development of new and effective models of collaborative working. However, if you as a teacher can spend less time on administrative and practical tasks, and more time on planning, reflection and collaboration, then pupil learning will benefit.

3.4 Career-long professional development

Teaching is far and away the biggest field of graduate recruitment in the UK. In 2006–07, over 39,600 people embarked on ITT courses. Graduate recruiters point to the increasing sophistication with which graduates assess various career options. Salary and status continue to be significant, but other qualitative factors such as work/life balance and development opportunities are also significant. New entrants to the profession have many reasons for choosing teaching, but CPD is an important factor in retaining the best teachers within the profession.

The international research literature has consistently shown that teachers' professional development is an essential component of successful school level change and development (Day 1999). It has confirmed that where teachers are able to reflect, access new ideas, experiment and share experiences within school cultures and with leaders who encourage appropriate levels of challenge and support, there is greater potential for school and classroom improvement. Improving schools invest in the development of their staff and create opportunities for teachers to collaborate and to share best practice (Harris 2002). Evidence also suggests that attention to teacher learning can impact directly on improvements in pupil learning and achievement. Where teachers have clear professional identities and have intrinsic as well as extrinsic rewards for their work, they are more satisfied and committed to their work. In addition, where teachers are able to expand and develop their own teaching repertoires, they are more likely to provide an increased range of learning opportunities for pupils (Joyce et al. 1998). In short, the research literature demonstrates that CPD has a positive impact on curriculum and pedagogy, as well as teachers' sense of commitment and their relationships with pupils (Muijs et al. 2004).

CPD is increasingly seen, then, as a key part of the career development of all professionals but particularly teachers. The concept is often left ill-defined, however, being in many cases conflated with the related concepts of in-service training and on-the-job learning. Both are more limited than CPD, as CPD can encompass a wide variety of approaches and teaching and learning styles in a variety of settings (inside or outside of the workplace). CPD is also distinguishable from lifelong learning, which is a broader concept in that it can include all sorts of learning whereas CPD is seen as related to people's professional identities and roles and the goals of the organization they are working for (Galloway 2000).

In this chapter we use Day's (1994: 4) definition of CPD. This definition encompasses formal and informal learning: 'Professional development consists of all natural learning experiences and those conscious and planned activities which are intended to be of direct or indirect benefit to the individual, group or school, which contribute, through these, to the quality of education in the classroom.'

One of the most striking findings from research into school improvement is that improving schools are marked by constant interchange and professional dialogue at both a formal and informal level (Harris 2002). Similarly, schools that are improving invest in professional development and are able to engage teachers in various forms of professional learning. It has long been argued that creating a collaborative professional learning environment for teachers is the single most important factor for successful school improvement and the first order of business for those seeking to enhance the effectiveness of teaching and learning (Little 1993). A particularly significant shift in the school improvement field in the last few years has been the burgeoning of network initiatives where teachers work closely together. Most recently, Hargreaves (2003: 9) has proposed:

> A network increases the pool of ideas on which any member can draw and as one idea or practice is transferred, the inevitable process of adaptation and adjustment to different conditions is rich in potential for the practice to be incrementally improved by the recipient and then fed back to the donor in a virtuous circle of innovation and improvement. In other words, the networks extend and enlarge the communities of practice with enormous potential benefits.

Consequently, it would seem imperative that teachers engage in collaborative forms of CPD that meet both the needs of individual teachers and the pupils they teach.

There are certainly opportunities and challenges associated with gaining access to professional development in teaching. In theory, it is inconceivable that a profession dedicated to promoting learning should not itself be a learning profession. In practice, it is fair to say that teachers' access to professional learning is still too variable, and too dependent on factors such as availability of funding and the priority attached to professional development by individual school leaders. There is an expectation that teachers will continue to learn and develop beyond their initial training, which is captured in the Professional Standards for new and experienced teachers (TDA 2007). The introduction of funding by the Training and Development Agency

(TDA) for qualified teachers undertaking postgraduate professional development on a part-time basis has been helpful in this respect. Nevertheless, this expectation is most likely to be met in a supportive environment. This might mean one in which teachers are supported to develop evaluative skills and to talk about teaching and learning; where time is made for observation, reflection and feedback; where teachers have access to research and evidence and the skills to interpret them accurately and draw on them in their practice; where performance management genuinely facilitates teachers' identification of their own development needs as well as allowing managers to pursue their needs of staff.

There are many schools with these characteristics, but it is possible for new teachers to find themselves in schools that do not attach sufficient importance to creating a culture that supports teachers' own continual learning. New teachers are perhaps of particular value to these schools because they come to teaching with expectations with regard to their own development. They may be joining schools in which expectations among experienced teachers are similarly buoyant, or they may encounter cultures where expectation has been dampened by thwarted aspirations or poor CPD experiences. It is essential for the health of the profession that new entrants retain high expectations in this area. If some schools are better at meeting such expectations than others, there are always other avenues beyond the school to explore. LAs, unions and subject or specialist associations may offer professional development opportunities, and a school might be part of a network such as a networked learning community or an Excellence in Cities (EiC) grouping with teacher learning goals. New entrants may also be aware of professional development opportunities offered by their ITT provider for qualified teachers. Some higher education institutions have developed links between ITT and courses of CPD to enable teachers to progress smoothly from one to the other. It may also be possible for projects completed during ITT to count towards other awards. Local schools may have been designated to play a role in the development of teachers beyond their own workforce, for example through the Leading Edge Schools initiative.

The Government is more attuned today to teachers' CPD needs than it has been in the recent past – it would be unusual for a government initiative not to consider the training implications for school staff when planning funding, lead-in time and so on. However, even the best school leaders who are committed to CPD may feel pressure to raid the CPD budget when finances are tight, if the alternative might be to increase class sizes or leave unfilled posts vacant. But most school leaders see professional development as an investment that will not only improve the quality of teaching and pupil learning but also help to retain and motivate staff.

An assessment of CPD provision needs to consider the quality of the learning as well as the extent of teachers' access to it. The term CPD may cover a diverse range of experiences from the traditional notion of a training day or a course, to participation in themed classroom observations, to touching base each week with a mentor. The GTCE has tried to capture this range in a Teachers' Professional Learning Framework, which is a map of diverse professional development experiences, opportunities and activities. The GTCE is among those advocating teachers' active engagement with the definition of learning needs, modes and preferred styles of learning. Its Teacher Learning Academy offers professional recognition and academic accreditation for those who seek it for teacher learning in a range of forms, placing a particular emphasis on collaborative approaches. Information about the Professional Learning Framework and Teacher Learning Academy is available on the GTCE's website (www.gtce.org.uk).

Task 3.4

Look at the GTCE's website and read the Teachers' Professional Learning Framework and the Engage network in detail.

The GTCE also highlights the benefits of peer development – teachers' involvement in the learning of their colleagues. New entrants to teaching will be acutely aware of learning from colleagues; they may be less aware of the extent to which experienced colleagues are learning from them. There will be topics on which students and NQTs have up-to-date knowledge of benefit to serving teachers, and new teachers will bring a fresh gaze to school practice. Most importantly, working alongside new entrants encourages experienced teachers to revisit and articulate their own pedagogy – to be confident and clear about the why and the how of teaching.

When you are applying for first teaching posts, one of the factors to take into consideration is opportunities for CPD available through the school, LA or nearby universities. This might be achieved by requesting a copy of the staff development policy, talking to the CPD coordinator, or asking about the schools' use of in-service training days. Student teachers can prepare for this task by finding out about CPD in their placement schools.

Increasing attention is being given to teachers' CPD, starting with an induction period to which newly qualified teachers are entitled. The statutory induction period was introduced in 1999 to provide resources for CPD and designated non-contact time. New teachers must pass induction standards at the end of the period, usually a year, to remain registered with the GTCE. To help them achieve this, they are entitled to a reduced timetable, the support of an induction tutor and a programme of observation and feedback on their teaching. Full details of the roles and responsibilities associated with induction can be found on the TDA website (www.tda.gov.uk) and it is worth becoming familiar with the induction arrangements before starting the induction period in order to be able to take early action if they are not properly in place. One of the most important ways of making this period of development effective is to make meaningful use of the CEDP which you will produce at the end of your training. The CEDP is designed to help you to think about your professional development at key points towards the end of ITT and during induction, thereby supporting the transition between the two, as well as preparing the way for the next phase of professional development.

ITT is an intensive undertaking and NQTs could be forgiven for breathing a sigh of relief when they gain QTS, and consider their development over for a while. It may be a challenge to think of induction as anything other than a further hurdle to jump. Nevertheless, in reality ITT and induction represent consecutive phases of development. Although there are expectations placed on NQTs undertaking induction, it may be helpful to think of induction as an entitlement to time, resources and support to consolidate and enhance professional practice. The period between induction and, for those who wish to do so, crossing the threshold (i.e. meeting standards set out by the DfES for experienced and effective practitioners) is now recognized as a coherent third phase of teacher development with it own expectations and entitlements. On the GTCE's advice, the Government piloted an early professional development (EPD) scheme between 2001 and 2004, which funded development opportunities for teachers in the second and third year of their professional practice. EPD is attractive as a means of consolidating the skills and knowledge of new professionals, establishing a culture of continuous professional learning and of retaining new teachers. To support it, the GTCE has developed Engage, one of three professional networks intended to link teachers nationwide. Engage, which can be accessed via the GTCE's website, provides support and networking opportunities for NQTs and teachers at an early stage in their professional development.

3.5 Multiple accountabilities

New teachers are entering the profession at a time of debate about the nature and extent of accountability. This is not a debate unique to teaching but common to all professions. It is customary for debates about accountability to suggest that the professions were once subject to too little accountability and that the pendulum has now swung so far in the other direction that processes of accountability can impede and curtail the activity for which people are being held to account (see, for example, O'Neill 2002).

Teaching takes place in a complex network of accountability. Teachers are individually held to account through performance management, which is the responsibility of their line manager working within a framework set by school policy. Ofsted inspection also passes judgement on the quality of teaching. Schools are expected to instigate their own processes of self-evaluation rather than relying solely on external judgements about the quality of their work, and teaching is scrutinized as part of these processes. LAs may also operate quasi-inspectoral processes, often in preparation for or in the wake of Ofsted inspections. Head teachers are accountable to school governing bodies and, through them, to stakeholders in the school. Finally, teachers are professionally accountable to their professional body, the GTCE. The Council issues codes of conduct and practice, and hears cases relating to competence and conduct. In addition to these structural accountabilities, teachers are acutely aware of feeling accountable or responsible to pupils, parents and colleagues. They may also describe more abstract but no less binding loyalties to, for example, their subject or their locality.

Making sense of complex accountabilities is a challenge for new teachers, and for their more experienced colleagues. Teachers' representative bodies seek a more streamlined, less labour-intensive system of accountability with an emphasis on supporting improvement. New entrants to teaching may find it helpful to think of accountability as giving an account of one's practice. This is a process with which trainees and NQTs are very familiar – it forms an important part of their formative professional learning. It is no less important for seasoned practitioners to be able to account for the multiple decisions taken while teaching – about curriculum content and organization, pedagogy, classroom organization, management and assessment. Teachers' best defence of their practice is an articulate, evidence-informed account of it, and the evidence on which teachers can draw is improving all of the time. Within the field of educational research there is a stronger emphasis on accessibility and, where appropriate, usability of research by practitioners and policy makers; and schools' interrogation of pupil and school level data is increasingly sophisticated (see Chapter 10). There is an emphasis on teachers being central to the process of school development and reform.

David Hopkins, Director of the Standards and Effectiveness Unit at the DfES, has stated:

> The emphasis on transformation is key – reform strategies can no longer take only an incremental approach to change. The raising of standards of learning and attainment for all of our students now needs to be seen within a whole school or systems context and to impact both on classroom practice and the work culture of the school.
>
> (Hopkins 2003: 3)

He refers to the latest phase of curriculum reform as 'Informed Professionalism' where teachers have a key role to play in the reform process. This principle should be supported and endorsed. Sustainable change is dependent on what individual teachers do in classrooms; to disenfranchise them from the process of designing and implementing curriculum reform would, at best, be unwise and, at worst, guarantee a continued legacy of failed curriculum initiatives and reforms.

In conclusion, teaching is a dynamic profession that can reward its members with a rich variety of experiences, within and beyond the classroom and school. Many of the current developments in education have the potential to be changes for the better. In any case, successive generations of pupils have reason to be grateful for teachers' ability to turn challenges into opportunities – to make extraordinary things happen without the benefit of an ideal environment, resources, or policy frameworks.

3.6 Recommendations for further reading and webliography

Hargreaves, A. (1994) *Changing Teachers: Changing Times*. London: Cassell.
Hopkins, D. and Harris, A. (2001) *Creating the Conditions For Teaching and Learning: A Handbook of Staff Development Activities*. London: David Fulton.
Joyce, B., Calhoun, E. and Hopkins, D. (1998) *Models of Teaching: Tools for Learning*. Buckingham: Open University Press.
Muijs, R.D. and Reynolds, D. (2000) *Effective Teaching, Evidence and Practice*. London: Paul Chapman.

www.gtce.org.uk
www.standards.dfes.gov.uk
www.tda.gov.uk

SECTION 2
Core professional competences

4

Understanding how pupils learn: Theories of learning and intelligence

Daniel Muijs

4.1 Introduction

In this chapter we will discuss the main theories on how children learn. This is, of course, an important issue in teaching, as to be effective we need to try and teach in a way that reinforces how people naturally learn. Theories of learning and intelligence are many and diverse, and we cannot look at all existing theories in one chapter. What we will do instead, is to focus on some of the theories that have been most influential in education over the years.

By the end of this chapter you should:

- know about the main theories on how pupils learn;
    - behaviourism;
    - Piagetian and Vygotskian learning theories;
    - IQ theory;
    - the theory of multiple intelligences;
    - cognitive and brain research;
- be able to make judgements on the relevance of these different theories to teaching and learning;
- be able to reflect on the extent to which these theories contradict or build upon one another.

4.2 Behaviourism

The first major theory of learning we will discuss is called behaviourism. Behaviourism was developed in the 1920s and 1930s by psychologists such as Skinner, Pavlov and Thorndike. While somewhat outdated now, this theory still has a strong influence on educational practice, if not theory.

Behavioural Learning Theory emphasizes change in behaviour as the main outcome of the learning process. Behavioural theorists concentrate on directly observable phenomena using a scientific method borrowed from the natural sciences. The most radical behaviourists, such as B.F. Skinner, considered all study of non-observable behaviour ('mentalism') to be unscientific (Hilgard 1995; O'Donohue and Ferguson 2001). In the later twentieth century, however, researchers and psychologists in the behaviourist tradition, such as Bandura (1985), have expanded their view of learning to include expectations, thoughts, motivation and beliefs. Learning, according to behaviourists, is something people do in response to external stimuli. This was an important change to previous models, which had stressed consciousness and intro-spection, and had not produced many generalizable findings about how people learn.

As I mentioned above, behaviourists imitated methods used in the natural sciences, especially experiments conducted with animals like rats and dogs as well as humans. This is because, being against 'mentalism', behaviourists think that it is largely external factors which cause our behaviour. The basic mechanism through which this happens is conditioning. According to behaviourists there are two different types of conditioning:

Classic conditioning occurs when a natural reflex responds to a stimulus. An example of this comes from another behaviourist's, Pavlov, experiments with dogs. In order to process food, dogs need to salivate when they eat. As all dog owners will know, what happens is that dogs will start to salivate even before eating, as soon as they have smelt or seen food. So, the external stimulus of food will cause the dog to salivate. It has become a habit: that is the response that is conditioned. When confronted with particular stimuli people as well as animals will produce a specific response.

Behavioural or operant conditioning occurs when a response to a stimulus is reinforced. Basically, operant conditioning is a simple feedback system: if a reward or reinforcement follows the response to a stimulus, then the response becomes more probable in the future. For example, if every time a pupil behaves well in class they gets a reward, they are likely to behave well next time. (It has to be mentioned here that while animal behaviour follows reliably from a stimulus, this is the case to a far lesser extent among humans.)

Rewards and punishments are therefore an important part of behaviourist learning theory. Initial experiments with dogs and rats convinced these psychologists of the importance of the use of rewards and punishments to elicit certain desired behaviours, such as pushing a lever, in these animals. Over ensuing decades these findings were further tested and refined with human subjects, and became highly influential in education. Pleasurable consequences, or *reinforcers*, strengthen behaviour, while unpleasant consequences, or *punishers*, weaken behaviour. Behaviour is influenced by its consequences, but it is influenced by its antecedents as well, thus creating the A(ntecedents)-B(ehaviour)-C(onsequences) chain. Skinner's work concentrated mainly on the relationship between the latter two parts of the chain (Skinner 1974; O'Donohue and Ferguson 2001), and these findings still form the basis of many behaviour management systems in schools, as well as much of the research on effective teaching (e.g. Muijs and Reynolds 2003).

While this movement remains highly influential, behaviourism has come to be seen as far too limited and limiting to adequately capture the complexity of human learning and behaviours. The idea that learning occurs purely as a reaction to external stimuli has proved to be inadequate. Activities such as recognizing objects (this is a ball), sorting objects (this is a rugby ball, this is a football) and storing information are clearly 'mentalist' activities; they occur in the head. While of course an external stimulus (perception of an object) is present, behaviourist theory cannot account for the information processing that occurs when we are confronted by stimuli. Behaviourism also cannot account for types of learning that occur without reinforcement – in particular, the way children pick up language patterns (grammar) cannot be explained using a behaviourist framework. Behaviourism also presents problems when the learner is confronted with new situations in which the mental stimuli they have learnt to respond to are not present. The fact that behaviourists do not study the memory in any meaningful way (they only talk about acquiring 'habits') is another major problem if we want to explain learning. If we want to really understand how people learn, we have to be 'mentalists' and look at what is going on inside the brain as well as measuring reactions to external stimuli.

Should we totally discount behaviourism? As mentioned above, behaviourism has been heavily criticized over the years. Much of this criticism is justified. Behaviourism is clearly too limited a theory of learning to properly account for how we actually learn. Not all the criticism is justified, however. Some of it seems to emanate from a dislike of the findings rather than a close look at the evidence. Behaviourism has little place for the role of free will and human individuality. This is never a popular view and, as we have seen, this determinism is clearly overdone in behaviourist theories. However, that does not mean that it is entirely inaccurate. While we always like to believe that we are entirely free, our behaviours can to an extent be predicted, in some cases by behaviourist models. That this is true is attested to by the continued usefulness of behaviourist methods in teaching, such as the use of rewards. Not liking certain research findings does not make them wrong, and it is not the job of research and science simply to tell us what we want to hear. Recently, it is fair to say that neobehaviourist theories have become popular among scientists looking at the role of evolution in the way we behave. If you read the work of Richard Dawkins (1989) for example, there are clear links with behaviourist psychology.

Task 4.1

Can you think of anything you can do or know that you have learnt in a way that conforms to behaviourist learning theory? Can you think of anything that you learnt in a way that clearly is not behaviourist? What does that tell you about behaviourist learning theories?

4.3 Piaget and Vygotsky

Jean Piaget: learning as qualitative change

As well as the behaviourists like Skinner and Watson, two other pioneering psychologists that have had a continuing influence on how we view learning are Piaget and Vygotsky.

Jean Piaget was a Swiss psychologist, who started his important work on how children develop and learn before the Second World War. In contrast to the behaviourists, who developed most of their theories using laboratory experiments and rarely looked at the real-life behaviours of children, Piaget's theories were developed from observation of children.

What these observations taught him was that in order to understand how children think, one has to look at the qualitative development of their ability to solve problems. Cognitive development, in his view, is much more than the addition of new facts and ideas to an existing store of information. Rather, children's thinking changes qualitatively; the tools which children use to think change, leading children and adults, and indeed children at different stages of development, to possess a different view of the world. A child's reality is not the same as that of an adult (Piaget 2001).

According to Piaget, one of the main influences on children's cognitive development is what he termed *maturation*, the unfolding of biological changes that are genetically programmed into us. A second factor is *activity*. Increasing maturation leads to an increase in children's ability to act on their environment, and to learn from their actions. This learning in turn leads to an alteration of children's thought processes. A third factor in development is *social transmission*, learning from others. As children act on their environment, they also interact with others and can therefore learn from them to a differing degree depending on their developmental stage.

According to Piaget (2001), learning occurs in four stages:

The sensori-motor stage (0–2 years): The baby knows about the world through actions and sensory information. They learn to differentiate themself from the environment. The child begins to understand causality in time and space. The capacity to form internal mental representations emerges.

The pre-operational stage (2–7 years): In this stage, children take the first steps from action to thinking, by internalizing action. In the previous stage, children's schemes were still completely tied to actions, which means that they are of no use in recalling the past or in prediction. During the pre-operational stage the child starts to be able to do this, by learning how to think symbolically. The ability to think in symbols remains limited at this stage, however, as the child can only think in one direction. Thinking backwards or reversing the steps of a task are difficult. Another innovation that starts to take place during this phase is the ability to understand conservation. This means that the child can now realize that the amount or number of something remains the same even if the arrangement or appearance of it is changed (for example, four dogs and four cats is the same amount). This remains difficult for children in this phase. Children in this phase still have great difficulty freeing themselves from their own perception of how the world appears. Children at this age are also very egocentric. They tend to see the world and the experiences of others from their own standpoint.

The concrete operational stage (7–12 years): The basic characteristics of this stage are: 1) the recognition of the logical stability of the physical world; 2) the realization that elements can be changed or transformed and still retain their original characteristics; and 3) the understanding that these changes can be reversed. Another important operation that is mastered at this stage is classification. Classification depends on a pupil's ability to focus on a single characteristic of objects and then to group the objects according to that single characteristic (e.g. if one gives a pupil a set of differently coloured and differently shaped pens, they will be able to pick out the round ones). Pupils can now also understand seriation, allowing them to construct a logical series in which A is less than B is less than C and so on. At this stage the pupil has developed a logical and systematic way of thinking which is, however, still tied to physical reality. Overcoming this is the task of the next phase.

The formal operational stage (12+): In this stage, which is not reached by all people, all that is learned in previous stages remains in force but pupils are now able to see that a real, actually experienced situation is only one of several possible situations. In order for this to happen, we must be able to generate different possibilities for any given situation in a systematic way. Pupils are now able to imagine ideal, non-existing worlds. Another characteristic of this stage is adolescent egocentrism. Adolescents tend incessantly to analyze their own beliefs and attitudes, and often assume that everyone else shares their concerns and is in turn analyzing them.

Piaget's theory has been hugely influential, but has been found wanting in a number of areas. His stages of learning are clearly too rigid. A number of studies have found that young children can acquire concrete operational thinking at an earlier age than Piaget proposed, and that they can think at higher levels than Piaget suggested, even to the propositional stage that Piaget believed only adolescents or adults could use. Piaget also underestimated the individual differences between children in how they develop, and the fact that some of these differences are due to the cultural and social background of the child. Piaget also did not take much notice of the way children can learn from others, seeing learning as largely dependent on their stage of development. Notwithstanding that, Piaget's theories have stood the test of time well, and are still a useful way of looking at children's development.

Vygotsky: the social side of learning

Vygotsky was a Russian psychologist, who worked at around the same time as Piaget (although he died younger) and was influenced by Piaget's work. During his lifetime he was not well known in the West, but after his death (in particular since the 1960s) he has become increasingly influential.

Vygotsky's main interest was the study of language development, which he believed initially develops separately from thought, but starts to overlap with thought more and more as the child grows up. According to Vygotsky, a non-overlapping part still remains later in life; some non-verbal thought and some non-conceptual speech remaining even in adults (Vygotsky 1978; Moll 1992).

A major disagreement between Piaget and Vygotsky was that Vygotsky did not think that maturation in itself could make children achieve advanced thinking skills. Vygotsky, while seeing a role for maturation, believed that it was children's interaction with others through language that most strongly influenced the level of conceptual understanding they could reach (Vygostky 1978).

Vygotsky strongly believed that we can learn from others, both of the same age and of a higher age and developmental level. One of the main ways this operates is through *scaffolding* in the *zone of proximal development* (ZPD). This latter concept, one of Vygotsky's main contributions to learning theory, refers to the gap between what a person is able to do alone and what they can do with the help of someone more knowledgeable or skilled than themselves. It is here that the role of teachers, adults and peers comes to the fore in children's learning, in that they can help bring the child's knowledge to a higher level by intervening in the ZPD. This can be done by providing children's thoughts with so-called scaffolds, which, once the learning process is complete, are no longer needed by the child. Children are not all equally *educable* in this respect, some being able to learn more in the ZPD than others.

Thus, for Vygotsky, it is *cooperation* that lies at the basis of learning. It is *instruction*, formal and informal, performed by more knowledgeable others, such as parents, peers, grandparents or teachers that is the main means of transmission of the knowledge of a particular culture. Knowledge for Vygotsky, as for Piaget, is embodied in actions and interactions with the environment (or culture), but unlike Piaget, Vygotsky stresses the importance of *interaction* with a living representative of the culture.

While Piaget has been criticized as being too strongly focused on developmental learning, Vygotsky's work is seen as suffering from the opposite problem. Vygostky wrote little about children's natural development and the relationship of that to their learning (Wertsch and Tulviste 1992). Vygotsky's theories are also in many ways rather general and overarching, and have not been fully worked out (that Vygotsky died at the age of 37 is one reason for this). Vygotsky's contribution lies mainly in his attention to the social aspects of learning, which clearly need complementing by what current research is teaching us about brain functions.

This view of learning as socially constructed strongly influenced the so-called constructivist theories that have followed since then, and has influenced classroom practice. His ideas about pupils' learning in their ZPD have been influential in the development of collaborative learning programmes.

Task 4.2

How do you think the theories of Piaget and Vygotsky should influence teaching? What can teachers do to take into account both Piagetian stages of learning and the importance of the ZPD?

4.4 IQ theory

Another theory that has had a lasting influence in education (whether this has been for the good is debatable) is Intelligence Quotient (IQ) theory.

IQ theory is mainly interested in the concept of intelligence, which is seen as determining people's ability to learn, to achieve academically and therefore to take on leading roles in society. IQ theorists, like William Stern, who was one of the developers of the theory in the early part of the twentieth century, claimed that core intelligence was innate. Many psychologists in America and England supported that conclusion. Using tests of intelligence, often developed for specific purposes such as screening for the US army or screening of immigrants, psychologists like Terman and Binet developed instruments designed to test people's innate 'intelligence', which were analyzed using the newest statistical methods such as factor analysis, developed by Thurstone and Spearman. These analyses showed that all the items (questions) in those tests essentially measured one big factor, called G, or 'general intelligence'. Therefore, the theory states that people have one underlying general intelligence, which will predict how well they are able to learn and perform at school (Howe 1997).

A major point of discussion is whether intelligence as measured by IQ tests is innate or learned, and to what extent. The initial theories largely stressed the innate nature of intelligence, seeing it as an inborn property. Subsequent research has, however, clearly shown that IQ can be raised through educational interventions, which means that it cannot be totally inborn. The successful Cognitive Acceleration in Science Education (CASE) programme in the UK, for example, does just that (Adey and Shayer 2002). Another fact that points to the mutability of IQ is that average IQ test scores have been increasing steadily over the past decades, in all countries where they have been studied (Flynn 1994). When we are testing someone's IQ, we are therefore testing his or her education level at least as much (if not more) than whatever innate ability they may possess. Also, it has become clear that children's IQ test scores are strongly influenced by their so-called cultural capital, that is their cultural resources (how many books they read, what media they access and so on). This in turn is strongly determined by their parents' socio-economic status, or their position in the social class system (Gould 1983; Howe 1997; Muijs 1997).

As well as the issue of whether IQ is innate or acquired, the whole theory of IQ has been heavily criticized for many years now. These criticisms focus on a number of areas. The first of these is the methods used to measure intelligence, which produced G. While we don't want to go into a discussion of statistics here, it is fair to say that the factor analysis method these researchers developed was specifically designed to come up with one big underlying factor, and usually does. If you use different methods, you are likely to find far more factors. Therefore, in many ways it is pre-existing theories which led to the development of methods designed to confirm these theories (Muijs 2004). The theory of intelligence also focuses purely on 'academic' intelligence, and so disparages other skills and abilities. As we will see, recent theories have taken a different approach to these matters (Gardner 1983). The idea that there is one measurable factor that distinguishes people has also been widely misused. One of the earliest uses of IQ tests was to look at differences in intelligence between particular groups in society, which were then said to be differently intelligent (and by implication more or less suitable to take on leading roles in society). The findings of these studies tell us far more about the societies in which they were carried out than about the 'intelligence' of different groups (which as a matter of fact does not differ significantly). Thus, in the US, research concentrated on finding differences between racial groups, in France on differences between genders (men scoring higher than women) and in the UK on differences in social class (the higher classes coming out as more intelligent than the working class; Blum 1980; Gould 1983).

Notwithstanding these criticisms, it would be wrong to reject wholly IQ theory. There is evidence that an underlying general aptitude influences how well pupils perform on a variety of subjects. There is a far stronger correlation between pupils' performance in maths and English than is often realized, for example. As we will see later, if conceptualized as just one of a number of possible 'intelligences', the study of the kind of intelligence measured by IQ tests may have some merit.

Task 4.3

Do you think there is such a thing as intelligence? Is it inborn, acquired, or both? In what ways do you think IQ theory has influenced educational practice?

4.5 The theory of multiple intelligences

As we saw in the previous section, the theory of IQ stresses the existence of one overarching intelligence, a view that has become increasingly controversial over time. For many decades, however, no alternative theory was able to overcome the dominance of IQ theory whenever ability and intelligence were studied. This changed in 1983 with the publication of *Frames of Mind* by Howard Gardner (1983), in which he set out his theory of 'multiple intelligences' (MI).

Gardner takes a view that is very different from that of IQ theory mentioned earlier. According to him, people do not have one general intelligence, but are characterized by a range of intelligences instead. So, rather than being globally intelligent, I may be particularly strong in certain areas, for example mathematics, while someone else may be particularly strong in another area, for example, physical sports.

Gardner (1983, 1993) distinguishes nine main types of intelligence:

1   **Visual/Spatial Intelligence.** This is the ability to *perceive the visual*. Visual/spatial learners tend to think in pictures and need to create vivid mental images to retain information. They enjoy looking at pictures, charts, movies and so on.

2   **Verbal/Linguistic Intelligence.** This is the *ability to use words and language*. These learners have highly developed auditory skills and are generally elegant speakers. They think in words rather than pictures. This is the ability that can be measured by the verbal part of IQ tests.

3   **Logical/Mathematical Intelligence.** This is the *ability to use reason, logic and numbers*. These learners think conceptually in logical and numerical patterns, making connections between pieces of information. They ask lots of questions and like to do experiments. The non-verbal portion of traditional IQ tests largely measures this intelligence.

4   **Bodily/Kinaesthetic Intelligence.** This is the *ability to control body movements and handle objects skilfully*. These learners express themselves through movement. They have a good sense of balance and eye–hand coordination. Through interacting with the space around them, they are able to remember and process information.

5   **Musical/Rhythmic Intelligence.** This is the *ability to produce and appreciate music.* These learners think in sounds, rhythms and patterns. They respond strongly to music and rhythm. Many of these learners are extremely sensitive to sounds occurring in their environment.

6   **Interpersonal Intelligence.** This is the *ability to relate to and understand others.* These learners can empathize and see things from other people's point of view in order to understand how they think and feel. They are good at sensing feelings, intentions and motivations. Generally they try to maintain peace in group settings and encourage cooperation. They can be manipulative.

7   **Intrapersonal Intelligence.** This is the *ability to self-reflect and be aware of one's inner states.* These learners try to understand their inner feelings, dreams, relationships with others, and strengths and weaknesses. Their strength lies in the ability to be self-reflective.

8   **Naturalist Intelligence.** This is the a*bility to recognize and categorize plants, animals and other objects in nature.* Learners with strong naturalist intelligence are good at recognizing, categorizing and drawing upon certain features of the environment.

9   **Existentialist Intelligence.** This is the *sensitivity and capacity to tackle deep questions about human existence, such as the meaning of life, why do we die and how did we get here.* Existentialist learners tend to have strong spiritual leanings and be interested in deeper underlying issues (Gardner 1983, 1993, 2003).

A misconception that exists is that one intelligence is necessarily dominant. This is not really the case, as all of us will possess all intelligences to some extent. It is also important to remember that doing something will usually require use of more than one intelligence.

To some, it might seem that this choice of different intelligences is somewhat arbitrary. Gardner's theories are sometimes seen as somewhat unscientific, a seemingly random selection of intelligences. This is a misconception, arising mainly from vulgarization and low-level application of his theories in education. In fact, Gardner (2003) uses a number of quite stringent criteria for defining an intelligence, taken from a variety of disciplines such as developmental psychology and cultural anthropology:

1   **Isolation as a brain function.** A true intelligence will have its function identified in a specific location in the human brain. This can increasingly be determined using the latest brain imaging techniques.

2   **Prodigies, *idiots savants* and exceptional individuals.** In order to qualify as an intelligence, there must be some evidence of specific 'geniuses' in that particular area, such as Maradonna (bodily kinaesthetic).

3   **Set of core operations.** Each true intelligence has a set of unique and identifiable procedures at its heart.

4   **Developmental history.** A true intelligence is associated with an identifiable set of stages of growth, and with a Mastery Level which exists as an end state in human development.

evolutionary history. A true intelligence can have its development traced through the evolution of our species as identified by cultural anthropologists.

6   **Supported psychological tasks**. A true intelligence can be identified by specific tasks which can be carried out, observed and measured by clinical psychologists.

7   **Supported psychometric tasks**. Specifically designed psychometric tests can be used to measure the intelligence.

8   **Encoded into a symbol system**. A true intelligence has its own symbol system which is unique to it and essential to completing its tasks.

Gardner's theory has proved both popular and controversial in education, and the two conditions are closely linked. As often happens in education, valid psychological theories are taken on board by educators or commercial consultants who do not understand them well and produce a low-level vulgarized version for use in schools. Gardner himself for a long time remained silent on the issue of use of MI theory in the classroom, but more recently has pointed to a number of misuses he sees of his theories in education:

1   Sometimes it is inferred that all subjects or concepts need to be taught using all nine intelligences. According to Gardner (1995), while most topics can be taught in a number of ways, it is usually a waste of time to try to teach a topic using all nine intelligences.

2   Going through the motions of using an intelligence does not in itself lead to learning. Gardner gives the example of some teachers getting children to run around as a way of exercising bodily/kinaesthetic intelligence!

3   Gardner (1995) also does not believe that the use of materials associated with a MI as background (e.g. playing music in the classroom) will do anything to aid learners who are strong in that area.

4   Sometimes teachers claim they are exercising pupils' MIs (in this case musical/ rhythmic intelligence) by getting them to sing or dance while reciting something like a times table. While this may help them remember it, Gardner (1995) describes such a use of MI as trivial. What educators should encourage instead is thinking musically or drawing on some of the structural aspects of music in order to illuminate concepts in other fields (like maths).

5   The use of various measures or instruments that grade intelligences is seen by Gardner as being directly in opposition to his views of intelligence as something that occurs when carrying out activities within cultural settings.

All this does not mean that Gardner sees MI as irrelevant to classroom teaching. The consequences he sees are the following (Gardner 1995):

1   The curriculum should be broadened so that schools cultivate those skills and capacities that are valued in the community and in the broader society, not just traditional academic school subjects.

2   Rather than going for a broad but shallow curriculum, schools should focus on

key topics, which can be explored in depth. Exploring key ideas in depth and in a lateral way should allow teachers to address different intelligences (although not all at once!).

3   Individual differences should be taken seriously. Education is most effective when it takes into account the different strengths and ways of thinking of different individuals.

One issue for teachers here is that they themselves will tend towards preferring certain intelligences and will, as a result of this, be likely to teach towards those intelligences, which may not correspond to those of their pupils. Being aware of what different learning styles exist among pupils, what one's own learning style is and how to teach to different learning styles are therefore important skills in this area (see Chapter 6).

While Gardner's theories have been widely influential in education recently (although, as mentioned above, not always in the most helpful way), they have also been subject to criticism. One criticism focuses on what is seen as a lack of testability of Gardner's theories. This is seen to result from an ambiguity of the theory, in that it is not clear to what extent the intelligences are supposed to operate separately or interconnectedly. The fact that the existence or not of an intelligence is not testable experimentally and cannot be accurately psychometrically assessed is also critiqued (Klein 1997), although Gardner would argue that this critique misunderstands the theory which sees intelligences as operating in cultural action. The lack of a clear definition of what intelligence is has also come under fire, with some authors stating that what Gardner is studying are in fact cognitive styles rather than intelligences (Morgan 1996). The criteria he uses have been described as somewhat arbitrary (White 1998), and Gardner is seen as not providing a clear explanation as to why these and not other possible criteria were chosen (Klein 1997). The fact that the number of intelligences he proposes regularly increases has reinforced these criticisms. Further evolution in brain science may allow us more accurately to assess the validity of the theory; what seems clear already is that in moving education on from traditional IQ theory, Gardner has done us a big favour.

Task 4.4

If you think about teaching you have done, or experienced, do you think the different intelligences of pupils have been addressed? Which ones were and which weren't? What could be done to address more intelligences?

4.6 Cognitive theory and brain research

What many of the older learning theories (like behaviourism and the theories of Vygotsky) were not able to incorporate was any theory of how the brain works (due to limitations in research methods at the time). More recently, however, brain research and the neurosciences have progressed greatly, and are informing learning theory and education to an ever greater extent. To some extent, these new methods are confirming theories that we discussed earlier, like Vygotsky's views on learning, but they are also offering us important new insights.

One of the first major theories of learning that explicitly based itself on our emerging knowledge of the brain was cognitive information processing theory. Especially important in this theory is the role of memory in learning processes. The memory consists of three parts: the sensory buffer, the working memory and the long-term memory.

The memory works as follows: one's experiences (tactile, visual or auditory) are registered in the sensory buffer, and then converted into the form in which they are employed in the working and long-term memories. The sensory buffer can register a lot of information, but can only hold it briefly. Some parts of the information in it will be lost, other parts will be transmitted to the working memory. The working memory is where 'thinking gets done'. It receives its content from the sensory buffer and the long-term memory but has a limited capacity for storing information, a fact that limits human mental processes. The working memory contains the information that is actively being used at any one time.

The long-term memory has a nodal structure, and consists of neural network representations, whose nodes represent chunks in memory and whose links represent connections between those chunks. As such, nodes can be equated with concepts, and links with meaningful associations between concepts. Together these form schemata, or clusters of information. Activating one item of the cluster is likely to activate all of them (Best 1999). This means that memorization and making connections are two crucial components of learning, according to cognitive information processing theory. Making connections is particularly important. The brain has literally millions of neurons that can be linked in neural nets in an almost unlimited number of ways.

Brain research is also telling us that the brain is a pattern maker. The brain takes great pleasure in taking random and chaotic information and ordering it. The

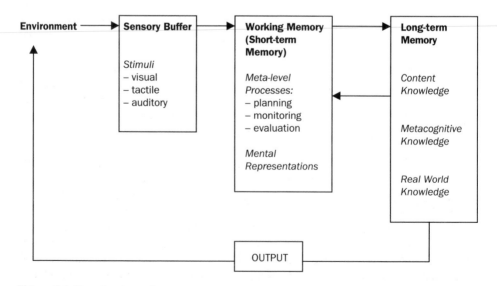

Figure 4.1 The structure of memory

implications for learning and instruction are that presenting a learner with random and unordered information provides the maximum opportunity for the brain to order this information and form meaningful patterns that will be remembered. Setting up a learning environment in this way mirrors real life, which is often random and chaotic (Lackney 1999). The brain, when allowed to express its pattern-making behaviour, creates coherency and meaning. Learning is best accomplished when the learning activity is connected directly to physical experience. We remember best when facts and skills are embedded in natural, real-life activity. We learn by doing. The implications of applying the findings of neuroscience related to coherency and meaning suggest that learning is facilitated in an environment of total immersion in a multitude of complex, interactive experiences which could include traditional instructional methods as part of this larger experience (Kotulak 1996; Lackney 1999).

Brain research also suggests that the brain is continually growing and changing throughout our life, but that this process is more pronounced at certain developmental stages, which can be seen as a 'window of opportunity' for learning. During childhood, this process of selectively strengthening and pruning connections in the brain is at its most intense, and it is therefore fair to say that this is a crucial period in development. Although this process continues throughout our lives, it seems to be most pronounced between the ages of 2 and 11, as different development areas emerge and taper off. During these critical periods, the brain demands specific and extensive (stimulating) inputs to create or consolidate neural networks, especially for acquiring language, emotional control and learning to play music. While one can learn outside of this period, what one has acquired during these windows of opportunity is crucial to what can subsequently be learned (Sousa 1998).

Another important finding relates to the strong evidence of individual differences between the brain functioning of different learners. While the basic brain architecture is essentially the same, brain scans have shown that, for example, 'while most people, when they recognize an object visually, show increased activity in the back part of their brains, the exact magnitude, location, and distribution of that increased activity varies quite a bit' (Rose and Meyer 2002: 64). Similarly, learners differ in the strategies they employ to make connections in the brain (Dall'Alba 2006). This is important for teachers, as it means both that, as constructivist educators have long claimed, each learner will construct knowledge in a slightly different way, and that teaching should be varied to address the different needs and strategies of learners, a finding that confirms the views of those who take a 'multiple intelligences' approach. This is not the same as saying that there are different 'learning styles', or that these can easily be categorized. An example of an idea based on learning styles is the use of the VAK categorization, very popular in England, not least following its support by the DfES (2004a). VAK stands for visual, auditory and kinaesthetic, the three main learning styles that are claimed to differentiate learners. It is claimed that learners predominantly use one of three 'sensory receivers' to process information, and that teachers should therefore make sure that their teaching addresses all three types (Dunn 1990). While using a variety of teaching methods is always sensible, there is actually very little evidence for the existence of the VAK styles, or indeed of many other learning styles that have been developed, and basing teaching methods on these is therefore not recommended (Coffield et al. 2004).

The final critical finding from brain research relates to the importance of emotion in learning. Emotions can both help and hinder learning. On the positive side, emotions help us to recall information from the long-term memory, through allowing any information received through the sensory buffer to be perceived as positive or a threat. Research suggests that the brain learns best when confronted with a balance between high challenge and low threat. The brain needs some challenge to activate emotions and learning. This is because if there is no stress the brain becomes too relaxed and cannot actively engage in learning. Too much stress is also negative, however, as it will lead to anxiety and a 'fight' response which are inimical to learning. A physically safe environment is particularly important in reducing overly strong levels of stress (Sousa 1998).

Brain research is a constantly developing research field, and it is highly likely that further developments will in future strongly inform our views on learning, and our teaching strategies. However, one caveat does apply: while I have presented a number of basic findings, this research area is diverse. Findings from different studies do not always agree with one another, and are usually far more subtle than I have been able to outline in this introductory text. Also, it is always dangerous to try and directly translate findings from brain research into the classroom. This type of research should clearly inform us, but we need to take into account that it has been conducted for very different purposes, and will always need to be matched to educational research findings on effective classroom teaching before it can be translated into effective classroom strategies.

4.7 Summary

In this chapter we have looked at some educationally influential theories of learning and intelligence.

Behaviourism was mainly concerned with how we learn from external stimuli. Using experimental methods, behaviourists looked at how behaviour can be conditioned, for example by providing rewards and punishments.

Piaget used observation to come to his theories of learning. His key concept is *maturation*, the unfolding of biological changes that are genetically programmed into us. A second factor is *activity*. Increasing maturation leads to an increase in children's ability to act on their environment, and to learn from their actions. An important finding of Piaget's is that growing up does not just mean knowing more, it actually entails a change in how we think.

Vygotsky concentrated on the fact that learning is a social process, and that we learn through interaction with others, both of the same age and of a higher age and developmental level. This process operates through *scaffolding* in the ZPD. The ZPD is the gap between what a person is able to do alone and what they can do with the help of someone more knowledgeable or skilled than themselves. Scaffolding refers to the way others can help us to bridge that gap.

IQ theory focuses on the concept of intelligence. According to IQ theorists there is one underlying, general intelligence that determines our capacity for learning. More recently, Gardner developed his theory of multiple intelligences. Rather than just the one intelligence, there are nine according to Gardner: visual/spatial, verbal/

linguistic, logical/mathematical, bodily/kinaesthetic, musical/rhythmic, interpersonal, intrapersonal, naturalist and existentialist. For most tasks, we need to deploy more than one intelligence.

Brain research is a fast developing area in psychology that is producing valuable findings for educators. One of these is that we learn best when challenged but not stressed. Another is the importance of pattern making in the brain. This implies that we need to provide children with the opportunity to create patterns. Finally, brain research confirms that while we can learn throughout our life, early childhood is a key period in developing (the capacity for) learning.

4.8 Recommendations for further reading

Best, J.B. (1998) *Cognitive Psychology*. New York: Wiley.
Gardner, H. (1993) *Multiple Intelligences: The Theory in Practice*. New York: Basic Books.
O'Donohue, W. and Ferguson, K.E. (2001) *The Psychology of B.F. Skinner*. Thousand Oaks, CA: Sage Publications.
Piaget, J. and Inhelder, B. (2000) *The Psychology of the Child*. New York: Basic Books.
Vygotsky, L., Vygotsky, S. and John-Steiner, V. (eds) (1978) *Mind in Society: The Development of Higher Psychological Processes*. Cambridge, MA: Harvard University Press.

5

Planning for learning

Paul Elliott

5.1 Introduction

It is necessary to understand what it is that teachers do in order to understand why planning is the activity that underpins success. This chapter will first explore the journey that teachers facilitate, from where the pupil is and has been (prior learning) to where they need to be (learning outcomes). Appreciating the range of approaches that can be used to help different types of learners on this journey is important, as is the ability to make conscious decisions about which are most appropriate in particular circumstances. Guidance will be given on how to construct a lesson plan and you will be shown how planning, at a very practical level, can help pupils' learning. Effective planning is also the best way to reduce the stress and anxiety you will feel in the classroom and ensure that things go smoothly for you. Only good planning will give you the confidence and clarity of purpose that will encourage the pupils to view you as someone in whose lessons they can learn. Since virtually all pupils want to learn, good planning will help you to build good relationships.

When you observe an experienced and successful teacher at work, it can be hard to appreciate how difficult teaching is. The lesson will proceed smoothly, all necessary resources will be at hand and the pupils will be interested in and engaged with the work. It is only when you try to emulate this performance that you are likely to discover how much experience the teacher was drawing on and/or how much effort they have put into planning their lesson. Great lessons do not just happen and they are not a product of good luck. Great lessons are a product of great planning, plus a little bit of inspiration and a tiny amount of good fortune. You can aspire to teach great lessons, but only if you are prepared to put time and intelligent effort into planning.

By the end of this chapter you should appreciate that good planning:

- starts with establishing 'where your pupils are';
- involves being clear about what you want them to achieve by the end of the lesson;
- requires you to think about how you can help pupils make progress;

- is something you can best demonstrate by producing a detailed written record of your thinking.

The principles of good planning discussed in this chapter are relevant to lessons at KS3, KS4 and post-16.

5.2 Establishing where pupils are

The success of your teaching is judged by the learning that your pupils do. Your first task is to establish what they already know, understand or can do: 'where they are now'. Two analogies can make the reason for this clear.

- **Bus stops**

    Think of yourself as a bus driver. You need to be clear about your destination. However, you also need to make sure that you stop at the right bus stop to pick up passengers. If you do not stop, very few of your passengers will be able to run fast enough to catch the bus.

- **Building bridges**

    Imagine that some of your pupils are standing on one bank of a river; other pupils are further back from the river while others are in midstream. The opposite bank is where you would like them to be. How are you going to get them there? Only a few will be capable of jumping across. The rest will need some help getting there. You need to build a bridge, or a number of bridges, to cater for the needs of all pupils. The bridges need to start where your pupils are and end up where you want them to be. The bridges need to be built carefully and probably in collaboration with your pupils otherwise some will fall into the river and be lost. Some scaffolding would be useful to construct the bridges.

It should be clear from both of these analogies that your lesson plan needs to take account of what your pupils already know, understand and can do. This applies at the start of a new topic, but is also likely to be the case at the beginning of lessons. You may think the content of the previous lesson will be clear in your pupils' minds, but remember that since they last saw you they will have been to several other lessons and subjects.

How can you find out where pupils are starting? There are a number of tactics that you can use:

1   Outside of the classroom

- Check what they have already studied by looking at SoW and the topics they have been taught prior to you taking the class. Cross-reference this information to the NC examination syllabuses.
- Look at pupils' exercise books to check the subject matter they have encountered and find clues about the level at which they have been learning and the range of support you will need to give.
- Ask to see assessment data for the members of the class.

2   Inside the classroom

- Question pupils on aspects of the topic with which they may already have some familiarity. Listen carefully to their responses (see Chapter 8).
- Set tasks to find out what they can do before you start (see Chapter 9).

  These could include pre-tests, quizzes, concept mapping exercises, sorting games and so on.
- Talk to pupils. Each individual will bring a different level of understanding to your lesson.

Try to avoid making assumptions about what a class will know or can do. If you do this, or misjudge where they are, you risk losing them by making too big a leap for them to follow or boring or patronizing them by covering work they have done before.

5.3 Identifying learning outcomes

Once you have established where your pupils are, the next step is to decide where they need to go next. Think in terms of what the pupils need to know, understand or be able to do at the end of a lesson or series of lessons, rather than what you are going to *teach* them. The input that you make should be determined by the outcome that is desirable. It is also crucial that you think in terms of how you will know that you have succeeded. What will characterize success and how will you *measure* it?

Planning can be based upon the behaviours that are the desirable outcome of learning. The intended learning outcome for a lesson can be framed in a way that describes a behaviour, preferably a measurable one. However, there will be differences between, and within, subject areas. For example, planning in RE might be more concerned with non-behavioural objectives which are more difficult to measure. This might involve introducing objectives related to values, attitudes or beliefs.

It would be easy to devise a learning objective for a history lesson on the English Civil War that read something like:

- *Understand the reasons for the rise of the parliamentarian movement.*

  While this may be a desirable outcome for the lesson, it is incredibly difficult to measure whether or not you have been successful. Whereas, by contrast:
- *Be able to describe at least three factors that gave rise to the parliamentarian movement.*

  This allows you to use questioning, output from class work, homework activities or testing to judge your success. The second version becomes part of the assessment cycle (see Chapter 9) and allows you to evaluate your own performance in terms of what your pupils have learned.

Bloom's Taxonomy (Bloom et al. 1956) is a useful way of categorizing the levels of demand in thinking and learning represented by different types of task. The taxonomy categorizes learning outcomes into three domains: cognitive, affective and psychomotor. The cognitive domain is broken down into six areas:

- knowledge
- comprehension
- application
- analysis
- synthesis
- evaluation.

It is helpful to draw on this approach during planning, to ensure pupils are being given opportunities to demonstrate what they have learned. For instance, in addition to the word 'understand', mentioned in the English Civil War example earlier, there are other terms that it is easy to use when phrasing intended learning outcomes which give only a poor indication of what outcomes might be expected; examples include:

know   *memorize*
become familiar with   *appreciate the significance of*

Figure 5.1 shows a range of terms that can be much more useful when trying to identify appropriate learning objectives. Note that these are in themes, related but not identical to Bloom's Taxonomy. The terms demonstrate a general increase in demand or difficulty as you go down the table.

Draw	State	Record	Recognize	Identify	
Sort	Describe	Select	Present	Locate information from text	
Decide	Discuss	Define	Classify	Explain what...	
Devise	Calculate	Interpret	Construct	Clarify	
Plan	Predict	Conclude	Solve	Determine the key points from...	
Formulate	Explain why	Use the pattern to...	Reorganize	Explain the differences between...	
Link/make connections between...	Use the idea of...to...	Use a model of...to...	Provide evidence for...	Evaluate the evidence for...	

(vertical label at right: General increase in demand)

Figure 5.1 Useful words to use for defining intended learning outcomes
(DfES 2002a)

Task 5.1

Choose a topic from your subject that might be taught in one lesson or a short series of lessons. Use the NC, exam syllabus or QCA SoW to work out what relevant prior learning pupils might have. Identify the learning that you would expect to take place when you teach the topic and try to devise statements that describe the outcomes in behavioural terms, using Figure 5.1 for guidance. What techniques could you use to assess whether the teaching had been successful?

5.4 How can you help your pupils get there?

Having established where your pupils are starting from (prior learning and attainment) and where you need to get them (intended learning outcomes), you need to determine a number of other things if you are to plan effectively.

First, you need to be clear how long you have with the class:

- the length of lessons will be determined by the school;
- the department's SoW will almost certainly specify the number of lessons to be devoted to the topic.

These factors will set the framework within which you work. Most departments have SoW in place for most topics and do not expect a trainee to create one from scratch. The SoW will normally be produced by a group of teachers who have collaborated to identify a route through the syllabus or curriculum that takes account of the learning that should take place, the resources and time available and the ideas and enthusiasms of the staff. However, you will have some degree of flexibility in how you interpret a SoW and should certainly aim to personalise aspects so that you can take ownership of it when you translate it into real lessons. You would be wise to plan to use slightly less time than the SoW indicates, because some of the learning may take longer than you anticipate and things like school trips, epidemics and tests can eat into available time. The time might also be needed to respond to feedback from formative assessment (see Chapter 9).

Pupils can be more efficient at learning early in the morning and earlier in the week, so check when lessons are and plan accordingly. Also, check what the pupils have done immediately before your lesson, since this will affect their attention and energy levels.

Homework should be integral to your planning and, used carefully, can allow you to devote time in the classroom to collaborative rather than individual learning.

Before going too far with your plans, you need to check what resources are available. Resources include props, ICT hardware and software, access to specialist teaching rooms and the human support of technicians, librarians, learning assistants and even external speakers. In some cases, you may have the chance to plan learning opportunities off the school site; for example, theatre visits, geography or science fieldwork, and visits to businesses or religious sites.

How are you going to assess how successfully pupils learn during the topic? You will almost certainly be preparing them for some sort of summative assessment, be it an end of topic test, a modular exam or coursework assignment and you need to be aware of the attendant requirements and expectations. You need to ensure that your pupils are properly prepared, but should avoid 'teaching to the test'. Concurrently, a major part of your planning should focus on how you are going to formatively assess pupils' progress during the topic. This should be guided by the intended learning outcomes, since you and your pupils need feedback on how effectively these are being met. It is also useful if you have some idea of where pupils are meant to be 'going next' since no topic that you teach will stand alone. Even if the factual content is not directly linked to any other part of the course, the development of pupils' skills will be. You need to know how the topic you are to teach will contribute to pupils' progression.

Really effective planning will also take account of what pupils are doing in other subject areas, especially where the learning in one subject supports pupil learning in another. For instance, work on graphs in maths should have some bearing on the graph work that is expected of pupils in science lessons. In this case, both science and maths teachers should be aware of each other's requirements and take account of these in their planning.

5.5 Planning for success

A huge amount of time during training is spent planning lessons. At times this will frustrate and exhaust you, but it is central to your success as a teacher. Carefully planned lessons are more likely to succeed. All your plans must exist in written form to provide evidence of the process you have been through. Mentors, tutors and external examiners will draw on them to inform judgements about your progress towards QTS. Your lesson plans will also be scrutinized if the school you are working in, or the course you are training on, is inspected. It can be difficult to reconcile the amount of time you spend putting your plans down in writing when more experienced teachers seem to get away with something far briefer. The truth is that good, experienced teachers are far more practised at teaching than you are and they automatically internalize aspects of the planning process. Even they have to put detailed plans on paper when producing a portfolio of evidence to cross the pay threshold or to achieve Advanced Skills Teacher status or when their school is being inspected.

The experienced teachers who you work with in school will give you assistance with lesson planning, but ultimately the plans need to be yours. Avoid trying to teach someone else's lesson, unless as a deliberate learning tactic. At the end of the chapter there are some websites from which you can download lesson plans, but you have to process the plans to tailor them to suit your pupils and your needs and strengths. If the plan is not really yours then you will not have engaged with all aspects of the planning process and will not feel fully committed to it.

Planning lessons is a complex business. Let us consider some of the fundamental processes that you need to engage in when planning a lesson.

Subject content and skills

First, you need to be clear what it is that your pupils are supposed to be learning. This will relate to specific subject-based information, but also to relevant skills, including those of literacy, numeracy and ICT. You then need to check that you have sufficient personal subject knowledge to help your pupils learn. If there are deficits in your knowledge, you will have to address them in advance of the lesson. At the same time you need to consider how you are going to make your personal knowledge accessible to Year 7, Year 10 and so on; you need to 're-shape ideas to represent knowledge in different ways' (Ellis et al. 2002: 34).

Planning for progression

Make sure you understand what pupils already know and be clear where they need to get to (intended learning outcomes). How will you differentiate your teaching and your expectations so that lower attaining pupils can still achieve something because of the support you give and the manageable tasks you set? Some pupils are likely to have individual education plans (IEPs), which you will need to consider (see Chapter 21). How will the more able in your class be challenged and stimulated by your lesson? It helps to consider what you want all, most or some to be able to do (see Chapter 6).

Resources

You will need to think about resources at least three times in your planning!

1   Identify the resources available to you that *could* be used to help your pupils learn.
2   Decide which of these is most appropriate to help pupils meet the intended learning outcomes.
3   Make absolutely certain that the resources you want to use will be available. Some you may need to order (e.g. science equipment), some you may have to book (e.g. ICT suite or drama studio), some you may have to collect for yourself (e.g. fresh fungi for an art lesson or leaflets from a medical centre for a Personal, Social and Health education [PSHE] lesson). An oversight in these areas is easy to make, but could be disastrous and very stressful. Check the minutiae: have you got the key to the room, have you got whiteboard pens, have you got spare pens to lend pupils, have you got something to light the Bunsen burners with?

Resources may need organizing well in advance of your lesson.

Safety should be incorporated into all planning, but for some subjects (e.g. PE, science, technology) this is a big issue and needs to be done overtly, in writing. In such subjects you will probably receive specialised training in risk assessment. In all cases the responsibility for safety in lessons lies with the normal class teacher, so it is in their interests to check your plan in advance of a lesson. You should have your plan ready sufficiently in advance of a lesson for the class teacher and/or mentor to check.

5.6 Structuring a lesson

So far, we have considered planning in a general sense, as it applies to any defined period of learning. For much of your time though, you will be preoccupied with the planning of specific lessons, so the rest of this chapter will deal with this.

The underlying sequence of events when planning a lesson should be:

Identify what the learning outcomes should be.
⇓
Identify and choose activities that help deliver the learning outcomes.
⇓
Determine what you have to do to facilitate these activities.

Be clear about the learning that needs to take place in the lesson, then investigate what activities might successfully bring this about, rather than trying to think of a justification for using an activity you have come across or had suggested to you. Next, think carefully about the lesson's exact structure. By adopting a clear structure for your planning you will find the task of helping pupils meet the learning objectives more manageable. You will also find that your pupils respond more positively if you have planned the learning as a set of discrete 'chunks' that will not test their powers of concentration for too long. If you make your pupils do any activity for too long, for example listening to you, writing, discussing, watching a video, you will start to see diminishing returns. By incorporating variety, you stand a good chance of maintaining their interest, motivation and momentum.

Lessons should have clear beginnings, middles and ends. It is surprising how many student teachers get bogged down with the 'middle' and neglect to plan for an effective start to their lesson or a discernible end. The Secondary Strategy in England has refocused teachers' attention on lesson planning and has sharpened the definition of 'beginning, middle and end', so that they have become 'starter, main activity(ies) and plenary'. A lesson should not necessarily contain only three phases, but these components are a useful tool in planning. Figure 5.2 overleaf represents various ways of structuring a lesson, but each is built on the principle of starter, main activity, plenary.

5.7 Starting a lesson

Before your lesson, your pupils may have been stimulated to the extent that their adrenaline is flowing and they find it difficult to settle. At the other extreme, they may have come from a stuffy, overheated classroom in which they were being bored to tears. If they have come to you after a break then anything is possible! You may not have seen them for days, in which case the topic of the last lesson with you may have dimmed in the memory. In all of these cases, your challenge is to get them learning. Some experienced teachers have their class so well trained that calling a register is effective in calming them down and establishing who is boss. For a student teacher, starting a lesson this way can present a class with an opportunity to challenge their authority. Even if you can do it effectively, it is still a pretty boring way to start a

Lesson plan structure 1

Starter	Main activity	Plenary

Lesson plan structure 2

Starter	1st main activity	Short plenary	2nd main activity	Longer plenary

Lesson plan structure 3

Starter	Whole class same task	Plenary 1	Whole class same task	Plenary 2	Whole class different task	Plenary 3

Lesson plan structure 4

Starter	Main activity Groups working on different tasks or circus of tasks	Plenary

Figure 5.2 Model lesson structures
(Adapted from DfEs 2002a)

lesson! It is much easier to take a register once pupils have engaged with a motivating task.

Reassure your pupils that you have a plan by sharing the purpose of your lesson with them. Since you cannot guarantee that all pupils will be paying attention, it is worth reinforcing this visually. The learning objectives you have identified for the lesson are unlikely to be in a suitable format for sharing with pupils, but can easily be translated into pupil-friendly language, displayed on a board and explained to them. You can also flag up any new or recently introduced key words at this stage. Pupils will also respond better if you give them an overview of the structure of the lesson, so that they understand better what is expected of them.

It is in your interests to start your lesson in a way that focuses attention quickly on the main theme of your lesson. Plan something that:

- you can start quickly;
- will stimulate your pupils' interest;

- will build bridges between relevant prior learning and today's lesson.

There are many tactics that can be used to start a lesson in a way that quickly engages pupils' attention, helps them to focus on the theme or purpose of the lesson and its objectives, but which do not take too much time. Table 5.1 offers a range of activities that can be employed to start lessons in ways that will achieve these aims. Try to employ a variety so that the starts of your lessons do not become predictable.

Table 5.1 Examples of starter techniques

Technique	Features
Sequencing	Put something on paper that has a sequential order to it. Give pupils envelopes containing the cut up sequence for them to order.
Card sort	Prepare sets of cards that can be paired up. Pupils work in small teams to see who can correctly pair them fastest.
Continuum	Pupils to position themselves on an imaginary line representing the range of views from one extreme to another (e.g. from *personal firearms should be banned* to *anyone has a right to carry arms*) or level of skill (e.g. from *extremely competent with spreadsheets* to *not sure what a spreadsheet is*).
Traffic lights	Pupils have a red, amber and green card. Teacher asks a question and provides a possible answer. Pupils hold up relevant card: red = false, green = true, amber = uncertain.
Mini-whiteboards	Teacher asks questions and pupils have to write the answer quickly on mini-whiteboards and display them to the teacher.
Five things	Give me the five key questions/key things/most interesting things/ most important things about . . . Teacher (or pupil) records the answers, which can then be used to recap prior learning.
Visual/audio stimulus	The teacher shows something thought-provoking (e.g. a piece of art, an artefact, a short science demonstration, a newspaper headline) and asks pupils to give their immediate response or raise questions about it.

Task 5.2

Identify appropriate intended learning outcomes for a single lesson in your subject. Identify some of the tactics in Table 5.1 that could be used to get the lesson off to a good start. Choose two contrasting alternatives from the table and prepare in detail, identifying any necessary resources. When you come to teach the relevant topic choose which starter activity to use and on the second occasion you teach it, use the other starter. Compare the responses.

ain activities

The main activity or activities in a lesson provide a time when you are probably not centre stage. Activities with the greatest educational value are very often not teacher-led, but teacher-facilitated. The teacher is then free to check that pupils are on-task and give them highly valuable individual attention. The activities need to be carefully planned so that they enable pupils to meet the intended learning outcomes of the lesson and are accessible to all pupils. Having identified a suitable activity ('task') you need to think about how long pupils should need to complete it ('time') and whether you want them to work at it as individuals, in pairs, groups of three or more or as a whole class ('team'). These are crucial decisions because they will affect the type of learning that takes place and have implications for classroom management and behaviour. Once you are clear about the activity, how long it will take and how pupils will be grouped, you need to plan how all this is going to be communicated to the pupils. It may be useful to remember the task-time-team triangle while planning to make sure that you have considered all three aspects (see Figure 5.3).

Remember to make use of a good variety of techniques to suit the range of learning styles preferred by different types of learner (see Chapter 6). You need to develop empathy for those pupils who learn in a different way to yourself, so that they are not disadvantaged in your lessons.

You should also consider the nature of evidence the activity will generate and how it can demonstrate whether learning and progression have occurred. Evidence may come from the way in which pupils engage with the activity, the output or both. The quality and quantity of evidence you collect will be influenced by:

- the way in which you communicate with pupils during the activity (see Chapter 8);
- the subject that you teach. This will influence the range of opportunities for pupils to demonstrate what they have learnt, but you should plan to incorporate activities within lessons and across a series of lessons that enable pupils with different learning styles and aptitudes to show you what they can achieve (see Chapter 6).

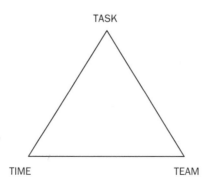

TASK

TIME   TEAM

Figure 5.3 The planning triangle

Once the structure of your lesson is in place, you need to review timing. Some student teachers find it really difficult to get this right. The most common problem is running out of time. There are various causes of this; the most usual are:

- underestimating how long pupils will take to complete a task. Until you get some experience of the speed at which pupils can be expected to work this is difficult to get right, but observing lessons and practice will help.
- failing to give pupils a clear indication of task-time-team, leading to confusion, uncertainty and lack of pace. This problem can therefore be avoided by good planning.
- failing to plan for all aspects of the lesson, for example, clearing away, setting homework, having a plenary.

5.9 Bringing a lesson to a close

How you end a lesson or a discrete portion of a lesson can have a profound effect on the overall quality of the learning that takes place. If you plan carefully how you will finish your lesson, or a portion of it, you can maximize the chances of pupils meeting the intended learning outcomes. The term 'plenary' is now widely used to describe this portion of a lesson.

Plenaries have a number of uses. They are:

- an opportunity to draw the whole class together;
- a chance to review what has been learnt so far, including progress against intended outcomes;
- a time to direct pupils to the next stage of learning (sign-posting);
- a time to help pupils reflect on how they have learnt;
- an opportunity for the teacher to make formative assessments, identify and explore misconceptions.

Successful lessons do not end with the teacher calling over the noise of pupils packing away '*That's all we've got time for today, don't forget to bring your homework in next lesson*'. As you can see from Figure 5.2, even if there are other plenary activities during a lesson, there should certainly be one at the end. In your lesson plan you should allow time for reflection so that pupils leave your classroom with a feeling that they have completed something and gained from the experience. This will build their confidence in you as someone who can help them learn. Yet ending lessons effectively is something that even many experienced teacher struggle with. Table 5.2 overleaf shows some plenary pitfalls and possible solutions.

5.10 Other planning issues

As well as planning your lesson so that it starts effectively, has appropriate main activities and a purposeful ending, there are a number of other factors that you need to consider and incorporate into your planning:

Table 5.2 Plenaries: common pitfalls and possible solutions

Pitfall	Suggested solutions
The class runs out of time and never gets round to a plenary.	1. Ask a pupil to be a timekeeper. 2. Stick to your planned times, even if some activities have not been completed. 3. Plan the plenary in detail.
Pupils feel the lesson is over when the main activity finishes and do not take the plenary seriously.	1. Sign-post what will be expected of pupils in the plenary. 2. Involve pupils in delivering the plenary. 3. Do not allow main activities to run until the bell rings.
'All I need to do is get them packed away, sitting in their seats and repeat the objectives and set the homework.'	1. Over a course of lessons vary your plenaries to re-engage attention. 2. Set homework at the beginning of the lesson.
'It's become dull because it's always the same routine.'	1. Plan for variety. 2. Design each plenary to fit the lesson and use it to revisit the objectives. 3. Use it to whet the pupils' appetites for the next lesson.
'You end up repeating everything and nothing is gained.'	1. Ask pupils to articulate the key points or consequences of the lesson. 2. Ask pupils to apply the learning to a new context. 3. Ask different groups to apply the learning in different ways.
'The learning is implicit in what has been covered.'	1. Ask pupils to identify the factors that have helped to achieve the lesson's objectives.

(Adapted from KS3 Strategy training materials, DfES 2003c)

- If you overlook the special needs or exceptional ability of one pupil, it can undermine your plans for the whole class.
- There should be opportunities for pupils to develop generic skills within the lesson, especially those relating to literacy, numeracy and ICT.
- There may be opportunities for your lesson to contribute to relevant cross-curricular themes such as education for sustainable development.

5.11 The best laid plans . . .

Ideally, by the time your lesson starts, your plan should be so familiar to you that you do not need to consult it during the lesson. If you need subject knowledge crib sheets, keep them separate, for example on index cards, so that they are easy to consult. Try to keep to your planned timing, especially allowing time for the end of lesson plenary. You may need to modify the plan during the lesson to take account of rates of progress, rates of learning, management issues caused by behavioural problems, interesting inputs from pupils and so on. Good planning will give you the confidence to deviate from your plan.

5.12 When it's all over . . .

Once a lesson is over, it is tempting to transfer your attention to the next. First though, you should try to learn from the experience you have just had. Part of this evaluation should focus on the lesson you planned as well as the lesson you delivered. How suitable did the plan turn out to be? Which parts of your planned lesson worked and which did not? Did you deviate from your plan and if so, why? Were the intended learning objectives met and how do you know? To develop your practice you need to make the time to ask these questions and answer them honestly.

5.13 Webliography

contentsearch.becta.org.uk/search/index.jsp?clear=y (links from the Becta website to quality-assured resources on the internet for use in teaching and learning)

www.standards.dfes.gov.uk/schemes3/subjects/?view (DfES-approved SoW for most subjects in KS1–3 and Citizenship at KS3 and 4)

www.teachernet.gov.uk/TeachingandLearning/ (a government site with links to thousands of free resources and lesson plan ideas)

6

Using differentiation to support learning

Liz Bills and Val Brooks

6.1 Introduction

It is a truism to say that all pupils are different and have different needs. Yet the comprehensive system aims to provide the best possible education for all its pupils and the teacher has to plan to teach them in groups of around 30. Whereas traditionally differences between pupils have been seen principally in terms of academic attainment, there is an increasing understanding that pupils also have legitimate differences of learning style and that helping pupils to fulfil their potential involves catering for these kinds of differences. This chapter will help you to understand your role as the class teacher in this process.

By the end of this chapter, you should:

- know what differentiation is and why it is an essential element of effective teaching;
- be familiar with different ways of differentiating in the classroom and at school level;
- be aware of issues raised by differentiation.

6.2 Case studies

To set the context for what follows in the rest of the chapter we would like you to think about three case studies. The following are descriptions of three pupils from the same Year 9 tutor group.

CASE STUDY 6.1 | Aisha

Aisha is a high achiever in most areas of the curriculum. She performs particularly well in mathematics and science, and also has very good literacy and language skills. She achieved a level 6 in English, maths and science in Year 6. Aisha grasps new concepts very quickly, however the material is presented, and she can be impatient with what she perceives as repetition. She likes to establish basic principles and to work from definitions; she is less interested in anecdotes or personal responses. Her strong analytical skills mean that she is often in a position to take a lead in group work, but she finds it difficult to work with those who grasp theoretical ideas more slowly or have priorities which are different from hers.

| CASE STUDY 6.2 | Daniel |

Daniel generally gets on well with people and is popular with his peers. Teachers find that he is happy to make constructive verbal contributions in lessons but that his attitude changes and he 'acts the fool' when they set a written task. In Year 7 he got off to a bad start with some teachers because he was invariably the last to arrive at a lesson and would usually give some excuse about being lost or having forgotten what time it was.

Daniel's difficulties stem from the fact that he suffers from dyslexia. His difficulties with literacy were recognized early in KS2 and most of his teachers were sympathetic and supportive, with the result that he did much better in his end of KS2 tests than originally expected. Provision was made for a reader/scribe in his maths and science tests and for part of English. He only managed to achieve level 3 in English but gained secure 4s in maths and science.

Daniel finds it difficult to read from the board, especially if he is some distance from it, and cannot copy from the board at any speed. He finds it difficult to communicate his ideas in writing and gets frustrated when this is the only way to demonstrate his understanding. Structuring a piece of writing is particularly difficult for him. He reads competently but slowly and often stumbles if asked to read aloud.

| CASE STUDY 6.3 | Ben |

Ben's performance data on entry to secondary school indicated that he was working below national expectation in key areas of the curriculum. He had achieved level 3 in all three NC tests (English, maths and science) and had a reading age 14 months below his chronological age. He did, however, gain a level 4 for teacher assessment in science. His Year 6 primary school report described Ben as a quiet child who needed to develop greater confidence in his own abilities. Ben has been placed in low sets for maths and English and a middle set for science. His reading age is now 10 months behind his chronological age following an intensive reading course in Year 8. Although Ben has made progress in KS3, he is unlikely to attain level 5 in end of KS3 tests.

Ben finds it difficult to concentrate during teacher expositions and doodles when required to listen for any length of time. He responds positively when visual stimuli are used to help him understand new concepts. Ben is left-handed and writes slowly and awkwardly, producing poorly formed script. In subjects which require extensive reading and writing, Ben is poorly motivated, slow to start tasks and gives up easily when he encounters difficulties. Written work is rarely completed. Ben does not seek help either from his peers or his teachers. In fact, he is at pains to avoid drawing attention to himself and always appears to be working assiduously whenever a teacher approaches. Ben does not enjoy group tasks, especially group discussions, and contributes little when he is obliged to work in a group. Although Ben's fine motor skills are poor, making intricate tasks difficult, he nevertheless enjoys practical activities. Ben likes investigating how things work and designing and making things.

Ben has an older brother, an able, confident boy in his final year in the sixth form. Throughout his school career, his parents and teachers have had expectations of Ben based on his brother's achievements. Unfavourable comparisons have dented his self-esteem.

Task 6.1

Analyze the aptitudes and needs of each case study pupil. Now pick a topic that is taught at KS3 in your subject. Imagine that you will be teaching this topic to a mixed ability group containing the three pupils described above. How might you adapt your basic scheme of work/individual lesson plans to cater for the needs of Aisha, Ben and Daniel?

Spend some time thinking about the characteristic features and demands of your own subject. (For example, English literature involves reading closely and reflecting on a text to analyze features such as theme, imagery and characterization. Mathematics involves solving problems by thinking logically and sequentially about the application of general principles.)

Identify the following:

(i)   distinctive features/demands of your subject;
(ii) types of learners who may be well suited to studying your subject;
(iii) types of learning difficulty or learning style preference which are likely to provide particular challenges for learners in your subject.

The exercise you have just completed replicates the kind of thinking required to plan for differentiation. Differentiation is the provision teachers and schools make to help each child to achieve their full potential. It entails teachers developing insight into individuals' learning style preferences, their needs and difficulties. It involves identifying the barriers to learning faced by some children and devising means of removing, or at least minimizing, them. It also entails identifying potential: the strengths and interests that each child brings to learning and finding ways to capitalize on these. Skilful differentiation relies on a sound diagnosis of what is required to improve learning and this is why differentiation and assessment are best viewed as twin activities that work in tandem. The best way to build a detailed picture of a child's learning profile is through formative assessment (see Chapter 9). Assessment helps a teacher to understand where a pupil currently is with their learning and to decide on next steps: what kind of experience, support or challenge will help them to progress. Information derived from assessment provides the basis for action and that is why differentiation and assessment are closely related processes. Differentiation is a set of strategies which aims to ensure that each pupil leaves a lesson having moved on with their learning: knowing more; understanding more and in more depth; confidently applying skills and wanting to learn more.

6.3 Differences between learners

All pupils are unique and it is easy to identify differences between any pair of pupils. However, not all differences between pupils are relevant to their lives as learners. It is helpful to have some idea about categories of difference that might affect the way you plan for pupils' learning.

Educational differences

At a very obvious level pupils' learning in any lesson is affected by what they have already learnt in previous lessons. This will be influenced both by the teaching that they have experienced and by the way in which they responded to it. Pupils in your class will have:

- attended different schools at KS2;
- been in different classes for your subject last year;
- been absent from lessons, worked with different partners, paid different degrees of attention both in class and to homework, attended to different aspects of the lesson;
- been more or less successful in achieving the learning objectives.

So even without taking account of differences in pupils' cognitive make-up, there are strong reasons to expect that pupils will come to the new topic differently equipped to learn it.

Most of the information about pupils' prior achievement that is mentioned above is available to you as the class teacher if you know where to look for it and are prepared to spend a little time interpreting it. Some is not, no matter how assiduous you are in collecting assessment information, and so there will always be a need to make ongoing assessment during the lesson and to adapt your plans accordingly. For example, you may need to provide support during the lesson for Ben when you find that he did not complete a unit of work from last year that you were relying on as background for the current topic. You may need to provide a more challenging task for Aisha when you find that she has encountered all the ideas in your introductory exercise already.

Psychological differences

It is a very common shorthand in schools to speak of pupils with 'high ability', 'low ability' or 'middle ability'. However, this terminology masks a great number of uncertainties and complexities about pupils' learning potential. The very existence of a characteristic which can be termed 'general ability' or 'intelligence' is hotly contested (see Chapter 4). Humans begin to learn as soon as they begin to exist and recent research into brain function has confirmed that, even more than was previously thought, the ability of the brain to learn is developed through its learning activity. In other words, cognitive ability is not set at birth but is developed through use. In this context, although it is possible to make statements about what pupils can do now (i.e. their attainment) it is not possible to be certain what they will be able to do in the future. For this reason it is more acceptable to describe a pupil who has been successful in their learning to date as a 'high attainer'. The use of this terminology is a reminder that there is nothing either innate or inevitable in a pupil's level of achievement.

In terms of differentiation at the classroom level, the notion of general ability, or even that of attainment in a general sense, is not particularly useful. It may help you to predict who will achieve a high score in the end of year assessment, but it doesn't tell you how to provide for the high or low attainer. What kind of learning do they prefer? Can they work effectively on their own or do they need a lot of input from an adult? What kind of problems or tasks will they excel at or find difficult?

Differences in learning style

Ability to learn might be characterized in terms of speed or capacity, but there is also much interest currently in different learning styles.

Learning styles have been conceived differently by different authors. However the two most common distinctions that are made are between *wholists* and *analysts*, and between *verbalizers* and *imagers* (see Riding and Cheema 1991). Wholists like to get an overview of what is to be learnt before they begin to fill in the detail, whereas analysts like to understand the detail before integrating the parts into the bigger picture. Verbalizers are most comfortable learning from words, whether spoken or written and can assimilate information most easily in this form. Imagers prefer to receive information in diagrammatic or pictorial form. There is a good deal of evidence that people have styles of learning which are common to the individual across different areas of learning. There is some debate over whether an individual's learning style remains constant or can be developed over time.

Learning styles differ from Gardner's MI (Gardner 1983; see Chapter 4) in that an individual's learning style goes across all the domains in which they learn, for example a verbalizer will prefer to learn using words whether they are learning about chemical reactions or poetry, whereas somebody with a strength in a particular intelligence will show an aptitude for associated areas of activity, for example a pupil with high musical intelligence will excel in that subject.

It may seem obvious that the best strategy for teachers is to try to adapt their teaching style to the learning style of their pupils in order to allow them to learn more efficiently. However, there is some evidence that a teaching style which is slightly different from pupils' preferred styles can actually help them to expand their repertoire of learning styles. The most effective differentiation strategy in these circumstances is to cater for different learning styles by making opportunities for wholistic thinking and analytical thinking, for verbalizing and using images. Schools tend to cater best for analytical thinkers and for verbalizers, so it makes sense to think about how that balance might be redressed. For example, it would be important to offer opportunities to Ben to learn through access to visual representations (diagrams, videos, posters) and to teach him methods of setting his ideas down in visual form, perhaps through 'mind maps' and annotated diagrams.

Social, cultural and gender differences

There is relatively little evidence that particular learning styles are more common for boys than for girls, or for pupils of some cultural backgrounds rather than others. There are some claims that girls tend to be wholistic rather than analytical thinkers (Head 1995) and that minority groups in America value particular forms of information (Guild 1994). However, it is very clear that differences within groups are much greater than differences between groups. So, for example, if you guessed that a pupil was a wholistic thinker on the grounds that she was a girl you would be only slightly less likely to be wrong than if the pupil were a boy. Paying too much attention to statistical links between certain learning styles and pupil characteristics can lead to dangerous stereotyping.

However, there are differences between pupils' interests and cultural experiences which can be very much linked to their sex and ethnic background. The teacher has the difficult task here of being continually aware, in particular, of how these interests and experiences might differ from their own. For example, a mathematics teacher who had based a probability lesson on examples using a pack of playing cards found that the lesson was inaccessible for a number of pupils. Some pupils in the class were unfamiliar with playing cards and others found them offensive on religious grounds because of their association with gambling.

Specific needs

Some pupils have been identified as having learning needs which make special provision necessary, or as having 'special educational needs'. Such pupils will have an IEP which sets out the differentiation strategies which are needed for that particular individual. For example, Daniel's IEP includes the following advice to his teachers:

> It is recommended that Daniel sits near the front in lessons where he can more easily read from boards and is more likely to build a positive relationship with the teacher through verbal interactions. Daniel will particularly benefit from opportunities to consolidate and demonstrate his understanding in ways that do not require a written response. Where possible written tasks should be short and employ techniques such as writing frameworks to help him organize his response. Teachers should avoid asking Daniel to read in class, because he is very embarrassed about his difficulty with this. Giving homework well before the end of a lesson will give Daniel time to copy it down correctly.

SEN can take a great many forms and it is not possible to do justice to the range of needs in a chapter of this nature. You will find more information in Chapter 21 which looks at SEN in greater detail.

6.4 Differentiation and planning

It is sensible to consider how differentiation affects the types of planning undertaken by student teachers: the medium-term planning of units and SoW and the short-term planning of individual lessons. Some aspects of differentiation are best planned for in the medium term. For instance, it may not be possible to cater for a wide range of learning styles and preferences within a single lesson, and to attempt to do so would fragment the planning. Therefore, it is helpful to think about catering for different learning styles and preferences as part of your overall planning for a SoW rather than attempting to tackle this on a lesson-by-lesson basis. Likewise, as well as having objectives for individual lessons, it is important to clarify longer-term aims for a SoW, distinguishing between essential knowledge, skills and concepts which all pupils will be expected to learn, additional materials which most pupils will assimilate and more advanced ideas and skills which some learners might master. This will result in a set of differentiated aims specifying what pupils must, should and could attain:

- all pupils MUST;
- most pupils SHOULD;
- some pupils COULD.

A similar process should take place at the level of individual lessons where it can be useful to distinguish between key, support and extension materials.

- Key material refers to information, concepts and activities which it is essential for all learners to address in some way.
- Support material refers to provision that supports pupils who find the key materials difficult for physical, psychological, emotional, behavioural or linguistic reasons. Support materials are not necessarily easier but they will have been developed with access in mind.
- Extension materials take the key materials to a higher or more complex level and are developed for those who find the key materials insufficiently challenging.

Differentiation can be considered in relation to lesson content, processes and products. The most commonly used differentiation strategies are described below.

- *Differentiation by task.* Pupils use similar resources but complete different tasks. For example, all pupils use the internet to research a topic but high-attaining pupils such as Aisha compile a report which requires them to synthesize and evaluate their findings whereas lower-attaining pupils with SEN such as Daniel follow structured guidelines and search for answers to specific questions.
  Pupils with learning difficulties often find tasks more manageable when they are analyzed into a series of small steps rather than being required to make one large step.
- *Differentiation by resource.* Pupils do similar tasks but use different resources. For

instance, all pupils produce a descriptive account of weathering during a geography lesson, but some base their account on reading about the process in written sources and others, such as Ben, base their account on watching a video.

- *Differentiation by time.* Similar tasks are undertaken but pupils have more or less time to complete them. Any subsequent tasks need to be purposeful and engaging to avoid acting as a disincentive to finishing promptly!

- *Differentiation by support.* In-class support could be provided by you or by assistants. At the planning stage, decide how your own time and that of assistants will be deployed. Some pupils will need help at the beginning to get going with tasks, others will need help intermittently and others still will need support throughout.

- *Differentiation by outcome.* Pupils work on similar tasks but the tasks are open-ended to allow for different outcomes. For instance, in a science lesson pupils are required to present the arguments for and against gas-fired power stations but a choice of presentational formats is offered including a poster, an audio recording of a speech and a written report.

These strategies can, of course, be used separately but they are more often used in conjunction with one another. Indeed, differentiation often involves a cluster of interventions designed to support and challenge children in their learning. For instance, Daniel's teachers make a point of monitoring his progress closely whenever he has to follow written instructions, a task that is made easier by seating Daniel near the front of the classroom. Teachers also find that it helps if instructions are printed on pastel-coloured paper, using a large font size and simplifying the language. In science and mathematics, Aisha often works with a small group of high-attaining pupils focusing on open-ended, investigative tasks where there is scope for taking risks in learning and devising creative solutions to problems.

Clearly, differentiation as part of lesson planning focuses on the detailed provision teachers make to meet the specific needs of individuals and groups within a class. Therefore, the requirements of children who have IEPs always need to be considered at the lesson planning stage. Thus, when Daniel's teachers set written tasks, they have to consider whether it would be appropriate for him – and other children who find writing difficult – to complete the same basic task by working in a different medium, possibly by word-processing a response or by producing a tape-recorded version. Alternatively, Daniel may be provided with a writing frame to enable him to complete the task or he may complete a variant. For instance, he may annotate a diagram rather than producing an extended prose response.

There are various organizational considerations to make too. For instance, Daniel benefits from sitting near the front of classes where he can more easily read from boards and has frequent opportunities to interact with teachers. Giving homework well before the end of a lesson gives Daniel time to copy it down correctly. Differences in temperament and attainment make it difficult for Aisha and Ben to cooperate on group tasks so the composition of groups needs careful consideration.

Differentiation at lesson level is also shaped by feedback from ongoing formative assessment (see Chapter 9). For instance, before they started their work on addition of fractions a class completed a pre-test. The results of the test suggested three broad starting points for this new topic. The understanding of equivalence of fractions needed to address addition was in place for over half of the group. However, over a quarter of the group had misconceptions that would need to be eliminated before they could tackle the work and a small group were already competent in addition of simple fractions with similar denominators and needed to extend their understanding. Pupils were assigned to groups based on their results in the pre-test and completed tasks tailored to their needs. The use of feedback to set individual and group learning targets is another example of the close relationship that should exist between assessment and differentiation. It is important to remember that where lesson objectives and learning targets have been differentiated, assessment criteria should also be adjusted so that different outcomes are recognized and valued.

6.5 Differentiation beyond the classroom

So far we have focused on what teachers can do inside their classrooms to help pupils to achieve their full potential. However, at national level, differentiation has been subsumed by two policy initiatives: personalised learning and *Every Child Matters* (DfES 2003e; see Chapter 20). Personalised learning is a nebulous concept which is easily misunderstood. The very name seems to suggest that each pupil should follow an individualized learning programme where they can work on their own at their own pace but the DfES has stressed that this is not what is intended. Personalised learning is presented as a 'philosophy' rather than 'a new DfES initiative' – one which some schools have embraced for many years. It is about

> tailoring education to individual need, interest and aptitude so as to ensure that every pupil achieves and reaches the highest standards possible, notwithstanding their background or circumstances, and right across the spectrum of achievement . . . What is new is our drive to make the best practices universal across all schools, particularly for children whose needs can be the most challenging to meet . . . giving every single child the chance to be the best they can be, whatever their talent or background.
>
> (www.standards.dfes.gov.uk/personalisedlearning/about)

Thus, although personalised learning is meant to address the needs of all children, including those who are gifted and talented, it is seen as having a particular role to play in raising the aspirations and attainments of disadvantaged children. It has been made a priority in the Primary and Secondary National Strategies and is backed by additional funding to help schools with its development. Thus, you are likely to encounter initiatives aimed at personalising learning during training and afterwards.

Personalised learning has five core elements which are 'supplemented by an enormous but loosely defined range of policies and practices' (Pollard and James 2004: 4). These are presented not as prescriptions but as a 'framework' and a 'set of tools', which schools are invited to consider with a view to improving their own practice. The core elements are listed below with practical examples to help make the concepts more meaningful.

1   **Assessment for learning** and the use of evidence and dialogue to identify every pupil's learning needs.

   - Teachers use feedback to plan lessons matched to needs and pupils are given individual learning targets;
   - Teachers use questions designed to stretch pupils, providing adequate thinking time for pupils to provide well-considered responses;
   - Pupils are trained to understand assessment criteria so that they can use them to assess their own and their peers' work.

2   **Teaching and learning strategies** that develop the confidence and competence of every learner by actively engaging and stretching them.

   - Teachers use a wide repertoire of teaching strategies including whole class interaction, guided group work and focused, one-to-one tuition for those who are experiencing difficulties;
   - Pupils engage with learning by reflecting on their own performance and identifying ways to improve it;
   - Peer tutoring schemes train same-age or older pupils to support the learning of other pupils;
   - Cognitive acceleration programmes focus on improving pupils' thinking skills.

3   **Curriculum entitlement and choice** that delivers breadth of study, personal relevance and flexible learning pathways through the system.

   - Groups of schools form consortia to provide greater curriculum choice at 14–19, with pupils moving between sites to access different parts of the curriculum;
   - New vocational GCSEs in subjects like engineering and health and social care;
   - Government-provided dedicated funding used for one-to-one and small group tuition of those children who have fallen behind in English and mathematics at KS3.

4   **A student-centred approach to school organization** with school leaders and teachers thinking creatively about how to support high quality teaching and learning.

   - Pupils are given a voice in decision making by, for example, more effective use of School Councils, allowing pupils a bigger role in setting agendas;
   - Pupils are given a real say in their learning, by being consulted about the effectiveness of teaching and learning and by providing feedback to teachers;

- The use of ICT to create a 'virtual school' which provides online materials and support to pupils outside normal hours.

5   **Strong partnerships beyond the school** to drive forward progress in the classroom, to remove barriers to learning and to support pupil well-being.

- Collaboration with employers to provide pupils with commercial and industrial experience;
- Creative partnerships which involve local artists or creative institutions working with pupils;
- Strengthening partnerships with parents and carers by, for instance, running workshops where parents can work alongside teachers and pupils to improve participation and progress.

Although the research community has broadly welcomed this policy, its response has been cautious and a number of questions have been raised. For instance, Pollard and James (2004) point to the speed with which personalised learning is developing, enquiring whether there is sufficient empirical support for the core components. How were they chosen? How well do they relate to one another? Are there other candidates for inclusion? They also emphasize the capacity of external and contextual factors to subvert the practice of schools, teachers and pupils arguing that: 'If Personalised Learning is to be introduced successfully, national government agencies, including OfSTED, NCSL, QCA and TTA, as well as the DfES will need to align their policies appropriately' (2004: 23). The 'Gilbert Review' published in 2007 (DfES 2007) responded to this need by making a range of suggestions for action by government, national bodies and local schools. Amongst the most radical were the provision of additional support beyond the school for pupils not progressing in English and mathematics and the availability of NC tests for pupils 'when ready' rather than at fixed times in their school career.

Schools also have a part to play in recognizing pupils as individuals and ensuring that their provision caters for different learning needs. Traditionally, differentiation has been seen as a response to ability, and so at school level it has involved the use of organizational strategies, 'setting' and 'streaming' being the most common. Streaming involves allocating children to a stream for all or most parts of the curriculum. It is an approach grounded in the notion of ability as 'general', that is that pupils will perform at a similar level in the various subjects that make up the curriculum. This is an outmoded view in the twenty-first century and streaming is a relatively unusual strategy in schools currently. Where it is adopted, this is often for pragmatic reasons to do with ease of timetabling. Setting involves allocating pupils to ability groupings on a subject by subject basis, allowing for variations in performance from one subject to another. Higher sets will, in theory, be set more demanding work using more sophisticated learning materials and more complex tasks. The 1997 White Paper, *Excellence in Schools* (DfEE 1997a) marked a shift in official thinking about organizational differentiation strategies, requiring schools to consider setting unless alternative approaches could be shown to be more effective. Despite this official endorsement, several concerns about setting remain. There are dangers that pupils placed in lower sets will be 'labelled' by themselves, their peers and teachers. Pupils can lose motivation when they are placed in the 'bottom set' and disaffection quickly spreads throughout the group creating an almost unteachable class. Setting can unfairly limit teachers' expectations for pupils in lower sets and sometimes leads to inequitable distribution of resources, both financial and human. Whatever mechanism is used for allocating pupils to classes, it is important to recognize that every group, however finely set, will contain children with a range of prior attainments and learning preferences. The only difference between a school practising 'setting' or 'streaming' and one using 'mixed ability' groups is in the spread of attainments and needs to be found within a group. Some researchers have raised doubts about the effectiveness of setting precisely because it allows teachers to assume that pupils in the class will work in the same way and at the same pace (see, for example, Boaler 1997).

Although school approaches to differentiation traditionally focused on ways of grouping pupils according to attainment so that pupils of similar ability could be taught together, some schools have experimented with grouping pupils according to learning style preference or, in responses to different learning styles observed amongst boys and girls, by gender. Schools have also become increasingly responsive to pupils as individuals and some of the approaches listed below demonstrate this. This list is intended to convey some of the principal ways in which schools are currently responding to the challenge of differentiation.

Target-setting

Target-setting takes place at different levels in schools. Chapter 9 considers target-setting as a feature of classroom life – the individual learning targets that are negotiated by teachers with pupils on an ongoing basis to enable children to progress in a subject. This day-to-day target-setting takes place within a framework of whole-school target-setting. Many schools run target-setting days where the timetable is collapsed to provide time for individual consultations between subject teachers, pupils and their parents. The aim of such meetings is to review a child's progress and potential and to establish targets for the medium term (e.g. the end of a KS or year). Once individual targets have been agreed, the information is collated and shared amongst relevant staff. Overall progress can then be monitored, for instance, by a pupil's form tutor, Year Head and School Assessment Coordinator. Continuous monitoring allows schools quickly to detect when an individual's progress exceeds or falls below expectations and to agree an appropriate intervention strategy.

Mentoring

Many people perform the role of mentor for secondary pupils, for instance, older pupils in a school, members of a school's senior management team, university students and business mentors from local workplaces. Although the role and responsibilities vary from scheme to scheme, mentoring represents an attempt to identify underperforming individuals whose learning may benefit from involvement in a mentoring relationship. Recommendations in the Gilbert Review take this much further by suggesting that the role of 'learning guide' should be established in all secondary schools with all pupils entitled to their own learning guide (DfES 2007: 44).

Support for the curriculum

The NC established pupils' entitlement to a broad and balanced curriculum. You will encounter a host of initiatives designed to support a broad and balanced curriculum by removing barriers and facilitating access for children with learning difficulties. For pupils who require additional challenge, the curriculum is extended in various ways. For instance, enrichment programmes may supplement the curriculum for high-attaining pupils whereas low-attaining pupils may be withdrawn from classes either for parts of the week, or for certain subjects, and taught by specialist SEN teachers or assistants. Sometimes pupils are withdrawn for several weeks at a time during which their education takes place in a special unit attached to a school. Alternatively, pupils may be provided with in-class support from a learning support assistant (LSA). Chapter 7 contains details of how the work of other adults in the classroom may be organized.

Modifications to the curriculum

The NC at KS4 (see Chapter 13) has been made more flexible, allowing schools to tailor provision to pupils' needs and aspirations. For instance, it is possible for high-attaining pupils to omit General Certificates of Secondary Education (GCSEs) in certain subjects and proceed immediately to Advanced Subsidiary (AS) level studies. Vocationally-related GCSE qualifications have also been introduced at KS4 to meet the interests and aptitudes of those who were poorly served by a narrowly academic curriculum. National vocational qualifications (NVQs) were originally conceived as work-related qualifications for those in employment. Schools are now able to offer a reduced NC alongside a regular work placement and/or NVQ qualification provided by a local FE college or other training provider for pupils who are in danger of leaving school with no qualifications, or of dropping out of the system altogether. A new specialised diploma is available from 2008 (see Chapter 19).

6.6 Conclusion

This chapter has provided a brief introduction to the many ways in which differences between individuals impact on their learning and to some of the approaches adopted by individual teachers and by schools in response to these differences. Responding to individual differences is possibly one of the most difficult aspects of a teacher's role and, if taken seriously, will provide you with challenges for the rest of your career.

6.7 Recommendations for further reading

Adey, P., Fairbrother, R., Wiliam, D., Johnson, B. and Jones, C. (1999) *Learning Styles and Strategies: A Review of Research*. London: King's College, London.

Kerry, T. (2002) *Learning Objectives, Task-setting and Differentiation*. Cheltenham: Nelson Thornes.

McNamara, S. (1999) *Differentiation: An Approach to Teaching and Learning*. Cambridge: Pearson.

Pollard, A. and James, M. (2004) *Personalised Learning: A Commentary by the Teaching and Learning Research Programme*. London: DfES (available at www.tlrp.org/documents/ESRCPerson.pdf).

Weston, P., Taylor, M., Lewis, G. and MacDonald, A. (1998) *Learning from Differentiation*. Slough: National Foundation for Educational Research (NFER).

7

Working with parents and other adults

Liz Bills

7.1 Introduction

As a teacher you will take sole responsibility for groups of pupils right from the start of your career. However, you will also need to be a team worker in many aspects of your professional life. As well as working alongside other members of the teaching profession, you will need to work in partnership with a wide range of other adults who have an interest in the education of the young people in your care. In order to be effective in teaching young people, you will need to understand the roles and interests of these other adults and to liaise with them to share information and make decisions. The key adults in a young person's life are their parents or carers. The first part of this chapter is devoted to looking at the means by which teachers and parents meet and communicate about individual pupils. In addition, teachers have dealings with a variety of other professionals. In the second part of the chapter we look in some detail at the skills needed for working with other adults in the classroom, and briefly at the roles of other professionals with whom you may come into contact in school.

This chapter aims to introduce you to good practice in reporting to parents and carers and in working with other adults in the classroom. By the end of this chapter you should:

- understand the principles of good report writing;
- feel more confident to take part in a parents' consultation event;
- understand the role of specialist support teachers and assistants and how the class teacher can most effectively work with them;
- be familiar with the roles of some other professionals who work with schools.

7.2 Parents and schools

In September 2006 Rawmarsh School in Rotherham made headline news because of a dispute between the head teacher and parents of some pupils at the school. Following the introduction of new 'healthy eating' rules about the content of school meals, parents began delivering hot food from local take-aways and passing it to their children through the railings around the school grounds. The two mothers at the centre of the story were said to be providing food to as many as 60 children who did not like the new menus in school. Yet a few years before, Ofsted had been able to say of the school that it was responsive to parents who approached it with questions or concerns and that the school worked well with parents to support pupils' learning.

Relationships between home and school vary enormously from school to school, from home to home and over time. They are, however, a vital part of the context in which pupils achieve or fail to make progress. The nature of the home–school partnership and the extent of the responsibilities of each to the other are frequently areas of contention.

Parents also play a key role in the development of the school in general, rather than just in the education of their own child. As an illustration of this, the National Confederation of Parent–Teacher Associations (PTAs), which is an umbrella body for individual schools' PTAs, reported that in 2005, PTAs helped state schools to raise £73 million.

Task 7.1

Which aspects of their child's life in school would you expect parents to be most concerned with? What are a parent's sources of information about school and the child's experiences of it? Note down your answers to these questions and then think about how this impacts on your role as a subject teacher and as a form tutor.

Since 1999 schools have been obliged by law to set up a home–school agreement which they should seek to have acknowledged by the parents or carers of all pupils. Such agreements should include school policies on:

- the standard of education;
- the ethos of the school;
- regular and punctual attendance;
- discipline and behaviour;
- homework;
- the information schools and parents give one another.

These agreements have been shown to be most effective when they are arrived at in consultation with both parents and pupils, and take account of the circumstances and value systems of different groups of parents. More details are given on http://www.standards.dfes.gov.uk/parentalinvolvement/.

7.3 Parents' consultation meetings

Parents' consultation meetings take a variety of forms. Parents may be invited to meet all their child's teachers on one evening, or to have a longer appointment with the pupil's form teacher who has received reports from all the subject teachers in preparation. The meetings may be timed during the school day, possibly with pupils off timetable to facilitate this, or in twilight or evening hours. Pupils may be invited to attend with their parents or asked to stay away.

Task 7.2a

As a parent, what might you hope to get from a consultation event? Information, advice, reassurance? Or to show support for your child and the school? To express concern to the teacher(s)? Given below are four parents' stories. Read through each in turn and ask yourself what this parent would be hoping to get from the consultation.

1. You are very concerned about Amir, who started secondary school this year. At primary school he was always very keen on science and usually got good marks. Since he started Year 7, he has been put in set two which upset you, and he seems to be showing little interest in the subject now. When you ask him about his homework, he says he has already done it. He still spends quite a lot of time looking at the night sky through his telescope, though. Science is your own area of interest and you hope that Amir will make a career in it too.
2. Brenda is in Year 13 and has always enjoyed school. She has plenty of friends and has recently had a major part in the school drama production. She sings in a rock group as well and is very keen on a career on the stage. She doesn't talk much about school work, apart from her drama lessons, but you've no real reason to be concerned except that she does seem to get very tired. You wonder whether you ought to be firmer with her about being home at a reasonable time on week nights.
3. Carl is in Year 9 and finds all school work difficult. You left school at 16 yourself and have never been keen on reading, so it is hard to help him. You know he needs to get some qualifications in order to get a job, but you are not very clear about what to expect. He seems to like his English teacher so you decide to ask her.
4. Danielle is in Year 8 and is in the top set for maths. It has always been her favourite subject and last year's teacher said she had a real flair for it. This year she seems to have become disillusioned with the subject. She says the lessons are slow and boring and that a lot of the other pupils 'mess about'. She often has no homework because she has finished it during the lesson.

Task 7.2b

Now imagine that you are about to meet one of these parents. The notes below will give you the teacher's perspective on each pupil. What would your priorities for the meeting be as a teacher? How would your actions meet their expectations? What are the likely difficulties in each conversation and how could you, as the professional, deal with them?

1. Amir is in your class for science in Year 7, that is the second set (out of five). He achieved a good level four for science in Year 6 which put him amongst the highest achievers in the small primary school that he attended. He seems to be having some difficulty adapting to the secondary school context and, although he is keen to answer questions in class, his written work is not as good and his homework usually appears rushed.
2. Brenda is in your Year 13 tutor group and is a very outgoing and lively personality.

Recently she has been involved with the school production and that seems to have taken up a lot of her time. You have encouraged her in this as you know she is very keen on drama. However, in the last fortnight you have had notes from four different subject teachers saying that Brenda is late with A level coursework, and you need to tell her parents about this at the consultation meeting. You have also noticed that she is often tired in the mornings during tutor period and you wonder whether the new boyfriend that her friend keeps teasing her about has anything to do with this.

3. You teach Carl in your Year 9 English group, set five out of five. He has struggled with literacy ever since primary school and has particular problems with spelling, punctuation and grammar. His reading and writing skills are both at level three. He seems to like English, though, perhaps because you always go out of your way to include him in lessons and to praise the little progress he makes. Other teachers say he is very withdrawn in their lessons.

4. Danielle is in your top set Year 8 maths class. She is very able and confident in maths and likes to show that she has got to the answer first. She is quite happy to show her disdain for the slower members of the class which makes it particularly difficult for you to manage the wide range of abilities in this class. To make matters worse, there is a small group of pupils in the class with very challenging behaviour. You have to spend a lot of time keeping them occupied which makes it difficult to pay much attention to the pupils who finish first. Danielle is usually amongst these. On the occasions when you do ask her to do some extension work she usually does not do it, especially if it is homework.

Thinking about these individual cases will, I hope, have helped you to develop some general principles for successful communication at consultation meetings. Some of the points you may have considered are:

Preparation

You need to be prepared in advance by having ready access to the pupils' grades on class work and homework, to information about their homework completion and to examples of their work. This would be very useful in, for example, telling Danielle's parents about the problem you have had in getting her to engage with extension work or for showing Amir's parents the quality of his work in comparison with the rest of the class. It may also be useful to have prepared what you want to say and some advice on the next stage for each pupil.

Positive start

Some parents will be arriving unhappy with some aspect of their child's experience at school, and others will be nervous about speaking to teachers. In either case, it is important to start by saying something positive about the pupil. This should have the effect of calming an aggressive parent or reassuring a nervous one.

Targets for future action

The interview will feel, and be, more purposeful if you can identify a target for future action resulting from it. This is especially effective if the pupil is present, but parents will also want to work out how they can help. For example, Carl's parents might be able to encourage him to read at home, and Brenda's parents will want to have a look at her coursework schedule with her.

Give parents a chance to talk

Parents' meetings can be a really good opportunity to find out about your pupils' home influences, their interests, motivations and aspirations. You might, for instance, find out about Amir's interest in astronomy. You also need to give parents a chance to ask questions and express their worries.

Be informative without using jargon

Many parents find assessment schemes, public exams and the curriculum bewildering. You will need to be very aware of parents' needs in this area and sensitive to their degree of expertise. Some of the parents that you talk to will be teachers themselves, of course.

Make a good first impression and keep to time

You need to look as though you have made an effort to look presentable, which can be a particular challenge at 4 p.m. after a day's teaching. Another aspect of showing your concern for your visitors is to keep to your appointment times. This can be very difficult as well, but it can be done if you do not 'fill time' unnecessarily and are firm about ending the interview on time, offering to find another time to speak to the parents if necessary.

7.4 Written reports for parents

The law requires that schools must provide a written report on progress and achievement at least once each academic year. At KS3/4 the report must include:

- comments on progress, highlighting strengths and development needs;
- general review of progress;
- information on absence;
- arrangements for the parents and/or pupil to discuss the report with teachers;
- in Year 9: in addition, NC levels;
- in Year 10: in addition, target grades for GCSE.

Schools are increasingly involving pupils in commenting on their reports before they are sent to parents, often as part of the academic tutoring system. Reports, then, are part of a cycle of assessment which involves pupils in self-assessment and target-setting. Chapters 9 and 10 will have more to say on these subjects.

Task 7.3

Schools use a wide variety of formats for written reporting, some of which involve ICT and comment banks. Make a note of three reasons why the use of comment banks might be advantageous, and three ways in which they might have a negative impact.

Below is an example of a report produced using an ICT-based 'writing frame'. Some parts of the report are the same for every member of the class, some phrases are chosen from comment banks and some are composed particularly for this pupil.

Name: Ruth Bridge   *Tutor Group 9SQ*
French

Students follow the 'Route Nationale' course and are assessed on their ability to listen to, speak, read and write the foreign language. In French, 'higher' levels of attainment mean National Curriculum Level 4 and above.

Subject specific comments:

In French, Ruth participates enthusiastically in oral work. She communicates with fluency and she can understand most things. In written work she conveys the meaning well with grammatical accuracy. She learns new vocabulary and language skills efficiently.

General subject comments:

Ruth consistently achieves higher levels of attainment;

- *she works well and is self-motivated;*
- *she is always well mannered and behaves in a responsible way;*
- *she is always punctual;*
- *she is always prepared for lessons;*
- *she can always organize her work effectively;*
- *she works well individually and within a group or team;*
- *she always completes homework properly.*

The excellent progress Ruth has made this year will be maintained by:

- *continuing the level of effort shown throughout the year;*
- *checking spellings thoroughly on completion;*
- *correcting mistakes to avoid repeating them;*
- *wider reading in the subject.*

Imagine yourself as Ruth's parent or carer. How would you respond to this report? How would it make you feel? Are there parts of it that are more informative than others? What questions does it leave you with? Are your comments about ICT and comment banks, both positive and negative, borne out by this report?

Your thinking about Ruth's parents' viewpoint may have led you to some general principles about good report writing. Perhaps the three most important things to remember are:

- Audience: avoid jargon and think about whether the language you are using will be easily understood by parents;
- Accuracy: draw on evidence and example so that your points are made more convincingly and with more clarity;

- Acclaim: praise and build on the positive, always including a suggestion as to how the pupil can make progress.

7.5 Other contact with parents

Contact with parents can range from a chance meeting in the supermarket, through an informal exchange at a school drama production to an individual meeting set up in school to discuss a particular problem. Take advantage of these opportunities as much as you can to make contact and to find out about your pupils' home backgrounds. This helps you to understand what motivates, interests and affects them. It is nearly always an advantage for pupils to feel that their teachers and parents know each other. Negative and positive messages from teacher to parent or vice versa are made more meaningful by personal knowledge.

As a subject teacher, your regular opportunities to communicate with parents are often limited. That means that any contact you do make is likely to have impact. A note written home, or a phone call, is an effective way of amplifying praise. Some teachers keep a stock of pro forma letters in their mark book so that in the lesson, or as they are marking work, they can add a few words which explain the reason for the letter and hand it over to the pupil there and then. Contact with home may also be appropriate for reinforcing a reprimand. This sort of contact needs to be treated with caution as it can result, at two extremes, in the parent responding aggressively to the teacher or over-reacting in their punishment of the pupil. It is not unknown for the same parent to make both of these responses. As a student teacher or NQT, it is wise to consult the pastoral team before making such a contact.

7.6 Other adults in the classroom

Between 1997 and 2002 the number of teaching assistants working in schools in England and Wales increased by 50 per cent and a slower increase has continued. Today's secondary school teachers are much more likely than in the past to be working with other adults in the classroom. Who are teaching assistants? What sort of work do they do? How will they expect you to behave to them? In order to get most benefit from the provision of teaching assistants for yourself and your pupils, you will need to understand the roles and skills of these other adults and how you can best interact with them as a teacher.

Changes in policy on inclusion have meant that an increased number of sources of funding are available to schools to enable them to provide in-class support for pupils with SEN and with EAL. In addition, the Remodelling Agreement signed by government and teachers' unions in January 2003 has meant changes to what teachers can be asked to do as part of their work. The agreement was followed in 2005 by a requirement on all schools to redesign their staffing structure to take changed roles into account. The increase in numbers and importance of support staff was consolidated by each of these changes.

In response to the recognition of the centrality of support staff to the workings of a school, the consultation paper 'Developing the role of school support staff' (DfES 2002b) signalled the beginning of the move to establish a national framework for conditions, qualifications and training for all categories of school support staff. In 2005 the remit of the Training and Development Agency for Schools was widened to include the professional development of support staff. Details about the qualifications framework and training opportunities are given on the TDA website at www.tda.gov.uk/support.

There is a large number of different terms used to refer to adults other than qualified teachers who work in secondary schools. The following glossary includes the main ones.

Support staff. This term is used officially to refer to all staff in schools who are not qualified teachers. So, for example, it includes office staff, librarians, cleaning and catering staff, school finance officers, technicians and others as well as staff who support the learning of individual pupils.

Teaching assistants (TAs). This is the chosen term for official use to refer to staff who directly support teachers in their work in classrooms.

Higher level teaching assistants (HLTAs). This was a term not used very much until 2003 when the Government began to encourage the creation of posts in schools which would involve more responsibility than had mostly been the case until then. Alongside the new name came a qualification and a set of 'standards' for HLTAs. This is part of the process of improving the career structure for TAs.

Learning support assistants. LSAs are usually employed to support the learning of a particular individual pupil or group of pupils who have been identified as having a SEN. They usually work under the direction of the school's SENCo. Especially in secondary schools, they form a large subset of those that the Government refers to as TAs.

Classroom assistants. This term is not used very much in official circles. It was used to describe the role of staff, usually in primary schools, who provided all kinds of practical support for teachers, from mounting display work to clearing up after art. Some consider it an undignified label.

Non-teaching assistants. Still in use in some schools, this term has more or less disappeared from official discourse. It was originally intended to distinguish teachers from other staff, but, perhaps rather confusingly, has been superseded by the term teaching assistants.

Learning mentors. The government initiative, EiC, developed the idea of a learning mentor in 1999, and it has now been taken up by a number of other projects. The role has something in common with that of TA, but a learning mentor is generally much more involved in the pupil's development outside school. Learning mentors are often paid much better than TAs, which is the cause of some ill-feeling.

EMAG teachers and assistants. EMAG stands for Ethnic Minority Achievement Grant. Staff are employed using this funding in order to support pupils who are learning EAL (see Chapter 22). Some of these staff are qualified teachers with a great deal of knowledge and expertise in language development. A major part of their role is to advise subject teachers on good practice. Others are employed to help specific pupils and are often bilingual.

You will have realized from scanning the glossary that TAs have many, varied roles. They fulfil a vital role in schools and yet they are often overlooked in terms of staff development and school management. In fact, some TAs report that teachers do not know their names or have any idea what they do. A survey of its members conducted by the National Union of Teachers in December 2002 concluded that:

- only one in seven teachers had received any training for working with TAs, and the proportion was less for secondary teachers; fewer than 2 per cent had received any training as part of their ITT.
- most secondary teachers spend less than one hour a week planning and preparing work with TAs who often plan their own work independently and take no part in assessment and recording.
- more than three-quarters of the respondents (and a higher proportion of secondary teachers) thought that the most important benefit of working with TAs was the additional support provided for individual pupils or groups of pupils.

Since this survey was carried out working with TAs has become part of every ITT programme and the Remodelling project (see www.remodelling.org.uk) has offered a lot of support to schools in re-thinking the way in which they deploy and support teaching assistants. Nevertheless it is easy to overlook the importance for you as a class teacher of working effectively with TAs.

In most secondary schools the work of TAs is organized by the SENCo who decides how to deploy the expertise and time of the TAs to best meet the requirements of the pupils identified as having SEN. This results in many different patterns of work for TAs. Three TAs described a typical working week like this:

Task 7.4

'In the course of the week I work with five different pupils. Most of them need my help because they have behaviour problems. I will often be with them for two or three periods in the day so I know them very well and know what has been happening for them earlier in the day.'

'Over the week I support between 40 and 50 pupils both in the mainstream and in the special unit. I see most of them only once or twice a week. During six periods a week I am on "rapid response" for one pupil. That means that if he gets into trouble in a lesson, I have to stop what I am doing to go and take him out to the unit.'

'I am the LSA for the maths department and I support whichever maths class most needs my help. I get to know the teachers and the curriculum very well, and have a lot of contact with some of the pupils as well. I take a major role in identifying which pupils need support and in differentiating work for them. I feel I am really involved in supporting the teachers as well as the pupils.'

How would you expect the skills and abilities of these three TAs to differ? What does that mean about how you could work with them most effectively?

The same TAs told me what they like most about their work:

'I get most satisfaction out of struggling with kids who don't want to be in school. If we can get to the end of a lesson and they say they've enjoyed it, that's really great. I can think that I've helped get them through a difficult day, because every day at school is difficult for them.'

'The thing I have enjoyed most recently was when I was working with a PGCE student with a mixed ability Year 7 class. She planned the lesson and she'd done a differentiated worksheet for the lowest ability pupils. I sat with them through the lesson and enjoyed the responsibility of teaching that group.'

'You get lots back from the pupils. I'm really pleased when they manage to achieve something. Of course, it's not always like that. You give a lot of yourself and that can be hurtful when it goes badly.'

I asked the group of TAs to tell me what teachers did to help them to work more effectively. Here are some of the replies:

'Involve me. Communicate. Not just about what the lesson is going to be but also where it fits in the scheme of work. It's usually done over a cup of coffee in the staff room. I like to get to department meetings. When I can get involved in the planning as well, I feel necessary and appreciated.'

'The most helpful teachers find time to give me a briefing before the lesson. Just a couple of minutes about what the lesson is going to be about. Giving me a copy of the worksheets at the start is really helpful. Otherwise I am turning up to the lesson not knowing what on earth is going to happen. Of course it's like that for the pupils. But it can make you feel really stupid and small.'

'The teachers who talk to you are the best. Otherwise you don't know whether they think you are helping. Everybody is different and has different strengths and preferences and if you don't talk then you never find out what they are.'

Communication is obviously a key issue. Plans for the lesson in which the TA is supporting your class need to be available to them in some form, but they will not have time to take in all the details of your lesson plan.

Task 7.5

Take a lesson plan that you have used recently and decide what would be the minimum information that you could pass on to a TA about the lesson in order for them to be able to operate usefully within it.

7.7 Support from other agencies

Every Child Matters (see Chapter 20) has had a major impact on the organization of the work of the variety of professionals who are concerned with children. Where there used to be a clear distinction between educational and social services for children, these are now part of an over-arching Children's Services provision. There is a very large number of other support services represented in schools with whom the subject teacher or form tutor might come into contact. Here I will mention just three.

Learning and behaviour support service

This service provides support for pupils who have reached the School Action Plus level of intervention for SEN. You can find more information about what this means in Chapter 21. They are the first port of call outside the school for advice on how to provide for the pupil's needs. As well as providing support for individual pupils, and advice for staff who work with them, they can also provide more general training for school staff on provision for SEN.

Educational psychologists

Educational psychologists are involved in assessing the needs of pupils with specific learning difficulties whose needs are more severe than can be met by provision under School Action Plus. They also provide advice and support to schools on how best to support these pupils.

Education social workers

ESWs, sometimes known as education welfare officers (EWOs), offer help to schools in enforcing school attendance. They are most likely to get involved in supporting pupils whose attendance is poor because they have been traumatized by bullying, bereavement or divorce, for example. They also advise on and follow up cases on child employment and child protection.

7.8 Conclusion

In this chapter we have looked at the relationships that you as a classroom teacher will have with a variety of other adults who have a legitimate interest in the pupils you teach. The keys to success in each of these relationships are communication and partnership. The time you spend considering and listening to the other partner's point of view will be the factor that makes the relationship work for the benefit of the pupil whose progress is everybody's concern.

7.9 Recommendations for further reading and webliography

Campbell, A. and Fairbairn, G. (eds) (2005) *Working with Support in the Classroom*. London: Paul Chapman.

Lee, B. (2002) *Teaching Assistants in Schools: The Current State of Play*. Slough: NFER.

O'Brien, T. and Garner, P. (eds) (2001) *Untold Stories: Learning Support Assistants and their Work*. Stoke-on-Trent: Trentham Books.

Rudney, G.L. (2005) *Every Teacher's Guide to Working With Parents*. Thousand Oaks, CA: Corwin Press.
Vincent, C. (1996) *Parents and Teachers: Power and Participation*. London: Falmer.

www.remodelling.org.uk
www.standards.dfes.gov.uk/parentalinvolvement/
www.tda.gov.uk/leaders/supportstaff

8

Communication in the classroom

Paul Elliott

8.1 Introduction

> Communication and the teacher-pupil relationship lie at the heart of teaching.
>
> (MacGrath 1998: 62)

The ability to communicate successfully with your pupils is central to your role as a teacher. Communication skills are very complex, but your success as a teacher depends upon them. We will consider the ways in which non-verbal communication occurs in the classroom, the features of verbal communication and, finally, take a detailed look at the art of questioning.

By the end of this chapter you should:

- appreciate that your ability to communicate effectively with pupils will play a major part in determining how successfully they learn;
- be aware of your scope for non-verbal communication in the classroom;
- be aware of the power of questioning as a teaching tool;
- be able to identify features of good practice in questioning technique.

If you communicate effectively with your pupils they will respond positively, but it is important to remember that communication is a two-way process. This means that when you are planning lessons you need to consider not only what you are going to communicate to pupils, but what you expect them to communicate to you, how they are going to do this and how you are going to respond.

Consider the following questions:

How do pupils know . . .

the intended learning outcomes of your lesson?
how they will achieve the outcomes?

whether they are on target to achieve them?

when they have achieved them?

what they need to do to progress?

And:

How do you know what your pupils know?

You cannot answer the questions above without a dialogue taking place. If communication involved one-way traffic from teacher to pupils, then teaching would be easy. Unfortunately, this ancient strategy of *filling empty vessels with knowledge* has proved ineffective.

To be a successful teacher, you need to plan what you are going to communicate and how you are going to communicate. A common mistake that student teachers make is to talk too much. If you talk too much, pupils will start to turn off from what you are saying and may miss the main messages. Successful teachers can facilitate quality learning with a minimum of words, but careful planning is essential if you are to achieve this.

8.2 Communication and power

Everyday conversation between people is characterized by particular features. Try listening to a conversation between two of your friends whilst thinking about how their conversation is structured. Their conversation will probably be punctuated by hesitations, interruptions, incomplete sentences that fade away and lots of facial interaction (even when one or both parties are blind). This is very different to many verbal classroom interactions involving teachers. Typically, teachers tell pupils: when to talk, when to stop talking, what to talk about and how well they have done it. In this traditional scenario much of the talk is centred on one individual pupil at a time and the teacher demands that the class pays full attention to what is being said. Either the teacher is talking or a pupil is responding to the teacher. This means that the teacher is in a very powerful position; there is a 'strong asymmetry of power in interactions between teachers and children' (Wood quoted in Norman 1992: 207).

By using the power of your position appropriately, you can build good relationships with pupils. When pupils trust you, you are in a good position to help them learn. To build such trust you need to communicate with:

- clarity, keeping sentences short and simple;
- appropriate vocabulary in terms of the complexity of the vocabulary and the degree of formality;
- the aim of building pupils' confidence and willingness to participate;
- honest and useful feedback.

If your communication lacks any of these features, your pupils will either fail to understand what it is you are trying to communicate or, worse, will feel threatened by it. Remember that you are the person in a position of power in the classroom; you are the person who possesses most knowledge and that you therefore have the responsibility to communicate effectively. It is a very common mistake to tell pupils they have not listened properly when, in fact, it is the teacher who has not explained properly.

8.3 Non-verbal communication

When you think of communication in a classroom, what form does it take? The first thing that probably comes to mind is verbal communication by the teacher. Classrooms throughout the land are full of teachers talking to pupils: explaining, questioning, instructing, praising, chastizing, pleading and so on. This verbal communication is central to your work as a teacher and most of this chapter relates to this skill, but there are other forms of communication between teacher and pupils and their importance should not be underestimated.

Simply by your presence in a classroom you are communicating with your pupils. In so many ways we send subtle signals to our pupils about:

- how we feel about ourselves;
- how we feel about them;
- how we feel about the subject matter of the lesson;
- how confident we are;
- how well organized we are;
- how competent we are likely to be at helping them learn.

These subtle messages are transmitted as a complex medley of signs and signals.

Compare the two sets of signs and signals that exemplify positive and negative messages:

Positive	Negative
Neat/tidy/stylish dress	Untidy/dishevelled/wildly eccentric or old-fashioned dress
Well organized paper work	Papers spilling out of bag, falling on floor
In the classroom before pupils arrive	Arrives after pupils
Cheerful, pleased to see pupils	Ignores pupils or scowls at them
Calm, confident	Flustered, tense

Think carefully about how others are likely to perceive you. As a student teacher it is important that you try to conform to pupils' expectations of what a competent teacher should be like. Teaching is a profession where there is room for individuality, but there are limits. You cannot expect simply to be yourself in the classroom. Observe experienced and successful teachers at work and then follow them into the staffroom after the lesson. As the staffroom door closes behind them, you will see that they metamorphose from the classroom version of who they are, their 'act', into the real person. The two persona will not be unrelated, but neither will they be the same!

Part of the communication between you and your pupils will be in the form of body language. This is a very complex language, but one in which it is well worth developing fluency. As with other forms of communication, it is about teachers' and pupils' behaviour. Neill and Caswell (1993) explore the subject in more detail. As a teacher, there are some simple guidelines that will help you:

- Stand or sit confidently – shoulders back, spine straight, and so on.
- Stand still! Shifting feet distract pupils and are a sure sign of nerves.
- Control your hands! However nervous you are feeling inside, try to avoid fidgeting with them.
- Try to show the pupils the palms of your hands and make confident, slow gestures with them while you talk.
- Try to be positive and expressive with your face: smile and nod regularly when pupils say or do anything positive.
- Have the confidence to approach pupils for an intimate discussion of their work, but avoid invading their personal space.
- With smaller pupils in particular, it is much better to squat next to them rather than lean over them when having a one-to-one interaction.

The way that you use your body will not only influence the way that you are perceived, but also the way that you feel. If you can act confident, even when feeling nervous, you are likely to end up feeling more confident.

8.4 The teacher's territory

The confidence with which you use the teaching space will also send a message to your pupils. A mouse that is feeling vulnerable tries to hide. If it has to be somewhere in the open, it will look for cover or stay close to walls at the edges of open spaces. As a new teacher, you may sometimes feel like using the same strategy in the classroom. Do you feel safest behind the teacher's desk? Would you prefer to avoid going anywhere near the back row? It is natural to feel this way when you start teaching, but it is behaviour to avoid if you are to communicate the right message to your pupils. However nervous you feel inside, there should be no 'no-go' zones in your teaching room.

Just as it is important to get your body language right, it is important to get your use of classroom space right: cower at the front and pupils will sense your fear. Here are some general guidelines that are worth remembering:

- Moving confidently around a classroom 'marks' it as your territory.
- Using posters, pictures and display work to personalise classrooms not only creates a more stimulating working environment but marks it as part of your territory.
- Addressing a class from different places in a room (this can be difficult in some small rooms) shows them that you are confident and at ease in the space.

- Talking to a class from the back of the room 'turns the tables' on those pupils hoping for a quiet life at the back.

- Moving amongst pupils to check their progress is important. It should be done soon after the start of a task to check that pupils have understood what they have to do.

- Whatever the layout of the room, you should make sure that all pupils are looking at you while you are addressing the class; this may mean that some or all will have to move around in their seat.

Some habits are best avoided:

- Walking around the room as you speak. This turns you into a moving target and will distract pupils from what you are saying.

- Turning your back on pupils for very long. If you stop to speak to one pupil, make sure that you scan the room regularly to check that everyone else is on task.

- Obscuring pupils' views of information on boards, overhead projector screens or interactive whiteboards. You do not want to become the excuse for pupils stopping work!

Task 8.1

Draw a sketch map of a room that you have taught in or are going to teach in. Think about how you could use the teaching space effectively and confidently. Mark on the map all of the places that you could stand or sit while addressing the class. These need to be places where you can scan the room easily and make eye contact with all pupils. Think also about suitable places in the room to place resources, to carry out demonstrations or to get pupils to engage in role play or other activities.

8.5 Types of teacher talk

Teachers need to talk to pupils for a variety of reasons. Their talk falls into three general categories: cognitive, procedural and managerial. Cognitive teacher talk concerns the content of the curriculum and will include the majority of the questioning and elucidation carried out by the teacher. Procedural talk concerns how the work in the lesson is to be done; so it is about the nature of tasks, the teams in which pupils are to carry out the tasks and the timing of the work. Managerial talk is that which relates to behaviour management, the giving of notices unrelated to the curriculum and so on. All of these categories of teacher talk are essential, yet much attention has been drawn to the need to shift the balance from procedural and managerial towards more cognitive talk. It has been suggested that two thirds of lessons are talk, two thirds of that talk is teacher talk and two thirds of teacher talk is about management and procedure rather than content (Norman 1992). As a new teacher you may well find yourself talking too much. Many new teachers are guilty of spending too long introducing content and explaining tasks, to the extent that pupils become bored and lose track of what is being said.

8.6 Pupil talk

There have been moves to encourage a shift in emphasis so that more teacher talk is about cognitive matters and more talk is by pupils. From 1987–1993 the National Oracy Project (see Norman 1992) developed and promoted strategies for encouraging on-task pupil talk and the Secondary Strategy has speaking and listening as one of its themes (see Chapter 16). Subject-specific materials have also been produced to promote the use of talk and argument, for instance, *Strengthening Teaching and Learning in Science through Using Different Pedagogies. Unit 1: Using Group Talk and Argument* (DfES 2004c). The pupil-to-pupil talk encouraged by these initiatives is valuable for a number of reasons:

- It gives pupils a chance to learn from and teach each other.
- It builds pupils' confidence by giving them the chance to verbalize their ideas about the work in hand and a chance to practise using the subject vocabulary.
- It is less daunting than talking to the teacher, especially in front of the rest of the class.
- It allows pupils to test ideas in an intimate setting before going public with them.
- It helps pupils to build social skills.
- It helps pupils to develop the ability to express themselves coherently and persuasively.

8.7 Your voice as a tool

You need to use your voice with precision and care if you are to get the best out of it. It also has to last you a long time, so it is important that you use it in a way that will avoid damage. Your voice is the main tool of your trade; think of it as a scalpel rather than as a sledgehammer!

Your voice has unique characteristics that make it distinct from anyone else's and you also have the ability to vary the way in which you speak. It is desirable to practise varying the way in which you use your voice to achieve different effects and emphases. Some people have voices that are easier to listen to than others, but there is a lot that anyone can do to maximize the potential of their voice. Volume, speed, pitch, projection and expressiveness are examples of the features of your voice that you can try to vary to achieve maximum impact.

There will be times when you need to be quite loud to get a class's attention but, once you have their attention, you can dramatically reduce the volume of your voice. If you insist on talking to a class with the volume of your voice raised, you will provide pupils with the cover they need to start their own conversations. If you speak at a volume that pupils at the far side of the room can only hear clearly by concentrating on what you are saying, it becomes hard for any pupil to start an illicit conversation. You should certainly avoid shouting. Pupils *hate* teachers who shout and you will end up with noisy classes and a sore throat. Loud teachers create loud classrooms.

You need to be able to make yourself heard on the far side of a classroom, but you should aim to do this by *projecting* your voice, not by shouting. It is possible to learn to project your voice effectively. Before you speak, take a deep breath, be clear in your mind what you need to say and then say it with clarity and conviction. Think about the tone of your voice as you speak so that you sound as if you are in authority rather than someone who is pleading with a class. A common mistake of new teachers is to talk too fast. If you do this, pupils may find it difficult to follow your explanations or instructions and sooner or later they will give up trying. Speak clearly and try using pauses to emphasize key points and to allow pupils to digest what you have said.

On becoming leader of the Conservative party, Margaret Thatcher was given voice lessons. The main aim of this was to teach her to lower the pitch of her voice and give her more gravitas. Her advisers knew that voices with a lower pitch tend to carry more authority and sound more confident. Speaking at a higher pitch can make projection in the classroom more difficult and, when you are under stress, the pitch will tend to rise further, making the situation worse. If you have a relatively high-pitched voice, you can try to practise using the lower end of your natural range and your training institution may also be able to arrange coaching to help you do this. The VoiceCare Network is also a useful source of advice (website address at page 112).

8.8 Less is more

Teacher talk is very important but it is the quality of what a teacher says, rather than the quantity, that matters. A lesson that is dominated by the teacher's voice is seldom a successful lesson. A lesson where the teacher says the minimum that is needed to interest pupils in the subject and explain the nature of a well-planned task or series of tasks that will engage their interest, can provide a powerful learning experience. Take the time to plan what you are going to say, make sure that it is clear, unambiguous and at a level appropriate to the listeners. Avoid unnecessary detail and repetition, check pupils' understanding and allow pupils the chance to check that they have understood you. Then let pupils get on with the task. Once pupils are on task you can circulate to talk to individuals or small groups. It is during these more intimate exchanges with your pupils that much of the highest quality learning can take place and you will be able to build effective working relationships.

Task 8.2

The next time you plan a lesson, think carefully about what you need to say. Try scripting part of what you are going to say and then edit the script down to the minimum that is needed to communicate clearly the cognitive, procedural and managerial aspects of the lesson. Aim to deliver the lesson with the minimum spoken input possible. Why not record the lesson and then evaluate how successful you have been?

8.9 The art of questioning

It is a little ironic that teachers spend so much of the time asking questions. In some ways it would make more sense for pupils to ask most of the questions, since it is teachers who have the knowledge and expertise. However, there are very good reasons why teachers should ask questions, most of which can come under the umbrella of 'assessment for learning' (see Chapter 9), for example:

- to establish what pupils already know about a topic or what skills they already have;
- to promote pupils' cognitive engagement with a topic;
- to check what pupils have learnt;
- to check the effectiveness of their own teaching;
- as a control technique.

Yet there should also be opportunities for pupils to ask questions. They need to be able to ask the teacher questions, but can also benefit from asking each other questions. However, the ability to ask questions effectively is a skill that needs to be nurtured in pupils. There are various strategies we can use to help pupils to identify, phrase and ask appropriate questions. Here are some ideas that you could try in the classroom:

- Get pupils to work individually, in pairs or threes to devise questions relevant to the topic for the teacher to answer. These could be placed in a box during one lesson and answered in the next. By making the process anonymous, you will encourage pupils to ask questions they might otherwise feel too embarrassed to ask and this system also gives you time to consider your answers.
- Create a climate of enquiry by encouraging pupils to ask questions during the lesson; for example, chunk lessons, providing opportunities for pupils to raise questions at the end of each phase.
- Give pupils 'answers' and ask them to suggest what the questions were.
- Use the 'hot-seat' technique. This is where pupils, rather than the teacher, take turns at fielding questions from classmates.

8.10 Types of questioning

There are various categories of question that you can ask. They place very different demands on pupils and achieve different things, so you need to develop an awareness of how you are using questions. Certain questions can be considered 'low-order', meaning that the cognitive response they elicit is relatively undemanding. Some questions merely require the pupil to **recall** something and so test existing knowledge or observations:

'In which parts of Brazil is coffee grown?'

This sort of question is often used at the start of a lesson to assess existing knowledge, but used too extensively it can bore or patronize pupils. It is important to develop a wider ranging repertoire of questions that require higher-order thinking. Slightly more demanding is the **comprehension** question:

'Why is Brazil a good place to grow coffee?'

and the **application** question which requires pupils to apply their knowledge to a different situation:

'What other parts of the world might have conditions suitable for growing coffee?'

High-order questions make greater cognitive demands and require pupils to analyze, synthesize and make evaluations. An **analysis** question might be:

'Why is Brazilia the capital of Brazil?'

A **synthesis** question demands that the respondent makes use of several pieces of knowledge to produce an answer:

'What would happen to Brazilia if Rio was made the capital of Brazil?'

An **evaluation** question requires the respondent to synthesize various pieces of information in order to make a judgement of some kind:

'Would Rio make a better capital city than Brazilia?'

These different types of question have been categorized according to Bloom et al.'s (1956) Taxonomy of Educational Objectives (see section 5.3).

Task 8.3

Choose a specific topic from your own subject area and devise six questions representing the categories exemplified above.

You will probably have heard of **open** and **closed** questions. Low-order questions tend to be closed questions, that is, there is only a limited number of correct responses and often only one. High-order questions tend to be open ones; pupils can make a wide variety of appropriate responses. Both open and closed, high- and low-order questions should have a place in your repertoire because they all have a part to play in effective questioning. However, pay particular attention to asking open questions which require elaborated answers in which pupils have to explain their thinking (Gipps 1994).

8.11 Planning questions

As with all aspects of teaching, it is best to plan your questioning strategy in advance. It should be linked to the intended learning outcomes for the lesson and should be designed to achieve specific things. For instance, you may want to use questions to establish what is already known, to stimulate thought or to set up the major themes of the lesson. You should also use questions to check learning and to reinforce learning that has taken place. By planning questions in advance, you can think about the way that you are going to ask them and take account of a range of options:

- *The sequence in which you will ask them.* It may be important to ask questions in a logical sequence. In most situations, it is wise to start with lower-order questions and build up to asking higher-order ones.
- *The language you will use.* Avoid ambiguity and try to get the level of vocabulary right for the class you are teaching.
- *Designing questions for particular pupils or groups of pupils.* It is important to involve all pupils in questioning, not just the most able. Try to differentiate your questions so that some are suitable for all.

Good planning will make you feel more confident during the lesson and better able to ask questions effectively.

8.12 Asking questions

Having planned your questioning strategy for the lesson, it is important to think about how you actually ask them. Whether you are asking questions of a whole class, a small group or just one individual, there are some basic principles of good practice to bear in mind. As with other communication with pupils, you need to remember that their use of language is almost certainly going to be less sophisticated than your own so questions need to be clear. The younger and the less able the pupils, the truer this will be.

Having asked your question, it is vital to allow pupils thinking or 'wait' time. It is very common for a new teacher to fail to do this because they are anxious to get the 'right' answer so that they can move on. Try to avoid this trap. Think how you would feel if someone was firing questions at you and failing to give you time to consider your response. By giving several seconds of thinking time, you provide pupils with a better opportunity to make a positive contribution to the lesson and thereby raise their self-esteem, making them feel good about being in your lesson. If you do not get a response, try repeating the question because this will give them a little longer to think about it and allows those who were not concentrating the first time a chance to refocus. You may also need to offer some prompts or clues to encourage pupils to have a go. There is also a danger that some pupils feel they have not had time to think because the teacher habitually accepts answers from those who raise their hands quickest or shout the answers out. Some teachers avoid this by operating a 'no hands' policy, giving children thinking time and then expecting everyone to answer if called upon (Black et al. 2002).

In a whole-class setting, you need to decide which questions to target at individuals or small groups and which to broadcast for anyone to attempt. If all of your questions are broadcast then you may only get responses from the most confident pupils. Whilst such pupils can be useful in helping to roll out your structured lesson, if you neglect to involve other pupils, this will leave them feeling isolated and you may miss the fact that the majority have lost the thread of the lesson. It is vital, therefore, to get in the habit of using both strategies to ensure that some questions are targeted at individuals and small groups. It is much easier to do this once you have learned pupils' names, but in the meantime you can employ other techniques such as:

- asking questions in sequence around the class;
- asking for a response from one of a group, for example 'Can anyone on the back left table tell me . . .';
- asking pupils to remind you of their name before they answer, so turning the session into an opportunity to learn some more names.

What you must avoid is asking only those pupils who are keen to answer, who are sitting immediately in front of you, who need to be kept occupied or whose names you can remember.

Pupils sometimes need longer to think about certain higher-order questions, especially those that require them to reflect on issues or consider their own opinions. You can help pupils to get the greatest benefit from these types of question by giving them the opportunity to discuss their answers before replying. A useful approach is to first ask them to consider their response privately for a short time, then to ask them to discuss their ideas in groups of two to four and finally to ask a spokesperson from each group to share their ideas with the whole group. This is sometimes known as the Private – Intimate – Public approach (P-I-P) and it is an excellent way of involving all pupils in responding to a question.

Questioning is an important assessment technique, but how do you know whether a whole class knows the correct answer to your question? Rather than getting pupils to respond verbally, you can get them to respond visually to very good effect. If individual pupils or small groups each have a small dry-wipe board, you can ask them to write answers on the boards and hold them up for you to see. You can also create a class set of true/false, yes/no cards and get pupils to indicate their response to statements that you make. Even simpler is to ask them to put 'thumbs up' to represent 'yes', 'thumbs down' for 'no' and 'thumbs horizontal' for 'not sure'. All of these techniques allow you to scan the classroom and get an impression of how confident the class is with the material and whether there are individuals that may need extra help with the work.

8.13 Receiving answers

It's not just how you ask questions that is important, but also how you receive pupils' responses. It is best to avoid answering your own questions (and it is surprising how often novice teachers do this!). Answering your own question has the effect of:

- frustrating those pupils who simply needed more thinking time before responding;
- suggesting that you did not expect anyone to be able to answer;
- denying pupils the opportunity to test their own understanding and develop their own communication skills.

After asking a question, it is very tempting to take the first appropriate answer and move on, but this can be a mistake in some situations. By allowing more than one pupil to respond to your question before you respond, you can get more ideas into the public arena and get a better feel for the understanding of the whole class. It is also good practice to invite pupils to evaluate each others' answers. This encourages greater pupil participation and active listening whilst allowing the teacher to spend more time listening, gaining a fuller picture of understanding within the group.

There are other choices to be made when responding to pupils' answers. First, you must decide whether to make a verbal response to a pupil's contribution. Generally, of course, you should, but there may be situations when it is best not to, for instance, when a clearly facetious response has been made. Sometimes an answer may be anticipating something that you wish to come to later, in which case it is best to acknowledge the contribution and note that you will come back to it later. It can be very useful to repeat the answer or the key element of it because this allows other pupils to keep up and gives them a second chance to listen to the answer or, indeed, to hear it for the first time if the respondent has a quiet voice. You may wish to rephrase an answer to make the point more clearly or concisely. It is certainly a good idea to praise contributions. If pupils receive praise for answers, they will be encouraged to make future contributions.

There will be occasions when the answers that you receive are erroneous. In these cases you will generally need to correct the pupil, but this needs sensitive handling or you may demoralize them and put them off making future contributions:

'Thanks for that, it's a really good suggestion, but it's not quite right . . .' is much better than:

'No, that's not what I'm looking for . . .'

In most cases it is a mistake to allow errors to pass because it may be assumed you are endorsing them as correct. Wrong answers can be just as useful to you as correct answers in providing clues to pupils' thought processes, so you need to listen carefully to them.

Some pupils will give you responses that are part-way to answering the question and in these cases it can be worth taking the time to gently probe them and encourage a fuller answer:

'That's an interesting idea, could you say a bit more about it?'
'That's an interesting answer, what exactly did you have in mind?'

By giving such opportunities you may discover that the pupil was not on the right track after all, but this would be a valuable thing to establish.

As you can appreciate, all of these different ways of responding to pupils' answers require you to be alert, sensitive and aware of what you are doing.

8.14 Avoiding questioning pitfalls

Questioning is a very powerful tool for promoting learning. A successful question and answer session can feel exhilarating and serve effectively to consolidate learning or move it forward. There are some common mistakes, in addition to those discussed above, that can cause such sessions to stall or lead to management problems. In general it is best to avoid:

- asking questions requiring yes/no answers, unless the whole class is required to respond with visual signals such as YES/NO cards;
- asking questions with several valid answers, unless you are anticipating this;
- asking questions in a way that may encourage calling out. Good examples of these are questions that begin with the phrases 'Who can tell me . . .' and 'Does anyone know . . .'. If you think about these questions you will see that the logical responses are not ones that you would want. It is much better to turn the question into an instruction: 'Put up your hand if you can tell me . . .';
- over-use of 'response-seeking' (Black and Wiliam 1998a), an approach which entails fishing for a desired response, ignoring or rejecting unwanted answers and then moving on as soon as the desired response is obtained. This promotes a surface approach to learning, encouraging guessing and the unthinking regurgitation of information that is poorly understood. It is also unhelpful to teachers because it fails to detect whether meaningful learning has taken place.

8.15 Theory into practice

You should now appreciate the importance of planning for effective communication with your pupils. Remember that it is about more than just what you say, but how you say it, as well as how you use your body and the space in which you teach. You should also realize that questioning is a powerful tool, but that you have to develop awareness of its finer points if you are to build successful relationships and promote learning.

8.16 Recommendations for further reading and webliography

Alexander, R. (2005) *Towards Dialogic Teaching. Rethinking Classroom Talk* (2nd edn). Cambridge: Dialogos.

Department for Education and Skills (DfES) (2004) *Strengthening Teaching and Learning in Science Through Using Different Pedagogies. Unit 1: Using Group Talk and Argument.* London: DfES.

Neill, S. and Caswell, C. (1993) *Body Language for Competent Teachers.* London: Routledge.

Norman, K. (ed.) (1992) *Thinking Voices: The Work of the National Oracy Project.* London: Hodder & Stoughton.

Wragg, E.C. and Brown, G. (2001) *Questioning in the Secondary School.* London: RoutledgeFalmer.

www.voicecare.org.uk/ (VoiceCare Network)

9

Using assessment for formative purposes

Val Brooks

9.1 Introduction

What image does the word 'assessment' conjure in your mind? A piece of work after it has been corrected and assigned a mark? A silent hall filled with serried rows of examination candidates? School 'league tables' splashed across newspapers following the publication of examination results? A teacher questioning a class and attending carefully to responses? The diverse images that spring to mind remind us that assessment is a multi-faceted activity. This chapter focuses on arguably the most important purpose of assessment – the use of formative assessment to enhance teaching and learning.

The organization of this chapter reflects the stages in a school placement: induction; obtaining information about prospective teaching groups; planning SoW; planning, teaching and evaluating lessons. It suggests ways in which assessment can enhance these activities. By the end of this chapter, you should:

- understand the concept of formative assessment;
- know why formative assessment is important;
- understand some of the ways in which assessment can be deployed to improve planning, teaching and evaluation;
- understand why and how to involve pupils in assessment.

9.2 Formative and summative assessment

Traditionally, formative assessment has been a neglected and poorly understood aspect of teachers' work (Black and Wiliam 1998a). Task 9.1 illustrates widely held assumptions that can hamper a teacher's ability to make effective use of assessment.

Task 9.1

Consider these examples taken from visits to student teachers during school placement.

Student teacher A had written an aide-memoire across the top of his lesson plan in bold print.

1   Tell them what they're going to learn
2   Teach it to them
3   Tell them what they've learnt.

Why is this approach flawed?

Discussion with student teacher B focused on planning a SoW. She had used the National Curriculum Programmes of Study to clarify learning purposes. Then she had planned for a variety of learning activities to cater for individual needs and the variations in learning style preference within the group. As her account made no mention of assessment, student B was asked how it would contribute. She pointed to a written assignment that pupils would complete at the end, explaining that it would be used to check what pupils had learnt.

How does student B view the role of assessment in her teaching? How else might she use it?

One of the problems with student A's approach is that he assumes that his pupils will learn exactly what he teaches them in exactly the way he intends them to learn. However, research, especially in conceptually difficult subjects like science, has found that it is common for pupils to understand a topic less well after teaching than they did before! The reasons for this are complex. For instance, pupils may start out with misconceptions that are incompatible with what is being taught. If teaching fails to address these misconceptions, confusion may be compounded when pupils try to assimilate new learning with pre-existing misconceptions. If a teacher does not attempt to find out what pupils already understand about a topic then they cannot help pupils to link the ideas in the current lesson to knowledge that they already have, often at an intuitive level. That means that the two sets of ideas remain separate and may be accessed by the pupil separately according to context. There is not a straightforward relationship between what teachers teach and what pupils actually learn. Therefore, you cannot, as student A did, tell pupils what they have learnt during a lesson. The only reliable way of finding out what pupils have actually learnt is to assess them. For student B, assessment is a terminal activity that takes place once teaching has been completed. It offers a final check on what has been achieved before moving on. This is a traditional, and very limited, view of the contribution that assessment can make to teaching and learning.

Following a paradigm shift, it is now recognized that assessment is most helpful when it is an ongoing and integral part of teaching and learning so that feedback can be used at each stage in the planning/teaching/evaluation cycle. To be formative, assessment must have a 'feedback' and a 'feedforward' function. This means that feedback from one stage should be used at the next stage to improve subsequent teaching and learning. Consequently, assessment could, and should, occur at any stage – even before anything has been taught! There are three aspects of this paradigm shift which represent a radical departure from traditional practice:

- the idea that assessment could come first, rather than last, in the sequence of events;
- the idea that it should be used continuously to monitor progress and adjust approaches to teaching and learning;
- the idea that to maximize effectiveness, pupils must understand, and be fully involved with, assessment.

Summative assessment provides a systematic summing up of attainment through, for example, an end-of-topic test or a piece of homework. Typically, it results in a grade or level and signifies the end of something such as a unit of work or a key stage. Formative assessment is more like a thread weaving its way through the planning/ teaching/evaluation cycle, binding the different elements and tailoring them to pupils' needs.

There are two common misconceptions about what distinguishes formative from summative assessment. The first is that the real difference is one of timing with formative assessment taking place during and summative taking place at the end of a learning event. Although that is often the case, it is not necessarily so and misses the key distinction between the two. The second misapprehension is that they involve different types of assessment. Summative assessment is often equated with external tests whereas formative is identified with what teachers do inside classrooms. However, test results can be used formatively and classroom assessment can be summative. For instance, a department that analyzes end of KS test results to identify strengths and weaknesses in pupils' performances, and then uses the feedback to alter the teaching of certain topics, is using test results formatively. In contrast, teachers whose marking is confined to giving ticks and recording marks in mark books exemplify a summative approach and their pupils will inevitably see the marks as a means of comparing themselves with classmates. Neither party uses the assessment to obtain information which can be used to improve future performance. The real distinction, then, is not one of timing nor of form but of *purpose* (Wiliam and Black 1996). Only if there is an attempt to use feedback to improve teaching and/or learning is assessment formative. To be formative, assessment has to lead to action – doing something differently as a result of what has been learnt from the feedback. For instance, a teacher uses a written exercise to check pupils' understanding of a new topic and discovers that a number of them are unable to complete the task because they are making the same basic error. Instead of pressing on with the final phase of the lesson as planned, s/he decides to use the remaining time to work through examples from pupils' work to illustrate and correct the problem. One way to check your own underlying purpose in carrying out an assessment is to ask yourself: 'Is this assessment FOR learning (formative) or assessment OF learning (summative)?'

Research published in the 1990s (Black and Wiliam 1998a) alerted the educational community to the capacity of formative assessment to improve teaching and learning, raising educational standards for all pupils. It focused on experimental studies, which produced measures of effect, showing that:

- the learning gains associated with formative assessment exceed those produced by most other educational interventions designed to raise attainment;
- formative assessment helps all pupils but is especially beneficial for low attaining pupils who it helps more than the rest;
- formative assessment reduces the spread of attainment whilst raising it overall.

Summative assessment, on the other hand, is often associated with 'high stakes'. Assessment is said to be high stakes when the results are regarded as very important (for instance, a community might judge a local school by its results in tests and examinations) or when the results have important consequences (for instance, the offer of a university place may rest on results at Advanced level [A level]). In contrast to formative assessment, high stakes summative assessment has been found to:

- narrow the curriculum and encourage rote learning;
- widen the gap between high and low achievers;
- promote high anxiety levels amongst pupils and erode the self-esteem of low attainers (Harlen and Deakin Crick 2002, available at http://www.eppi.ioe.ac.uk).

These findings provide powerful reasons for making the development of formative assessment a top priority during training.

9.3 School induction

Useful first steps at the start of a placement include identifying a school's assessment coordinator and obtaining a copy of the assessment policy. The policy should specify preferred approaches to target-setting, monitoring progress and providing feedback to pupils. Your department may have produced its own subject-specific guidance so check whether there is also a departmental policy. In secondary schools, where pupils may be taught by ten or more teachers, a consistent approach is important to avoid confusion so use these policies to ensure that your own practice is consistent with requirements.

When I trained as a teacher, conventional wisdom held that pupils should be allowed to make a fresh start with a new teacher who should avoid preconceptions about their capabilities. Although this principle was meant to apply to behaviour, one consequence was that student teachers possessed very little information about pupils' attainments and needs when they assumed responsibility for their learning. Nowadays, serving teachers can expect to receive a wealth of assessment data on teaching groups at the beginning of an academic year. Transferring data from one teacher to another has many advantages. It provides a smoother transition between years, helping teachers to pitch work appropriately from the outset. Knowing what children should be capable of saves time that would otherwise be wasted rediscovering information that is already known. Similar principles apply to teaching placements so

Remember!

14.99
14.99
19.5
35
27.0
1.99
800

familiarize yourself with assessment data held on groups you will be the
following information is likely to be available:

- test results and targets;
- the regular teacher's most recent assessment of pupils' current working levels;
- assessments of attributes like organization and whether examination coursework is on target;
- reading ages;
- details of children on the SEN register, including IEPs;
- details of children identified as gifted and talented.

These prior assessments will help with differentiation (see Chapter 6) and pitching work at an appropriate level. There is also a case for undertaking your own assessment before finalizing SoW.

9.4 Assessment for planning

Traditionally, assessment played no part in the planning stage of the teaching cycle. The difficulties to which this can lead are illustrated by Case Study 9.1.

CASE STUDY 9.1

Student teacher C taught a science lesson in which pupils investigated the factors affecting the strength of an electromagnet. To undertake the experiment, pupils needed to be able to construct a line graph to plot and interpret their results. When he marked pupils' accounts of the experiment, student teacher C realized that the point of the investigation would have been clearer if he had reinforced previous work on lines of best fit and their use in identifying trends and making predictions *beforehand*. He decided to go over the work again in the following lesson to reinforce learning objectives which had been only partially achieved.

Student teacher C obtained feedback from pupils *after* he had taught them whereas this feedback would have been most useful to him *before* he finalized his plan. It would have helped him to appreciate the prior learning that would play a key part in making the lesson meaningful and thus he could have avoided having to repeat work.

Is there any hard evidence to support this way of working? A large-scale American study is interesting in this respect (Black and Wiliam 1998a). It involved a fresh intake of kindergarten children, most of whom came from disadvantaged home backgrounds. Socio-economic background and academic attainment are known to correlate closely, with more advantaged backgrounds correlating positively with educational attainment whereas the opposite is true of educational attainment and disadvantaged backgrounds. Each year, many of these children were identified as having SEN at an early stage in their schooling. The purpose of the research was to determine whether a different approach to teaching could reduce the incidence of special needs referrals.

The research involved splitting the intake into two groups. One group was treated as a control group and taught as normal. The other group was placed on an eight-week experimental programme. Their teachers were trained to carry out baseline assessments before they did any teaching so that teaching could be matched to children's needs from the outset. After two weeks, pupils' progress was reviewed and teaching plans were modified in response to the feedback. There was a further review after four weeks when teaching plans were adjusted yet again. Thus, over the course of the programme, children were assessed three times: baseline assessment plus reviews after weeks 2 and 4 and, on each occasion, teaching plans were adapted in the light of the feedback.

To determine whether the experimental approach made a difference, both groups were given pre-tests in reading, maths and science to establish a baseline for them. At the end of the programme, outcome tests in the same skills were used to measure whether there were any differences in their progress. The results showed that children's baseline scores provided a good indication of how well they would do in the final tests, that is those who did best in the baseline tests were also likely to do best in the outcome tests. Nevertheless, the experimental group made significantly greater gains than the control group on all three subject tests. However, the key research question was whether the experimental approach had made a difference to the incidence of SEN referrals. Over a quarter of the children in the control group (1 in 3.7) was identified as having special needs. Did the experimental approach improve the performance of the other group? And if so, how big a difference did it make to special needs referrals? Make your own prediction and then turn to note 1 (page 126).

Research such as this provides compelling evidence that pupils learn more effectively if teachers fine-tune their plans to learners' needs. Ausubel (1968: 36) explained this phenomenon thus: 'The most important single factor influencing learning is what the learner already knows; ascertain this and teach him [her] accordingly.' Assessment is the only reliable way of obtaining this information. It also helps teachers to develop a clearer understanding of how the learning jigsaw fits together and which pieces of prior knowledge need to be in place before a new topic is introduced. Prior learning is particularly important in 'hierarchical' subjects where progressing to the next level is dependent on the acquisition of a hierarchy of knowledge, skills and concepts (i.e. science, modern foreign languages and mathematics). However, it is a fundamental educational principle that learning should start from the point where the learner is. Therefore, assessment for planning is a critical component of formative assessment in all subjects.

Task 9.2

Identify some strategies for implementing assessment for planning. Two examples are given as a starting point.

1.   Consider whether an end-of-topic test is suitable for use as a pre-test. A well designed pre-test can identify commonly held misconceptions and gaps in learning. It also provides a useful indication of progress when pupils are re-tested at the end.

> 2. Analyze a topic to identify necessary prior learning and knowledge, skills and con-
>   cepts to be taught. Using pupil-friendly language, produce a list of key learning
>   points for pupils to 'traffic light'.[1]
>
> [1] Traffic lights involve using the colours red, amber and green. Their purpose is to identify those
> pupils whose knowledge and understanding are secure making them ready to move on (green),
> those who need to repeat work (red) and those whose learning is not yet secure so they would
> benefit from consolidation (amber). Traffic lights can be used in many ways, for example they
> provide a highly visual record-keeping system and pupils can use them to self-assess work prior to
> submission.

Information gained from assessment for planning can be used to:

- identify prior learning that need only be revised, rather than wasting time repeating what pupils already know;
- identify strengths that can be used as a foundation for building new knowledge
  and skills;
- reorient a scheme of work to pay particular attention to gaps in knowledge and
  misconceptions that are widely shared;
- differentiate to meet the particular needs of individuals;
- identify concepts and skills that will be required which are not subject-specific
  (e.g. the literacy and numeracy demands of a topic).

9.5 Building assessment into schemes of work

It is known that:

- effective teachers monitor pupils' progress closely (Harris 1998);
- pupils benefit from receiving rapid, regular feedback (Black and Wiliam 1998a).

These research findings suggest that assessment needs to be carefully considered
during medium-term planning so that it can be properly integrated into SoW. Close
monitoring and rapid feedback are particularly important when new material is being
introduced or when the subject matter is conceptually difficult. Opportunities for
both should be identified on SoW. Formative assessment requires teachers to view
their medium-term plans as flexible working documents which can be adjusted in
the light of feedback. If assessment is treated as a bolt-on extra, there is likely to be
insufficient time to do justice to it and insufficient flexibility in the scheme to respond
to feedback. This approach invariably raises concerns about the deployment of time.
Under pressure to cover programmes of study in a limited amount of time, teachers
worry about 'wasting' valuable teaching time on assessment. However, as Case Study
9.1 shows, assessment can make teaching and learning more efficient, reducing the
amount of reinforcement and repetition involved so it does not necessarily require
more time. If it also makes teaching and learning more effective, it should not be
dispensed with on the grounds of wasting time!

Planning a SoW is also an opportunity to take an overview of the role of assessment. The principles of variety and match are as important in planning for assessment as they are in planning for learning. Therefore, the assessment demands that will be made of pupils, and the opportunities they will be offered, should be considered. Just as pupils have different learning style preferences so too they favour different approaches to assessment. Indeed, some assessment techniques have been shown to display a gender bias. For instance, girls do better on extended writing tasks and boys on multiple-choice tests (Gipps and Murphy 1994). Likewise, some pupils perform better in one medium than another. A written medium favours those with well-developed literacy skills. Others may understand something just as well but would benefit from being able to demonstrate competence in a different medium, for example an oral or a practical task or by using computer software.

Task 9.3

Take a SoW (preferably your own). If assessment has been considered, analyze the assessment demands and opportunities. Alternatively, published examples are available at www.standards.dfes.gov.uk/schemes3/.

- Have points where progress should be monitored and pupils should receive feedback been identified?
- Are approaches varied or is there over-reliance on particular strategies (e.g. testing) or one performance medium (e.g. writing)?
- Are there opportunities for pupils to become involved in assessment?

If assessment has been overlooked, how could it be used to improve the scheme?

9.6 Assessment at the teaching stage: questioning

Questioning is, perhaps, the most useful and versatile assessment technique available. Because understanding can falter at any stage in the learning process, teachers need to be able to monitor progress continuously so that they can intervene promptly if problems arise. Questioning is easy to use and provides immediate feedback, making it very effective for monitoring progress. Unlike other commonly used assessment techniques such as tests and homework, questioning doesn't require elaborate preparation or forewarning pupils about its use. It can be used as and when needed, providing instant feedback and allowing teachers to make on-the-spot decisions about how to proceed. Questioning also gives teachers access to the processes of learning as well as the products. When a teacher assesses a finished product (e.g. written work), although errors may be apparent, the reasons behind them may be hidden. Questioning has a diagnostic function, allowing teachers to probe pupils' reasoning and gain insight into thought processes that are causing difficulties. Skilful questioning has been described as: 'the single most important factor in students achievements of high standards, where questions were used to assess students' knowledge and challenge their thinking' (Ofsted 1996a: 23). It, therefore, ranks among the top priorities for development by student teachers.

Chapter 8 includes an extensive section on questioning. Some of the points made there are particularly relevant to questioning as a means of assessment. For example:

- using open questions to elicit elaborated answers;
- allowing wait time;
- avoiding response-seeking;
- obtaining feedback from all members of the class;
- listening carefully to right and, perhaps especially, to wrong answers;
- providing honest feedback to pupils;
- providing opportunities for pupils to evaluate each others' answers;
- encouraging pupils to ask questions about what they are learning.

Task 9.4

Research suggests that teachers devote insufficient attention to developing high quality questions which challenge or extend pupils' ideas, promoting higher-order thinking (Black and Wiliam 1998a).

Select a topic from your own subject and identify aspects that children are likely to find demanding. Devise questions which will help pupils to engage with the demands in a thought-provoking way.

Consider ways in which questions could be tackled (e.g. orally in pairs) and responses shared (e.g. 'hot-seating').

9.7 Peer and self-assessment

Formative assessment only achieves its full potential when pupils become engaged with the process through self-assessment. Pupils who become skilled in self-assessment make impressive learning gains. For instance, in one study where pupils were trained to make regular, usually daily, use of self-assessment in mathematics, over a 20-week period the group made almost double the progress of a control group which did not practise self-assessment (Black and Wiliam 1998a). Findings such as this led Black and Wiliam to conclude that self-assessment is 'essential' rather than 'a luxury' (1998b: 19). However, self-assessment is a difficult undertaking beset with misunderstandings. For instance, teachers who claim to use self-assessment are often confusing it with a process better described as 'self-marking' (Ofsted 1998) where pupils mark their own work against a predetermined mark scheme (Freeman and Lewis 1998). Some teachers worry about allowing pupils to allocate grades, believing them to be incapable of marking their own work reliably or honestly. Again, this represents a misunderstanding of the purpose of self-assessment which is not about transferring the grading function from teachers to pupils. The real purposes of self-assessment are to equip pupils with:

- insight into the assessment criteria that will be used to judge their work;

- realistic notions of quality so that they can recognize 'excellent', 'good' and 'satisfactory' work;
- awareness of the gap between standards embodied in the assessment criteria and their own attainments.

Equipped with these understandings, pupils are able to regulate their own performance and tackle the attainment gap. Unfortunately, pupils also find self-assessment difficult and may take a long time to learn to use it effectively (Black 1998). Black and Wiliam have concluded that self-assessment is too difficult for pupils to attempt without first honing their skills through peer assessment.

- Share assessment criteria with pupils *before* they embark on a task;
- Make assessment criteria accessible by converting official language into a pupil-friendly idiom. Simplify criteria by using concise checklists or questions against which pupils can assess their performance;
- Use exemplification material to take the mystery out of assessment by providing concrete examples of what success looks like;
- Ensure that standards are well-illustrated by providing examples of pupils meeting criteria with varying degrees of success. (Sources of exemplification material include the National Curriculum in Action website [www.ncaction.org.uk] and model scripts with examiners' commentaries produced by awarding bodies (Assessment and Qualifications Alliance [www.aqa.org.uk], Educational Excellence [www.edexcel.org.uk] and Oxford, Cambridge and RSA [www.ocr.org.uk]));
- Model assessment processes for pupils by sharing peer-assessment exercises with them;
- Introduce self-assessment once pupils have become competent peer assessors;
- Use peer and self-assessment *during* a unit of work so that pupils have an opportunity to reflect on work while it is in progress and put what they learn into practice while it is *still* relevant.

Figure 9.1 Developing peer and self-assessment skills

9.8 Written feedback

Constructive feedback is vital in helping pupils to progress. Nevertheless, one review of the literature on feedback found that two out of every five feedback effects were negative (Black and Wiliam 1998a). Given that feedback has both a negative and a positive potential, a key question concerns the types of feedback that are most likely to be helpful. One study investigated the impact of three common feedback types on pupils' progress and motivation (Black and Wiliam 1998a). It also explored whether the effects were influenced by ability. The experiment entailed a large sample of high-attaining and low-attaining 11-year-olds selected from a number of schools. For the purposes of the experiment, pupils were assigned to one of three groups that were mixed by school and ability. Their group determined the feedback children received:

- one group received individually composed comments on the level of match between their work and the assessment criteria which were described to all beforehand;

- the second group were given grades only;
- the final group received a grade and a comment.

The children's performance and motivation were then monitored over a series of tasks to determine which feedback type was most beneficial. Which group made most progress and were best motivated? Make predictions before turning to note 2 for the results (page 126).

Providing constructive feedback is a sophisticated skill. Figure 9.2 overleaf identifies approaches which have been shown to be effective and those likely to have a deleterious effect.

Target-setting is another means of converting feedback into feedforward.

9.9 Feedforward through target-setting

Setting targets for the end of a KS is considered in the next chapter. Although end-of-KS targets are a natural focus for attention, they can only be achieved by identifying the sequence of smaller steps children must take to achieve their long-term goals. Therefore, it is individual learning targets, set on a day-to-day basis, which play a critical role in raising attainment (see Figure 9.3 on page 125). These targets are important for the following reasons:

- Having a general aim to improve is almost as unhelpful as having no aim at all (Black and Wiliam 1998a).
- Ofsted (1998) reports that teachers find it difficult to provide feedback which combines honesty about the shortcomings in pupils' work with a positive tone. Instead they avoid comments that might appear negative, producing feedback which is over-generous and misleading in its appraisal of the quality of pupils' work.
- Pupils often ignore feedback, failing to act on its suggestions for improvement.

Target-setting can address these difficulties. By taking a defect, and converting it into a target, the need for explicit criticism is obviated. Instead of dwelling on difficulties, target-setting looks to the future, offering guidance on how to improve. It has been found to increase pupils' motivation and sense of purpose and accelerate rates of progress (Black and Wiliam 1998a).

9.10 Feedforward through lesson evaluation

Student teachers frequently fail to make the link between assessment and evaluation. Evaluations are often written before assessments have been completed. Even where assessment data is available, evaluation is completed without reference to it. Most lesson evaluation is impressionistic, based on students' personal perceptions of how well lessons went. Assessment offers an additional source of evidence of the extent to which objectives have been achieved. It can add rigour to evaluation, either corroborating or refuting personal impressions.

Constructive	Counterproductive
✓ **Prompt feedback** The ideal is immediate feedback provided during performance so that pupils have an opportunity to implement what they have learnt before the work is completed.	✗ **Delayed feedback** Most likely to be ignored if pupils have already moved on to a new topic.
✓ **Written comments** When used to provide a clear explanation of ways in which work is successful and how future performance could be improved.	✗ **Marks and grades** A powerful form of feedback which 'overrides' comments. Encourages complacency in the able and despondency in the less able.
✓ **Task-involving feedback** Focuses on the knowledge, skills and concepts relevant to succeeding with a task.	✗ **Ego-involving feedback** Encourages pupils to focus on themselves, how well they are performing and comparing themselves with others.
✓ **Criterion-referenced assessment** Assessment is linked to explicit criteria which are clarified before pupils embark on a task.	✗ **Criterion-weak assessment** Criteria are muddled (Ofsted 1998) or tacit.
✓ **Scaffolded feedback** Creates a 'state of mindfulness' (Black and Wiliam 1998a: 51) with regard to the feedback, giving pupils as much help as they need to progress but no more.	✗ **Corrective feedback** Least helpful where teachers correct every error so that pupils are not encouraged to think about or apply the feedback.
✓ **Balanced feedback** Strengths and achievements are set against areas for improvement without dwelling unduly on either.	✗ **Unbalanced feedback** Dwells on the positive or the negative without properly acknowledging the other dimension.
✓ **Positive tone** Can be created by acknowledging achievements first and treating weaknesses as targets for development.	✗ **Negative tone** Can be created by drawing attention to what is wrong with work first or offering critical comments with no indication of how to improve.
✓ **Feedforward** Can be achieved by providing time for pupils to read and respond to feedback and by following up on previous feedback next time.	✗ **Feedforward absent** Where teachers neglect the links between feedback and future performance, pupils are encouraged to do likewise.

Figure 9.2 Providing feedback

Assessment also plays a part in evaluating teaching over longer periods of time. Patterns and trends can be detected in large bodies of data (e.g. the information for a year group over a full year) which are not apparent in small amounts of information. The analysis of large-scale pupil performance data is dealt with in the next chapter. It is mentioned here to show that evaluation at the microcosmic level fits into a bigger picture. The analysis that takes place at departmental and whole-school level is an extension of the scrutiny to which class teachers subject their groups and teaching methods. At both levels, the key questions are:

> To what extent are all pupils achieving their full potential?
> How could teaching and learning be improved?

Effective targets:

· are few in number;

· offer precise, measurable guidance on what pupils need to do to improve (compare 'Improve your presentation' with 'Improve the layout of your work by providing a margin, starting each new line next to the margin and using a sub-heading [underlined] for each section');

· are realistic and achievable in the short term, to maintain motivation;

· are task-related, focusing on knowledge, skills and concepts necessary to complete a task;

· are accompanied by regular opportunities for review;

· are those which pupils have been involved in selecting so they feel some ownership;

· are used as a reference point (e.g. pupils are reminded of them before embarking on a task and then offered feedback on their success in achieving them);

· involve pupils in deciding when targets have been met so that they become self-regulating.

Figure 9.3 Effective targets

The thesis of this chapter is that formative assessment plays a key role in improving teaching and learning. Thus, all new teachers need to view 'assessment literacy' (Gipps 1994) as a priority for their own professional development.

9.11 Recommendations for further reading and webliography

Black, P., Harrison, C., Lee, C., Marshall, B. and Wiliam, D. (2003) *Assessment for Learning: Putting it into Practice.* Buckingham: Open University Press.

Brooks, V. (2002) *Assessment in Secondary Schools: The New Teacher's Guide to Monitoring, Assessment, Recording, Reporting and Accountability.* Buckingham: Open University Press.

Clarke, S. (2005) *Formative Assessment in the Secondary Classroom.* London: Hodder Murray.

Centre for Educational Research and Innovation (2005) *Formative Assessment: Improving Learning in Secondary Classrooms.* Paris: Organisation for Economic Co-operation and Development (OECD).

www.aaia.org.uk (website of the Association for Achievement and Improvement through Assessment)

www.qca.org.uk (an area of the QCA's website is devoted to 'Assessment for Learning')

Endnote 1

Only 1 in 17 children from the experimental group was identified as having SEN. This reduction was achieved by using assessment to inform planning. The study provides evidence of the learning gains to be made by tailoring planning to meet children's needs.

Endnote 2

Group	Performance	Motivation
Comments only	Raised and the improvement was sustained over the series of tasks	Followed a broadly similar pattern to performance but was also influenced by ability.
Grades + comments	Steady decline across the series of tasks	• High achievers maintained a high level of interest irrespective of feedback type.
Grades only	Initial improvement which was not sustained	• Low achievers who received grades quickly lost interest.

Note that both feedback types which used grades were associated with a deterioration in performance and motivation.

10

Using assessment data to support pupil achievement

Chris Husbands

10.1 Introduction

Task 10.1

It's approaching the beginning of the Autumn Term. You are preparing your teaching for a Year 8 group. One of the pieces of information you have received is pupils' reading ages. How might the following information support your planning and teaching?

Table 10.1 Reading ages for a Year 8 class

Adam	10.1	Lauren	13.8
Aysha	14.6	Manisha	12.4
Craig	11.1	Miranda	13.4
Georgina	12.1	Richard	9.5
Ian	11.4	Samantha	11.5
Inderjit	10.7	Sarah	11.9
Irma	11.1	Sirinan	9.3
James	9.8	Syrha	11.11
Jimmy	11.5	Tara	9.10
Jo	12.00	Toby	8.1
Kimberley	11.7	Vikki	7.9
Laura	12.2	Yasin	7.8

Several features of the group are noteworthy:

- All but three of the pupils (Aysha, Lauren and Miranda) have reading ages below their chronological age;
- Three pupils (Yasin, Vikki and Toby) have reading ages which are more than three years below their chronological age;
- Girls have higher reading ages, across the group, than boys;

- Two girls (Aysha and Lauren) have reading ages which are much higher than the rest of the class.

The reading age data you have been given is an example – in fact a relatively simple and crude example – of information which will help you to consider appropriate teaching methods, reading materials and suitable writing activities for the group. It will also help you to consider other issues which could support your teaching: seating and grouping arrangements and individual learning plans for pupils in the group. It should help you to refine learning and outcome targets for pupils. In short, this sort of data should help you to plan learning more effectively. In using evidence in this way, you are beginning to make active use of attainment data in order to support planning for pupil achievement.

This chapter explores ways in which teachers can use data to support pupil achievement. In particular, it sets out to introduce:

- the range of data which is available to teachers;
- the ways in which schools use that data;
- the target-setting process.

10.2 The range of data available

In the example above, we used reading ages to make initial judgements about teaching and learning. Although reading age data is valuable, and helps teachers to think about the sort of curriculum materials which learners can access, it is also rather crude. Few schools now depend only on reading age material to help them plan. There are a number of difficulties with reading age data: it measures only one aspect of learners' attainments; it quickly becomes out-dated; and there is evidence that some groups of children perform less well on reading tests than others. Pupils whose first language is not English, for example, may perform far less well on a reading test than their attainment would suggest. Different curriculum areas use language, and written materials, in different ways: reading age data may be relatively unhelpful in supporting mathematics, science, music or art teachers. Since the mid-1990s, the range, quantity and quality of data available to teachers have expanded enormously. They now have access to comprehensive data on pupil performance, progress and achievement, and they are able to make use of this to track pupil progress and identify appropriate targets for learning outcomes. Most schools will have in place sophisticated tracking strategies which draw together a range of attainment data and allow teachers to map their strategies against a range of data, as well as to track the extent to which learners are making expected progress.

New teachers face particular challenges in making the best use of the range of data available. They need to find ways of making judgements about the reliability of information available and about methods of deploying information to support good teaching and learning, and they need to work out how to integrate data, and schools' strategies for using it, with their routine planning activities. This has become more pressing as schools have begun to explore the issue of personalising teaching and learning (see Chapters 6 and 26), since effective personalisation depends on the availability and use of reliable data about pupils' attainment.

Since the introduction of NC tests in the 1990s, schools have been able to access a vastly increased quantity and quality of information on pupil attainment, and to compare the performance of both individual pupils and groups of pupils in school against other groups within the school, previous performance and national performance patterns. At KS3, pupils are assessed against an 8-level scale on the basis of national tests and teacher assessment in English, mathematics and science and on the basis of teacher assessment in foundation subjects. Schools are required to report formally against the 8-level scale at the end of KS2 (at age 11) and at the end of KS3 (at age 14). By the end of KS2, pupils are expected to achieve a level 4 in English, mathematics and science, so that a pupil who achieves level 4 is said to be working 'at national expectation', whilst a pupil working at levels 1, 2 or 3 is working 'below national expectation'. Because KS2 assessment data covers the whole of the NC, and is supported by both test and teacher assessment data, it provides secondary teachers with a range of assessment information which can inform decisions about teaching and learning at KS3. All this means that in addition to reading age data, the school will have available NC performance data on the pupils in your Year 8 teaching group, and it will have been able to use that data during Year 7 to make judgements about the ways in which these pupils can access the secondary curriculum. Table 10.2 sets out the sort of assessment data profile which a secondary school might receive on two pupils.

This is clearly a wider variety of data than that provided by reading scores alone, and it begins to point up some issues for teaching. Mayuresh, for example, appears to

Table 10.2 Key Stage 2 attainment profiles

	Mayuresh		Kirsty	
	Test	Teacher Assessment	Test	Teacher Assessment
Overall Subject Level: English	4	3	2	3
AT1: Speaking and Listening		4		3
AT2: Reading	3	3	2	3
AT3: Writing, including spelling and handwriting	4	3	2	2
Mathematics	5	4	3	3
Science	4	4	3	3
Design and technology		4		4
Information and communication Technology		4		3
History		3		2
Geography		4		2
Music		3		3
Art and design		5		4
Physical education		4		3

be working at or above national expectation in core subjects, but his reading score, at level 3 on both test and teacher assessment, suggests that there are potential difficulties in reading. Kirsty is working below national expectation and there appears to be a particular difficulty about writing. Multiplied across cohorts of learners, this data on entry to secondary school is a potentially rich source of information. During Year 7, it will be confirmed or revised by continuing teacher assessment.

However, the use of KS2 assessment data is far from straightforward. Persistent doubts have been expressed about its reliability, particularly near the boundaries of levels, and about the relationship between test results and teacher assessments. Given the extent to which primary schools are held accountable on the basis of their pupils' performance in KS2 tests, considerable effort is expended in Year 6 on boosting pupil performance, as a result of which many secondary schools treat the results with some caution. Finally, the data are rather crude – there are eight levels, but 90 per cent of pupils entering secondary school are assessed at level 3, 4 or 5, so test results provide little discrimination between pupils. As a result, schools have become adept at looking below 'headline levels' at the ways in which levels are made up, at discrepancies between test and teacher assessment and at patterns across subject areas, in attempts to make NC test data more usable.

Task 10.2

Look at Table 10.2 and consider the implications of this data for planning work in the first term of Year 7 for Mayuresh and Kirsty.

Given the difficulties of reading ages and NC scores, schools have turned to other assessment devices to provide more robust data on their pupils. There is now an exceptionally wide range of such data available. The most widely used sources of datasets which can support schools' uses of attainment evidence are those provided by the National Foundation for Educational Research (NFER; http://www.nfer.ac.uk), the Curriculum, Evaluation and Management (CEM) Centre at the University of Durham (http://www.cem.dur.ac.uk), and the Fischer Family Trust (www.fischertrust.org). NFER and CEM both provide standardized testing materials which schools can purchase, and a calibration/benchmarking service which enables schools to compare individual pupil and cohort characteristics with those of pupils nationally. NFER Cognitive Abilities Tests (CAT) and CEM Year Eleven Information System (YELLIS) and Middle Years Information System (MidYIS) are essentially cognitive reasoning tests which are not content- or syllabus-dependent. Administered across ranges of schools, they provide comparative data for schools of pupils' attainments, allowing schools to compare an individual's performance with that of a large sample of pupils, or to understand in more detail the make-up of their intake in comparison with overall performance patterns. Both NFER and CEM present learners' profiles in cognitive domains: MidYIS tests permit assessment of vocabulary, maths, non-verbal and skills. MidYIS, which is used in over 1500 schools, standardizes results nationally with 100 representing the average score. Pupils are sorted into four equally sized bands from A (the highest) to D (the lowest). This analysis allows schools to examine their own cohort in relation to the national cohort and, drawing on previous years' MidYIS, KS3 and GCSE data, to make predictions about pupils' KS3 and GCSE outcomes. Information is confidential to the school, and not used for publication.

The Fischer Family Trust data work in a slightly different way, since no additional testing is involved. Although, like CEM and NFER, Fischer data is based on using pupil progress data to predict likely performance in subsequent tests, the Fischer datasets are all derived from NC and GCSE performance. The Fischer approach is based on findings that there are high levels of association between pupils' attainments at KS2 and the same pupils' attainments in Year 9, and high associations between KS2 attainment and pupils' attainments on NFER CAT or CEM MidYIS tests taken in Year 7. Based on these starting points, the Trust's researchers explored the performance of different groups of pupils in KS3 assessment, examining the influence of gender, entitlement to free school meals and those for whom English is an additional language, and looking in detail at pupils whose performance was much higher or much lower than expectation. From this, the Trust developed data systems which allow local authorities, schools and teachers to explore pupil performance against expectation based on looking at all pupils nationally, pupils in similar schools and pupils in higher-performing schools. The Fischer Family Trust profiles are widely used in school self-evaluation and, in conjunction with other data, provide a powerful tool for mapping pupil progress.

Task 10.3

Table 10.3 (overleaf) summarizes the range of entry data for some of the pupils in the Year 8 group we began by looking at. Study it to determine what more you can surmise about these learners' capabilities than was apparent from reading age data alone. How might you use this information to inform your planning and teaching of these pupils? What difficulties and pitfalls do you see?

Taken together, NC, CEM or NFER and Fischer Family Trust analyses put in the hands of schools powerful resources which can be used to map, analyze and predict pupil performance and to implement interventions where pupil performance is below expectation. Schools have available datasets which permit the analysis of pupil performance in fine detail. Used together, such data allow schools to establish assessment management systems which track performance in relation to expectation and to challenge teachers and pupils to seek to exceed expectation. As pupils move through their secondary career, the school will be able to flesh out data profiles in increasing detail, adding further information to track performance, and to use this to intervene to support improvement in pupil performance. Although we are looking here at the patterns exhibited by individuals, schools will want to identify patterns amongst year groups to help direct support and resources. This range of data across a cohort or class allows schools to make initial judgements about grouping strategies or teaching needs of groups of pupils. Schools will rapidly supplement this data with their own within-KS data to build up an increasingly sophisticated pattern of information which allows them to track pupils' progress.

Table 10.3 Year 7 entry data

| Pupil | Reading age | National Curriculum | | | MidYIS | | | |
		NC Eng	NC Maths	NC Sci	Vocabulary	Mathematics	Non-verbal	Skills
Ian	10.04	3	4	3	101	108	100	104
Inderjit	9.7	3	3	2	97	92	103	101
Samantha	10.05	3	3	3	95	94	95	96
Lauren	13.8	5	4	4	116	105	110	112

The real power of these datasets derives from their predictive power. We know that the most powerful single influence on learners' attainment is their prior attainment. National datasets allow us to examine this in more detail. Pioneering work to develop predictive datasets was done with the A level Information System (ALIS) which was the precursor of MidYIS and YELLIS. Schools submitted pupil-level examination data at 16+(GCSE), and then the A level performance of the same pupils two years later. This data was used to explore patterns of pupil performance and, over a number of years, to track with some degree of certainty the A level outcomes for learners with a given level of GCSE performance. Over a number of years, and over a large number of sites, this developed into a robust dataset which allowed schools to explore the performance of their pupils as a whole or sub-groups (e.g. boys, girls, those studying mathematics, those studying English, etc.) against the performance of a large cohort. ALIS enabled schools to explore extremely good performance and patterns of under-performance and to feed the results of this analysis into their planning. YELLIS and MidYIS applied the principles of ALIS earlier in pupils' careers, using very large datasets to predict GCSE outcomes for pupils with given YELLIS profiles.

NC tests provide a national dataset for benchmarking purposes, and are made available to schools by the Fischer Family Trust materials and the Key Stage National Data, formerly known as the *Autumn Package* (http://www.dfes.gov.uk/standards). The *Autumn Package* was developed by the DfES statistical service from the performance of pupils across the country and allows comparison with previous years' data. For example, the 2006 KS3 results can be compared with the 2003 KS2 results, or the 2006 GCSE results with the 2004 KS3 results. In order to do this statistically, the levels are turned into scaleable totals: a level 3 scores 21 points, a level 4, 27 points and so on, whilst a GCSE A* scores 8 points, an A, 7 points and so on. The DfES collates scores nationally and tracks the outcomes secured by pupils for given levels of input. Figure 10.1 from the 2006 national data presents the GCSE/GNVQ outcomes for given levels of performance in 2004 KS3 tests. Individual pupils will have very different profiles, and the best fit line (the solid line) shows the *likely* outcome for a pupil with a particular intake profile. It also presents a tolerance band (the dotted line) around the best fit line. Performance within the tolerance line is broadly in line with expectations. Within a very short space of time, this sort of benchmarking has come to be seen as rather crude; again, as we have seen, the Fischer Family Trust, CEM and NFER materials allow secondary schools to undertake sophisticated analyses of pupil performance at whole cohort, group or subject level and to make decisions about appropriate teaching interventions.

Nonetheless, the national data allow us to examine the process involved in a relatively simple way. To demonstrate how this can work, take a pupil, Marcus, who scored a level 5 in English, a level 5 in mathematics and a level 4 in science at KS3. Converting into points on the agreed scale would give Marcus 33 + 33 + 27 = 93, or a mean of 31 points (see Table 10.4). Using Figure 10.1, we would expect a pupil scoring 31 points at KS3 to score approximately 34 points at GCSE. Marcus's GCSE profile gave him 43 points (see Table 10.4). In this sense, Marcus exceeded expectations, or, put it differently, the school *added value* for Marcus.

Once again, the exercise we have just traced, for a single learner, turns on a number of assumptions, and, again, the NC data are relatively unhelpful in performing

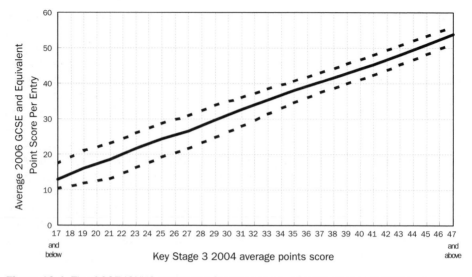

Figure 10.1 The GCSE/GNVQ outcomes for given levels of performance in KS3 tests (http://www.teachernet.gov.uk/)

the calculations. In order to make comparisons between NC and GCSE data, both had to be converted into a scaleable number. Critics have pointed out that this calculation involves some doubtful assumptions. In the first place, there is an assumption, which has never been validated, that the steps between NC levels are equal. By setting the numbers (27, 33, 39, etc.) at the same intervals, it is assumed that the difficulty of moving up from a level 4 to a 5 is the same as the difficulty of moving from a 5 to a 6. There is no reason why this should be so. Second, it is assumed that all level 5s, in whatever subject, can be regarded as being at the same level of difficulty: again, there is no reason to suppose this is the case. Third, in the same way, by converting GCSE grades into numbers we make assumptions that gaining an A★ (8 points) is twice as difficult as obtaining a grade D (4 points). The calculation could be done quite differently if a G were given 1 point, an F 2 points, an E 4 points, a D 8 points and so on. Fourth, the graph and predictions assume that these figures can be compared

Table 10.4 Marcus's Key Stage 3 and GCSE outcomes

Subject	Key Stage 3 test scores	GCSE subjects	GCSE results
English	L5 (33 points)	English Lang/Lit	B/B (12 points)
Mathematics	L5 (33 points)	Mathematics	B (6 points)
Science	L4 (27 points)	Double Award Science	C/C (10 points)
		History	C (5 points)
		Resistant Materials	B (6 points)
		French	D (4 points)
Mean	31 points	Total	43 points

against each other, whereas there is no direct connection between NC levels and GCSE grades. Finally, the national data line of best fit in Figure 10.1 is based on summary data. Although the national data makes crude comparisons possible, critics argue that the statistical manipulations by which these comparisons are achieved make the exercise fundamentally flawed, and that only comparisons between identically structured tests could provide evidence on whether a pupil is making greater or lesser progress than might be expected. Nonetheless, this sort of data have been extremely influential in schools.

The data we have so far seen are summary data. What might be of more interest to schools is the ability to examine this data against the performance of different groups of learners. Consider the data in Figure 10.2, which presents a simple version of an input/output attainment diagram for School A. The school has compared pupils' performance on a test at entry to the school with their performance on tests at the end of their school career. Each '♦' marks the performance of a single pupil, showing their performance on the exit test against their performance on the input test. A best fit line is applied to the data. This line shows the overall trend and the expected outcome for a pupil at each level of input performance. Every pupil below the line has performed below expectation for their level of input performance and every pupil above the line has performed above expectation. What the school will wish to do is to analyze at group and individual level those pupils who performed *substantially* above or below expectation, and to look for any common characteristics between these pupils. For example, it might explore the difference between expected and actual performance separately for girls and boys, and discover that girls were disproportionately represented amongst those under-performing. It might also analyze the performance of different ethnic and language groups within the school. It might analyze the outcome based on different teaching groups, and discover that pupils in groups taught by one teacher did particularly well: the school would then want to identify and disseminate

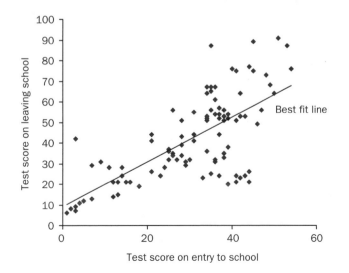

Figure 10.2 Entry and Exit Test results for a year group of pupils

that teacher's good practice. It might analyze the outcome based on individual factors. In particular cases – such as pupils whose performance was disappointing given their starting point – it may wish to call on the specialised knowledge of their tutors. It might discover that their performance was the result of traumatic events, such as the experience of divorce. Schools will also expect staff to examine the performance of pupils with moderate or severe learning difficulties in their classes and ensure that their progress is as good as possible. Local authorities carry out area analyses of performance, looking at the experience of individual schools with particular groups of pupils to inform overall thinking about performance within the authority, and its improvement. These analyses are an essential part of school life, but there are real dangers in over-interpreting data which may be based on small cohort sizes or which are not sensitive to pupil characteristics. Predictive data do not always take account of the moderating effect of special educational needs or pupils with EAL. Pupils may enter secondary school with poor KS2 results and leave with far higher GCSEs than would have been predicted because they have radically improved their command of English along the way. This is recognized nationally and the contextual value added (CVA) calculations (see below) add a value to raise the expectations for particular categories of EAL learners.

National policy has largely absorbed the potential of attainment data to support school level analysis of trends in performance as a tool for school management. As practice has developed, tools have become much more sophisticated. Schools have been benchmarked against national and LA norms, against patterns of prior achievement and against the performance of schools in the same free school meals band. In 2005, the sophistication of comparative analysis was further enhanced by the introduction of CVA measures. CVA models school performance taking into account pupil prior attainment, gender, special educational needs, first language, ethnicity, measures of deprivation, measures of pupil mobility, age distribution and the number of 'looked after' children in the school. CVA patterns underpin the development of a very sophisticated national ICT tool for analyzing patterns of performance in schools, the RAISE programme (Reporting and Analysis for Improvement through School self-Evaluation) being commissioned by Ofsted (www.raiseonline.org) at the time of writing.

We have now looked at the basic technical and conceptual tools for data analysis and target-setting in school and, before considering how they might be used, it would be sensible to review them. In the first place, schools have an array of different sorts of evidence available to them which can be supplemented by internally generated data. Sorting and using this data effectively presents schools and teachers with a significant challenge. Second, data exist which allow schools and teachers to make initial judgements about the needs of individuals and groups of learners. Third, national datasets also exist which allow schools to make predictions about pupil learning outcomes based on very large datasets and thus to set realistic targets for pupil outcomes based on national expectation and local knowledge. Finally, the use of statistically-based data on pupil outcomes is fraught with complications which may generate unreliable conclusions.

Task 10.4

Find out how the assessment manager in your school draws together assessment data and find out the cycle for using such data to map pupil progress in Year 7 and Year 8.

What steps are taken to challenge pupils who are not performing at least to expected levels of performance?

10.3 Using data to support achievement

The challenge for schools is to turn this data into a dynamic driver for improvement which supports interventions into learning and teaching. All that we have seen so far is that data can be used descriptively to analyze pupil needs and patterns of attainment and to identify patterns of over- and under-attainment rather than to support achievement. There are two challenges here: interpreting and analyzing data in ways which are helpful to teachers and learners and developing frameworks for target-setting.

Target-setting deploys a set of techniques which turn essentially static perform-ance data into a dynamic process involving negotiation between teacher and learner. It uses the data available to schools to make realistic but challenging judgements about what individual learners can achieve. This, of course, does not follow from analyzing data in itself. The use of national datasets could easily promote a fatalistic approach about what might or might not be possible: a pupil with a particular input score might easily be written off given the predictions about what pupils with that input score might expect to attain by the end of their schooling. Data could provide ceilings on achievement rather than floors. The challenge, therefore, is to use data to demonstrate to learners that if the majority of pupils with a given profile will end up with a particular outcome, then application, commitment, effort and good teaching can help them to do better than that. Schools have approached this in a variety of ways. Some have thought about targets in the 'comfort' and 'challenge' zones; others have con-sidered 'minimum targets' and 'extended targets'; others have used national data to demonstrate what some pupils, whatever their level of entry performance, can poten-tially achieve. The effectiveness of target-setting depends on teachers' ability to trans-late the data available into short- and medium-term targets which learners are motivated to achieve. This, in turn, depends on skilled teaching and active mentoring: identifying with learners what their potential is and then working to identify the barriers to achieving this potential. In most schools, responsibility for using data to promote achievement is shared between subject teachers and pastoral staff. The chal-lenge is to take the data and, having made it comprehensible and usable, to deploy it to define challenging targets which encourage learners to aspire to succeed. Too many targets, or over-ambitious targets, will demotivate learners just as much as inadequately challenging targets. We looked at Marcus's KS3 and GCSE results above, but it is likely that during Year 11 Marcus received a report containing some of the information in Figure 10.3, giving him both target minimum grades and poten-tial grades. Once data have been used to identify potential success, the task passes back to teachers to deploy all their professional skills and abilities in motivating and supporting pupils, removing barriers to learning, making material accessible and defining tasks in ways which help pupils meet, and if possible exceed, their targets.

	Target Minimum Grade	Potential Grade
English Lang/Lit	D/D	B/C
Mathematics	D	C
Double Award Science	C/C	C/B
History	D	C
Resistant Materials	D	C
French	D	C

Figure 10.3 Extract from Marcus's Year 11 report

10.4 Conclusion

In this chapter we have explored the increasingly sophisticated ways in which schools and teachers can make use of a huge range of data in support of effective teaching and improved learning. The range of data available and the number of techniques deployed to make best use of it have increased enormously over the last decade and it is almost certain that schools will become even more sophisticated in using new techniques over the next decade. There are obvious dangers in an over-reliance on quantitative data, and your responses to the tasks will have alerted you to some of these. Data can help to map outcomes and trajectories but it normally, at best, can only diagnose areas for further investigation and analysis. It will suggest areas on which teachers and pupils can work productively; it will not in itself tell you or your pupils what to do. The important thing in using data, as in all other areas of school life, is to focus on supporting pupil achievement, raising pupil expectations and maximizing potential.

Acknowledgment

I am grateful to Fiona Hammans, Principal of Banbury School, and to Ian Clayton, Headteacher at Thorpe St Andrew School, Norwich, for their comments on earlier drafts of this chapter.

10.5 Recommendations for further reading and webliography

Hedger, K. and Jesson, D. (1998) *The Numbers Game: Using Data in the Secondary School.* Shrewsbury: Shropshire County Council.
Gray, J., Hopkins, D., Reynolds, D. and Farrell, S. (1999) *Improving Schools: Performance and Potential.* Milton Keynes: Open University Press.
Neal, A. (1999) *Measuring Added Value.* London: Secondary Heads Association.
Fitzgibbon, C.T. (1996) *Monitoring Education.* London: Cassell.

www.cem.dur.ac.uk (the Curriculum, Evaluation and Measurement Centre at Durham University manages MidYIS, YELLIS and ALIS)

www.dfes.gov.uk/standards (the DfES standards website is a regularly updated source of statistical data and examples of good practice in using it).

www.nfer.ac.uk (The NFER website provides information and guidance on Cognitive Ability Tests)

www.raiseonline.org (the OFSTED link for the RAISE online project which replaces PANDAs and Pupil Assessment Trackers)

11

Positive approaches to supporting pupil behaviour

Jo Crozier

11.1 Introduction

All teachers need to be able to manage behaviour in the classroom effectively in order to promote learning and the well-being of learners and this is an area of concern for many student teachers. The basis of effective classroom management lies in good professional practice. It entails:

- teachers who have high expectations of pupils;
- the delivery of well-prepared lessons appropriately matched to pupils' learning needs;
- opportunities for pupils to succeed and to have both academic and social successes recognized;
- teachers who offer good role models and whose behaviour promotes mutual respect.

The role of the teacher is both to promote positive learning behaviour and to respond effectively to incidents of undesirable behaviour. Teachers acquire a tool kit – strategies that they employ almost automatically – and that resource is constantly replenished from the experiences they have every day, in and out of school.

These skills continue to develop throughout a teacher's career and even the most experienced teachers continue to learn. Effective teachers are able to reflect on their own practice in order to develop their skills.

This chapter aims to enable you to:

- be aware of some research findings about schools, teachers and pupils;
- take a critical look at a range of theoretical stances;
- consider a range of strategies for positive classroom management.

The focus in this chapter is on prevention and proactive planning rather than on reaction and punitive responses. It will reflect the emphasis in the current standards for QTS (TDA 2007) which are underpinned by the five key outcomes of *Every Child Matters* (see Chapter 20) and an emphasis on supporting each individual learner to realize their potential. To meet the requirements of the most recent standards for QTS, in place for all new trainees from September 2007, teachers need to have constructive relationships with learners based on high expectations, awareness of relevant legislation, respect for diversity and commitment to achievement. Self-awareness, adaptability, identification of professional needs and commitment to professional development are key attributes for teachers entering the profession (see Figure 11.1).

Student teachers draw on their own experience as learners in school, in work and in family contexts to build up their tool kit. These experiences offer transferable skills and inform student teachers' approaches and responses. The key to making effective use of these skills is to develop a critical awareness of the aspects of previous experience that are helpful or unhelpful in a school context. The ability to be critically self-aware is fundamental to learning the craft of teaching and to developing as an effective classroom manager.

Pupils who behave badly are not a new breed of monsters; they were there when you were at school. As when you were young, part of the process of growing up involves challenging, or at least renegotiating, relationships with parents and teachers who have been authority figures. In addition to the difficulties of adolescence, some

---

Those recommended for the award of QTS should:

Q1 Have high expectations of children and young people including a commitment to ensuring that they can achieve their full educational potential and to establishing fair, respectful, trusting, supportive and constructive relationships with them.

Q2 Demonstrate the positive values, attitudes and behaviour they expect from children and young people.

Q7a) Reflect on and improve their practice, and take responsibility for identifying and meeting their developing professional needs.

Q10 Have a knowledge and understanding of a range of teaching, learning and behaviour management strategies and know how to use and adapt them, including how to personalise learning and provide opportunities for all learners to achieve their potential.

Q21b) Know how to identify and support children and young people whose progress, development or well-being is affected by changes or difficulties in their personal circumstances, and when to refer them to colleagues for specialist support.

Q25 d) Manage the learning of individuals, groups and whole classes, modifying their teaching to suit the stage of the lesson.

Q29 Evaluate the impact of their teaching on the progress of all learners, and modify their planning and classroom practice where necessary.

Q31 Establish a clear framework for classroom discipline to manage learners' behaviour constructively and promote their self-control and independence.

Figure 11.1 QTS standards specially concerned with behaviour management (TDA 2007)

young people bring 'baggage' into school from difficult lives. Chapter 20 points to the emphasis of *Every Child Matters* on the holistic needs of children and young people and the need for teachers to be aware of the wider dimensions of young people's lives and the impact on their learning. Teachers need to be sensitive to pupils' experience and see their behaviours in context, rather than 'labelling' them as disruptive. The ways in which we categorize pupil behaviour are notoriously imprecise and subjective and the behaviour that one teacher finds infuriating may be seen by a colleague as good fun.

Task 11.1

a)   Remember some of the things you or your friends did at school that would be seen as disruptive or undesirable. How did you feel about this behaviour at the time? Do you feel differently now?

b)   Look at these quotations.

'We tightened a pupil's head in a vice.'
'We locked a teacher into a store cupboard.'
'We climbed through the loft hatch and banged on the ceiling of the classroom below.'
'We coated the drawer handle of the teacher's desk with syrup.'
'I organized a pupil rebellion in which we refused to attend lessons.'

Who were these miscreants?
Two head teachers, two university lecturers and one Chief Education Officer.

11.2 Research perspectives

This section will look briefly at what research tells us about the whole school, teacher and pupil factors that influence the effective and positive management of behaviour in the classroom.

First, research tells us the culture of schools matters and impacts on teacher effectiveness. Schools with similar intake profiles have very different behaviour outcomes. Important features are:

- effective leadership and shared values across the school community;
- teachers with high expectations and self-esteem;
- good relationships between school, pupils and parents;
- a focus on the prime importance of teaching and learning;
- clear and consistent behaviour policy and practice that includes positive systems for rewarding pupils as well as sanctions.

(Sammons et al. 1995; Watkins and Wagner 2000)

The individual classroom is influenced by the larger context of the school with its distinctive characteristics and ethos. In terms of behaviour, the ethos of the school is signalled in relationships across the school community, in the organization of rewards and sanctions, in the pastoral system, in the support available to teachers and TAs and in the school's relationships with the wider community.

Research also tells us that individual teachers make a difference. Jordan (1974), cited in Hargreaves et al. (1975), identified two models of teacher belief and behaviour, given in Figure 11.2. In the first model the teachers found that pupils behaved in deviant ways in class and that attempts to deal with the behaviour made things worse. In the second model, teachers found there were relatively few problems in class and that attempts to manage behaviour were effective. All teachers will behave in ways that draw from both of these models at times, but the study illustrates the importance of positive expectations for effective classroom management and, old as it is, remains salient today.

Finally, research tells us that pupils have a clear idea of what they want from teachers. Cowley, in her book *Getting the Buggers to Behave 2* (2003), gives an account of the views of secondary school students about what makes a good teacher. 'Firm but fun' is preferred – a teacher who tells them what is expected rather than asking or pleading, who is clear about the school rules (e.g. uniform) and who delivers interesting lessons with a variety of activities. Above all, they want to be treated as equals and to feel that the teacher likes them. Kinder et al.'s study (1996) of pupils with a history of truancy or disruption found that 'relationships with teachers' was high on the list of factors that pupils said caused truancy and disruption. Lack of respect and injustice were key teacher characteristics that they raised as underpinning poor relationships.

'Deviance-provocative' type

- believed that pupils did not want to work and that there was nothing the teacher could do about it;
- believed that the only way forward was for the pupils to change;
- expected that pupils would behave badly, be anti-authority and hostile;
- spent a lot of time in class giving ultimatums and referring pupils to senior staff for sanctions to be applied;
- talked negatively about their pupils in the staffroom and avoided contact outside the classroom.

'Deviance-insulative' type

- believed that pupils do want to work;
- believed that if pupils were not working that was a cue for the teacher to examine the lesson content and organization to see how the conditions could be changed so that pupils would be better engaged;
- showed respect and concern for the pupils and were able to tell them so, happily talking to them outside class and taking an interest in them as individuals;
- saw all pupils as potential participants in the lesson, including deviant pupils;
- were firm and had clear and explicit classroom rules;
- were able to avoid confrontations and when they did have to impose sanctions, did it in a way that enabled the pupil to 'save face'.

Figure 11.2 Models of teacher belief and behaviour
(Jordan 1974)

11.3 Background theories

Approaches to addressing the complex issues involved in managing classroom behaviours are informed by a wide range of theories about what causes pupil misbehaviour, how to assess behaviour and what interventions are effective.

This section will look briefly at three fundamental underpinning approaches to the issue of pupil behaviour. There is not space to do justice to the scope and value of theoretical ideas, and you are recommended to follow this up with further reading (for example, Ayers et al. 2000 and Porter 2000; see pp. 155–6 for details). Theories link to different stances about the social world and human behaviour and you will be able to make links between your own belief systems and some of these ideas. Most teachers make flexible and eclectic use of strategies that derive from each of these approaches, but are selective in working with strategies that fit with their own philosophical ideas.

Behavioural approaches

The behavioural model addresses the observed behaviour rather than seeking explanations in cognitive or psychological causes. You can read more about behaviourism as a theory of learning in Chapter 4. Pupils have learned negative behaviours and need to unlearn them. Behaviour is influenced by the antecedents – the environment in which the behaviour occurs – and is reinforced by the response it gets. The model uses an ABC formulation:

- A for Antecedent;
- B for Behaviour;
- C for Consequences.

Changing behaviour may involve changing the antecedents (e.g. reorganizing seating arrangements), observing precisely the frequency and context of the behaviour and looking at what reinforces it. To increase the incidence of good behaviour, the teacher needs to notice and respond to this, while unwanted behaviours should be dealt with by use of sanctions but not rewarded by lots of attention.

Many schools have adopted whole school approaches such as Assertive Discipline or Discipline for Learning as a main method of behaviour management. These programmes seek to enable teachers to respond schematically to behaviours with a clear tariff of responses. Within the classroom a discipline plan allows for clear rules that are taught to the pupils, positive recognition of pupils for following the rules, and a system of consequences for not following the rules. Much effective behaviour change has been achieved by these approaches – not least because they are accompanied by training of all the staff and support staff, the development of a coherent policy and consistency in application of the approach.

There are some concerns that arise with this approach – do the pupils internalize the better behaviour or is it bound to the context? For some it works well. Better behaviour enables better learning, so it is possible that the passing of time, the better educational achievement and consequent improvement in self-esteem will enable some pupils to pass through difficult periods. Others, especially some who are having a difficult time outside school, may need approaches that give them more space to look at feelings (see Chapters 14, 24 and 25).

Cognitive approaches

A further set of theories attaches more importance to the child's experience and to understanding its impact on behaviour. Cognitivists believe that young people's perceptions, their understanding of a situation, their emotional state, the stage of their development and the context all impact on their behaviour. Interventions are targeted at helping them think through irrational, distorted or impulsive responses. Pupils with behavioural problems may not have the cognitive skills they need for appropriate interactions with their peers or with teachers and other staff. Problem-solving training and social learning approaches can help pupils develop new behaviours.

How people feel about themselves determines their self-esteem. Self-esteem plays a significant part in the ability of pupils to be effective learners and pupils with low self-esteem are vulnerable to failure and to criticism. A young person with high self-esteem can take risks in their learning and in their relationships. Low self-esteem means playing very safe and avoiding trying out new things. There are ways in which teachers can help protect and develop the self-esteem of vulnerable pupils (see Figure 11.3).

Supporting self-esteem:

- Learn names and use them;
- Use praise – specific and personal;
- Reprimand the behaviour, not the person;
- Repair the relationship;
- Apologize if you are wrong;
- Look after your own self-esteem;
- Develop sensitive practices – for example, let pupils choose whether they read aloud;
- Don't show pupils up by making comparisons and/or mocking them.

Figure 11.3 Supporting self-esteem

The ecosystemic model

The ecosystemic model is based on systems theory, which sees the school as part of interconnected systems, each part influenced by change in the other parts. Porter (2000) characterizes this as one of the 'democratic' theories. These look at young people and teachers as equal actors in the teaching and learning enterprise and as each having rights to have their needs met, albeit in different roles. Relationships lie at the heart of these theories, and the emotional needs of participants in learning are included in the framework. Central to the ecosystemic model is the idea that different people have different understandings of the same events and that any event may be subject to various interpretations. Some interpretations are more useful to enabling progress than others.

To change the situation, we need to look at where it is stuck and seek ways of understanding it that will encourage change. Teacher and pupils can get locked in a negative cycle: this theory would encourage the teacher to look at the situation from the pupils' perspective and seek ways to cooperate with them. The assumption is that there are different interpretations of a situation, each equally valid, and the behaviour of teachers and pupils draws on those interpretations. The technique for thinking about a problem from a different perspective is called 'reframing' and requires the teacher to think of alternative explanations for the behaviour and ways in which they might respond differently. Teachers who took part in research by Tyler and Jones (2002) found that, in spite of initial resistance and scepticism, there was an improvement in dealing with entrenched problem behaviours and that they were more relaxed and so were their classes.

In summary, it is useful to reflect on the different goals that underpin these theories. Behavioural approaches seek for pupils to comply with external controls, while cognitive approaches (often combined with behaviourism) seek internalized compliance and control over emotions. Systems theory looks for cooperation and integrity in the interactions in school (Porter 2000). Practice based on theories that assume the teacher is a calm and objective judge of the situation and plays a neutral role in any conflict do not invite an emphasis on self-awareness and self-evaluation. Effective teachers are often able to reflect on where their own behaviours have contributed to a conflict situation and this awareness is itself a useful contribution to positive teacher–pupil relationships based on mutual respect.

A further perspective on behaviour is to do with biological explanations for behaviour. Attention Deficit Hyperactivity Disorder (ADHD) is seen as having a biological base and is increasingly being treated with drugs. Autism is believed to have an underlying biological basis (Ayers et al. 2000). For both these conditions, behaviour management approaches, often drawing on behavioural and cognitive techniques, are widely used.

11.4 Strategies

Task 11.2

As you read the next section try to link strategies with the theoretical frameworks outlined above.
Note where they fit neatly and where there is a lot of crossover.
Think about your own beliefs and how well these approaches suit the sort of teacher you want to be.

Teachers need strategies to enable them to plan for positive behaviour, to prevent the onset of poor behaviour and to respond effectively when such incidents occur. Although almost all young people want to learn and mind if their learning is impeded by other pupils' disruptive behaviour, the same pupils are able and willing to take advantage of a chance to reduce a lesson to chaos.

The Elton Report (DES 1989: 69–70) – still an excellent and relevant read – reports evidence that: 'teachers' group management skills are probably the single most important factor in achieving good standards of classroom behaviour' and that 'those skills can be taught and learned'. Skills and strategies are essential and can be learned through 'the right kinds of training, experience and support'. Applying them depends on a pragmatic assessment of the context and it is not the purpose of this chapter to offer strategies as blueprints. You need to consider them, try them out, add those that work for you to your tool kit, and pursue further skills through reading and observation of experienced colleagues. There are excellent resources to draw on in pursuing the development of your skills. Behaviour4learning is a website supported by the TDA which seeks to enhance the development of skills and understanding in trainee teachers (see details at page 156).

Task 11.3

Remember someone you thought was a good teacher from your own school days:
- Make a list of the key features that you think made them memorable.
- Identify how many of those features were linked to the lesson content, to class-room management skills, to personality? What other categories?
- What qualities or skills of that teacher do you share?
- What qualities or skills would you like to develop?

The interactions between a teacher and the group of pupils in any particular class-room are determined by key features that you as a classroom teacher can influence. Important things that you need to think about are:

- whole school behaviour policy;
- high expectations;
- good relationships between teacher and pupils;
- planning for behaviour management;
- setting up a system of routines and rules;
- planning the lesson to meet the needs of all the pupils;
- organizing the physical environment;
- rewards and sanctions;
- support for the teacher.

We will look at each of these in turn.

Whole school policy

Starting in 2003, the behaviour and attendance strand of the SNS KS3 has sought to build on previous initiatives to support whole school development of effective approaches to behaviour, requiring all schools to review their policies about behaviour and attendance and identify areas for improvement. As well as including specific support for schools in particularly challenging circumstances, the Strategy focuses on whole school perspectives, identifying and sharing best practice in order to develop consistent and effective policy to secure positive behaviour and attendance.

Schools are not seen in isolation. The local community has a part to play:

> sharing best practice across schools to promote effective strategies to improve behaviour and attendance for learning, engaging the wider community in a more coherent and imaginative approach to local pupils, particularly those that are disaffected; this could include parents, local shopkeepers and residents, who may be encouraged to support extended school activities.
>
> (*Behaviour and Attendance Strategy, KS3*)

The Strategy emphasizes the importance of this strand in improving standards.

Whole school behaviour policies also address the school's response to issues of bullying, including racial and sexual harassment. The recent Race Relations Amendment Act, discussed in Chapter 22, requires all educational institutions to put in place anti-racist policies and practice.

It is very important that new teachers and trainees should familiarize themselves with their school's policies on behaviour and attendance as part of their induction, and their own practice should be constantly informed by the policy.

Policies underpin school rules or codes of conduct, which are usually expressed positively, signalling what is required, rather than the list of 'don'ts' which you may remember from your schooldays. Thus, 'Walk in the corridors', is seen as more positive in promoting desired behaviour than 'Don't run' which focuses on the negative. In many schools you will see a written 'code of conduct' displayed in strategic locations and these provide a shared framework for promoting good behaviour. Look up the KS3 Strategy and you will notice that all current material reflects this emphasis on the positive.

High expectations

We saw earlier that teachers' expectations have an impact on pupils' behaviour and on their learning. High, but realistic, expectations should inform your approach and you need to signal this in the way you address pupils both as a group and individually.

The negative impact of 'labelling' has been seen as a key influence on negative outcomes for some pupils, particularly the most vulnerable – and remember that the acting-out and acting-up pupil may be vulnerable although it may not feel like that to you.

Labelling links to the idea of positive and negative expectations and to the idea of self-fulfilling prophecy. Figure 11.4 shows how this works. There is an opposite phenomenon, called the 'halo' effect which brands some pupils as 'good' and picks up the evidence that confirms that image.

- The teacher expects Jaz to behave badly – probably because she has been warned in the staffroom;

- Every time Jaz steps out of line she notices because it confirms her negative expectations;

- Because of her preparedness she is alert to Jaz even though he may not be behaving worse than other pupils;

- By the end of the lesson she is convinced that Jaz is a troublesome pupil, thus confirming her original expectations;

- At the same time, Jaz will have experienced that he cannot do anything right and that, although no worse than others in the class, he gets a bad name, so what is the point of trying.

Figure 11.4 How labelling can lead to self-fulfilling prophecy

The sibling phenomenon is associated with labelling theory. Pupils may arrive in secondary school already labelled by their association with their older siblings. The staffroom is often the locus for this process. There is a difficult balance to strike between the information that it is useful for you to know about your pupils as a new teacher and the labelling effect that staffroom talk may encourage.

Positive relationships

Relationships need to be based on confidence that you have the right to manage the class while signalling that you respect the pupils and their points of view. Genuine liking for and interest in young people is important and pupils will be aware of this at once. Knowing and using names is very important in showing interest in the pupils, as is learning about pupils' personalities and enthusiasms. Listening to pupils carefully signals respect and will help you to learn about them.

How you present yourself is important. A calm sense of determination that you are in control of the lesson and expecting the best from your pupils will contribute to a positive outcome. You do need to *look* like a teacher, rather than like a student or a fellow-pupil, and for some this can be difficult. It is important to create an identity that signals 'grown-up in charge' both to the pupils and to yourself. For the impoverished student teacher this might involve a trip to the charity shop to acquire a jacket in order to look and feel convincingly authoritative. As Chapter 8 notes, body language and voice are important too, as key tools in managing a class effectively. The use of tape recording, or better still, video, in reviewing how you come over is invaluable, even if scary in prospect.

The teacher's self-conviction is an important signal to pupils while the opposite, self-doubt, is an open invitation to create trouble. The conviction underlying this chapter is that warmth and genuine engagement with pupils is an important quality and a valuable tool. However, some student teachers have found that a natural desire to be chummy with pupils, particularly at the outset during initial visit days, sets up relationships that are hard to shake off when they become responsible for managing the class. While the old adage 'don't smile till Christmas' seems extremely grim these days, it is prudent to adopt a teacher persona right from the outset, even when it feels awkward.

> A simple and very effective idea from Bill Rogers is his use of the word 'thanks', rather than 'please', 'Everyone looking this way, thanks' or 'Books open at page 43, thanks' signals the expectation that the students will comply. 'Please' is less assertive in the classroom context. Try it out in your interactions – it signals to the listener your expectation of compliance, and at the same time makes you feel more in control.
>
> (Rogers 1998)

There is useful guidance on developing good communications skills in working with young people, and indeed with their parents and carers, in The Common Core of Skills and Knowledge for the Children's Workforce (easily accessed through the *Every Child Matters* website, see page 156). which looks at key aspects of effective communication – listening, summarizing and explaining, consulting and negotiating.

Planning for behaviour management

Planning for behaviour management is as much a part of lesson planning as the subject content. You need to establish rules and expectations within the framework of the school policy and practices.

Most effective teachers anticipate and prevent disruption by careful planning for key stages of the lesson:

- Beginnings of lessons:
  - Try always to be there first, properly prepared, with everything you need;
  - Control the entry to the classroom by standing at the doorway to greet pupils, remind them of the rules (e.g. coats off, bags at the back);
  - Have an initial activity ready for them to get on with, either on the board, OHP, whiteboard or worksheet, so that they are occupied while you settle everyone and get the main lesson started.
- Transitions between activities:
  - Make sure everyone stops what they are doing to listen to your instructions; do not talk over them;
  - Tell them you are going to issue instructions and that they are not to move until you tell them to;
  - Give clear instructions; check they have understood.
- Handing out resources and equipment:
  - Use reliable pupils to hand out books and equipment, otherwise it holds up the flow of the lesson.

- Dealing with interruptions by minimizing their disruptive impact:
  - Politely ask someone who comes in to wait while you get to a point where you can talk to them;
  - Plan how you will respond to requests to leave the room (check whether there is guidance on this in the school behaviour policy);
  - Respond to disruptive behaviour by talking quietly to the pupil individually, avoid public showdowns and if necessary ask them to see you after the lesson.
- Ending lessons:
  - Anticipate so there is plenty of time left for reviewing learning, setting homework and clearing up;
  - Warn the group that they will go when you tell them, not when the bell rings;
  - Make sure that pupils leave chairs tidy and pick up litter;
  - Give positive feedback;
  - Let pupils go in groups or rows, when they have tidied up and are ready and quiet.

Routines and rules

Bill Rogers has a very user-friendly approach to setting up rules, routines and responsibilities and it is well worth looking at his books, videos or DVDs (see page 156). Rogers makes the important point that you are establishing routines right from the beginning, so you need to plan for this. If pupils are carrying on talking when you are talking, then you are establishing that it is acceptable. While Rogers' work includes dealing with very difficult behaviour, his emphasis on routines, on clarity, on reinforcing desired behaviour and on dealing with problems in the least intrusive way is useful for most situations.

As well as establishing routines it is useful to establish rules. Rogers (2006) suggests four to six rules focusing on:

- treatment of others in class (peers as well as adults);
- communication (this includes systems such as hands-up, but also how people speak to each other in class);
- learning behaviour (including cooperation and support, accessing support from teacher);
- movement about the class (entry and exit, respecting other's space);
- problem-solving (including settling disputes).

Establishing these rules in discussion with the class provides a sense of ownership. Posting them on the classroom wall provides a point of reference and allows for an early preventive reminder ('Rosie, remember our rule about . . .').

> **Task 11.4**
>
> Write a list of classroom rules, no more than five in number, to cover the key features of: entry to the classroom and readiness for the lesson; movement within the classroom; getting teacher's attention; teacher's cues for whole class to attend; responses to and behaviour with other pupils; closure systems for ending lesson.
>
>   The rules should be easy to understand and suitable for putting up on the class-room wall. Make sure they are expressed positively.

Planning to meet the needs of all pupils

This is a challenge and an opportunity for teachers in the current climate of inclusion (see Chapter 21) and in the light of *Every Child Matters*, discussed in Chapter 20. Inclusion embraces the idea that the school community should be representative of and include all the community members of school age. This means that in schools and in individual classrooms teaching approaches and management strategies need to be based on the individual learning needs of pupils. Differentiation to meet pupils' needs and the planned and effective use of classroom support are key elements in preventing disruption. Work pitched at too low a level will bore pupils and at too high a level will make some defensive and anxious. Both may lead to disruptive behaviour. *Every Child Matters* focuses on the concept of pupils' 'well-being' and its link with achievement and social change – 'doing well in education is the most effect-ive route for young people out of poverty and disaffection' (DfES 2003e: 1). Key to achievement is participation – pupils have an active role to play in planning their learning.

Organizing the environment

When you go round a school you will see that some classrooms signal good regard for the work going on in them. Many school buildings are scuffed and scruffy, but a teacher can do a lot to make the classroom a welcoming environment. Organizing the environment includes thinking about seating plans for individual and group work, keeping an eye on the temperature and opening or closing windows, and attractive wall displays, including displays of pupils' work.

Rewards and sanctions

- Catch them being good: notice and respond to desirable behaviours as well as to academic achievements. Use praise generously and specifically, so that the pupil (and all the pupils in earshot) knows what was praiseworthy. As pupils get older it is more appropriate for praise to be more private as public praise may have a negative effect.

- Praise is rewarding, as are positive comments in written feedback on work or in homework books. Some teachers write letters home to acknowledge good behaviour. Giving pupils responsibility can reward good behaviour. Some schools have whole school or year systems which you can use to acknowledge merit for positive behaviour as well as for good work.

- Recognize 'baggage': however carefully teachers plan a lesson, they cannot control the baggage that a pupil may bring in from home, from an earlier lesson or from relationships with peers that may make them disruptive. As well as establishing routines and rules, any teacher needs to be ready to respond when disruptive behaviour occurs.

- Relate to whole school policy: responses to poor behaviour need to take into account the whole school policy. Serious problems will invoke the school systems, which probably include referral to year head or senior management, time out, detentions, letters home and, as a last resort, exclusion. There should be clear lines of support for students and new teachers in a school that spell out how to get help to deal with major difficulties. Find out at an early stage what the back-up systems are and how to access them.

- Respond early and lightly: most difficulties will be dealt with within the classroom by the individual teacher. Initial reactions to signs of disruption need to start at the early signs of disruptive activity and very low on a tariff of responses. A lot of behavioural problems can be spotted early and deflected effectively with very small interventions (see Figure 11.5).

Where low tariff interventions have not succeeded in dealing with problem behaviour and tensions rise, teachers need to employ strategies to keep calm. Angry or exasperated responses can easily exacerbate tense situations and a shouting match is not going to improve the situation.

- Take a few deep breaths to calm yourself;
- Own what you are feeling: 'I am angry because . . .';

Tariff of interventions:

- The look;
- Proximity control (standing next to a pupil who is disruptive and delivering the lesson from there);
- Praise to person adjacent who is on-task;
- Private word – less confrontational if delivered from same height (i.e. crouching down) rather than towering over seated pupils;
- Restatement of task;
- Use of humour (not sarcasm which puts the pupil down);
- Rule reminder – 'remember our rule about calling out';
- Direct questions – 'What are you doing?' 'What should you be doing?' (Avoid 'Why are you doing that?' questions);
- Offer choices (Rogers 2006) 'If you choose not to put the magazine away, I will have to ask you to stay behind at break.'

Figure 11.5 Tariff of interventions

- Use assertive language: 'I don't swear at you. That language is unacceptable here';
- Lower your voice as soon as possible;
- Allow cool-off time for both parties: 'We will follow this up tomorrow morning';
- At a meeting with the pupil, explain what made you angry at the time, listen to the pupil's perceptions, refer to relevant rules, discuss how to make reparations, or deal with a similar incident next time;
- Repair and rebuild the relationship (Rogers 2006).

Support for the teacher

You need to ensure that you have systems of support in place as a student or a new teacher. Some or all of these will be useful to you:

- A member of the senior management team usually has responsibility for pastoral and discipline matters;
- The SENCo or, in some schools, behaviour support specialist teacher, has particular knowledge about pupils with behavioural difficulties and their needs;
- School mentors can offer advice, demonstrate skills, point you in the direction of other skilled teachers;
- Peers can offer excellent support, including peer observation as a basis for discussion about your approach;
- Reading, making use of websites, watching videos/DVDs and trying out new ideas can all be helpful;
- Use stress-busting techniques such as exercise, relaxation, playing in a band, talking to friends and eating chocolate!

Task 11.5

Ryan

a)   Think about the following situation and how you would react:

You are teaching in your first week of school placement when Ryan, a pupil you have not met before, comes in and walks deliberately and slowly across the front of the room between yourself and the pupils you are addressing.

b)   Consider how your reaction to the situation would be affected if you knew that:

- Ryan is regular troublemaker who frequently tries to 'needle' teachers;
- Ryan has been asked to take a message around the school by his Head of Year;
- Ryan is six feet tall;
- Ryan is small for his age and his mother says he is very nervous – often too frightened to come to school;

- Ryan has Asperger's Syndrome (a form of autism);
- It is a science lesson and you are demonstrating a potentially dangerous experiment;
- The mentor has warned you not to stand any nonsense from this group and especially not from Ryan who rarely comes to school;
- The class laughs uproariously;
- The class falls silent.

Underlying teachers' responses to pupils are sets of assumptions and pre-suppositions which can get in the way of responding to pupils' needs and building positive relationships. If you can, as a teacher, strive to avoid jumping to conclusions, be sensitive to pupils' needs and *listen carefully* to what they have to say, you stand a good chance of promoting positive behaviour and avoiding disruption and conflict.

11.5 Conclusion

This chapter has introduced you to some ideas about managing pupil behaviour in a positive and planned way. The central resource in this process is you, the individual teacher and your skills, working within a framework of the school community, its ethos and its policy on behaviour, which is in turn informed by government policy. Your skills will take time to build up and you will learn most from reading about and observing a range of practices and selecting approaches that fit the sort of teacher you are becoming.

Good teachers are constantly reflecting on their own practice and seeking ways to develop new approaches that fit with their value system and suit their personal style. It is tempting, and easy, to blame the pupils when a lesson goes wrong. The trouble is that this does not help you to make the sorts of changes that might improve things. A teacher can change the lesson plan, vary seating arrangements, alter the order or content of the lesson, or vary the activities or the pace, to meet the needs of a particular group or a group at a particular time. Flexibility to respond to the context is an important part of the teacher's skill and preparation for a range of eventualities is invaluable for beginning teachers.

11.6 Recommendations for further reading, viewing and webliography

Ayers, H., Clarke, D. and Murray, A. (2000) *Perspectives on Behaviour: A Practical Guide to Effective Interventions for Teachers*, 2nd edn. London: David Fulton. Outlines eight major perspectives and their implications for assessing and planning interventions in the classroom. Includes a section on the biological perspective with particular reference to ADD/ADHD.

Cowley, S. (2003) *Getting the Buggers to Behave 2*. London: Continuum. Useful introductory book for initial ideas on such topics as meeting a class for the first time, keeping control, reasons for pupil misbehaviour and classroom organization. Draws on interviews with pupils.

Porter, L. (2000) *Behaviour in Schools: Theory and Practice for Teachers*. Buckingham: Open University Press. An overview of theoretical approaches to behaviour management, schematically presented with case studies and an emphasis on preventive approaches.

Rogers, B. (2000) *Cracking the Hard Class: Strategies for Managing the Harder than Average Class*. London: Paul Chapman. More useful and practical material from the prolific Bill Rogers.

Rogers, B. (2006) *Classroom Behaviour: A Practical Guide to Effective Teaching, Behaviour Management and Colleague Support*, 2nd edn. London: Paul Chapman. Very useful practical approach to effective behaviour management, looking at setting up systems with a new class, dealing with challenging pupils, managing anger – pupils' and our own – and strategies for when things get difficult.

Watkins, C. and Wagner, P. (2000) *Improving School Behaviour*. London: Paul Chapman. Looks at whole school as well as classroom dimensions of planning for and responding to pupil behaviour in addition to exploring individuals and their behaviour.

Videos/DVDs

Rogers, B. (1995) *Managing Behaviour*. Newbury: Quartus. Four titles in this series of useful talks and illustration of key techniques: Prevention; Repair and Rebuild; Positive Correction; and Consequences, set in Rogers' native Australia. Worth looking at and still available in libraries.

Rogers, B. (2000) *Cracking the Challenging Class* DVD set. Expensive, but useful and set in the UK context – one to look for in libraries or teachers' centres.

Websites

www.behaviour4learning.ac.uk (a major resource, established by the TDA to support student teachers and teachers, useful links to up-to-date articles, reports, research and lots of practical help)

www.everychildmatters.gov.uk (policies and strategies to improve outcomes for disabled children)

www.standards.dfes.gov.uk/secondary/keystage3/issues/behaviour/

www.teachernet.gov.uk/professionaldevelopment/classroompractice/supplyteachers/ (access to materials prepared for supply teachers including classroom and behaviour management)

www.teachersupport.org.uk (information, support and even counselling for teachers)

12

Using ICT to support learning

Mick Hammond

12.1 Issues in using ICT in school

This chapter discusses the use of Information and Communications Technology (ICT) in teaching your subject. First, I present three case studies of student teachers using ICT followed by a discussion of your own use of ICT. Finally, I point you to further sources of information. By the end of this chapter you should be:

- aware of different motives for using ICT in school;
- able to assess the contribution of ICT to teaching and learning;
- able to plan for using ICT in your own teaching.

12.2 Different motives for using ICT

I will consider three examples of student teachers using ICT in their placement schools. These examples illustrate a range of ICT applications as well as different levels of planning and evaluation. I will use them to consider the planning, implementation and evaluation of ICT in teaching, and how classroom experience can be used to inform future planning. These examples or 'case studies' are necessarily rooted in the teaching of particular subjects but they raise general issues so please do not skip them even if the subject context is unfamiliar.

Task 12.1

Before reading the commentary that comes after each case study, ask yourself:
What is ICT contributing to pupils' learning?
What are the strengths and weaknesses of each teacher's approach?

| CASE STUDY 12.1 | Anthony using ICT to motivate pupils |

Anthony, a student teacher of English, was worried about several aspects of his teaching and fretful about his relationships with pupils which were often confrontational. He freely admitted to becoming interested in the use of ICT as something that might get the pupils interested in working in class and in his own words 'bring them over to my side'. He booked the ICT room and planned a lesson based on pupils' understanding of *Romeo and Juliet*, the play they had been reading. Pupils would be asked to prepare a 'pitch' trying to persuade a production company to make a film of the play. Pupils would use presentation software – in his school this was the programme PowerPoint. He had used PowerPoint in his own work many times before and felt confident of being able to demonstrate its use and deal with any problems pupils had. He asked a colleague, a student teacher of ICT in the same school, to give him a short demonstration of how to log on and save work on the school network. This colleague volunteered to be on hand to deal with any technical hiccups which might occur during the lesson.

Anthony prepared and used his own PowerPoint slides to explain the aims of the lesson. He set pupils to work in pairs at their machines. He monitored their work and tried to prompt them into recalling the key events of the play and move them away from investigating Clip Art and other images, and embellishing text. At the end of the lesson he asked for volunteers to talk through the work they had done in front of the rest of the class. His evaluation of the lesson was not extensive or formal. However, he felt the lesson had been a great success as pupils seemed much more positive and relationships with pupils had been far less stressful. Nevertheless, although pupils had been 'on-task', he was not quite sure what they understood the task to be. They had spent a lot of time 'playing on the computer' rather than addressing the subject learning goals. He could see that pupils would need more time to finish the presentation, something he had not predicted, and decided to try to book the room next lesson.

Commentary

This case study hardly represents an ideal model of introducing ICT into your teaching but it is consistent with the haphazard way in which many teachers get started with ICT. It is worth remembering that computers and computer programmes are rarely produced with schools in mind – teachers are adapting widely available tools for their own use and settings. This may sound like an indictment of Anthony, and of schools in general, but it is not meant to be. Anthony faced a challenge in the classroom so he looked around and used what was available to try to address this issue. Having said that, his planning of the lesson was rudimentary. He took pupils' skills very much for granted. Fortunately, he chose a software application which had a 'low entry threshold' (one pupils could start using without long and detailed explanation) and one with which they were, in fact, familiar. Again he was fortunate in getting a colleague to support the technical side of the activity – any hitches would have been very difficult to address by himself first time through. He was unsure of the learning goals of his lesson and hence did not set out his objectives very clearly. He could have structured the presentation more clearly. For example, he could have made clear that he wanted to see a synopsis of the plot and a statement about why the play would still be relevant to today's audiences. He could have encouraged pupils to focus on specific scenes or on how language was being used. On the positive side, he sensibly used PowerPoint to model the presentation and asked pupils to work in pairs. This had the advantage of reducing the number of pupils asking for technical assistance and as they were encouraged to help each other. More importantly, it would prompt pupils to discuss their ideas and their understanding of characters and themes in the play. Pupils were asked to present their work using bullet points so there was not a lot of waiting while one entered text and the other watched.

Anthony saw the lesson as a success as pupils had been on-task, or at least they had not disrupted his lesson or his teaching. He was very preoccupied with his own role as a teacher and relied on his own 'gut' feelings to evaluate the lesson. Of course, the introduction of ICT is not a guarantee of increased motivation but it is a common observation, and a commonly reported finding, that many pupils do enjoy using ICT. Why this is the case is not always clear, pupils often find their enjoyment of ICT difficult to articulate. However, they do seem to take satisfaction from making decisions and seeing the consequences of those decisions on screen. For example, in Anthony's lesson pupils could add and delete text, insert images and introduce sound and animation quickly and easily. The use of the computer opened up opportunities which were not there using pen and paper. ICT has an expressive quality which seems to motivate pupils. Many, though by no means all, young people feel at home with digital gadgetry and Anthony wanted to show that his world as a teacher was not as removed from that of his pupils as they might have thought.

It was doubtful whether Anthony's subject teaching aims in the lesson had been fully met or even properly articulated. Pupils were as much focused on format as content. He learnt valuable lessons from this class. In doing this kind of work again, he would need to focus pupils' attention on the content of their work. Next time he would stress the need for a simple, uncluttered and consistent background and work to a series of writing 'frames' to help pupils plan their presentation. He would need to think about timings, to make pupils aware of the timescale to which they were working and to book the room over two lessons not one. He realized that he was fortunate to have ICT support but in the future he would need to prepare in more detail. He needed to know how to use the software on the machines the pupils were going to use, not simply on his machine at home. He also needed a contingency in case the network broke down – this was something he had not thought about before pupils had told him of its unstable performance.

| CASE STUDY 12.2 | Baljit using ICT to address learning objectives |

Baljit, a student science teacher, had a specific focus on her pupils' subject learning in her use of ICT. She was aware that pupils had spent a long time collecting data manually in their laboratory work and were not sufficiently focused on drawing conclusions from experiments. She felt it was important that pupils could 'tell stories about data' if they were going to develop their information handling skills. She planned two lessons based on software with which she was familiar from training events she had attended. In the first she introduced data logging software to help pupils explore the many variables involved in determining the speed of a vehicle rolling down a ramp. Trolleys and ramps were set up in the laboratory with light gates to measure the speed of the trolley as it reached the end of the ramp. Pupils released the trolley from different points on the ramp and measurements were taken and entered on a spreadsheet. Graphs of the results were displayed. To support pupils, Baljit gave a short demonstration on using the software and provided a brief help guide. Each group of pupils was asked to discuss their results and to give an explanation of why the speed of the vehicle changed with the distance it had travelled. As an extension, pupils could look at the relationship between speed and other variables such as the height of the ramp or distance travelled on leaving the ramp.

A follow-up lesson gave pupils an opportunity to extend their work on interpretation of data. Baljit set up a circus of activities using temperature sensors. The first investigated the effect of surface area on cooling. Here temperature sensors recorded the temperature of two hot potatoes, one large, one small, every five seconds. A second experiment involved wrapping a temperature sensor in cotton wool and comparing the cooling effect of different liquids, including alcohol and water. A third investigation examined the insulating properties of different materials by recording the temperature of water inside containers insulated by cotton wool, paper and other materials chosen by pupils.

Pupils were asked to focus on the key variables in each experiment, to describe the relationship between these variables and provide an explanation to account for any relationships they had identified. In fact, each experiment raised challenging scientific concepts which Baljit would need to develop later. For now, she was concerned that pupils generated and justified their own hypotheses about the events they were investigating.

Baljit evaluated the two lessons as successful as she had uncovered many misconceptions about interpreting data which she was able to address in whole class discussion and in one-to-one work. Pupils had supported each other in using the software. The area that worried her most was the social dynamic within groups and dealing with whole class discussion at the end of the activity. Not all pupils had contributed to the discussion and she had not left enough time to develop her response to pupils' ideas.

Commentary

Unlike Anthony, Baljit had planned her use of ICT in detail and had a clear idea of how it could contribute to pupils' learning about science. In this case, the automatic features of the programme gave pupils opportunities to capture data over very short time periods, something they could not do accurately by hand and eye. The software took away the repetitive graph-drawing work and allowed pupils to focus on higher order skills of interpretation. The use of the technology was nicely staged so that all pupils could get experiences of using the data logging software before the circus of activities. The software had a relatively low entry threshold and any difficulties were addressed through help sheets, peer support or occasional teacher intervention. The case study illustrates how a very simple and long-established approach – data collection – can work really well to support teaching of higher order skills. Pupils are unlikely to take advantage of opportunities for reflection and discussion without teacher intervention. Although Baljit had built discussion into her planning, she would need to fine tune her approach during her placement, for example, developing ideas for plenary sessions.

| CASE STUDY 12.3 | Carlton using ICT to support out of school learning |

Carlton, a student teacher of geography, was enjoying his school placement and receiving good feedback on his teaching. His major area of concern was how much time he seemed to spend setting, chasing up and marking homework. The results seemed disproportionate to the effort he was putting in. He worked in a school that was highly committed to ICT and had attended an after-school session which had introduced him to the learning resources on the school's own intranet or 'virtual learning environment'. Already one department, religious education (RE), had built up a substantial set of resources and links to outside sites. He wondered if he could build a similar site for his pupils to support them in their homework or what he now wanted to call independent learning tasks. Perhaps he could even produce simple quizzes that could automatically mark work and send finely tuned feedback?

After much discussion with the ICT coordinator, he scaled down his plans. He would focus on one topic, population growth, which he was covering with a GCSE class. He would post files of presentations about the topic to the site and set up links to resources he had found on both the BBC and the Geography Association website. He saw that an attractive feature of these external sites was the generous use of images and small video clips. He would try to guide pupils by setting weekly tasks, such as to report on population growth in countries or cities he had specified. These were mini investigations which required pupils to search for material and draw conclusions from it. They could tackle these tasks any time they wanted over the week. He would encourage pupils to mail each other in a discussion area he had set up and to mail him at any time if they needed help.

The innovation met with mixed results. One good thing was that the creation of the website turned out to be easier than he had imagined as he had an existing template from which to work and ICT support from within the school. The key point was to reference other sites as far as possible rather than spend hours duplicating material. He monitored pupils' work. He found that most pupils were mailing him their investigations but much of their work was cursory and, where extended, pupils seemed to have simply copied and pasted text from existing sites. He did, however, find that the initiative had reduced the stress of cajoling pupils to do their homework not least because no one could say they had lost their handouts as they were all available on the web. One or two did email him to ask for clarification and this seemed to have enabled them to complete the task, though he had not considered where he would find the time if this side of the innovation took off. At the end of the placement, Carlton sought more formal feedback from the pupils and designed and carried out a questionnaire survey. He discovered that web access was not a problem for most pupils – they could access his site at home or through school machines during lunch or at the end of the day. He was surprised at how often pupils did use the internet on their own initiative and how often they mailed each other using free accounts they had set up. The web was a pupil resource of choice but it was not going to be easy to direct pupils within this environment. Most pupils were positive about the innovation and liked the greater access to pictures and moving images. However, they frequently found the text within the sites was too difficult to understand, again something he had not fully considered.

Commentary

Like Anthony, Carlton was attempting to use ICT tools to motivate his pupils as much as to address specific subject learning objectives. Carlton had latched on to the idea of developing online support through work he had seen in another subject. Nonetheless, the potential contribution of ICT to his subject teaching was considerable. It would provide pupils with access to materials and access to discussion.

There were limitations in his planning. First, he had not thought in advance how those without access to the internet would fare, though in the event this was not a serious difficulty as all pupils could access machines at school or at friends' houses. He had not communicated to pupils what was involved in the shift from setting homework to providing 'independent learning tasks'. The latter he associated with pupils making choices so that they find their own way through the resources at their own pace. However, he had not modelled how this would happen or been precise in what he wanted pupils to do with the resources once they had been located. Here, there was a major difficulty with pupils' information handling skills. He assumed that pupils were advanced information handlers because they appeared to be familiar with the World Wide Web (WWW). In fact, they lacked the knowledge and skills to be able to analyze the information they accessed. They could not identify key points within a text or transform information for another audience. The reading age of external materials was another problem. The innovation left him with more questions than answers but Carlton decided to pursue his investigation further as pupils really did seem interested in using the internet.

12.3 Planning your use of ICT

These case studies show some of the starting points teachers had for using ICT and some of their experiences. They are summarized in Table 12.1. Below I draw together some of the lessons from the case studies in the form of key questions to ask yourself in planning your use of ICT within a lesson or series of lessons.

Table 12.1 Summary of issues in the use of ICT in the three case studies

Case study	Problem	Planning	ICT knowledge and skills	Contribution of the technology	Implementation	Evaluation methods
Anthony	Motivation of pupils	Minimal	Familiar with software, assumed pupils would know how to use it	Expressive of relevance, provisional nature of text (easy to alter)	Computer room, pair work, some whole class teaching	Monitoring, teacher focused
Baljit	Focus pupils on interpreting data	Extensive – lessons build on one another	Familiar with software, demonstrated use to pupils	Automatic data collection and display	Laboratory, group work, whole class starters and plenaries	Scanning class, use of question and answer, plenary, pupil writing
Carlton	Development of out of lesson learning	Extensive – teacher needed to extend ICT knowledge and skills	Taught how to use the software, assumed pupils would know how to use it	Storage of multimedia resources, interactivity through electronic communications	Machines accessed in school and at home, pupils have high level of control over what and when to access resources	Monitoring, questionnaire survey

What does ICT contribute to teaching my subject?

First and foremost consider what you are expecting the use of ICT to contribute to your teaching. For example, ICT may enable:

- storage of information (in particular, multimedia material);
- automatic functions (for example, logging data, recalculating within spreadsheets);
- interactivity between user and software or between fellow learners using electronic communications;
- provisionality (for example, rapid deletion and reformatting of text).

A further feature of ICT is the speed at which functions are carried out so that it allows the user to do things it would be very difficult to do otherwise. ICT also has an expressive quality so that it is, at least initially, seen as new and potentially exciting.

A key issue to consider is whether you want to use these attributes of ICT to help you carry out what you normally do as a student teacher or whether you are using ICT as a springboard to introduce a deeper change in teaching and learning. Anthony wanted to use the storage and interactivity of ICT to engage pupils in his lessons. In a similar way, a student teacher who feels under constant pressure when carrying out whole class teaching might look to the electronic whiteboard (EWB) to engage pupils' attention. Of course, in both these cases, the use of ICT will open up new opportunities which may not have been anticipated. For example, Anthony found it natural to use pair work around the computer, something he was normally more resistant to doing. Similarly, users of EWBs often get pupils in front of the class to demonstrate to their peers in a way they would not consider when using an ordinary whiteboard. However, these changes are modest when compared to Carlton who wanted to use ICT in order to develop a more investigative approach to homework. There was nothing wrong with this, but Carlton was very unlikely to succeed as he had not communicated his expectations to pupils. In contrast, in the second example, Baljit was much clearer in her mind about how ICT could contribute to refocusing pupils' learning on higher order skills. The conclusion from the case studies is that, as you plan your use of ICT, you need to think carefully about what ICT has to offer. Consider what changes, if any, you are making to your teaching style and how you are going to convey your expectations of learning outcomes to pupils. If you are not clear about your subject aims, then pupils might easily end up focusing on the technology or using ICT for its own sake.

Are pupils supported in crossing the ICT skills threshold?

You will want to ensure that pupils have easy access to ICT. This means that they have the necessary knowledge and skills to use the software. If not, provide simple demonstrations and help sheets in support. Think carefully if you are planning to use software which has a high entry threshold.

Are you confident in your ICT knowledge and skills?

Enthusiasm, learning by trial and error and a willingness to admit to lack of knowledge all go a long way in working successfully with ICT. But the lesson from the case studies is to make sure you can use the software using school machines. Ensure that you have technical support for your first attempts in working with pupils.

How will pupils have access to machines?

All three teachers had to plan around access to machines. Carlton assumed pupils had out of school access; you will need to check this for yourself. If you intend using the internet, make sure you are familiar with any school policies. In school you will need to book a computer room or organize access to portable machines or to departmental resources. What do you see as the pros and cons of each approach? If you have a limited number of machines then pupils will need to work in pairs or groups. Is this desirable in the lesson you are planning or is it a constraint?

Have you planned work away from the machines?

The same rules apply to using ICT as in any other lesson. If you think whole class starters and plenaries are a good idea then use them when the lesson involves ICT. Move pupils away from machines so you have their full attention.

Have you planned a contingency?

Have you got contingency materials if the network fails? Can you quickly adapt if getting started takes much longer than you thought (for example, the network is slow, pupils have forgotten passwords, their skills are not as you imagined)? Can you use the computers for a follow-up lesson if you need to?

How are you going to monitor and evaluate pupils' use of ICT?

The case studies showed that question and answer, intervention with groups and plenaries were all good monitoring tools. How can you use your monitoring and evaluation of pupils' work to inform future planning? Would a short questionnaire survey on pupils' use of ICT be appropriate?

Task 12.2

Plan for the use of ICT in a lesson in school. Address all the focus questions in the above section.

Task 12.3

Carry out a search of the WWW to locate resources which support teaching your subject. Comment on the value of these resources and how you would adapt them for a class you are going to teach.

12.4 Where can I find out more about using ICT in my teaching?

You will almost certainly have been directed to online and paper-based reading on the use of ICT in your subject. To explore more general issues, you may want to look further afield, for example, Leask (2001). To get a more contemporary perspective on the use of ICT look at Futurelab reports (see the address at page 167). Here you can find overviews in the form of literature reviews on several topics including ICT and creativity, mobile learning, digital video games and learning and e assessment.

The issue of curriculum change with ICT is debated at length by academics many of whom are asking why (at least from their perspective) ICT seems to have had so little impact on teaching and learning (e.g. Reynolds, Treharne and Tripp 2003). A perennial concern is whether we are too apt to focus on the teaching and development of ICT skills rather than the use of ICT in subject teaching. This is discussed, for example, by Watson (2001), while Selwyn (2001) has expressed scepticism about the Government's agenda for using ICT, seeing information technology policy as lacking a curriculum focus. Other writers worry about lack of fit between curriculum and attributes of ICT. In North America, Cuban et al. (2001) have asked why it is that when school meets computer, school wins. Further insight on this issue is provided by The British Educational Communications and Technology Agency (Becta) supported ICT Test Bed project (Somekh et al. 2006). This was a project which provided an account of special circumstances, i.e. schools with high access and high support. ICT was seen as making a positive contribution to learning outcomes and there was some evidence that teachers made most use of applications such as EWBs which they could most easily incorporate into their everyday teaching routines. This research came on the back of previous work (Comber et al. 2002; Harrison et al. 2002; Somekh et al. 2002) which Becta had commissioned into the impact of ICT on educational attainment in English schools. This research suggests that ICT has a positive impact on pupil learning and highlights children's use of ICT in the home.

If you are interested in the specific contribution of ICT to teaching your subject, have a look at your subject association website – most will suggest relevant links. For use of ICT in the classroom, explore Teachers TV and enter 'ICT' in the search box. At the time of writing, there are classroom examples of using web quests, pod casts and discussion of the contribution of ICT to personalised learning. As capability of machines increases, multimedia presentations using sound and moving images become increasingly viable. Short digital video clips, either those captured by pupils themselves, or those produced by public service providers, for instance, Pathe News, are very appealing to pupils. Find out more from Becta.

If you are interested in the use of data logging, this is well documented in many publications; see, for example, Newton and Rogers (2001). Again, look at Teachers

TV for up to date examples of classroom practice. If you would like to set up a virtual learning environment, many LAs have developed their own learning grids for pupils (find these through a web search). You might be able to gauge the development of school websites by seeing past winners of the Becta/the *Guardian* UK Education Web Site Awards within the Becta website. Finally, if you are interested in practical applications of EWBs, consult the multimedia resource sponsored by the National Endowment for Science, Technology and the Arts (Nesta 2004).

12.5 Recommendations for further reading and webliography

Becta is supported by the UK Government to research and promote the development of ICT in education. Its site (www.becta.org.uk/) contains advice and curriculum materials on the use of ICT. Its research reports are also posted to the site and can be easily located using the internal search engine.

Broadcasters provide many resources for schools (BBC bite size can be found at www.bbc.co.uk/schools/gcsebitesize/).

Futurelab is a not for profit organization which promotes innovative use of ICT (go to www.futurelab.org.uk/). Literature reviews are found in the research section of the site.

Pathe News has a library of historical film clips some of which are freely available and easily incorporated into several subjects (go to www.britishpathe.com for more information).

Teachers TV is an expanding resource for all aspects of teaching and learning; search for programmes relevant to ICT by using the internal search engine.

Multimedia resource:

Nesta (2004) *The Good Guide to Interactive Whiteboards*. Hull: University of Hull.

Paper-based reading:

Cuban, L., Kirkpatrick, H. and Peck, C. (2001) High access and low use of technologies in high school classrooms, explaining an apparent paradox, *American Education Research Journal*, 38(4): 313–34.

Leask, M. (ed.) (2001) *Issues in Teaching Using ICT*. London: RoutledgeFalmer.

Newton, L. and Rogers, L. (2001) *Teaching Science with ICT*. London: Continuum.

Reynolds, D., Treharne, D. and Tripp, H. (2003) ICT – the hopes and the reality, *British Journal of Educational Technology*, 34(2): 151–67.

Selwyn, N. (2001) Why the computer is not dominating schools: a failure of policy or a failure of practice? *Cambridge Journal of Education*, 29(1): 77–92.

Somekh, B., Underwood, J., Convery, A., Dillon, G., Harber Stuart, T., Jarvis, J., Lewin, C., Mavers, D., Saxon, D., Twining, P., Woodrow, D. (2006) *Evaluation of the ICT Test Bed Project, Annual Report*. Coventry: Becta (www.evaluation.icttestbed.org.uk/reports)

Watson, D. (2001) Pedagogy before technology: re-thinking the relationship between ICT and teaching, *Education and Information Technologies*, 6(4): 251–66.

SECTION 3

Secondary schools and the curriculum

13

What should we teach? Understanding the secondary curriculum

Chris Husbands

13.1 Introduction

The curriculum is one of the most obvious aspects of schools. Not only does the curriculum describe what pupils learn, but the daily routines of secondary schools are marked by the division of the curriculum into subjects for study: English, mathematics, science, PSHE, music, art, humanities and so on. Their staffs are organized into curriculum teams, either through conventionally described school subjects ('the biology department', 'the English department'), or through broader curriculum areas ('the humanities faculty', 'the language area'). Student teachers themselves are trained, above all, to teach a secondary school subject, normally defined in terms of their own degree specialism or closely related to it. The curriculum, in many ways, defines what school is about. 'What did you do at school today?' is one of the most routinely asked – and routinely avoided – questions of a child's life! We all know what goes on in school: pupils learn and teachers teach. What they learn, and what they teach, is defined by the curriculum. As we shall see, however, the curriculum is far from straightforward, and in many ways is one of the most complex and least obvious aspects of school life. Understanding the curriculum involves far more than understanding the list of subjects which goes to make up the school timetable. It involves exploring questions about what is taught, how it is taught and organized, and, more controversially, why the things which are taught in schools have been selected as being significant and worth teaching to young people. These questions are difficult enough in themselves, but they derive from two more fundamental questions, about which there is always considerable disagreement between teachers, within schools and throughout society: what should children learn in school, and how should they learn it? These are difficult and complex questions not just because there is always more material which could be taught than there is time available to teach, but because they raise fundamental questions about the purposes of education itself. As a result of studying this chapter, you should have:

- developed a clear understanding of different ways of thinking about and organizing the curriculum;

- built up ideas about what the school curriculum is for;
- begun to explore how the curriculum is changing.

13.2 Curriculum debates and disputes

Before exploring the organization and structure of the school curriculum in England in detail, it is useful to identify some of the underlying debates about the curriculum which shape policy at national and at school level and which are resulting in pressures on the curriculum. Three are of particular importance. They are to do with the purposes of the curriculum, with learners' entitlement and with who should decide what is in the school curriculum.

Perhaps the most fundamental issue in discussions about the curriculum relates to debate about its purposes. The school curriculum is one of the main ways in which a society socializes its young into knowledge and ways of thinking. Any curriculum is a selection from all the things that might be taught, and the way in which a curriculum is developed will depend on ideas about its purposes. Because this is in itself controversial, disagreements about the purposes of the curriculum are often ferocious. Children learn different sorts of things in schools: they build up knowledge, they develop skills and they acquire attitudes. There are those who regard the primary purpose of education as the acquisition of certain types of knowledge. For example, this may entail inducting children into a cultural heritage, emphasizing the significance of making great literature, music or art accessible to the next generation. There are those who see the primary purpose of education as being the acquisition of transferable 'skills for work' which will prepare young people for the demands of the workplace. There are those who stress the significance of education in developing learners' sense of their own capacities and abilities. Of course, a simple response to these debates is to argue that the curriculum must serve different purposes: it must transmit knowledge, develop useful skills, and produce rounded individuals. However, the different balance we give to these different goals will go a long way to shaping both the organization of the curriculum and the teaching of individual subjects. For example, we might debate both the place of music in the school curriculum, and the extent to which the subject should be concerned with talent-spotting musical giftedness, developing the skills of concentration and col-laboration, and offering all young people opportunities to enjoy the capacity to make music.

A second issue relates to learners' entitlement. Most of us have views, even if we cannot clearly articulate them, about the basic entitlement which should shape learners' experience in school: we have views on those minimal things which we expect schools to teach every learner. Politicians often talk about the importance of the 'basics'. By this, they normally mean that they expect every child to be taught to read, to write and to attain basic numeracy. In the nineteenth century, this concep-tion of entitlement led to the idea that schools were fundamentally about the 'three Rs': reading, (w)riting and (a)rithmetic. Although this sense of 'the basics' is still prevalent – for example, in the Government's targets for primary school pupils' attainments in literacy and numeracy and the National Strategies – few serious com-mentators would now regard this as an adequate account of the basic curriculum entitlement in a complex, advanced society. Most teachers and educationalists would extend the list.

Task 13.1

What did you not learn at school that you wish you had? What did you learn at school which you have since found no use for?
What would you include as compulsory elements in a curriculum for all learners at the beginning of the twenty-first century?

Your own list might include some or all of the following. You might have defined the basic entitlement as including facility with ICT – an addition to the entitlement which could not have been foreseen by the Victorian advocates of the 3 Rs. You might have considered that schools have an obligation to prepare pupils for the world of work by teaching them a range of transferable skills, including the abilities to work collaboratively in groups, to apply knowledge to the real world and to take responsibility for their own learning. In a society in which many adults will change employment frequently, you might consider that an essential component of the curriculum is to lay the foundations for lifelong learning. Looking at other areas, you might consider that schools have failed their pupils if they have not prepared them for independence in adult life: this might include the teaching of basic cookery skills, or the rudiments which will enable them to understand their cars. Given the notorious difficulties which parents have in exploring issues relating to sex education or drug and substance abuse with their own children, your entitlement curriculum might include the expectation that all schools will offer PSHE. By now, your list of entitlements is extending. It may not be complete. You may have taken the view that in a complex, multicultural and diverse society, schools have an obligation to undertake some political or citizenship education. You may well feel that the ability to make sense of the modern world through an understanding of history, geography, sociology or economics is an essential component of the curriculum.

This list of potential entitlements is by now a long one. It is difficult, in the absence of hard cases or criteria, to argue that any of these areas is inessential. For example, are you content with school leavers who have no understanding of how our democracy works, or how to boil an egg, or of strategies to prevent sexually transmitted diseases? But it is also apparent that the list of entitlements has become almost impossibly large. In building curricula, choices have to be made. If the entitlement is too large, then there is no room for choice, and some pupils will become disaffected by having to learn things which do not connect with their own lives. If the entitlement is too small, then schools run the risk of premature specialisation, that is of ruling out of the entitlement for pupils important elements which will enable them to make informed choices later on. They also risk the emergence of different curricula for children labelled as 'academically successful' or 'academically unsuccessful'. The debate about entitlement is a long one. The 1944 Education Act, which made provision for a free secondary education for all children, introduced different types of school providing different types of entitlement curriculum to supposedly different types of children. 'Grammar' schools offered an academic curriculum to the supposedly most able 15–25 per cent, technical schools offered an applied curriculum to those deemed at 11 to be technologically-oriented and secondary modern schools offered a 'practical' and 'vocational' curriculum to the rest. One of the main impetuses for the reform which introduced comprehensive schools was recognition that this sort of divisiveness from the age of 11 was inadequate, ineffective and unfair. Despite the widespread promotion of curriculum specialism for secondary schools – specialisms now include technology, science, mathematics and computing, performing arts and humanities – the principle of selection by ability or aptitude has not re-established itself in the secondary system.

Debates about entitlement intersect with debates about the *purposes* of the curriculum. We might argue, for example, that all young people have a shared entitlement to a broad, balanced curriculum throughout their schooling. At the other extreme, we might argue that the entitlement curriculum might differ for different groups at different stages of their schooling dependent on interest, attainment and motivation. There is at the time of writing a lively debate about the place of modern foreign languages in the curriculum. Until 2003, modern foreign languages were a core part of the 14–16 NC for secondary schools. The removal of modern foreign languages as a core component at 14–16 was largely based on the argument that there was little purpose in teaching languages to those adolescents who had neither the inclination nor aptitude for learning them. However, national concern about the consequential decline of languages at GCSE led to the establishment of a government task force chaired by Lord Dearing. To the frustration of some, Dearing's 2007 report did not recommend restoring languages to the core at 14–16 but did recommend the extension of an entitlement to learn languages at primary school. The debate about modern languages is a good case study in disagreement over entitlement and purposes: it involves issues about when is the best time to start teaching languages, about how interest might be kindled, about whether all, or simply some, pupils need to develop facilities in speaking several languages. It also involves debate about which languages should be taught and why – whether the traditional pre-occupation with French and Spanish should be replaced by Chinese (given the rapid growth of the Chinese economy) or Gujarati, Hindi and Bengali (given the polyglot make-up of the UK). Mathematics is a part of the compulsory curriculum for learners from 5 through to 16 and, at the time of writing, there are tentative proposals to develop entitlement to mathematics as part of the 14–19 curriculum. Nonetheless, some mathematics educators have argued that the subject is ill-served by its 'privileged' status, and that learners should be given choice as they mature about whether to learn mathematics. Once we have decided which subjects should be taught and when, there are similar debates about purposes which translate into often bitter disputes about particular issues within school subjects: whether in a multicultural society the balance of school history should focus on British history or global history, whether and how Shakespeare should be a compulsory element in the English curriculum and so on. There is no 'right' answer to questions like these, which depend on different views about the purposes of the curriculum. You will encounter these debates in the teaching of your own subjects.

Behind these disputes lies a third area of disagreement, about *who should decide* the content of the curriculum. It could be argued that teachers should decide the content of the curriculum: they, after all, have professional expertise in the management of pupil learning. This, indeed, was the belief which underpinned curriculum policy making in England between about 1944 and 1988. David Eccles, Conservative minister for education in the early 1960s, spoke of the 'secret garden of the curriculum, into which ministers wandered at their peril', and Government largely devolved curriculum management to the Schools Council, which had a majority of teacher professional association representatives. Alternatively, it could be argued that parents should be able to control the content of the curriculum: we might argue that it is parents who know best about their own children's needs. In the Netherlands, considerable curriculum authority is devolved to parents, who can attract state support to set up schools. In the UK, in the 1990s, there was a powerful strand of policy discussion which suggested that parents might have considerable control over the curriculum. Schools are still required to consult parents over the content of sex education provision, and parents can exercise the right to withdraw their children from religious education and sex education in school. We might regard other groups as having an important place in decision making over the curriculum: religious and community groups, universities or employers – who, after all, employ pupils after they leave school – or, perhaps most radically of all, pupils themselves. There is, of course, another key influence on the curriculum: the Government. At different times, and in different ways, Government has claimed to represent the views of parents or of employers, or of other social groups in its planning for the curriculum, and a number of studies have tried to explore the ways in which Government reflects different influences in its curriculum policy (Graham 1993; Elliott 1997; Chitty 2002).

13.3 The National Curriculum

In retrospect, however, what seems most surprising is how slow Government was to take direct control of the curriculum in English schools. Only in the 1988 Education Reform Act did Government assume power to establish a National Curriculum (NC). Established between 1988 and 1991, the NC has been substantially revised on three occasions. The first was in 1994, in response to widespread teacher protests about what was seen as an unworkable initial specification. Subsequent revisions in 2000 and 2006–2007 were part of scheduled reviews.

The NC provides a basic curriculum structure for schools, though, as we shall see, it has become more complex as waves of reform and implementation have overtaken it. As we explore the NC, you might want to consider the balances it strikes between entitlement and choice, between different purposes and between the influence of different power groups in the education system. Table 13.1 sets out the basic structure of the NC. Compulsory schooling is divided into five stages, from Foundation (introduced in 2000) to KS4. At each stage, curriculum requirements set out targets for pupil attainment in a range of subjects.

Learning to teach the NC is a demanding task for new teachers. There is content to master and issues of planning to overcome. The formal requirements of the NC must not only be addressed through well-focused teaching, they must be addressed in

Table 13.1 An overview of the National Curriculum

Stage	Age	School year
Primary education		
Foundation Stage	3–5 years	
Key Stage 1	5–7 years	Years 1 and 2
Key Stage 2	7–11 years	Years 3–6
Secondary education		
Key Stage 3	11–14 years	Years 7–9
Core subjects (English, mathematics, science)		
Foundation subjects (ICT, history, geography, citizenship, Art and design, music, PE, design and technology, modern languages)		
Plus RE (outside National Curriculum)		
Key Stage 4	14–16 years	Years 10–11
Extended Core (English, mathematics, science, ICT, citizenship, PE, work-related learning)		
Entitlement areas (which must be made available to students who wish to study them): arts, design technology, humanities, modern languages		
Plus RE (outside National Curriculum)		
Specialised (i.e. vocational) diplomas (Level 1 and Level 2) are being introduced from 2008 (see Chapter 19)		

ways which engage and support the learning of all pupils. However, the NC does not describe the full range of the school curriculum. The NC is itself a part of the wider school curriculum and many elements of the school lie outside its formal requirements. RE, although a compulsory element of the school curriculum for all pupils in school from 5–19 since the 1944 Education Act, is not a part of the NC. Before 1988, ironically, RE was the only subject schools were required to teach and in 1988 it was felt to be too controversial for the Government to prescribe the content of RE. Schools are also at liberty to add subjects to the curriculum. Many primary schools already make provision for modern foreign language teaching, even though languages are not due to become part of the KS2 entitlement until 2010. Secondary schools may add subjects such as business studies, Latin or Greek to the KS3 or KS4 curriculum. More radically, schools may decide to restructure the curriculum around organizing themes, intersecting with the requirements of the NC.

At KS4, much of the provision is outside the NC, which requires only the teaching of an Extended Core (see Table 13.1). Thus, history, geography, art and music are elements of the NC at KS3 but not at KS4, whilst vocational elements of the curriculum, such as work experience or vocationally-related courses are likely to feature at KS4. The post-16 curriculum (see Table 13.2) lies entirely outside the NC (save for the legal requirement, in practice often ignored, for post-16 pupils in schools to study RE). At the time of writing, the Government is reforming the 14–19 curriculum, in an attempt to develop a more coherent phase of learning, with a clearer

Table 13.2 Post-16 education

Stage	Age	School year
Post-16 (sometimes referred to as KS5)	16–19 years	Years 12 and 13
Curriculum 2000: 4 or 5 AS levels (3 units each) in Year 12 plus Key Skills		
3 A2 levels (3 units each) in Year 13		
3 AS units + 3 A2 units combine for 1 A Level (other qualifications include the International Baccalaureate, the European Baccalaureate, the Specialised Diploma, Level 3, and a variety of workplace-based training and education programmes.)		

articulation of pupil entitlement, which maps progression routes through a variety of learning provision, including a stronger vocational offer (see Chapter 19).

Task 13.2

Read the NC Order for your own subject. (If you are training to teach a non-NC subject, use a GCSE or other examination syllabus in your subject.) How does this document reflect wider ideas about the content and purpose of the curriculum?

13.4 Beyond the National Curriculum

The NC can thus be seen as nesting within the school curriculum, and schools are encouraged to use curriculum freedoms to give a distinctive flavour to the curriculum which reflects the ethos of the school, for example, reflecting specialist status as a language college or a business and enterprise college, or responding to particular features of the school's location or intake. Increasingly, schools are asked to articulate the basis for their curriculum planning and to take responsibility for developing distinctive elements to the curriculum. In this sense, the school's *planned* curriculum is a tool for combining their responsibilities to deliver statutory elements of the curriculum – the NC, RE and PSHE – with the non-statutory elements which it wishes to emphasize. The planned curriculum will need to be much more than a list of contents. It will need to clarify the aims of the school's curriculum and to identify mechanisms for translating those aims into practice, defining knowledge, skills and concepts. It will also need to identify an 'organizational' framework for achieving these aims, as well as a set of assessment and evaluation arrangements for establishing the effectiveness of the curriculum. At present, for example, some schools are looking beyond AS/A2 assessment and making use of the International Baccalaureate as an assessment device at post-16. The planned curriculum adapts the National and whole curriculum to resources, learners and school ethos. However, the *planned* curriculum typically differs from the *delivered* curriculum. No school ever quite teaches what it plans to teach in its curriculum statements. There are a number of reasons for this, some of them quite accidental and unpredictable. Changes in staffing, long-term staff absences, unexpected opportunities to become involved in curriculum development projects, local or national initiatives and circumstances may all affect the delivery of the planned curriculum. Finally, the curriculum *experienced* by individual learners may differ markedly from the curriculum experienced by other learners. Again, this can happen for a variety of reasons, perhaps due to the school's decision to differentiate provision for different groups, or due to learners' decisions to take different routes through the school's planned curriculum.

Task 13.3

Find out about the range of possible curricula which different learners at KS4 might follow using www.qca.org.uk (or www.aqa.org.uk, www.edexcel.org.uk and www.ocr.org.uk).
Why do you think schools are so strongly committed to choice in curriculum for pupils post-14? What dangers might there be in wide choice?

We have seen that the school curriculum is a complex construction, comprising the whole curriculum, the NC, the planned curriculum, the delivered curriculum and the experienced curriculum. However, to understand learners' experiences in school, one further concept needs to be considered: *the hidden curriculum*. The hidden curriculum is the term generally used to describe the implicit, often unintended and often very subtle, messages schools convey about learning, knowledge and achievement. The hidden curriculum is very powerful, but often difficult to pin down. It is made up of the assumptions about how learning is to be conducted which schools convey unconsciously through, for example, the way classrooms are organized and work is presented. Messages about sorts of achievements which are worthy of praise are communicated through notices and honours boards which can be seen around schools and in the kinds of achievements which are praised in newsletters. There are often hidden messages about an implied hierarchy of subjects. For instance, school reports are normally presented loose leaf, with English, science and mathematics at the front and art and music at the back. Underlying messages can also be detected in the organization of staff handbooks and in how well-equipped different subjects are. Some commentators have argued that this is not just about a hierarchy of subjects and achievement in schools, but something more fundamental about schooling, conveying messages about what counts as knowledge in our society, and how that knowledge is organized and presented.

Task 13.4

What other ways might there be in which schools communicate a 'hidden curriculum' to learners? How can schools and teachers become more aware of the 'hidden curriculum'?

At the time of writing this chapter, there are enormous pressures for change on the curriculum. The balance between subject areas has been changed by, for example, the removal of modern languages from the core curriculum at KS4 and the introduction of new subjects such as citizenship, and will change further as the vocational offer in schools is extended. Increasingly, policy makers and schools are under pressure to develop curriculum solutions to what are seen as pressing educational difficulties. There are pressures for more 'relevance' to the world of work in what is taught, the way it is taught and its assessment: schools are being asked to place greater emphasis on vocational training and to enhance the quality and range of work experience. There are pressures to use the curriculum as one tool for combating social exclusion and disaffection, as a result of which schools are looking at their provision of personal and social, drugs and sex education and developing links with out-of-school agencies such as the Connexions service. The *Every Child Matters* agenda (see Chapter 20) involves schools in reviewing the ways in which their curriculum contributes to its five agreed outcomes for all children: that they enjoy and achieve; stay safe; remain healthy; achieve economic well-being and make a positive contribution. There are pressures on all curriculum areas to make increased use of new technologies for learning as part of a strategy for preparing pupils for a changing world. There are continuing pressures on improving standards of educational performance, which involve schools in making adjustments to the curriculum to improve the performance of individuals and groups of pupils so that learners can achieve the best possible measurable outcomes. These pressures translate into specific curriculum innovations, some of them discussed in detail elsewhere in this book. There is a significant expansion of specialist schools all teaching the NC but with a clear focus on technology, performing arts, languages, business and enterprise, mathematics and so on. At the same time, the Government proposes an expansion of faith-based schools, again, schools with an obligation to teach the NC but with the curriculum underpinnings provided by faith values. Proposals to reform the 14–19 curriculum seek to develop and strengthen vocational elements of the curriculum, but to improve the opportunities for learners to move between vocational and other pathways as they progress through their 14–19 curriculum. Policy makers and schools are becoming more interested in the scope provided by ICT to individuate learning, and to tailor provision to the needs of individuals. As your career develops, these and other issues will be matters for lively discussion and decision making. The ways in which they are resolved in the schools in which you work will depend on a number of things. They will, of course, depend on patterns of national policy and local provision. However, they will also depend on the answers you and the teachers you work with give to questions about what should be taught, what pupils' entitlement should be, what the curriculum is for, and who has the power and authority to develop it.

13.5 Recommendations for further reading and webliography

Moon, B. (2001) *A Guide to the National Curriculum.* Oxford: Oxford University Press.
White, J. (ed.) (2003) *Rethinking the School Curriculum: Values, Aims and Purposes.* London: Routledge.

www.14–19reform.gov.uk (the full text of the Working Group on 14–19 Reform: Principles for the reform of 14–19 Learning Programmes and Qualifications, July 2003)
www.nc.net (the full text of the National Curriculum for England)
www.qca.org.uk (the QCA website: QCA has overall responsibility for curriculum monitoring in England)

14

Spiritual, moral and cultural development

Judith Everington

14.1 Introduction

> Education influences and reflects the values of society, and the kind of society we want to be. It is important therefore to recognise a broad set of common values and purposes that underpin the school curriculum and the work of schools. Foremost is a belief in education . . . as a route to the spiritual, moral, social, cultural, physical and mental development, and thus the well being of the individual.
>
> (DfEE/QCA 2000: 10)

This chapter will focus on spiritual, moral and cultural development. By the end of the chapter you should:

- understand what is meant by spiritual, moral and cultural development in the context of the secular secondary school;
- know the legal and professional requirements relating to spiritual, moral and cultural development;
- understand how spiritual, moral and cultural development can be promoted in teaching and pastoral work;
- know how to obtain guidance on and ideas for promoting spiritual, moral and cultural development.

14.2 Spiritual, moral and cultural development – what's all that then?

'That's RE isn't it, and assemblies?'

'Moral development sounds like something to do with cold baths and keeping idle fingers busy!'

'Spiritual development is surely a very private thing and I'm worried about interfering in it.'

'I'm interested in the idea of cultural development but my subject isn't "arty".'

Task 14.1

What do you associate with each of the terms spiritual, moral and cultural development? Write a list of immediate thoughts and feelings. Are they negative or positive? Where have they come from?

In this chapter you will find 'official' definitions of the terms. However, when approaching these complex and sensitive dimensions of teaching and learning for the first time, it is important to be aware of the understandings that you have already formed and the feelings that are associated with these. For example, some students' experience of school and higher education may have convinced them that they have little or nothing to contribute to one or more of the areas of development. Others will have attended faith-based (for example, Islamic, Roman Catholic and Church of England) schools and may have understandings that are different from those that are current in secular secondary schools. Through a recognition of preconceptions and existing attitudes, it is possible to set these aside in order to develop a critical openness to new definitions and possibilities.

Whatever your responses to the task above, you may have been inclined to skip over this chapter. Research indicates that student teachers tend to be most interested in those aspects of their training course which have to do with teaching their subject effectively, controlling their classes and forming good relationships with pupils. They take less interest in matters which fall outside these concerns. However, in this chapter you will be asked to consider the view that a teacher's ability to teach, manage and relate to pupils effectively is greatly enhanced by her or his ability to take account of and draw upon pupils' spiritual, moral and cultural lives, and provide opportunities for development.

14.3 Requirements and responsibilities

The quotation at the beginning of this chapter is from the introduction to the NC which restates the 1988 Education Reform Act requirement for the school curriculum to promote pupils' spiritual, moral and cultural development (SMCD). Schools document their provision for SMCD and Ofsted inspects this provision and its outcomes. In recent years, a great deal of attention has been paid to the promotion of SMCD in subject teaching. However, it has been made clear that SMCD are to permeate the whole of school life and should be reflected in every aspect of teachers' work, including their relationships with pupils and with other people who work in the school. This whole school perspective will be outlined in statements about the school's ethos that appear in its prospectus and policy documents.

As a student teacher, you will be expected to demonstrate that you can contribute to SMCD in your work with pupils. In terms of formal assessment, the national standards for QTS do not make specific reference to SMCD, but a number clearly refer to spiritual, moral and cultural matters. For example, students are required to:

- have high expectations of those children and young people they teach and establish fair, respectful, trusting, supportive and constructive relationships with them (Q 1.1)

- demonstrate the positive values, attitudes and behaviour they expect from children and young people (Q 1.2)

- understand that the progress and well-being of learners is affected by a range of developmental, social, religious, ethnic and linguistic influences (Q 2.1)

- know how to make effective provision for all those they teach, including those for whom English is an additional language, and how to take practical account of diversity and promote equality and inclusion in their teaching (Q 2:2).

(TDA 2007)

The Standards for practising teachers also include these expectations.

14.4 Defining spiritual, moral and cultural development

To what does the term 'spiritual' refer?

In one definition it is said to refer to 'a dimension of human existence which applies to all pupils' and as 'something fundamental in the human condition which is not necessarily experienced through the physical senses and/or expressed in everyday language' (SCAA 1995: 3). Other definitions refer to an inner life or self; our non-tangible personality or our self awareness (Bigger and Brown 1999: 6).

Spiritual development

Of the three areas considered in this chapter, spiritual development is the most difficult to define. There is a vast body of literature devoted to exploring such slippery questions as, 'Is there such a thing as a human spirit?' but what matters for most teachers is having a definition that is clearly related to the context in which they are working.

Some student teachers will undertake one or more of their school placements in faith-based schools and some will eventually take up posts in such schools. In faith schools, guidance related to spiritual development will reflect the religious beliefs and values associated with the origin of the school and this guidance will need to be consulted. In this chapter, the context considered is the secular school which is responsible for the development of young people from a wide range of backgrounds and with a wide range of attitudes to religion – from fervent atheism, to mild curiosity, to profound commitment to a religious faith. Mindful of the need to provide guidance that is inclusive, those who have offered definitions appropriate for the secular school stress that spiritual development should not be viewed as synonymous with religious development. At the same time, it must include pupils who will view spiritual development in relation to their religious development. The Standards for QTS (TDA 2007) indicate that teachers need to know something of the backgrounds, personal beliefs and attitudes of pupils if they are to recognize and deal sensitively with individual spiritual needs.

In what aspects of their lives do or can young people develop spiritually?

It has been suggested that young people develop spiritually in and through their:

- **beliefs and values:** as they develop personal (for some, religious) beliefs and values, but also begin to understand the beliefs of others and how individual and shared beliefs shape people's lives and identities and lead to decisions and actions;

- **feelings, emotions and inner experiences:** for example, the sense of being moved by beauty or kindness or angered by injustice; a sense of awe, wonder and mystery – in response to the natural world or to a sense of a reality beyond the material world and the limitations of human understanding;

- **search for meaning and purpose:** for example, asking 'why' when reflecting on hardship and suffering or on the origins and purpose of life, or responding to the challenging experiences of life such as death or loss of love and security;

- **self-knowledge:** an awareness of oneself in terms of thoughts, emotions and experiences and a growing understanding of one's own identity as a unique individual, but also as a member of groups and communities;

- **relationships:** recognizing and valuing the worth of each individual; building trustful relationships with others and developing a sense of the responsibilities that trust entails;

- **creativity:** exploring and expressing innermost thoughts and feelings through art, music or creative writing and using the imagination, inspiration, intuition and insight.

(based on SCAA 1995: 3–4)

Like most definitions of spiritual development, those above have been arrived at by adult professionals. However, research undertaken in a range of comprehensive schools found that Year 9 pupils' own understandings of 'spiritual' and 'spiritual development' were 'uncannily similar' to the kind of adult definitions provided above. It was also found that, even when pupils struggled to find words, they 'communicated a great depth of understanding and feeling' in their responses to questions about spiritual matters (Wintersgill 2002: 8).

Moral development

Like spiritual development, moral development is not easy to define, is the subject of much controversy and debate and, in faith schools, will reflect the religious beliefs and values associated with the origin of the school. However, in the context of the secular school, the guidance offered by Government and other authorities has suggested two major strands of pupils' moral development:

1   knowledge, understanding (and at least implicitly) acceptance of the moral values

and codes and conventions of conduct which are promoted within the school and which reflect those promoted in society;

2 knowledge and understanding of criteria for making moral judgements and the ability to employ these in making their own judgements, in relation to personal behaviour and moral issues.

Between the first and second strands there is a tension and potential for conflict. This reflects one of the most fundamental and enduring tensions within education and within the teacher's role – the tension between 'training' young people to become 'good citizens' and providing them with the tools to think for themselves and make their own judgements and decisions.

At school level, the extent to which there is tension or conflict between moral 'training' and 'empowering' will depend on many factors, including the ways in which moral values and development are presented in school ethos statements and are interpreted by school managers and other members of staff. However, in any school it is difficult to avoid the fact that there will be times when teachers will be enforcing the school's moral values and code, and other times when they will be encouraging pupils to look critically at the moral arguments put forward by adults and develop confidence in making their own moral judgements.

This difficulty is illustrated in the definitions of moral development drawn up by Ofsted, with reference to the role of schools and to pupil characteristics. The school related definitions begin with a statement that leans strongly in the direction of the 'training' view of moral development. So, schools that are encouraging pupils' moral development are likely to be 'providing a clear moral code as a basis for behaviour which is promoted consistently through all aspects of the school' (Ofsted 2004: 18). In the list of characteristics of pupils who are becoming 'morally aware', the emphasis is much more on independent thinking and the individual's will to act in accordance with moral principles. So, pupils will be developing:

- an ability to distinguish right from wrong, based on a knowledge of the moral codes of their own and other cultures;
- a confidence to act consistently in accordance with their own principles;
- a commitment to personal values in areas which are considered right by some and wrong by others;
- a willingness to express their views on ethical issues and personal values;
- an ability to make responsible and reasoned judgements on moral dilemmas;
- an understanding of the need to review and reassess their values, codes and principles in the light of experience.

(Ofsted 2004: 17)

Leaving aside the issue of consistency, the characteristics above reflect the Government's current emphasis on the empowerment of pupils and, as we shall see, play an important role in citizenship and PSHE (see Chapters 18 and 25).

Cultural development

The term 'culture' is used and understood in different ways, in different contexts. In everyday speech, to refer to someone as 'cultured' often implies that they are well educated in and appreciative of the Arts. Another common usage of the term is in 'multicultural', although this is being replaced by the more flexible term, 'cultural diversity'. In sociological debate the term 'culture' is fiercely contested, but there is some agreement that it refers to the expression of the fundamental concepts and values of a community, and that these are subject to continuous development and change.

Attempts to define cultural development in an educational context have drawn upon these differing understandings of 'culture/cultural'. The report of the National Advisory Committee on Creative and Cultural Education, *All our Futures* (1999), has been an influential work in this area. The report identifies four central roles for education in the cultural development of young people. In their guidance, Ofsted provide a commentary on each of these and outline their view of the characteristics of pupils who are becoming 'culturally aware'. These are summarized below.

1 *To enable young people to recognize, explore and understand their own cultural assumptions and values.* Pupils need to understand their own culture. This gives them a sense of identity and a language with which to communicate, receive and modify the shared values of the culture. Such language embraces customs, icons and images, artefacts, music, painting and sculpture, dance and technology, as well as verbal and literary forms. There will also be agreed norms of behaviour and opportunities to participate in celebrations which mark key ideals or events. Pupils who are becoming culturally aware will be developing an ability to understand the meaning and significance of, and to use, the various forms of cultural 'language', and a willingness to participate in and respond to artistic and cultural enterprises.

2 *To enable young people to embrace and understand cultural diversity by bringing them into contact with attitudes, values and traditions of other cultures.* Within any culture, there will be sub-cultures and the dominant culture of any one group of people is only one among many in the world. With improvements in communication, we are also beginning to recognize a 'world culture' which people need to understand and feel comfortable with. Pupils who are becoming culturally aware will be developing an ability to appreciate cultural diversity and to accord dignity to other people's values and beliefs, thereby challenging racism. They will be developing an openness to new ideas and a willingness to modify cultural values in the light of experience, and a sense of personal enrichment through encounter with cultural media and traditions from a range of cultures.

3 *To encourage a historical perspective by relating contemporary values to the processes and events that have shaped them.*

4 *To enable young people to understand the evolutionary nature of culture and the processes and potential for change.* Cultures are always changing and growing. Pupils who are becoming culturally aware will be developing an understanding

of the processes of cultural development and change and an appreciation of the inter-dependence of different cultures. This will involve understanding the influences that have shaped their own cultural heritage, and facing the prejudices which lead to dismissing or marginalizing unfamiliar traditions (Ofsted 2004: 23–6).

The emphasis on cultural diversity in the summary above may seem alarming to student teachers whose lives and educational experiences have provided little opportunity to learn about a range of cultures. At the end of this chapter, you will find references to websites which provide material on a wide range of religious and cultural matters and practical guidance on cultural development. During your training, you should be given opportunities to learn about cultural diversity. You may also be able to gain knowledge and understanding through a placement in a school in which a range of cultures is represented.

During your school placements, you may wish to consider the extent to which the schools actively promote the kind of cultural development described above. However, the very considerable emphasis that is given to cultural diversity in Government policy documents, and the fact that schools are inspected in relation to cultural development, means that all teachers need to gain sufficient knowledge and understanding to reflect cultural diversity in their teaching.

Task 14.2

- Look back at your initial responses to the terms spiritual, moral and cultural development. How do they compare to the descriptions above?
- Which of the aspects of SMCD above do you feel most and least comfortable with, and equipped to deal with? Make a note of the things that you will need to find out about before and during your training course.
- Make a quick-fire response to the question, how could your specialist subject promote spiritual, moral and cultural development?

14.5 What does it all mean in practice?

In this section we will look briefly at the relationship between SMCD and the *Every Child Matters* agenda. We will then consider the four overlapping areas of a teacher's work in which there are opportunities for pupils' SMCD: subject teaching; citizenship and PSHE; pastoral work; and assemblies/collective worship. Each area will be considered in a separate section, but in 'real life' there is no clear separation between these, and the opportunity or need to contribute to pupils' SMCD can crop up at any point in a teacher's day. In 'real life' too, the distinction between spiritual, moral and cultural development breaks down. The following example is intended to illustrate these points.

CASE STUDY 14.1

Spiritual, moral and cultural development in a teacher's day

Stuart gets in to school to find a fight brewing between two girls in his tutor group. One is accusing the other of spreading rumours about her 'sex life'. Stuart intervenes and reminds both about the importance of respect for others and self respect.

At the staff briefing, all Year 7 teachers are asked to support the sponsored 'Silly Hair Day' organized by the pupils in aid of 'Children in Need'.

At the Year 9 assembly and act of collective worship, some of Stuart's tutor group read out their own poems on 'Being on the Outside'. The Head of Year follows her short talk with a minute's silent reflection on how it feels to be an outsider, and what each of us can do to break down barriers and enable everyone to feel included.

During the second lesson, a Year 10 pupil asks Stuart why they need to spend 'so much time looking at the situation in other countries'. Stuart reminds the whole group that to be at the cutting edge these days, it is crucial to have a global perspective.

At lunchtime, Stuart attends a meeting to discuss plans for the cross-curricular field trip to Stonehenge.

In the afternoon, his Year 8 pupils are put into groups to explore and come up with solutions to a conflict between three families who live in adjoining flats, but have very different lifestyles and needs.

In the evening he downloads the lyrics of a song that is well known to his Year 11 groups and that he will use to help them explore the idea that the effects of a single action go far beyond the intentions of the actor.

As a student teacher, you will not have to cope with all the situations described above. However, you will encounter many like them and you will be expected to demonstrate that you can contribute to SMCD in your work with pupils, as outlined below.

Every Child Matters

Chapter 20 provides a full account of the government initiative referred to as *Every Child Matters* and of the five intended 'outcomes' for children and young people: that they enjoy and achieve; achieve economic well-being; stay safe; be healthy; and make a positive contribution. The key point to be made here is that the ideals and aspirations reflected in these outcomes and those of SMCD are the same. Ofsted now inspect spiritual, moral, social, emotional and cultural development in the context of the school's performance in promoting pupils' enjoyment and achievement and enabling them to make a positive contribution (Ofsted 2005). The case study above provides some examples of what this might mean in the daily life of a teacher. However, commentators have been quick to point out that all of the *Every Child Matters* outcomes involve pupils' SMCD. For example, in order to enable pupils to 'stay safe' and 'be healthy', schools will need to provide opportunities for them to develop their self-esteem, to reflect on what is meant by and contributes to a 'healthy mind', and to consider the consequences of drug and alcohol abuse for themselves, others and society. If pupils are to be encouraged to achieve 'economic well-being', they will need to develop a belief in their own value and potential but also to explore the factors that contribute to inequalities and how these might be addressed at a societal and global, as well as a personal level.

Subject teaching

The extent to which subject departments and teachers actively promote SMCD in their planning and teaching will vary from one school to another. However, there is considerable pressure for them to do so. Ofsted inspectors report on SMCD in subject teaching and some LAs encourage departments to refer to these matters in their SoW. Awarding bodies are required to make explicit reference to the ways in which their GCSE and GCE courses contribute to SMCD.

Leaving aside external pressures, there is some evidence that planning SMCD into SoW and lessons can improve the quality and outcomes of learning. A research project, undertaken by secondary school teachers in Bristol, found that when SMCD were planned into lesson objectives, and teaching and learning strategies were geared to achieving these, pupils' discussion and critical thinking skills developed and they became more engaged and motivated in their learning (Midgley et al. 1999: 3).

How can all subjects contribute to SMCD?

The arts and humanities are often viewed as the natural subjects to promote SMCD. However (and despite teaching which has disguised the fact), there is a long tradition of exploring such matters in maths and the sciences. In subjects which straddle these categories, opportunities for SMCD are being recognized and developed, and support is provided in an increasing number of SMCD-related websites. Adult perceptions of 'SMCD friendly' subjects may also be challenged by those of pupils. For example, there is research evidence to suggest that some pupils view PE and sport as important in their spiritual development (Wintersgill 2002: 6).

Whatever the subject, there are two main ways in which SMCD can be promoted:

- through the topics that are taught;
- through the teaching and learning methods used.

Topics at Key Stage 3

At KS3, teachers of most subjects will be covering topics dictated by the NC programmes of study. Opportunities for SMCD are more obvious in some of these than in others, but can be identified in the process of interpreting the programmes of study to produce units of work and lesson plans. When the teachers involved in the Bristol-based research set out to plan SMCD into lessons, they found no difficulty in identifying opportunities for development in the content of existing SoW and/or in the application of content (Midgley et al. 1999: 2).

Table 14.1 indicates the kind of topics or aspects of topics that can provide opportunities for SMCD, in their content or application of content.

Table 14.1

	Spiritual development	Moral development	Cultural development
Maths	Mathematical principles behind natural forms and patterns	Calculation of amount of paper used in the lesson related to the number of trees needed	Analysis/presentation of numerical data on family expenditure in differing cultures
Science	Role of scientific discoveries in changing people's lives and thinking	Why sustainable development is important	Relationship between culture and nature of scientific exploration
Art & design	Exploring ideas and feelings in creative work	The role of A&D in political propaganda	Cultural variations in the representation of universal themes
D&T	Aesthetics in the design of a product	Environmental impact of products	Analysis of cultural influences on design
PE	Developing pride in skills and an ability to cope with losing	Exploring/developing values of cooperation and inclusion in sport	Performing dances from differing cultures
MFL	Expressing personal feelings and opinions in the target language	Reading/responding to 'Problem page' letters in the target language	Learning about the culture of the target language country
Geography	Human responses to environmental hazards	Reasons for changes in the distribution of economic activities	Population distribution and change – why, how and the consequences
History	The power of religious beliefs in people's lives and deaths	'Myths of racial superiority' in events past and present	The development of 'multicultural' Britain
RE	Religious/non-religious views of what happens at death	Differing perspectives on the development of 'cloning' techniques	Cultural variations in the interpretation of religious texts
English & drama	Expressing a personal 'vision for the future' in creative writing	Creating dramas that explore conflict between the values of family members	Exploring the content and style of poems from differing cultures

Topics at GCSE and AS/A level

At this level, the topics taught are determined by national criteria and by the examination specification (syllabus) that the department has chosen. Awarding bodies are required to provide specifications which cover spiritual, moral, ethical, social and cultural issues and to identify the opportunities for these. The kinds of topics indicated in Table 14.1 often appear in KS4/5 specifications, but you can further your understanding of SMCD in your specialist subject by reading the relevant sections of the specifications that appear on exam board websites. For example, in GCSE IT pupils might explore issues related to privacy and the confidentiality of data, and use the technology to obtain, analyze and report on data related to the distribution of wealth. In business studies, they might consider non-financial reasons why people work in organizations; ethical stances of those who control or try to influence businesses, and the workings of multinationals across cultural divides.

Task 14.3

- What do you think of the suggestions for your specialist subject in the section above? How do they compare with the ideas that you suggested in response to Task 14.2?
- What advantages and disadvantages might there be in focusing on SMCD in subject teaching?

Teaching and learning methods

Although the content of some subjects is more obviously related to SMCD than that of others, teachers of all subjects can and do promote development through their teaching methods. These methods need to be of the kind that encourage pupils to think for themselves. Opportunities to work with others are important, but activities which enable pupils to reflect 'privately' are also needed. Examples of both kinds of activity are:

- expressing opinions and listening to those of others;
- exploring and discussing issues from a range of perspectives;
- simulations, for instance, role plays;
- working collaboratively, for instance, to solve problems;
- reflecting privately on issues, experiences and feelings;
- sharing experiences and feelings in 'safety', for example, in friendship pairs.

In all cases, teachers need to create a learning environment in which pupils feel sufficiently secure and confident to express and explore their views, feelings and experiences.

Citizenship and PSHE are explored in Chapters 18 and 25, but they are considered here because both play an important role in promoting SMCD.

Citizenship

Citizenship became a statutory subject in secondary schools in 2002. The programmes of study and non-statutory SoW for the subject reflect the three interrelated
strands of citizenship: Social and Moral Responsibility, Community Involvement and
Political Literacy. Spiritual, moral and cultural matters are so deeply embedded in
these strands that it would be difficult for teachers to contribute to citizenship effectively without promoting SMCD. The titles of units from the KS3 SoW (for example,
'Why is it so difficult to keep peace in the world today?'; 'Debating a global issue';
and 'How do we deal with conflict?'; QCA 2001: 27), illustrate the intertwining of
citizenship and SMCD.

These units of work can be delivered through subjects, but schools are encouraged to deliver citizenship in a variety of ways. During your school placements you
might be asked to support your tutor group in their 'democratic decision making'.
You might be involved in a cross-curricular project, such as creating a 'peace
garden' in the school grounds. You might also be able to teach or observe a dedicated
citizenship lesson on an SMCD-related topic such as 'human rights'.

Personal, Social and Health Education

There is substantial and deliberate overlap between PSHE and citizenship and
schools must demonstrate how both promote SMCD. PSHE has been part of the NC
since 2000 and there is a national framework for the subject. This identifies three
major areas of pupils' development:

- developing confidence and responsibility and making the most of their abilities;
- developing good relationships and respecting the differences between people;
- developing a healthy, safer lifestyle.

(QCA 2000b)

SMCD permeate all three areas and can be seen clearly in the non-statutory programmes of study which supplement the PSHE framework. For example, under the
first heading, spiritual development will be promoted as pupils are enabled 'to recognise the stages of emotions associated with loss and change caused by death, divorce,
separation and new family members and how to deal positively with the strength of
their feelings in different situations'. Cultural development is strongly represented
under the second, 'relationships' heading, which includes teaching about stereotyping, prejudice, bullying, racism and discrimination, and how to challenge these assert-
ively. Opportunities for moral development are to be found here, as pupils are taught
to 'resist pressure to do wrong, to recognise when others need help and how to
support them', and under the third 'health' heading, where sex education is set in the
context of 'the importance of relationships' (QCA 2003: 1–3).

Topics such as those described above and in the citizenship section, are clearly
sensitive and require very careful 'handling'. The QCA has produced guidelines on
teaching sensitive and controversial subjects (QCA 2001: 44). Schools deliver the

PSHE curriculum in a number of ways: through dedicated lessons and PSHE events; through other subjects; and through the pastoral system and assemblies. These latter opportunities will be considered in the final sections of this chapter.

Pastoral care and guidance

Pastoral matters are examined in Chapter 24, but this section will focus upon one aspect, that is 'pastoral casework'. 'Pastoral casework' covers work with individual pupils on any aspect which affects their development and attainment. It includes supporting pupils when they have personal problems, are in need of encouragement, or want to talk about experiences, feelings or issues that they are grappling with. In many schools it is expected that teachers who act as pastoral tutors will be a 'first port of call' for pupils in their tutor group who want to talk. However, any teacher may be sought out by a pupil in need.

As a student teacher you will not be given sole responsibility for a tutor group, and all tutors should hand over serious problems (such as suspected child or drug abuse) to senior pastoral staff. Nevertheless, you may find that pupils choose to speak to you about personal matters. You should find guidance on managing these situations in the school's staff handbook, but an awareness of the spiritual, moral and cultural dimensions of young people's experience and development will be important in enabling you to respond to pupils with sensitivity. For example, we have seen that adolescents can be interested in, or even deeply concerned about, spiritual matters. In the spiritual development research referred to above, a number of the pupils who offered lengthy and very thoughtful accounts of their spiritual feelings and experiences made it clear that they would not feel able to share these with other pupils. An awareness of this may help teachers to recognize and encourage pupils who need or would benefit from opportunities to talk about spiritual matters.

Young people from religious backgrounds may hide their beliefs, practices and special events from their peers, but may need or just want to talk to someone about these. A teacher who has some knowledge and understanding of pupils' backgrounds, and of religious and cultural beliefs, practices and sensitivities will be in a position to respond sensitively to these matters.

Moral development issues raised by pupils can be difficult for teachers caught between their 'training' and 'empowerment' roles. However, an awareness of the tension can be helpful, especially in situations where pupils are not in trouble, but want to explore issues with a teacher. A PGCE student found herself drawn into an informal discussion with Year 12 pupils about 'soft drugs'. She recognized the pupils' right to hold their own views and to discuss such matters openly. At the same time, she was able to raise questions about the 'down-side' of getting involved with such drugs and to keep her own pro-legalization views to herself!

Assemblies and acts of collective worship

The assembly is a traditional part of school life and, at one time, was synonymous with the act of worship. Now, however, a distinction is drawn between the two.

Schools can provide 'secular assemblies' whenever they wish, but are required by law to provide a daily act of collective worship.

Large group (for instance, year group) assemblies are an important means of bringing pupils together to share an 'inspirational' experience and a sense of belonging to the school community. They are also a useful means of covering aspects of citizenship and PSHE. Careful planning and good speakers can produce genuinely 'moving' assemblies. However, there is an increasing emphasis on the involvement of pupils as presenters or even as organizers and leaders of assemblies. This approach has the advantage of encouraging pupils to view the assembly as 'their time', rather than as an opportunity for senior staff to rant about the state of the school site!

Assemblies usually include an act of collective worship, although in secular schools it is rarely possible to have more than one large group assembly a week and this leads to difficulties in meeting the requirement for a daily act of worship. However, the law allows for flexibility in the timing of, and grouping for collective worship, and one option is for tutors to set aside a few moments during the daily registration or tutor period for quiet reflection/worship. In practice, many schools have simply failed to meet the requirement, and this is one reason why head teachers have called for changes in the law and guidance relating to collective worship. Other reasons, shared by many in and outside the teaching profession, have to do with opposition to the very idea that pupils in a secular school should be required to attend an act of worship.

In fact, parents have the right to withdraw their children from collective worship and teachers have the right to withdraw on 'grounds of conscience'. In practice, very few parents exercise their right. The reasons for this are complex, but a major factor has probably been the creative way in which schools have interpreted the requirements. Few would accept the idea that young people who have no belief in God should be forced to worship or pray to God. However, all pupils are capable of reflecting on spiritual and moral matters, if these are of a kind that have meaning for them and are presented in ways to which they can relate. An inclusive act of worship will allow for a spiritual response from some pupils, and a worshipful response from others. This may mean that pupils will begin by listening to a presentation on a spiritual/moral theme. They will then be invited, either to reflect quietly on what they have heard (or on a related thought or question), or to offer their own prayer. The benefits to pupils of this opportunity for a moment's stillness, reflection or prayer make it likely that even if the law is changed, many schools will continue to build some 'private time' into assemblies.

Task 14.4

- How do you feel about those aspects of a teacher's work which involve guiding pupils in and through matters which are very personal to them?
- Do you have any concerns about how you will be able to remain true to your personal beliefs, values and attitudes and promote the spiritual, moral and cultural development of your pupils?
- Note down your responses to these questions so that you can give more thought to these and perhaps share some in your training sessions.

At the beginning of this chapter you were asked to consider the view that 'the teacher's ability to teach, manage and relate to pupils effectively is greatly enhanced by her or his ability to take account of and draw upon pupils' spiritual, moral and cultural lives and provide opportunities for development'. What do you think now?

14.6 Recommendations for further reading and webliography

Bigger, S. and Brown, E. (eds) (1999) *Spiritual, Moral, Social and Cultural Education: Exploring Values in the Curriculum*. London: David Fulton.

Mackley, J. and Draycott, P. (2000) *Active Learning Strategies to Support Spiritual and Moral Development*. Derby: Christian Education Movement (CEM). This book of practical classroom strategies does not take a religious stance. As a publisher, CEM is now called 'RE Services' reflecting its long-standing commitment to promoting broad educational principles and a multi-faith/cultural approach.

SMSC Online at www.smsc.org.uk (aimed at teachers and includes guidance on all spiritual, moral, social and cultural matters, including examples of good practice)

Multiverse at www. multiverse.ac.uk (provides teacher educators and trainee teachers with a comprehensive range of resources focusing on the educational achievement of pupils from diverse backgrounds)

Respect for all: valuing diversity and challenging racism through the curriculum at www. qca.org.uk/ca/inclusion/respect_for_all/ (includes policy documents, guidance for teachers (including subject guidance) and examples of good practice)

RE-Net at www. re-net.ac.uk (a one-stop web portal for teacher educators and trainee teachers that will provide links to a number of sites that deal with SMCD matters)

15

Raising standards: the Secondary National Strategy

Alan Howe

15.1 Introduction

The Secondary National Strategy (SNS) for school improvement is part of the Government's major reform programme for transforming secondary education to enable children and young people to attend and enjoy school and achieve personal and social development and to raise educational standards in line with the *Every Child Matters* agenda (see Chapter 20). The aim is to create a dynamic and diverse education system built on high expectations and a commitment to the needs of every child, underpinned by a new teacher professionalism. The SNS is right at the centre of this drive to raise standards, and is part of a 0–19 national initiative to support and challenge the education system at all levels – national, local and individual schools and settings – in order to achieve this.

By the end of this chapter you should:

- understand the significance of the SNS as a major government initiative, and the policy context in which it sits;
- know what the SNS offers schools and individual teachers and how to access key materials, resources and support;
- have considered some of the implications for your own teaching and professional development.

The SNS grew out of the KS3 Strategy (2001–2005), which in itself was a development from the initial national drive to raise standards of literacy and numeracy in primary schools (the National Literacy Strategy [NLS] began in 1998 and the National Numeracy Strategy [NNS] in 1999). The KS3 Strategy was made up of different strands, focusing on the core subjects of English, mathematics, science and ICT, but extending to the Foundation Subjects as well through some important work on teaching and learning strategies. An additional strand of work on behaviour and attendance was introduced in 2003, designed to help schools to address barriers to learning caused by unsatisfactory behaviour, high absence and persistent truancy.

By the time of the extension into KS4, the Strategy had added another layer of development to its work, which supported schools in implementing Whole School Initiatives (WSI) designed to contribute to the improvement of standards overall. The WSI were focused on key cross-curricular policies and approaches: Assessment for Learning (AfL); ICT as a means of learning across the curriculum (ICTAC); literacy and learning (LAL); and an innovative approach to the development of thinking and learning skills called Leading in Learning (LiL). Running alongside all of these developments was some important thinking on classroom pedagogy, which we will return to later in this chapter, and support for schools in developing coaching and mentoring as ways of improving the quality of teaching and learning. A number of influential pilot programmes which develop and then disseminate cutting edge approaches – for instance on supporting improved attainment and achievement by particular ethnic minority groups – have also been running as part of the Strategy. A significant element of the Strategy, introduced in 2005/06, was the establishment of the School Improvement Partners (SIPs) programme. SIPs are individuals with recognized expertise in school leadership, often head teachers themselves, who are appointed to offer advice to schools. They provide a school head and leadership team with an additional element of challenge and support, and are part of the DfES commitment to a 'New Relationship with Schools'.

15.2 What does the Secondary National Strategy stand for?

The SNS has the following overall key strategic aim:

> *To raise standards of achievement for children and young people in all phases and settings.* Specifically this involves: improving the quality of teaching and learning in all schools; improving the effectiveness of the management and leadership of schools in order to deliver the best possible outcomes for learners.
>
> (DfES 2006a: 3)

It is worth noting that the aim goes beyond just improving teaching and learning, although it remains at the heart of what the SNS stands for. As well as improving the classroom experience of all pupils, the right kinds of leadership in schools is needed if changes in teaching are to be sustained. The following extract from an internal Strategy paper clarifies the approach taken to these two inter-related issues:

> The Strategy puts learners at its heart. Everything we do is only of value if it benefits them. They need the best teaching and learning practice available if they are to acquire the high level of skills they need in the twenty-first century. We aim to raise expectations by raising their confidence and engagement and our quality of teaching. The Strategy is about classrooms and what goes on in them. We address management, theory and materials only in so far as it supports the central business of learning.

Underpinning the Strategy are four main principles:

- **Expectations:** establishing high expectations for all pupils and setting challenging targets for them to achieve;
- **Progression:** strengthening the transition from KS2 to KS3 and ensuring progression in teaching and learning across KS3 and KS4;
- **Engagement:** promoting approaches to teaching and learning that engage and motivate pupils and demand their active participation;
- **Transformation:** strengthening teaching and learning through a programme of professional development and practical support.

These aims are part of a wider policy context. Alongside *Every Child Matters*, the White Paper *Higher Standards, Better Schools for All* (DfES 2005a) sets out a vision of further improving schools through increased personalisation of learning. In particular, the White Paper identifies some key approaches which will lead to greater personalised learning:

- exciting whole class teaching, which gets the best from every child;
- extra small group or one-to-one tuition for those who need it, not as a substitute for excellent whole class teaching, but as an integral part of the child's learning;
- innovative use of ICT, both in the classroom and linking the classroom and home.

Each of these approaches is central to the way the SNS supports schools.

15.3 Raising standards in secondary schools: the challenge

There has been an interest in 'standards' for as long as there have been public examinations, but serious policy interest can probably be traced back to the 1960s when researchers first began to make international comparisons and governments were able to ask questions about how UK pupils performed compared to their peers in other countries. In recent years you will have been aware of an annual debate as the KS test and GCSE results are announced as to whether standards are genuinely rising or not. It is always legitimate to ask questions about whether tests are easier or harder to pass than in the past, and some people would argue that even this question does not make sense since the context in which pupils live and learn changes so quickly. However, when you look at the pattern of pupil attainment over the last decade or so the evidence of a significant rise in recent years is pretty compelling, as Figures 15.1 and 15.2 show. The general trend at KS3 in all three subjects for pupils achieving level 5 or above is upwards and at GCSE a similar pattern emerges. In 1988 when GCSEs began, 29.9% achieved 5+ A–Cs. Since 1997, over 350,000 additional pupils have achieved 5+ A*–C GCSEs than would have done if the pass rate had remained the same.

However, look at the lower line in Figure 15.2 which shows the increase in the percentage of pupils achieving five good GCSEs with English and mathematics. It is improving, but at a slower rate, and the gap between the two measures is wide. It isn't a matter of whether standards are rising or not; but whether they are rising fast enough, and for all pupils. Still too many are left behind; too many from specific

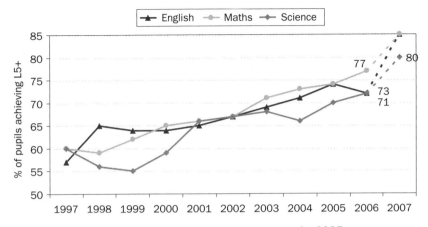

Figure 15.1 Key Stage 3 test results 1997–2006 and targets for 2007

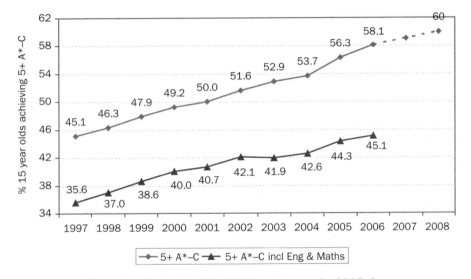

Figure 15.2 GCSE results (5+ A*–C) 1997–2006 and targets for 2007–8

groups in our society underachieve; too many fail to reach their full potential – with all of the consequent problems that this causes for both individuals and society as a whole. Good qualifications in English and mathematics for young people about to move on to post-16 study or vocational learning, and about to take their place in a knowledge-rich world, are essential.

Look also at the dotted lines on both figures. These represent the Government targets for 2007: for 85% of 14-year-olds to achieve level 5 or above in English and mathematics, and for 80% to do this in science; and for 60% to get five GCSE passes at grade C or above. These targets are indicative of the improvement challenge that the SNS has been established to support. They are also a measure of the aspiration that has been set for the nation's young people.

Task 15.1

- Find out the pattern of attainment at both KS3 and GCSE in either the subject you teach, or a core subject at your school. Compare it to the national data. You can find the latest information at the DfES Research and Statistics Gateway (http://www.dfes.gov.uk/rsgateway/DB/SFR/index.shtml).
- What is the gap, in your school, between attainment of 5 A*–C grades at GCSE in all subjects, and attainment of 5 A*–C grades at GCSE with English and mathematics included?

There is one more slice of data that it is important to know about, as it explains further why the Government is so committed to the targets for improvement mentioned above. Table 15.1 shows the percentage of pupils who, in 2005, made at least two levels of progress from level 3 to level 5 or above, and also those who moved at least one level from level 4 to level 5 or above, over the three years of KS3. The 'conversion rates' are revealing. Whilst over a third of pupils moved two levels in English and mathematics from level 3, far fewer did in science. Most only moved one level. And a significant proportion (33%) of those who start secondary school at level 4 in science – the national expectation – don't make even one level of progress. Why does this matter? There are many reasons, but one of the most compelling is the correlation between attainment at the end of KS3 and at GCSE as Table 15.2 shows. This compares subject conversions in 2005. In other words, 58% of pupils went on from level 5 in English to grade C or above, whereas only 25% did so in mathematics. Level 6 in mathematics is really essential if a pupil is to have a good chance of a grade C or higher at GCSE.

A pupil's chances of getting five GCSE grades at A*–C are below 10% if they leave KS3 at level 4 in English, mathematics and science. This increases to over 50% with level 5 in the core subjects, and to 94% with level 6.

Table 15.1 National KS2 to KS3 conversion rates 2005

English		Mathematics		Science	
KS2 L3 to KS3 L5+	KS2 L4 to KS3 L5+	KS2 L3 to KS3 L5+	KS2 L4 to KS3 L5+	KS2 L3 to KS3 L5+	KS2 L4 to KS3 L5+
37%	85%	31%	89%	10%	67%

Table 15.2 National KS3 to KS4 conversion rates 2005

English		Mathematics		Science	
KS3 L5 to GCSE C+	KS3 L6 to GCSE C+	KS3 L5 to GCSE C+	KS3 L6 to GCSE C+	KS3 L5 to GCSE C+	KS3 L6 to GCSE C+
58%	93%	25%	79%	39%	86%

Task 15.2

- Find the data for the prior attainment of pupils, especially in English and mathematics, in one of the classes you are, or will be teaching.
- Do your pupils, especially those who are working below national expectations, have specific learning targets in key aspects of literacy, numeracy and learning skills? Talk to your school-based mentor, and/or the relevant head of department about how the school sets specific *curricular targets* for individual pupils. Remember, however, that it's not *setting* a target that's important, but having strategies in place to help pupils achieve it.

It is, of course, possible to raise questions about this type of data. For instance, questions have been raised about the extent to which tests and examinations are valid and reliable (e.g. Black 1998). Broader questions about whether such forms of assessment measure educational standards in their wider sense or standards of test performance are also debated (e.g. Gipps 1994). Nevertheless, the patterns of achievement demonstrated above show how important measured achievement is at KS2 and KS3 for predicting qualifications at KS4.

The sets of data shown above also highlight why the SNS continues to be central to the Government's drive to improve further the progress of all pupils. Despite everyone's best efforts not all pupils progress or attain equally. A child receiving free school meals is currently half as likely to get five good GCSE passes as other children. A child who grows up in care is five times less likely. A child with special educational needs is nine times less likely. There are stubborn disparities among some ethnic groups (see Chapter 22). There are also problems of under-achievement by boys, whose progress often slows sharply in the early teenage years, so that boys are ten percentage points behind girls at GCSE (see Chapter 23).

The data are a spur to the system, to identify new ways to develop talent and overcome low expectations.

The SNS has been established in order to help schools to do this and to make a difference:

- to support those who start secondary education already struggling with basic literacy and numeracy;
- to maintain momentum for those at risk of slowing in the progress they make;
- to ensure that all those who are already achieving at a high level continue to be challenged.

This extract from an internal Strategy document captures this sense of high aspiration and drive to do the best for all young people:

The purpose of education is to create adults who have the capacity to fulfil their personal, social and economic potential. The emphasis is on entitlement, inclusion and holding in. We believe most pupils 'can do' even if they 'haven't yet'. We don't give up on any pupil. That's why our targets are high: they reflect our belief that most pupils have it in them to reach the standard of their peers, and that we can find ways to challenge past difficulties, underprivilege, negative experience, social factors and poor teaching in the past.

15.4 What does the SNS offer?

The SNS is not statutory. Schools are encouraged to select and prioritize from its materials, guidance and support. The 'offer' is available in a number of different ways, and is directed at different people in schools. Here are some of the key features of that 'offer':

- Head teachers and senior leaders are provided with a termly set of 'Headlines' which sets out the main priorities for the coming term and gives them instant access to the Strategy support that is available.

- Schools should have a senior colleague who takes on the role of school Strategy manager and whose main task is to know about what is on offer, and to ensure that the Strategy support is woven into the school improvement plan. The person who adopts this role will be extremely important to you as a student teacher and when you enter employment in a school. Strategy managers attend regular briefing and development meetings run by local authority Secondary Strategy managers, at which key developments are discussed, materials disseminated and good practice at school level shared.

- Subject leaders in English, mathematics, science and ICT are supported directly via national materials and termly development meetings run by local authority consultants. These are designed to support subject leaders in leading improvement in their departments and to make best use of Strategy guidance and resources.

- Strategy consultants who work for local authorities are a major ingredient in the way the Strategy works: it has invested in the establishment of a major national and local infrastructure of expert support that schools can call on. Local authorities target consultancy at those schools which have the largest number of low attaining pupils, or where there is significant underperformance.

- Classroom teachers may well be directly involved in Strategy developments through contact with a consultant; via actions being taken at department level; and/or as part of a whole school focus on, for example, assessment for learning, or a whole school approach to literacy.

- If you are a teacher of English, mathematics, science, ICT, design and technology or modern foreign languages, you are also likely to encounter the Strategy via the use of a Framework for Teaching at KS3. The emphasis of the Strategy is not on *what* is taught but rather on *how* it is taught. The frameworks identify teaching and learning objectives for Years 7 to 9, which are based on the content prescribed in the NC or agreed syllabuses. They are designed to support planning so that you can ensure you are focusing your teaching on critical steps in learning, with high expectations of pupils, and so that they make good progress.

To view and download the Framework relevant to your subject go to the DfES Standards Site (www.standards.dfes.gov.uk/keystage3/respub/).

- Another important strand of Strategy work is in providing support for pupils who have fallen behind. The Strategy has produced a suite of materials for both teachers and teaching assistants to support intervention in schools:

  - *The Intervention Toolkit* outlines all of the teaching guidance and classroom materials that is available from the Strategy for use with these pupils. You will find it very relevant, especially as it outlines approaches and materials that can be used with small groups of pupils. It is available to view/download at: www.standards.dfes.gov.uk/keystage3/respub/ws_intvstrat

  - *Progression Maps in English and mathematics* are web-based resources to help teachers identify curricular targets for their pupils and teach effectively towards them. The progression maps also help teachers make effective use of the wide range of materials that have been developed by SNS. The progression maps are available online at: www.standards.dfes.gov.uk/ progressionmaps/

Task 15.3

Discuss with your head of department, or school-based tutor, what your school provides as a programme of support for pupils who start KS3 at level 3, or who need additional support in Years 8 and 9, or who would benefit from 'intervention' support at KS4. How are they supported through additional programmes? Discuss how you can support their learning in your subject lessons. Remember that intervention support is a combination of support in mainstream classes and through additional small group help.

As has already been mentioned, the SNS has teaching and learning at its heart, and one of the most widely welcomed aspects of the Strategy has been the way that it has created a professional dialogue about lesson structures, learning design and the most effective teaching approaches in secondary schools. You will find many common messages coming through about pedagogy in the SNS materials. The following extract (DfES 2002c: 22) has been used in a number of Strategy publications for schools and gives a good overall summary:

WHAT'S DISTINCTIVE ABOUT A NATIONAL STRATEGY APPROACH IN THE CLASSROOM?

Pupils come into the classroom and there's **something to do right away**. There's a puzzle on the board, a challenge on the desk, something to think about. Right away, the teacher has the class on the ball. There's no dead time, no opportunities for bored talk or 'mucking about'. The lesson is off to a flying start.

The first ten minutes are spent on a mini-activity to catch the imagination and focus attention. This is the **starter activity**. In English, they might think of 10 alternatives to the words 'said', 'asked' or 'exclaimed' to use when they write a dialogue, or in mathematics they might work out and explain the pattern in a sequence of numbers on the board. Very often, this starter will be picked up later, in the main part of the lesson. But even ten minutes into the lesson, the pupils already feel as though they've learnt something.

The main part of the lesson will be kicked off by the teacher, who always starts by **telling the pupils what they are going to learn**. They won't just be 'getting on with the novel' or 'doing some calculations'. Pupils will be told exactly what it is they are going to learn: 'Today we're going to learn how to substitute an integer into a simple formula' or 'Today we're going to consider how the writer builds suspense'. Lessons now have focus. The learning points in lessons are borrowed from a 'Framework of Objectives' supplied by a national team of experts. If you asked a pupil coming out of a lesson what they had learnt, they could tell you.

Another feature is the **active teaching**. For example, pupils aren't expected simply to 'get on' with writing; now, the teacher will demonstrate on the board how to compose a particular type of writing, and the pupils will be drawn in to contribute. Instead of heads buried in workbooks, pupils in mathematics lessons are now looking up, being engaged and thinking. **The teacher is not afraid to be an expert.**

The main change from the pupils' point of view is that the lessons are **much more active and engaging**. Pupils are always expected to participate. They are frequently asked to stop, think, suggest and explain themselves. They might have a moment to talk to a partner and come up with a suggestion. They might have to work out a simple problem and hold up an answer on individual whiteboards.

A key feature of this approach is asking pupils to explain their thinking or working out: 'You're right. Tell the class how you worked it out.' There is an **emphasis on thinking**, demonstration and showing how good learners operate, suggesting how the same method can be used in other subjects.

The teacher moves quickly to get the pupils to **apply what they've learnt**, for example in group work or pair work. This part of the lesson may last around 15–20 minutes. In the past, teachers might have waited for pupils who get stuck to put their hands up. Now, they are more likely to sit with one group for several minutes, guiding them through the work and helping them to apply new skills.

The teacher practises **assessment for learning**, keeping an eye on individual development, so that lessons can be tailored to individual needs, and move at the optimum pace. The teacher knows pretty well what each pupil can do, and sets individual targets to maintain their focus and their motivation to move on.

If there is a teaching assistant in the classroom, she has known about the lesson in advance, and knows what her role is. She's even attended training about it. She may be sitting with a group of pupils to help them keep up with the work, or observing which of the pupils is struggling with a task, so they can be targeted in a later lesson. **The teaching assistant is well-prepared and has her own special role in the lesson.**

The teacher closes the lesson with a **plenary session** in which the teacher draws out the key points. Pupils do most of the work. They are encouraged to explain what they've learnt and how it can be used in future, perhaps in other lessons.

These 'strategy' lessons are popular because they are interesting. As a result, **behaviour is constructive** and pupils' confidence grows. Boys especially like it when the lessons are more lively, when they can talk about the ideas, and they also like knowing exactly what they are learning.

Task 15.4

Think about a lesson you have taught recently or are soon to teach. Use the account above as the basis for identifying one aspect of the lesson plan you will adapt, or change in order to improve the learning experience for the pupils. For instance, you might aim to improve the way the lesson starts; or make sure you build in time towards the end for a plenary session that ensures the pupils are clear about their learning.

For further guidance and materials on classroom pedagogy, the Strategy has produced a major self-study resource that you can use, either on your own or (better) in collaboration with other colleagues, to develop your teaching approaches.

See the webliography at the end of this chapter for details.

15.5 What is the evidence of impact?

The SNS is evaluated annually by Ofsted. Some key findings from the 2006 evaluation are:

- The implementation of the SNS was good in half the schools.
- The impact of SNS on teaching and learning was good or better in the majority of schools but was still not consistent or sufficiently focused on learning in too many schools. Often, schools had implemented the mechanics of lesson planning and structure without significant impact on pupils' learning.
- Strong school leadership, with clear direction and purpose, led to effective implementation of the SNS.
- The SNS had most impact where schools integrated it into planning for the improvement of teaching, learning and achievement and where there were consistent expectations of all teachers and subjects.
- Weaknesses in self-evaluation and the identification of areas for improvement were often associated with less effective implementation of the SNS.
- Assessment remained the weakest area of the SNS's impact. Too often, there was no central coordination of developments in assessment for learning (AfL) leading to a lack of consistency in approach but with isolated pockets of good practice.
- The quality and impact of intervention strategies varied widely between schools.
- Provision for literacy and ICT across the curriculum remained underdeveloped.

- Relatively few schools in the sample had identified behaviour and attendance as a priority but those that had done so reported good progress, especially in improving attendance in conjunction with other funded initiatives.

- Schools continued to have better arrangements for the induction of pupils and social aspects of transition into Year 7 than for progression in the curriculum and continuity in learning.

As a result of this picture, Ofsted recommends that schools should:

- ensure that the SNS is integrated carefully into plans for improving teaching, learning and achievement rather than treating it as a discrete initiative;

- ensure that the SNS is properly focused on improving learning and not just the mechanics of lessons;

- improve the consistency and effectiveness of assessment so that it has a clear impact on pupils' achievement;

- develop coherent and consistent policy and practice for literacy and ICT across the curriculum to aid pupils' learning;

- ensure that pupils are appropriately identified for intervention according to their particular needs and that programmes provide effectively for these needs.

15.6 What does this mean for me?

One way of reading this Ofsted evaluation report is that the Strategy is now at a critical phase of development. It began as an immediate response to concerns about standards in English, mathematics and science in KS3, and to ensure that the gains in attainment achieved in primary schools would transfer through to secondary education. Successive layers of development since then have led to the SNS becoming an inclusive whole-school improvement strategy, with a much greater emphasis on leadership and whole school systems that aim to enable greater consistency of practice and a better all round experience for all pupils. The list of recommendations above underlines the ongoing challenge of tackling low attainment, the underperformance of some groups of pupils and the overall quality of teaching as a whole school. Where schools have responded positively to the SNS, they have taken ownership rather than simply responding to it.

As a beginning teacher you should aim to reflect on the support that the Strategy could offer you in your subject teaching, as well as look critically at the whole Strategy and the role it plays in wider educational policy matters. Many of the Strategy materials could be of immediate value to you in your training, as well as when you start your induction year, and as a support system as you develop your professional career. Most importantly, the SNS offers all teachers a route map to CPD that you can access at different stages of your career. Research into the kinds of professional activity that are most likely to lead to sustained change and have the greatest impact on pupils' learning singles out three key features:

- Teachers engage in frequent, continuous and increasingly concrete and precise talk about teaching practice ... building a shared language adequate to the complexity of teaching.

- Teachers frequently observe each other teaching and provide each other with useful evaluations of their teaching.

- Teachers plan design, research, evaluate and prepare teaching materials together (Fullan 2001).

The SNS has been developed as one of the most ambitious reform programmes seen in education anywhere in the world. It has high aspirations, as we have seen, and is having an impact in all secondary schools, to a greater extent in some than in others. As beginning teachers, as NQTs and as experienced practitioners, you will need to make informed decisions as to how it will influence and support your own practice.

Task 15.5

Log on to the DfES Standards website, then locate the SNS website and find the relevant sections that will support you in your own teaching.

15.7 Recommendations for further reading and webliography

The current version of the Secondary Strategy website is at www.standards.dfes.gov.uk/keystage3/

DfES (2004) *Pedagogy and Practice: Teaching and Learning in Secondary Schools.* London: DfES Publications. (This consists of and includes units on: structuring learning; teaching models; lesson design for lower attainers; lesson design for inclusion, starters and plenaries; modelling; questioning; explaining; guided learning; group work; active engagement techniques; assessment for learning; developing reading; developing writing; using ICT to enhance learning; leading in learning; developing effective learners; improving the climate for learning; classroom management and a leadership guide.) (Available as separate booklets from Prolog, or to download from the DfES Standards site: www.standards.dfes.gov.uk/keystage3/respub/sec_pptl0)

Department for Education and Skills (DfES) (2004) *Teaching and Learning for New Teachers in the Secondary School* DVD ROM (DfES 0733–2004DVD). (This is an interactive version of the *Pedagogy and Practice* materials for all new teachers.)

16

Literacy across the curriculum

John Gordon

16.1 Introduction

Spend any amount of time wandering around a school, down corridors or into class-rooms, and the chances are you will encounter some physical manifestation of Literacy Across the Curriculum (LAC). You may see examples of pupils' writing in display cabinets; you may notice laminated cards of subject-specific vocabulary decorating the walls; and you may spot phrases that help pupils structure their writing arranged carefully in sequence on various whiteboards. All schools, to a greater or lesser degree, are language-rich environments, where words are put to diverse purposes, in speech, in writing, or encountered on the page or screen.

In this chapter you will:

- reflect on what is meant by both 'literacy' and 'Literacy Across the Curriculum';
- learn about the context of whole school literacy initiatives;
- be introduced to the official strategy of LAC, its purposes and content;
- consider LAC in relation to your own subject;
- learn about some current thinking concerning key approaches to reading, writing, speaking and listening that may be helpful to teaching in your subject.

16.2 What is meant by LAC?

You have just read a description of a school environment demonstrating cross-curricular literacy practices in action. What thinking lies behind these signs of LAC? Surely it can't be the case that attention to standards of reading, writing and oral communication in schools is a new idea?

Lewis and Wray (2000) assert that the present interest in the development of literacy throughout the secondary school has to be seen as part of a cycle that follows from the report *A Language for Life*, otherwise known as the Bullock Report (DfES 1975), though just prior to that books such as *Language, the Learner and the School* (Barnes et al. 1969) had considered whole school language policies. The Bullock

Report itself begins with some contextualizing historical detail, citing the Newbolt Report's findings (1921) that employers were disappointed to find young employees 'hopelessly deficient in their command of English' and that they considered the teaching of English in schools of the day to produce 'a very limited command of the English language'. Reflecting on the school's role in the same period, in the report *English for the English*, George Sampson (1921) stated 'all teachers are teachers of English because every teacher is a teacher in English. That sentence should be written in letters of gold over every school doorway.' Whole school literacy was as important then as it is today, its purposes contested and its effectiveness alternately criticized or vigorously defended just as they are now.

If pupils' aptitude and facility with language – their literacy skills – have been often debated in terms of the national economy and state of the workforce, discussion has also extended into other concerns. The 1921 quotation describing 'deficient' levels of skill could paraphrase more recent statements concerning adult literacy: 'seven million adults in England cannot locate the page reference for plumbers in the Yellow Pages' (DfES 2001b: 1). In this instance it becomes evident that literacy is not just about employability, it is about functioning in day-to-day life, and this gives rise to the concept of 'functional literacy'. Some commentators take the scope of literacy still further, to contend that literacy is about so much more than basic skills. Richard Hoggart, for example, presents a view of literacy as inseparable from social justice, democracy and true citizenship (Cox 1998). More recently, similar ideas have been espoused in discussions of 'new literacies' (Cope and Kalantzis 2003), developed in the context of globalization and the new forms of communication that arise from developing technologies.

In the light of these debates it becomes difficult to conceive of whole school literacy as anything other than a priority. There is room, though, for a number of different responses to the official strategy for 'literacy across the curriculum' and you will want to form your own views about its purpose and nature and how that relates to your role – to paraphrase Sampson – as a teacher of literacy.

The training materials devised for the Strategy provide an account of literacy as 'vital to function in a modern, communications-led society, for personal pleasure and for intellectual growth' (DfEE 2001a: 1). They describe the whole school approach as a response to functional illiteracy, the low levels of adult literacy identified in Britain relative to other countries (DfEE 1997), and to slower than expected progress of pupils in English across the secondary phase, where boys seem to fall further and further behind girls in their attainment. Asking 'what's in it for departments?' the materials: propose that literacy supports learning; make claims for its links with motivation, behaviour and esteem; present literacy as central to cognition and 'thinking skills'; and state that reading allows us to 'learn from sources beyond our experience'. Literacy, according to this view, is all-pervasive, affecting every domain of school life and pupils' experience of it. It also presents a significant challenge for teaching staff.

Have all of these points in mind as you read this chapter. Thinking about what the word 'literacy' can mean is essential to developing your ability to support pupils in the way they engage with and respond to your own subject area, and to contribute to 'literacy across the curriculum' in a manner that will be enriching both to your pupils and to your school.

Task 16.1

Before you read any further, attempt the following activities:

- Consider and write down your own definition of literacy.
- Identify three activities, common in your subject, which you believe develop pupils' literacy skills likely to be applied a) elsewhere in school and b) in contexts beyond school.

16.3 LAC – the official framework and recommended strategies

The framework of recommendations for LAC was disseminated to schools in 2001 (DfEE 2001a), through documentation covering several dimensions of literacy teaching in the secondary phase.

The different areas identified align with a view of literacy that encompasses spoken language (see sections headed 'the management of group talk' and 'listening') as well as more conventional associations with the page or screen ('writing style', 'spelling and vocabulary'). Literacy is presented as integral to teachers' assessment practice ('marking for literacy'), to inclusive education ('support for EAL learners'), and to pupils' thinking skills ('active reading strategies', 'making notes'). The overt treatment of non-fiction ('writing non-fiction', 'reading for information') and the role of the school library ('using the library') signal connections across subject special-isms, and the possibility of common approaches to texts and resources. These con-nections were more fully outlined in the collection of Literacy Progress Units (DfES 2001c) first issued in the same year. These units described precise programmes of intervention and support for pupils considered to be working below expectations of average attainment in reading and writing at KS3, providing material on phonics, writing organization, information retrieval, reading between the lines, spelling and sentences. That these were intended for teaching in small groups by specially appointed staff and not English teachers is indicative of an effort to make the organi-zation and implementation of literacy teaching a whole school issue. The content of the units itself often draws on examples across subjects, from geography to science to history. In practice, staffing for teaching these units has involved teachers from any subject area, specialists in special educational needs, and school librarians.

Organization of whole school literacy approaches – of personnel and resources – presents one of the biggest challenges to head teachers, school leadership teams and departments, hence there is specific guidance in the framework on 'whole-school implementation'. Schools were encouraged to identify a member of staff with respon-sibility (sometimes acknowledged with dedicated remuneration) for coordinating approaches to whole school literacy, usually involving an audit of literacy teaching across subjects and of the literacy needs of pupils across the school, and the identifica-tion of whole school priorities for literacy work to guide the selection and prioritizing of strategies and interventions at classroom level. Examples of such cross-curricular priorities might be, for Year 8, to 'combine clauses into complex sentences, using the comma effectively as a boundary signpost and checking for fluency', or for Year 9, to 'discuss and evaluate conflicting evidence to arrive at a considered viewpoint' (both

DfEE 2001a: Chapter 1, Handouts 1.2 and 1.3). These examples highlight the broader implications of the strategy, which required training for staff around very specific aspects of literacy education, sometimes entailing reflection on points of grammar but also likely to require consideration of the relationship between pupils' use of language and their thought processes. This illustrates the overlap between the whole school approach to literacy and another cross-curricular consideration, that of 'thinking skills' (DfES 2005b).

Since the initial impetus for LAC, its treatment in schools has had to absorb and adapt to further initiatives, such as The Learning Challenge (DfES 2003f), Assessment for Learning (DfES 2004d) and a plethora of further guidance for literacy teaching, often comprising material to support subject teaching according to the specific literacy demands of each specialism. All of these require professional training. It is likely that even if you do not experience dedicated literacy-oriented training in your early teaching career, literacy education will be an implicit part of your professional development.

16.4 Thinking about literacy in your own subject

When you begin to think about how pupils use words in your subject, think also of what they need to do in your subject that they perhaps don't do in any other area of school life. What type of writing are they asked to do? Are there specific *genres* of writing that they must write, such as reports, instructions or diaries? Are there very specific *purposes* for which they write: to explain, to persuade, to describe or to speculate? In what contexts do they usually write: with a computer, in books, on worksheets? The same principles apply to reading. What sort of texts do they commonly encounter? Are these electronic or paper-based? Do these combine words with images, with pictures, maps or diagrams? Again, the concepts of *genre* and *purpose* become relevant: it may be that pupils look at particular forms of text to find equally distinctive types of information. Speaking and listening activity is no different: do pupils talk to hypothesize, to predict or to recount? Do they need to develop skills of negotiation or collaboration? In each arena of literacy you will ask pupils to do things pertinent to your subject and perhaps *only* to your subject within the whole school setting. By recognizing your role as a teacher of literacy you are acknowledging LAC. A step further is to recognize what literacy means in your subject, to develop expertise in 'literacy for history' or 'literacy for art', for example. Perhaps we should begin to think instead of *literacies* across the curriculum, given that each area makes unique demands of pupils.

Of course literacy in your subject is not just about what you ask pupils to do. It is also about the attitudes you foster towards language use and the general atmosphere of your lessons. How do you use display space? If you display key vocabulary on classroom walls, do you ever refer to it as you teach, or ask pupils to interact with the information? How do you introduce pupils to pages in books or details in worksheets? Do they have time to scan for information? Do you give helpful directions, for example guiding the group to the third paragraph down? Do you make good use of presentational resources, of an overhead- or data-projector, to display the text that pupils maybe have in front of them on their desks? Do you take care with your own handwriting on the board or in books? How do pupils feel in your lessons about asking about spellings? How do you respond to inaccuracies of pupil spelling that occur when they attempt to use unfamiliar or ambitious vocabulary in their writing? How do you organize pupil talk? Do they share ideas prior to writing, have thinking time before putting pen to paper or finger to keyboard?

Each question here deserves careful reflection. The ways in which you respond, and what you actually do as a teacher, culminate to affect how pupils communicate with each other and with you. To some extent you determine the value they attach to words and activity with language, with a bearing too on their propensity and facility to communicate in environments not only beyond your lessons but also beyond the world of school.

16.5 Key words in your subject

A good place to begin in your consideration of subject-specific literacy is at the level of individual words. The important words, often the jargon of subjects, have come to be known as 'key words', and it is often these that you see presented around the school environment, in specially demarcated areas of a whiteboard or across classroom walls. How do pupils come to understand the concepts conveyed by the words, and how do they begin to use them in context, in their own talk and in their own writing?

In her book about the language needs of EAL learners, author Norah McWilliam (1998) details an excellent and versatile strategy that has merits across subjects and for all learners. She calls it 'rich scripting', a process which involves pupils bringing their existing knowledge of language to bear on words they encounter in subject-specific settings. Sometimes these words may be familiar to them in other contexts, but can have very precise meanings and uses within a specialism. McWilliam provides the example of 'peak' in geography, which pupils may already know through everyday idioms such as 'peak performance' or 'career peak'. Other examples might include 'scale', used differently across maths, music and art, possibly known to pupils beyond school as a concrete noun (e.g. as in bathroom scales, dragon scales), or as a verb ('to scale the rock face'). McWilliam's strategy is about making explicit the associations and resonances of any given word, so pupils can understand better its distinct meaning in the subject context, but also so that in heard speech they can distinguish it from homophones – words that sound the same – so that they fully understand its use in the immediate context (returning to an earlier example, a peak in geography is not the same as 'a peek'). Addressing such subtleties can be helpful in support of EAL learners, but also valuable in making all pupils alert and sensitive to the nuances of words, in creating language-rich classrooms.

If you use key words on displays to enrich the environment, use them to aid your teaching and to assist pupils. Quick reference to a word in print to support spoken use can be of help to pupils who benefit from visual learning strategies. The connection may help them to assimilate the spelling of the word by seeing its letters and remembering its shape. You may also wish to present different classes of word on different coloured paper, for instance yellow for nouns ('bunsen burner', 'test tube', 'tripod') and green for verbs ('react', 'liquefy', 'combust'). If pupils are to be helped to learn about these different classes, a common colour code is probably best adopted consistently across a school.

No doubt you will wish to support pupils in accurate spelling of key vocabulary. Ensure you appraise yourself of the various ways in which individuals learn spellings: some prefer to see words written down, some need them sounded out, others have to know how it feels to write the word themselves, while others remember through mnemonics or word games (e.g. to get the commonly misspelt 'necessary' right, remember 'one collar, two sleeves'). At the same time, try to understand the reasons why words are misspelt. Does the pupil make a guess based, perhaps reasonably, on how the word sounds? Has the word been confused with a commonly used homophone? Does the pupil regularly forget to double consonants where they should?

16.6 Supporting pupils with reading in your subject

It is likely that a significant amount of the information with which pupils are asked to engage in your subject is encountered through the verbal mode in print or on screen. Often written text will be combined with other visual items such as photographs, flow charts or illustrations. Even within written text, graphic elements such as typography, headings and spacing influence how the text is read and sometimes dictate how it should be approached.

If we come to such material as experts well versed in our specialisms and familiar with their text types, it can be easy to assume that pupils also know how to approach them. However, we should appreciate that pupils may not understand what we take for granted. Many textbooks, for instance, are not designed to be read from the top-left corner then across and down, line by line, every word to be taken in. Instead they often comprise columns and figures, between which the reader's gaze may move back and forth, and it may be the case that different parts of the page can be rapidly scanned while others require close reading. Such approaches to reading need to be made explicit to pupils, and ideally demonstrated (or 'modelled') so that all have equal opportunity to access curricular content. For this very reason one of the initial Literacy Progress Units focused on 'information retrieval' and contained a section on the reading skills of scanning and skimming, with geography and science textbook extracts for consideration. With this in mind, it is worth reflecting too on the demands of internet reading, where texts incorporate moving images and sound, and which are organized in complex, non-linear arrangements. Some commentators reflect on such reading in the context of 'multiliteracies' (Kress 2003) or 'new literacies' (Cope and Kalantzis 2003), stressing that it is rare for contemporary texts to isolate the verbal mode. It thus becomes important to understand how readers approach and make meaning from a non-verbal item such as a diagram, just as it is useful to consider how it is understood in relation to any accompanying verbal text. Unsworth (2001) is especially pertinent in this respect, offering detailed analyses of specialised school textbooks and identifying distinct grammars of design for each.

Having reflected on how you help pupils orient themselves to the texts relevant to your subject, it is probable that you will want them to read for specific purposes and for particular information. But how do you prevent reading becoming a relatively passive activity, where, even though eyes glance over a page, detail may not be assimilated? 'Directed Activities for Reading and Thinking' (or 'DARTs'; see Guppy and Hughes 1999) is a term used to describe strategies that marry literacy skills with thinking skills, requiring pupils to engage deliberately and often interrogatively with the texts before them, usually in pairs or groups rather than in silent, individual reading. Examples of DARTs include:

- providing pupils with a prose text that has been disrupted, perhaps with paragraphs presented out of sequence, which pupils must restore to chronological order;
- asking pupils to shape a given number of questions about a text, possibly requiring some that relate to factual or literal details within the text (reading the lines), some that respond to bias or inferred meanings (reading between the lines) and some that consider the text in context, for instance how it came to be written or how it might be used (reading beyond the lines); and
- summarizing the text in a given number of words (necessitating selection of detail), or representing it in a different form (e.g. transforming a series of instructions into a flow chart).

All require careful attention to the detail of texts, invite discussion and promote higher-order cognition (according to Bloom's Taxonomy: Bloom et al. 1956, see Chapter 5), and most approaches can be applied to a variety of texts across many subject disciplines. They are all likely to influence pupils' engagement with your subject.

Task 16.2

Identify five genres of text encountered by pupils in your subject. For each, try to articulate the reading strategies employed by readers when approaching that genre.

16.7 Supporting pupils with writing in your subject

Pupils write differently in different subjects. In some areas they are frequently asked to write quite lengthy extended prose; in some, short answers of only a couple of sentences, even one or two words, may be legitimate. Elsewhere pupils may be asked to write poems, letters, create newspaper articles, make posters. Expectations of how their work will be presented will also vary. In some instances, much of their writing will be considered 'draft', not intended for public viewing or 'best' formal presentation. At other times they may be writing for display on the classroom wall, or for sharing on a school website or in a discussion forum. Behind each purpose for writing and mode of presentation lie numerous decisions, assumptions and skills: as with reading skills these need addressing overtly with a class.

Research into the written responses of pupils in examinations (Ofsted 2003a), and more general consideration of their writing across several genres (Lewis and Wray 1998) has suggested that pupils are not always familiar with the conventions of the types of writing they are asked to do in school. Furthermore, if they have at least some success with any given genre, they often have difficulty sustaining the quality of their writing across a whole piece, with concluding sections often relatively weak. It also seems that facility with different genres can relate to gender. Generalized findings suggest that boys, through their reading, may be relatively comfortable with quite a range of non-fiction forms, and that girls tend to be more at ease with a broader repertoire of fiction and 'literary' forms.

The strategy for LAC offers a range of responses to this background. To ensure pupils are familiar with the conventions of, say, fieldwork report writing in geography or match report writing in PE, it is recommended that teachers provide pupils with 'models' for these types of writing. These are examples of successful writing in the chosen genre, which the teacher can use to illustrate important conventions essential to the text type. This might involve looking closely at the organization of the text, noting the focus of each paragraph and common phrases that contribute to the clarity of the piece, perhaps drawing attention to a sequence ('First . . .', 'Second . . .', 'In summary . . .') or to the juxtaposition of statements ('On one hand . . .', 'Conversely . . .', 'In contrast with . . .'). Each genre will have its own distinct phrases. In the jargon of LAC these are known as connectives, and are considered essential to a pupil's ability to present and develop ideas in writing, and to their likelihood of writing successfully within the conventions of the genre at hand.

Not only can teachers present 'models' so that pupils have a sense of how their finished writing might look, they are also advised to model the *process* of writing in the given genre. This can involve demonstrating the writing process via a whiteboard, overhead projector or interactive board, shaping sentences in front of pupils and articulating the decisions you make as a writer. What thinking lies behind the sentence you have just written? Why is the next sentence important in developing the idea? Why have you decided on those particular areas of focus for the six paragraphs that make up the main body of the writing?

A complementary approach to the writing process is the use of 'writing frames', formats which provide a scaffold for pupils' own attempts at writing in a given genre. Generally these identify the key organizational elements of a text, usually through boxes arranged on a worksheet, and include conventional phrases, often connectives, which act as a prompt for a pupil's writing. Such frames can provide a means of differentiating support for writing in your lessons, and can be designed to include varying degrees of detail. It is important, however, that the frames do not become inhibitive. If not carefully presented they can restrict pupils' responses as discussed in a paper by Fones (2001), which describes a process of developing writing frames to support able writers within English without limiting their thinking.

Task 16.3

Choose one genre in which pupils are likely to write in your subject. Create a writing frame to support them in recognizing the structural features and connectives relevant to the genre.

16.8 Supporting pupils' speaking and listening in your subject

Like writing, the talk-based activity you ask pupils to do can be considered along the lines of genre. In what types of talk do you ask pupils to participate? Do they give talks to an audience, perhaps with presentational devices such as posters, flipcharts or PowerPoint? Are they asked to work through formal debates, opposing teams thrashing out an issue? Do you want them to take part in role plays, for example as members of a community debating an issue at a council meeting? Do they solve problems in groups? Once more, the types of talk they engage in have specific demands, particular organizational features and distinct turns of phrase, and may also require a certain register of speech (some may necessitate Standard English, in others a colloquial idiom will be apt).

The same principles of 'modelling' apply. In the case of a formal debate, maybe pupils should see an extract of a debate in the Commons, noting conventions of address ('With respect to the Right Honourable gentleman . . .', 'Mr Speaker . . .', 'Objection!'); in the case of a presentation to other members of the class, perhaps give a short talk yourself, use examples from video, or invite another pupil (a sixth-former?) to demonstrate. If you are using a complex group work activity be sure that at the first attempt the process is highly structured and regard it as a model for future work: it will take time for pupils to understand and be comfortable with the procedure. In each case you may find it helps to give pupils prompt sheets of the key phrases that support discussion, especially in group situations. Do pupils know how to signal polite disagreement with one another or how to put an opposing view without offence or aggression? Can they build on the comments of others ('Just like Mary said, I think . . .'), or open the floor for peers ('Is there anything you'd like to add . . .')? Prompts like these can contribute to pupil talk becoming self-sustaining, with less need for teacher intervention, just as writing frames support individual responses on the page.

Bear in mind the relationship between talking in groups and thinking skills. In this respect, the work of Vygotsky (1986) is relevant (see Chapter 4). Especially important is the idea that talk acts as a means of rehearsing, clarifying and refining ideas and these processes support the assimilation of those ideas in the mind of the individual ('intramentally'), aiding understanding and recall. The way in which you organize groups will be very significant, and factors to consider include the propensity of pupils to share ideas or, conversely, to refrain from involvement; potential clashes of personality; the ability of pupils to manage and sustain their own conversation; and the knowledge and confidence of individuals in relation to the topic in hand. You are unlikely to leave the selection of groups to chance: the decisions you make cannot be separated from principles of behaviour management, differentiation or inclusive education.

Task 16.4

Identify a talk-based task in your subject that could be conducted through group work.

(contd)

a) What ground rules do you need to establish for the task?
b) List phrases that are likely to help pupils organize the discussion, for beginning their contributions and for inviting others to speak.
c) Try to identify the thinking skills developed as part of the task, with particular attention to those developed through pupils' dialogue that would be unlikely to occur in individual writing activities based on the same topic or idea.

16.9 Conclusion

Whether or not an initiative such as LAC has a profile in schools or government thinking, literacy is always an issue for a teacher, whatever their specialism. It is intimately connected with pupil engagement and enjoyment of a subject, and in turn with their self-esteem. Literacy skills are at the heart of every pupil's ability to find a way into subjects, to access curriculum content; and often too they are central to a pupil's ability to succeed in assessments, especially formal and summative assessments, in a system where responses written on paper in silent exam conditions predominate. Ultimately literacy is about communication, and because communication is about our relationship with others, it is about identity and participation. Literacy is an issue for education in the broadest sense, part of the 'hidden curriculum' as much as the overt curriculum, always there.

16.10 Recommendations for further reading and webliography

Klein, C. and Millar, R.R. (1990) *Unscrambling Spelling.* London: Hodder and Stoughton.
Lewis, M. and Wray, D. (eds) (2000) *Literacy in the Secondary School.* London: David Fulton.
McWilliam, N. (1998) *What's in a Word?* London: Trentham Books.
Sage, R. (2000) *Class Talk: Successful Learning through Effective Communication.* Stafford: Network Educational Press.
Unsworth, L. (2001) *Teaching Multiliteracies Across the Curriculum.* Maidenhead: Open University Press.

Teachers TV – literacy microsite: www.teachers.tv/literacy
Standards Site for Literacy Across the Curriculum materials: www.standards.dfes.gov.uk/keystage3/respub/lit_xc
Literacy Progress Units: www.standards.dfes.gov.uk/keystage3/respub/en_lpu_w
David Wray: www.warwick.ac.uk/staff/D.J.Wray/index.html
Thinking Skills: www.teachernet.gov.uk/teachinginengland/detail.cfm?id=524

17

Numeracy across the curriculum

Chris Bills and Liz Bills

17.1 Introduction

Numeracy, like literacy, has been identified as a basic skill for adult life, and, moreover, one which is underdeveloped in a high proportion of adults. It is tempting to think that numeracy is not as fundamental to functioning in modern society as is literacy, but in fact research carried out for the Basic Skills Agency found that people without numeracy skills suffered worse disadvantage in employment than those with poor literacy skills alone. They left school early, frequently without qualifications, and had more difficulty in getting and maintaining full-time employment (Basic Skills Agency 1997: 27). So numeracy skills are important to pupils, but surely they can be left to the mathematics department? Why should they be a concern for other teachers?

There are three main reasons why you need to be involved in developing numeracy skills even if you are not a maths teacher. The first is that numeracy is about being able to apply mathematical and arithmetical skills in real contexts. To become confident with this pupils need to see and take part in applications of mathematics outside the maths classroom. They also need to see teachers who are not maths specialists using mathematical concepts confidently within their own subject area. The second reason is that in order to develop confidence in their skills, pupils need to experience some degree of consistency in the ways in which they are expected to apply their mathematics. As you will see later in the chapter, that does not mean insisting on the same procedures for calculations, for example, but it does mean being open to pupils' own methods. Thirdly, pupils need to rehearse their numeracy skills as often and as widely as possible, and the opportunity to do so in other areas of the curriculum is important for embedding new skills.

One of the barriers to the development of numeracy is fear of mathematics in general and arithmetic in particular. This fear often arises from a perception that right or wrong answers are all that matters in numeracy, that there are set procedures that must be followed and that there is a limited time to produce the right answer. Teachers of other subjects as well as mathematics teachers, have a role to play in helping pupils to overcome these fears or, preferably, not to develop them at all. This chapter sets out to help you to be equipped to do this.

It will help you a great deal if you understand a little about the way in which mathematics is and has been taught to your pupils. In this chapter you will be introduced to the National Numeracy Strategy (NNS), followed in primary schools, and the mathematics strand of the SNS (originally the KS3 National Strategy), hereafter referred to as the Mathematics Strategy (MS). The implementation of the NNS in primary schools from September 1999 and the MS in state secondary schools from September 2001 has had a major impact on both the content and style of mathematics lessons. In particular, the way in which children now make calculations may be quite different from the way you were taught at school.

A key principle of both the NNS and MS is that pupils should use methods which they understand. The implication for teachers of other subjects is that pupils may be using a variety of methods that appear less efficient than the standard written calculation methods that may have been their own only technique. Young children are encouraged to use mental calculations whenever possible and progress to informal written methods before more efficient written algorithms (rules for calculation) are introduced. One purpose of this chapter is to introduce these different methods of calculation (mental and written) in order that teachers might support pupils in methods the pupils are confident with, rather than impose algorithms that might make little sense to pupils.

In the second part of the chapter we will consider the Numeracy Across the Curriculum initiative and its implications for KS3 teachers.

By the end of this chapter, you should:

- understand the thinking behind the NNS and how it was developed in the Mathematics Framework for KS3;
- be familiar with approaches to mental and written calculation taken in the Strategy;
- be ready to consider the numeracy opportunities and demands in your own subject area.

17.2 A brief history of the Mathematics Strategy

The New Labour Government, elected in May 1997, saw education as a priority for action. An early initiative was the implementation of a national strategy for improving standards of literacy and numeracy at KS2. The public face of this was the 'literacy hour' and 'numeracy hour' and an emphasis on 'the basics'. However, beneath this media image lay a radical change in the way teachers were required to organize their lessons. The NLS and the NNS also gave much more detailed guidance on the content of literacy and numeracy lessons than is given by the NC in English and maths.

The National Numeracy Project (NNP) had been set up in 1996 to pilot teaching and learning approaches aimed at improving children's understanding of number and number operations. Mental calculation was to be given much higher priority, with the intention that written calculation should be built on children's understanding of mental strategies. Oral work and 'whole-class interactive' activities were seen as preferable to individual work on published mathematics schemes. This project was intended to last for five years in pilot schools and, after it had been thoroughly evaluated, recommendations would be made for the teaching and learning of numeracy in all schools. In fact the NNS which built on the NNP was published as early as 1998, for implementation from September 1999. Although the main ideas behind the NNP were based on research, many claim that the design of the NNS was influenced by political imperative as well as research findings (Brown et al. 1998).

Since the NC requires the teaching of mathematics and not 'numeracy', the other strands of the mathematics NC (algebra; shape, space and measure; and handling data) were added to the NNP's draft framework for teaching numeracy. Thus the *Framework for Teaching Mathematics from Reception to Year 6* (DfEE 1999), usually referred to as the NNS Framework, was produced. After much debate, the NNS Framework said what it meant by numeracy: 'Numeracy is a proficiency which involves confidence and competence with numbers and measures . . . and an inclination and ability to solve number problems in a variety of contexts' (DfEE 1999: 4).

The development of the KS3 MS was equally rapid. Draft materials for a mathematics framework for Year 7 were piloted in some schools from September 2000 but, before extensive evaluation was conducted, the decision was taken to implement the strategy nationally from September 2001. The resulting KS3 National Strategy, *Framework for Teaching Mathematics: Years 7, 8 and 9* (DfEE 2001a) and the underlying principles of teaching and learning that it espouses, were largely untested in secondary schools. The popularity in schools of the Reception to Year 6 model on which it was based was enough to drive the KS3 initiative forward. Thorough evaluation of the effects of the NNS are only now becoming possible (Brown and Millett 2003; Earl et al. 2003; Kyriacou 2005). They point to evidence of improved attainment during the years that the NNS has been in operation, but also to different effects on different groups of pupils (middle attainers have made the most progress) and to the difficulty of attributing effects to particular causes. In other words, while we might accept that test results have improved overall, it is difficult to know whether this is due to changes in curriculum, more time spent on maths teaching and learning, different teaching methods, much more centralized testing regimes or any number of other changes.

At KS3, the word numeracy is dropped from the title of the Strategy and, according to the KS3 Framework, the definition of numeracy is extended: 'to take account of pupils' growing appreciation of mathematics and the demands of the Key Stage 3 curriculum' (DfEE 2001a: 9). As if to underline this, the training given to KS3 mathematics teachers by KS3 mathematics consultants in the first two years of the Strategy focused on algebra, geometry, handling data and problem solving. Little time was given to calculation, though there was an emphasis on 'proportional reasoning'.

A key to the popularity of the MS is that schools are not obliged to use it. The 'Introduction' to the Framework set the tone:

> The government believes mathematics teachers in KS3 will find the Framework a valuable tool for reviewing and adjusting their practice . . . However schools should make a professional judgement about this, once they have studied the Framework, reflected on their training, and reviewed their current practice.
>
> (DfEE 2001a: 2)

The KS3 Framework has been widely welcomed as a valuable resource for planning and teaching. It lists the key objectives for each year based on progression through the NC levels. Year 7 pupils are expected to work mainly at level 5, Year 8 start level 6 work and Year 9 work mainly at level 6. This may not be over-ambitious in terms of progression but teachers are expected to differentiate the objectives and some pupils are expected to be working at levels 7 and 8 in Year 9. Low achieving pupils might be working at levels below the year group norm. In addition to the key objectives, the Framework gives more detailed objectives in a yearly teaching programme.

When the first statutory NC was introduced in 1989, most mathematics teachers found it too prescriptive and the detailed list of statements of attainment with an example of questions pupils should be able to answer (nearly 300 of them) was overwhelming. The early revisions of the NC (1991, 1994, 2000) substantially reduced the number of level descriptors, leaving a framework which was not detailed enough to use as a planning tool. The KS3 Framework, which unlike the NC is not statutory, has thus been seen by some mathematics departments as helpful in providing more detailed guidance on the curriculum. It gives over 60 objectives for each year group in KS3 with a supplement of examples of what pupils should be able to do if the objectives are achieved. Other departments, of course, saw it as overly prescriptive and felt de-professionalized by the extent to which adoption of the Framework took decisions out of the hands of teachers.

In order to give guidance on how the yearly teaching programme should be organized, the Strategy provided a 'sample medium-term plan' which sets out the way in which the units of work might be scheduled through the year. Although it was designed only to give guidance, this 'sample' has been adopted by the majority of mathematics departments. Although teachers develop their unit plans in a variety of ways, the use of this schedule of units means that most schools will be doing 'Algebra 3', for instance, at approximately the same time.

17.3 Mental calculation

The NNS and MS start from the premise that an ability to calculate mentally lies at the heart of numeracy and that mental calculation should be the first resort when a calculation is encountered. Only if mental calculation, perhaps supported by jottings, is impossible should a formal written algorithm be used. When the focus of the lesson is not written calculation methods then calculators are used when mental calculation is not possible.

Task 17.1

Try this. Quickly calculate 56 plus 27.

Now reflect on how you did it. If possible ask someone else as well and compare methods. If someone else could ask you to add two 2-digit numbers, so that you do not see them written, you might find that you respond differently.

You may have just known the answer – use of 'known facts' is often an appropriate calculation strategy. If not, you may have mentally calculated, used a written algorithm or used your calculator. Which is the most appropriate?

For an addition of two 2-digit numbers, mental calculation is regarded as the appropriate method of calculation since it should be quicker than either a written algorithm or calculator. People who were taught formal written calculations when they were very young often perform this calculation in their heads by imagining the calculation as if they were doing it on paper. They see the two numbers written vertically, one beneath the other. They then add the units digits and 'carry the ten' before adding the tens digits. This is not so much a mental calculation strategy as an effective way of doing the calculation without paper that relies on an ability to apply the written algorithm.

The KS3 Framework notes that: 'Many countries, and in particular those which are more successful at teaching number, avoid the premature teaching of standard written methods in order not to jeopardise the development of mental calculation strategies' (DfEE 2001a: 11). Many children will develop their own mental calculation methods but they can also be encouraged to adopt more efficient methods. The NNS provides a booklet for guidance on mental strategies: *Teaching Mental Calculation Strategies: Guidance for Teachers at Key Stages 1 and 2* (QCA 1999a). This lists strategies and also encourages the use of a device referred to as the 'empty number line', which is a means of recording and supporting different mental methods (see Figure 17.1). Pupils are encouraged to describe their methods and these can be illustrated with the empty number line. For example, 56 add 27 can be tackled in a number of ways depending on how the numbers are 'partitioned'. The first two show 'bridging through a multiple of ten'. Here the 7 is partitioned to make a step to the next multiple of ten. The third diagram partitions into tens and units. The last diagram shows adding 30 instead of 27 then 'compensating' for having added 3 too many.

Subtraction can also be illustrated in this way.

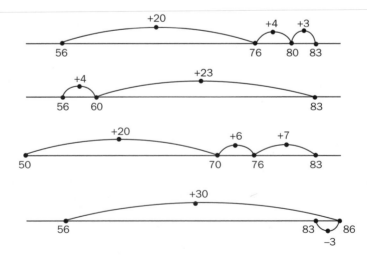

Figure 17.1 Some mental addition strategies

Task 17.2

How would you calculate 75–26? Now consider different strategies and try to illustrate them on a number line.

Some possibilities are shown in Figure 17.2. The first three do subtraction as 'take away' whilst the last finds the difference between 26 and 75 by adding-on to get from 26 to 75.

Methods of multiplication can use similar 'partitioning' and 'compensation' techniques. For instance:

$$8 \times 17 = 8 \times 20 - 8 \times 3 = 160 - 24 = 140 - 4 = 136$$

$$\text{or} = 10 \times 17 - 2 \times 17 = 170 - 34 = 166 - 30 = 136$$

$$\text{or} = 8 \times 10 + 8 \times 7 = 80 + 56 = 100 + 36 = 136$$

Division is taught as the inverse of multiplication so children learn their multiplication and division facts together. The following are related facts:

$$3 \times 4 = 12 \qquad 4 \times 3 = 12 \qquad 12 \div 3 = 4 \qquad 12 \div 4 = 3$$

If pupils know the ways in which multiplication and division are related, then they need only learn one of these facts, not all four. In a similar way, pupils can expand their 'repertoire' of calculations if they know that these give rise to other 'derived facts':

$$30 \times 4 = 120 \quad 0.4 \times 3 = 1.2 \quad 1200 \div 40 = 30 \quad \text{etc.}$$

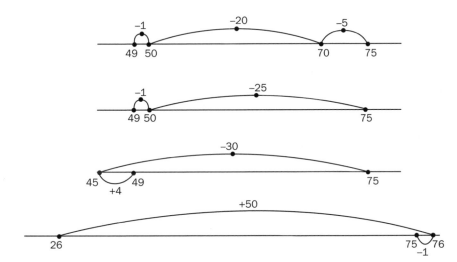

Figure 17.2 Some mental subtraction strategies

For mental division calculations where you do not know the answer as a learnt or derived fact, different techniques are needed. For example, the calculation $1000 \div 7$ may be done by 'building up' to 1000 in sevens:

$100 \times 7 = 700$

$40 \times 7 = 280$

$2 \times 7 = 14$

so $142 \times 7 = 994$

hence $1000 \div 7 = 142$ remainder 6.

Mental calculation methods are discussed and practised throughout KS1–3 with methods developed and refined often in the oral and mental starter activities in mathematics lessons. Mental mathematics is not exclusively calculation and other starter activities include mental algebra and mental visualization related to shape and space. For further information on mental mathematics see Bills (2002).

17.4 Written calculation

The NNS also provides a booklet for guidance on written calculation: *Teaching Written Calculations: Guidance for Teachers at Key Stages 1 and 2* (QCA 1999b). The standard written algorithms for calculations in columns are expected to be taught at KS2 but teachers are encouraged to refine these from expanded recording methods. It is important that the meaning of the number is retained when written algorithms are followed so, for instance, 36 is talked of as 30 and 6 not '3' and '6'. The expanded written addition and subtraction calculations are illustrated in Figures 17.3 and 17.4.

Multiplication and division methods are similarly developed through expanded versions. The 'area' or 'grid' methods for multiplication (see Figure 17.5) are used by many children at KS2 and they may feel confident to continue with this before moving to a conventional column method. Notice that in the 'area' method the numbers are partitioned into tens and units and the individual multiplications may be thought of as the areas of the partitioned rectangles (not drawn to scale).

The standard written algorithm for division is based on the mental calculation technique of 'chunking'. Division is seen as a process of repeated subtraction. So $578 \div 17$ is taken to mean, 'How many 17s can be taken from 578?' Children take as big 'chunks' of 17 as they are confident with (see Figure 17.6).

```
  3  7  6        might first be      300   70   6       or        3  7  6
  2  4  8 +      written as          200   40   8+                2  4  8 +
  6  2  4                            500  110  14                    1  4
    1  1                                                          1     1  0
                                          = 624                   5     0  0
                                                                  6     2  4
```

Figure 17.3 Progression in written addition

```
   6
3 ⁷1̄6    might first be    300  60  16   or    3  7  6
2 4 8 –   written as        200  40   8 –        2  4  8 –
1 2 8                       100  20   8               -2
                                 = 128          3  0
                                              1  0  0
                                              1  2  8
```

Figure 17.4 Progression in written subtraction

The 'area' method:

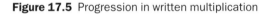

	40	6
50	2000	300
7	280	42

The 'grid' method

×	40	6
50	2000	300
7	280	42

46 × 57 = 2622

May become:

```
expanded version                      compact version
                 4  6                                  4  6
                 5  7 ×                                5  7 ×
6 × 7            4  2                   46 × 7        3  2  2
40 × 7        2  8  0                   46 × 50      2  3  0  0
6 × 50       3  0  0                                2  6  2  2
40 × 50    2  0  0  0
           2  6  2  2
```

Figure 17.5 Progression in written multiplication

```
expanded version using chunking        compact version
    5 8 7                                  3 4 r 9
 –1 7 0   10 × 17                      17 ) 5 8 7
    4 1 7                                  5 1 0
 –1 7 0   10 × 17                            7 7
    2 4 7                                    6 8
 –1 7 0   10 × 17                             9
    7 7
 –  6 8   4 × 17
      9
  so 587 ÷ 17 = 34 remainder 9
```

Figure 17.6 Progression in written division

Standard written algorithms were intended to be 'foolproof'. It was intended that they could be used by clerks who would achieve speed and accuracy through frequent repetition. This level of automaticity is no longer necessary in a calculator age. The NNS and MS recommend that children only use methods they understand. If they do not understand a compact written method they should be encouraged to use a method they can understand. The NNS suggests that children should work towards knowing and understanding a compact standard method for each numerical operation so that they are secure with these by the end of Year 6. It is important to realize that children will have different levels of confidence with these methods in KS3 so that teachers need to be prepared to work with methods that individual pupils can understand rather than a one-method-fits-all approach.

In a snapshot survey in one secondary school in Oxfordshire, conducted in April 2003, 220 Year 7 pupils were asked to perform a single calculation for each operation. The questions were:

$$376 + 248 \qquad 376 - 248 \qquad 46 \times 57 \qquad 1000 \div 7$$

In the addition question 79 per cent used the standard, vertical written algorithm. Seventy-six per cent of pupils used the standard, vertical written algorithm for subtraction. For multiplication, 31 per cent used the standard, vertical written algorithm whilst 69 per cent used a variety of less formal methods. A quarter of the pupils did not attempt the division question but of those who did 53 per cent used the standard compact division algorithm and 47 per cent used methods such as chunking. A selection of non-standard methods is illustrated in Figures 17.7 and 17.8, see pp. 227 and 228.

17.5 Numeracy across the curriculum

Cross-curricular projects are not new. Before the NC was introduced it was not uncommon for schools to have cross-curricular themes to which departments could contribute. For instance, in the 1980s one school in Berkshire gave over one week of lessons for Year 8 pupils to study Didcot Power Station. Lessons in history, geography, science, mathematics, design technology, music and English all focused on different aspects of the station, culminating in a visit. Another school chose 'Canals' as a theme and another made 'One World Week' an opportunity for pupils to engage with moral issues in a variety of lessons.

The introduction of the first NC brought a flurry of cross-curricular activity as departments struggled to cover the content in the available time. Some schools gave inter-departmental meeting time for comparison of content to check for repetition across subjects. If density was in the science curriculum, it need not be repeated in mathematics. Geography made use of scales but could leave it to mathematics teachers to teach it. Mismatches in the timing of subject content were also revealed. For instance, science teachers thought pupils needed to be able to calculate the area of a circle in Year 7 but mathematics teachers taught this in Year 9.

The KS3 Mathematics Framework encourages mathematics teachers to use examples drawn from other subject areas. The supplement of examples gives suggestions for links. For instance, work done in science lessons can provide examples of proportionality. Data collected from geography field trips or athletics performances might be analyzed in mathematics lessons.

In addition to mathematics teachers contextualizing mathematics skills in this way, the Framework suggests that mathematical skills can be consolidated and enhanced when pupils have opportunities to apply them across the curriculum. The potential for non-mathematics teachers to support pupils in their learning of

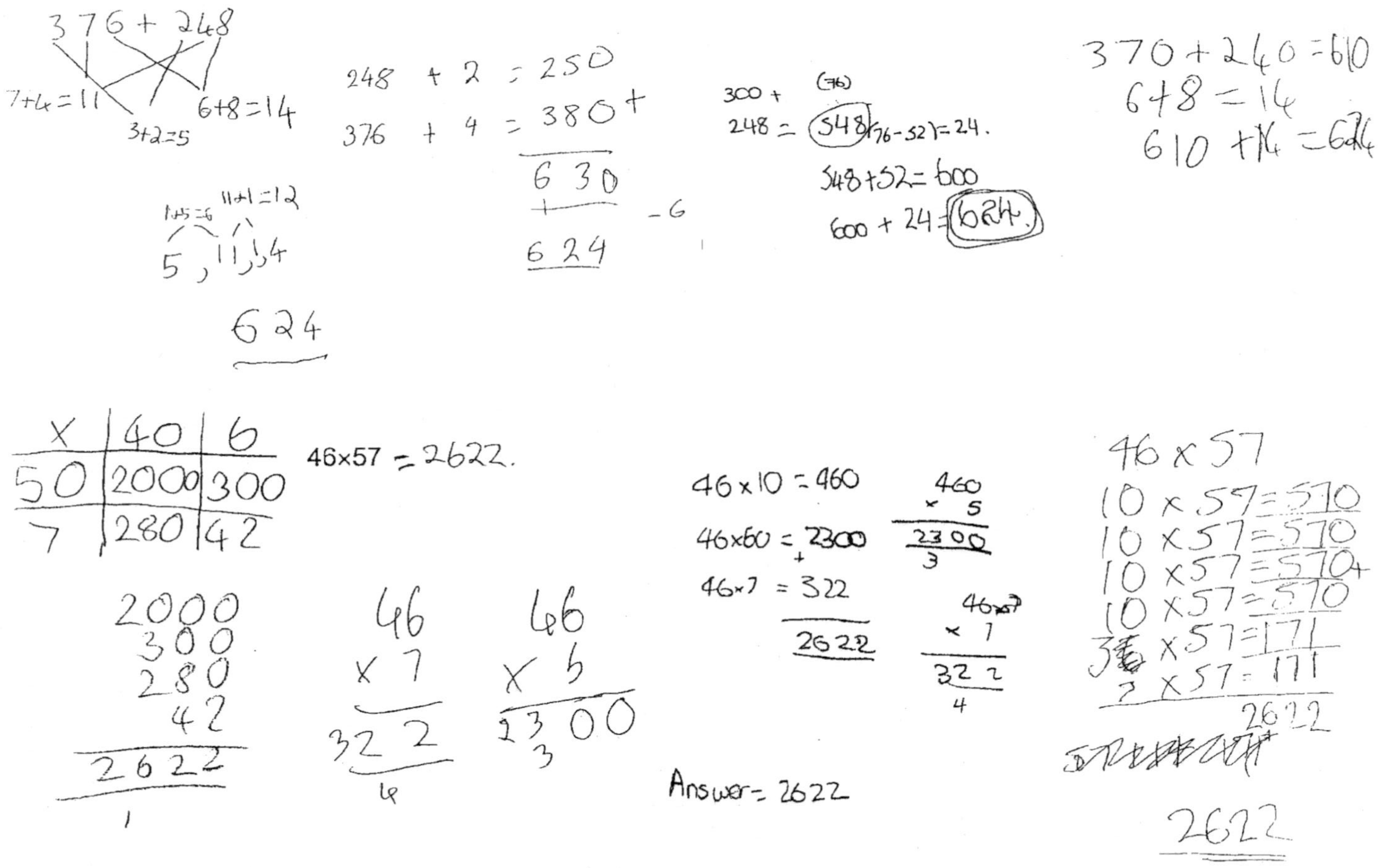

376 + 248
7 + 4 = 11
6 + 8 = 14
3 + 2 = 5

248 + 2 = 250
376 + 4 = 380 +
         630
          - 6
         624

1+5=6 11+1=12
5, 11, 14
624

376 + 240 = 610
6 + 8 = 14
610 + 14 = 624

300 +
248 → (348) 76 - 52 = 24.
348 + 52 = 600
600 + 24 = 624

46 × 57
10 × 57 = 570
10 × 57 = 570
10 × 57 = 570
10 × 57 = 570
3 × 57 = 171
3 × 57 = 171
? × 57 =
2622

$$46 \times 57 = 2622.$$

×	40	6
50	2000	300
7	280	42

2000
 300
 280
  42
2622

46
× 7
322
  4

46
× 5
1300
 3

46 × 10 = 460
46 × 60 = 2300
46 × 7 = 322

460
× 5
2300
  3

46
× 7
322
  4

2300
+
 322
2622

26 22

Answer = 2622

Figure 17.7 Informal methods for addition and multiplication

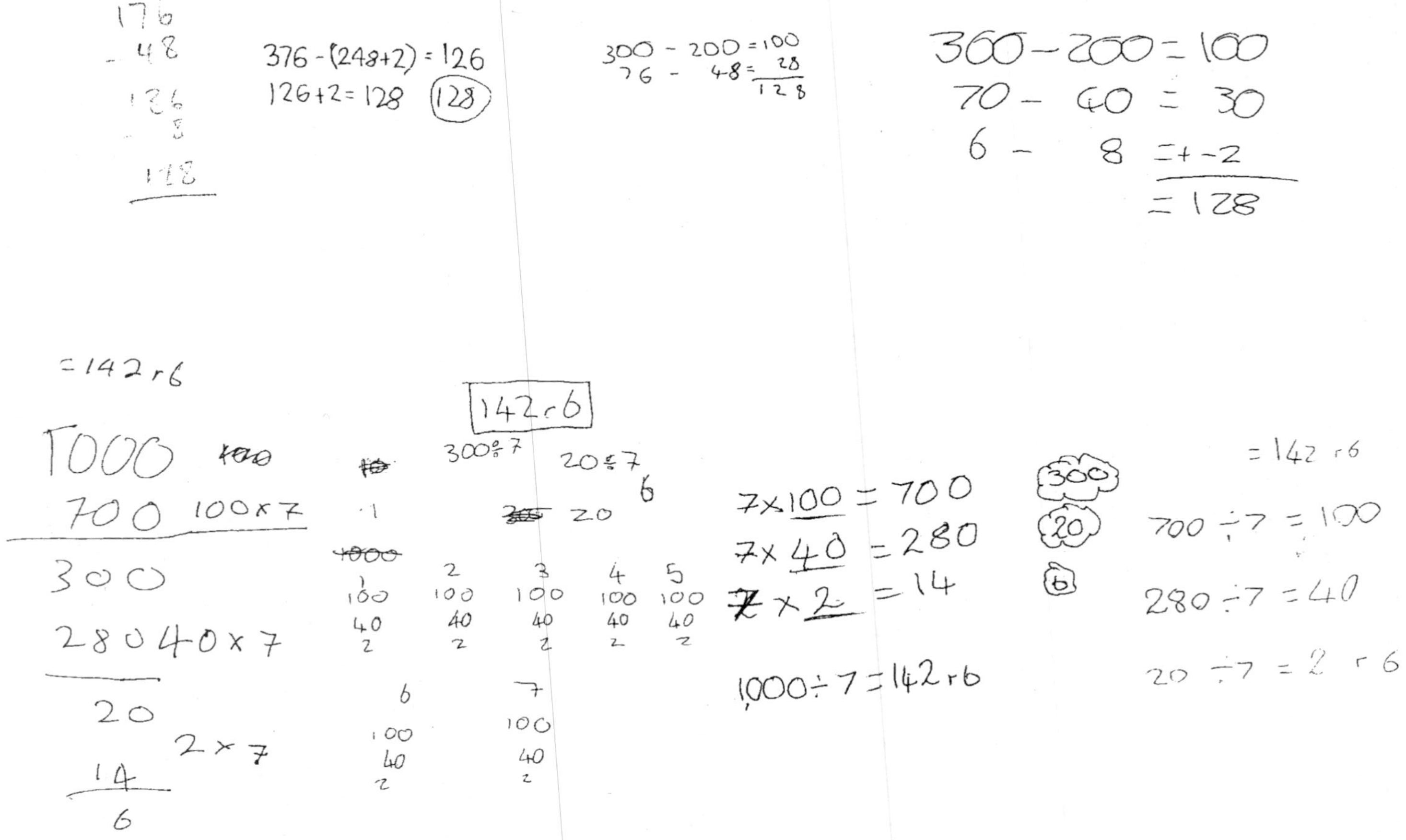

Figure 17.8 Informal methods for subtraction and division

mathematics is emphasized when the mathematics concepts inherent in many other subject areas are considered. In order to open up this issue and raise awareness, there was a need for cross-curricular training and discussion.

For the academic year 2001/2002, an extra 'closure day' was given for whole school training. Schools were asked to devote one day to Literacy Across the Curriculum (LAC) and one day to Numeracy Across the Curriculum (NAC). The implementation was patchy. Some schools gave one day to LAC in the autumn term but decided they could not spare one of the usual five closure days for NAC in the spring term. Others gave a half day to each or ran them as twilight sessions.

The NAC file of notes for school-based training, with a video and resources for training activities, was distributed to all schools (DfES 2001c). The materials were intended to be used by the head of mathematics and the senior management team to run in-school sessions, in the first instance to raise awareness of the importance of numeracy across the curriculum. This could then be followed up by more detailed work on calculation strategies for those subject teachers for whom it was appropriate. There was an underlying assumption that a numeracy working group with cross-department membership would be formed to develop cross-curricular activities. Members of the mathematics department might also work with individual departments to audit the possibilities for collaboration.

So much is history, but there is a potential benefit for pupils if all new and experienced teachers in all subjects support them to improve their numeracy. Teachers can assist this by using approaches to calculation consistent with the ethos of the NNS and MS and by highlighting the importance of numeracy in their own subjects. This will be achieved through active inter-departmental collaboration and initiatives between individuals.

You will find it useful to refer to the NC for each subject for references to mathematics.

Task 17.3

Check the NC for opportunities for numeracy in subjects other than mathematics. Check first the 'links to other subjects' which are given as margin notes in each programme of study. For instance, Citizenship KS4 2a builds on Ma4/5k. Look more carefully at the programme of study for your own subject to identify other opportunities for numeracy. For instance, the PE KS3 'Breadth of study' includes, 'create and perform dances using a range of complex movement patterns'.

You can also check the QCA 'schemes of work' for each subject which list links to mathematics and application of number (www.standards.dfes.gov.uk/schemes3/).

Here are some suggestions for numeracy activities in subjects other than mathematics given in the NAC file (DfES 2001c).

Art and design	Perspective and scale. Geometric designs.
Design and technology	Accuracy of measurement and calculation. Graphics.
Geography	Direction and position. Handling data.
History	Timelines. Graphs and charts.

ICT	Spreadsheets and databases. Modelling and simulation.
Languages	The language of reasoning and proof. Language patterns in counting numbers.
Music	Fractions for relative values of notes. Rhythm patterns.
Physical education	Patterns in movement. Performance data.
PSHE, RE, Citizenship	Risk assessment. Biased data. Financial applications.
Science	Formulae and graphs. Data logging.

17.6 Numeracy demands and opportunities

If you are to make the most of opportunities to enhance pupils' numeracy skills through the work they do in your subject, as well as using those skills to help them in their learning of the concepts that you want them to master, then you need to be aware of several things. The first is the possibilities from your own subject SoW for developing and exploiting numeracy skills. The second is what kind of numeracy skills you can expect pupils to have already which might be relevant to the work you want to do with them. The third is how relevant mathematical concepts might have been presented to pupils and understood by them.

The first of these obviously requires a more detailed understanding of the SoW within which you are operating than can be tackled in a chapter of this nature. If you are lucky, the department in which you are working will already have thought through and identified a good number of such possibilities. The second, acquiring an awareness of the kind of skills that pupils might have, is quite challenging, but there is plenty of information around that might help you. It is very common for teachers of other subjects to overestimate the numeracy skills that pupils might be expected to have, especially if they base their judgements on what seems easy or obvious to them. The best source of advice on this is the maths department in your own school. They will be able to tell you quite specifically what pupils have been taught and how it might have been presented to them, as well as common difficulties that pupils might have with these skills and methods for overcoming them.

If you cannot get this kind of help from the maths department for any reason, then the *Framework for Teaching Mathematics: Years 7, 8 and 9* (DfEE 2001a) offers quite a good alternative source of information. The most useful section from this point of view is the Supplement of Examples which, as the name suggests, gives examples of the kind of tasks that pupils should be able to do at each stage. They are organized under topic headings (e.g. graphs of functions, number operations or fractions, decimals and percentages) so that it is relatively easy to find the kind of skills you are looking for. For example, suppose that you wanted pupils to be able to construct a graph using some data relevant to the topic you are teaching. Then the examples on Processing and Representing Data would give you some idea of what pupils will have come across in maths by the end of Years 7, 8 and 9.

Task 17.4

Look at the *Framework for Teaching Mathematics Years 7, 8 and 9* supplement of examples (available in schools and at: www.standards.dfes.gov.uk/keystage3/respub/

mathsframework/). Choose an aspect of mathematics which might be encountered in your own subject and check the examples which indicate the progression for pupils in KS3.

Repeat this with the *Framework for Teaching Mathematics from Reception to Year 6* (available in schools and at www.standards.dfes.gov.uk/primaryframeworks/mathematics/). This will give you an indication of what is expected of pupils before Year 7.

The third issue, of how concepts might have been presented to or understood by pupils, is much more subtle. You will never have as much information about this as you would like. We have spent some time in this chapter looking at approaches to mental and written calculation in order to increase your familiarity with methods in these areas. But there is a lot more to numeracy than calculation. The best source of information about how pupils understand a concept is, of course, the pupils themselves. When pupils are using numeracy skills in your lesson, you can help them to gain confidence and enable yourself to understand pupils' skills by:

- discussing the mathematics with pupils;
- building on what they already know and can do;
- asking questions such as 'How did you get that answer?', 'Does it seem reasonable?', 'How do you know?';
- encouraging pupils to share ideas and discuss their thinking and strategies;
- encouraging reasoning and justification;
- not dismissing pupils' own methods of calculating or working, even if they are different from yours;
- not reducing the mathematics involved to procedures to be remembered;
- listening to pupils.

17.7 Conclusion

Numeracy is an important life skill and numeracy is more than just maths! In order to be numerate, pupils need to be able to apply their mathematical skills outside the maths classroom, and therefore the role of other subject teachers in developing pupils' numeracy is vital. It is your responsibility to:

- Think through how numeracy skills are relevant to your subject;
- Familiarize yourself with the kind of skills that pupils can be expected to have at different ages;
- Encourage pupils to make links between the mathematics they do in your lessons and the mathematics they do in maths lessons by asking them about their methods and building on what they can already do.

17.8 Recommendations for further reading and webliography

Askew, M. (2001) Policy, practices and principles in teaching numeracy: what makes a difference?, in P. Gates (ed.) *Issues in Mathematics Teaching.* London: Routledge.

Gammon, A. (2002) *Key Stage 3 Mathematics: A Guide for Teachers.* London: BEAM.

Mathematical Association (2001) *Numeracy Across the Curriculum.* Leicester: Mathematical Association.

Ollerton, M. and Watson, A. (2001) *Inclusive Mathematics 11–18.* London: Continuum.

Perks, P. and Prestage, S. (2001) *Teaching the National Numeracy Strategy at Key Stage 3.* London: David Fulton.

The following websites are useful sources of information:
www.standards.dfes.gov.uk/keystage3
www.standards.dfes.gov.uk/primary/mathematics

18

Citizenship

Alison Kitson and Terry Haydn

18.1 Introduction: What is citizenship?

Task 18.1

Before you start to read this chapter, think about what you understand by the term 'a good citizen'. Cover a sheet of A4 or A3 with as many characteristics of a 'good citizen' as you can think of.

There is no single definition of a 'good citizen', of course. Instead, there are competing definitions which can be grouped together under two broad headings. The *liberal tradition*, emerging from popular revolutions in Britain, France and America, lays particular stress on individual rights. People, according to this tradition, have certain rights and the state must respect this. Fundamentally, the right that defines a citizen is the freedom to accrue wealth. Under the Thatcher Government in the late 1980s and early 1990s, this became a fashionable definition (remember Thatcher's famous phrase, 'There is no such thing as society') although the rights of an individual were coupled with an individual's civic responsibilities and obligations, coined as 'active citizenship'. In this definition, however, the state is meaningless – the rights and responsibilities of an individual have primacy over the state. The other, classical, definition of citizenship is the *civic republican tradition*, which emphasizes duties and responsibilities. This is the tradition which characterizes New Labour's philosophical approach with an emphasis on 'civic morality'. In this definition, an individual assumes certain civic responsibilities *in partnership* with the state.

Task 18.2

*   Look again at your response to Task 18.1. Were your characteristics predominantly about individual *rights* or about an individual's *responsibilities* towards others and to public life in general? Can you begin to group them in this way?

- Now think of other ways you might be able to group or categorize the characteristics you identified. Here are some possible categories to get you started:
  - values;
  - identity;
  - participation;
  - political/economic/social/religious;
  - life skills.
- You may wish to add more characteristics as you begin to categorize them.

Having a definition of a 'good citizen' is not, however, the same as defining what exactly we mean by 'citizenship education'. Is it about educating pupils *about* citizenship (in which case, it might entail, say, teaching them about how Parliament works) or is it about educating pupils *through* citizenship (in which case, it might involve lots of community work) or is it about educating pupils *for* citizenship (so that pupils *become* good citizens)? The Final Report of the Advisory Group on Citizenship states that: 'Citizenship education must be education for citizenship. It is not an end in itself, even if it will involve learning a body of knowledge, as well as the development of skills and values' (QCA 1998: 8). It is therefore education *for* citizenship that dominates the approach of the current citizenship curriculum, though this clearly embraces education both *about* and *through* citizenship.

At a common-sense level, being a good citizen means being able to lead a happy, successful and ethically sound life in the society you will be a part of when you leave school. Although there has been a considerable amount of pressure put on schools in recent years to improve pupil attainment in school subjects, the *Every Child Matters* agenda (see Chapter 20) makes it clear that there is more to education than examination performance. Teachers must address the well-being of the child as a whole, and ensure that all pupils have the opportunity to fulfil their potential and are able to 'make a positive contribution' to society when they leave school. Being a citizen means being 'a grown-up', with the civic and social responsibilities which that entails. It means being intellectually autonomous and socially responsible, being able to interact effectively and appropriately with other adults, and act within generally accepted codes of behaviour, whilst possessing the intellectual faculties to examine those codes critically, and an understanding of how one might reasonably act to 'change things for the better'. If you have spent time inside schools, you will know that there are many pupils who will need help in 'getting there' and developing these attributes by the time that they leave school.

By the end of this chapter you will have:

- considered and reflected on different definitions of citizenship and citizenship education;
- explored reasons why citizenship education has become one of the current educational priorities;
- examined the citizenship curriculum and different models of implementing it in schools;

- reflected on the opportunities and challenges posed by the requirement to deliver citizenship education in schools;
- developed a fuller understanding of the range of ways in which you can contribute to the citizenship education of the pupils in your care.

18.2 The development of citizenship education in the UK

It is helpful to have some understanding of the ways in which citizenship education has evolved in the UK in recent years. Traditionally, citizenship education in Britain has not received a great deal of attention, at least at state level. The first official publication devoted to citizenship was published in 1949. The next did not appear for a further four decades! This latter document was entitled *Curriculum Guidance Eight: Education for Citizenship* (National Curriculum Council 1990) and offered help to schools who were required to take account of citizenship in their teaching. This was because citizenship was one of several 'cross-curricular' strands of the new NC. The thinking behind such strands was that they should somehow infuse classroom teaching. It was never entirely clear, however, exactly what the citizenship strand might entail. A survey completed in 1997 suggested that citizenship featured in many schools' curricula – or at least, they claimed it did – but that the amount and quality of citizenship education being offered was inconsistent (Kerr 1999). In the same year, the Labour Government's first education White Paper – *Excellence in Schools* (DfEE 1997a) – placed citizenship firmly on the educational agenda. David Blunkett, then Secretary of State for Education, pledged to 'strengthen education for citizenship and the teaching of democracy in schools'. It was clear from this statement that the conception of citizenship education would have a strong political slant.

The Advisory Group on Education for Citizenship and the Teaching of Democracy in Schools was formed in 1997 under the chairmanship of Sir Bernard Crick. Its final report came out the following year and the Citizenship National Curriculum Orders, published in 1999, emerged out of this. Citizenship was introduced in primary schools from September 2001 as part of the non-statutory framework alongside PSHE. A year later, in September 2002, it was introduced as a statutory foundation NC subject at KS3.

It is worth considering why, on the one hand, a formal requirement to teach citizenship took so long to establish in this country and, what, on the other, influenced its timing. Amongst the reasons for the former, a fear that schools might attempt to indoctrinate pupils can be detected from very early on and, as recently as 1996, the Education Act required LEAs, governors and head teachers to forbid 'the promotion of partisan political views in the teaching of any subject in the school'. Teachers, understandably, became nervous about tackling issues in the classroom which might lead to accusations of bias. The existence of a degree of apathy and even antipathy towards politics, especially amongst the young, also played its part. Heater (2001) has outlined further reasons, including the absence of specialist training for teachers, the limited nature of democracy in Britain and a lack of any developed consciousness of citizenship as a concept (which would be different from France, for example).

So why did citizenship emerge as a priority in the late 1990s? The underlying reason appears to be a fragmentation of social values and community identity in Britain, brought on by a period of rapid economic and social change. Numerous research studies have, according to one study, 'concluded that there is a perceptible decline in civic culture in English society, in contrast to other countries and a marked absence of a political and moral discourse in public life' (Arthur et al. 2001: 8). Although examination results have improved in recent years, there has also been an increase in youth crime and various forms of anti-social behaviour. Increasing numbers of young people appear to be unable to live up to the model of good citizenship which you constructed in Task 18.1. Margo and Dixon (2006) also point to an increasing level of apathy towards public life and the political sphere. There is a greater reluctance to vote, for example, as demonstrated by recent low turnout figures in national, local and European elections. The turnout in the 1997 general election (at 71 per cent the lowest in the post-war period) contributed to the concern emerging in the late nineties. More recent general election turnouts have been even lower (59% in 2001 and 61% in 2005). Furthermore, failure to vote is highest in the 18–24 age group. Another manifestation – though of course it is hard to isolate the cause precisely – is increased anti-social behaviour in schools, leading to an increase in exclusions (Arthur et al. 2001). Overall, therefore, it might be argued that citizenship has been introduced in order to redress the balance between an individual's self-preoccupation and their responsibilities towards society or, to put it another way, between an individual and the public sphere, whether at community (including school) or national level.

18.3 The Crick Report

The Final Report of the Advisory Group on Citizenship (commonly known as the Crick Report) was published in September 1998. In its introduction it outlined what it saw as the main aims of citizenship education. You might like to reflect on the clues this extract provides about the Group's definition of a 'good citizen'.

> We aim at no less than a change in the political culture of this country both nationally and locally: for people to think of themselves as active citizens, willing, able and equipped to have an influence in public life and with the critical capacities to weigh evidence before speaking and acting; to build on and to extend radically to young people the best in existing traditions of community involvement and public service, and to make them individually confident in finding new forms of involvement and action among themselves. There are worrying levels of apathy, ignorance and cynicism about public life. These, unless tackled at every level, could well diminish the hoped-for benefits both of constitutional reform and of the changing nature of the welfare state. To quote from a speech by the Lord Chancellor earlier this year (on which we end this report): 'We should not, must not, *dare not*, be complacent about the health and future of British democracy. Unless we become a nation of engaged citizens, our democracy is not secure.'

(QCA 1998: 7)

The report went on to identify the crucial areas which should inform the citizenship curriculum. Borrowing from T.H. Marshall's definition (Marshall 1950), which highlighted three elements of citizenship (the civil, the political and the social), the report recommended that any citizenship curriculum should be based around:

- **Community involvement**. This is fairly self-explanatory. It was argued that pupils need to understand their place as a community member as well as an individual. This brings with it certain responsibilities or duties. The community might be the school or the local area.
- **Political literacy**. This is a broader term than simply 'political knowledge', though it does imply the teaching of some factual knowledge. In addition to knowing and understanding about our political systems and other areas – such as the justice system – pupils also need to develop the skills of debating, decision making and critical thinking.
- **Social and moral responsibility**. At its most basic level, this is about the way we behave towards each other and our environment and in particular, the *values* which underpin this behaviour. This might range from the way children interact in the playground to the attitudes young adults have about the law or about sustainability.

It will be clear that the Report did not envisage a citizenship curriculum which was primarily about learning facts. Their definition was a more active one in which knowledge, understanding, skills and values all had a part to play. Figure 18.1 overleaf illustrates how the essential elements are inter-related.

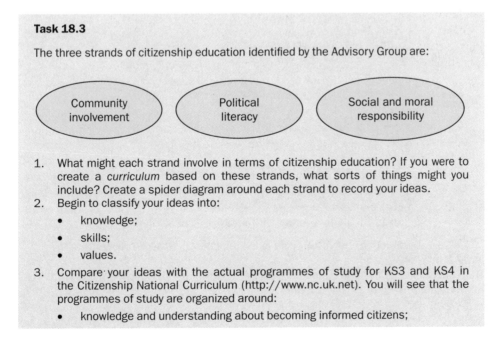

Task 18.3

The three strands of citizenship education identified by the Advisory Group are:

Community involvement   Political literacy   Social and moral responsibility

1. What might each strand involve in terms of citizenship education? If you were to create a *curriculum* based on these strands, what sorts of things might you include? Create a spider diagram around each strand to record your ideas.
2. Begin to classify your ideas into:
    - knowledge;
    - skills;
    - values.
3. Compare your ideas with the actual programmes of study for KS3 and KS4 in the Citizenship National Curriculum (http://www.nc.uk.net). You will see that the programmes of study are organized around:
    - knowledge and understanding about becoming informed citizens;

- developing skills of enquiry and communication;
- developing skills of participation and responsible action.

As you study the NC Orders, think about how the programmes of study deal with issues of:

- rights and responsibilities: *where does the balance lie?*
- identity: *how plural is it (i.e. how much account is taken of social diversity)? Is it a British/English/European/global identity?*
- values: *what values underpin the whole document? How far do notions of democracy and democratic values infuse it?*
- autonomy: *is citizenship education about producing compliant and conformist young people or critical and active citizens? To what extent can it be both?*

4. Using *only* the programmes of study for KS3 and KS4, define what a good citizen is in one paragraph. Compare this with your original definition in Task 18.1. What are the similarities and differences? Can you explain them?

This cube may help to reinforce the inter-relationship of the essential elements and to confirm the need to approach them in a developmental and sequential way through the four Key Stages. This approach underpins the learning outcomes, as set out by Key Stage, that follow.

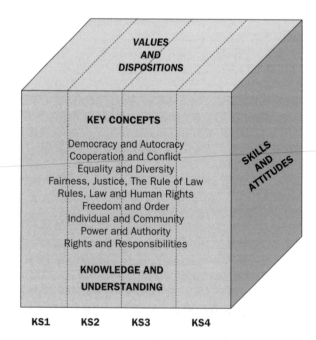

Figure 18.1 Diagrammatic representation of the relationship between elements of the citizenship curriculum
(From *Education for Citizenship and the Teaching of Democracy in Schools*: final report of the Advisory Group on Citizenship, QCA 1998)

It is important that you have a sound grasp of the three strands of citizenship outlined by the Crick Report. Not only does the Report provide a clear structure for delivering citizenship education, it provides a rationale and a mandate for teachers to work in these areas. Margo and Dixon (2006) argue that societal change in the areas of the family, religion and employment paths point to an increasing need for teachers and schools to provide guidance to young people in how to live their social and civic lives post-school.

18.4 Implementing the citizenship curriculum

You should now have a clearer sense of what the citizenship curriculum looks like, why it has been introduced and what influences have been brought to bear on it. Creating a citizenship curriculum is only half of the story, however. Implementing it in schools is a different challenge altogether. You may be teaching in schools which approach the teaching of citizenship in radically different ways, and you should be prepared to work effectively within any of the differing approaches to citizenship education. This section will examine different models of implementing the citizenship curriculum, together with some reflections on how this is working in practice.

Citizenship was introduced as part of the non-statutory PSHE framework at KS1 in September 2001. In the following year, it was introduced at KS2 (again, as part of the non-statutory PSHE framework) and at KS3, where it became a statutory part of the NC. In September 2004, it was introduced as part of the statutory KS4 curriculum. Obviously, citizenship cannot be statutory after Year 11 because not all pupils will remain at school. However, the Final Report recommended strongly that citizenship education should continue to have a presence beyond KS4.

It is expected that citizenship will take up 5 per cent of the available curriculum time at KS3 and KS4. The Final Report recommended a number of different approaches to allocating this time. Citizenship, it stated, could be delivered in blocks, modules, during tutorial time, as part of general studies, in a discrete weekly period or through existing subjects. The Teacher's Guide published by QCA (2001), alongside its Official Schemes of Work for Citizenship, also outlined a number of different approaches:

- Discrete citizenship provision taught by a specialist in separate curriculum time;
- Citizenship taught as part of a timetabled PSHE course by a specialist team;
- Citizenship taught within and through other subjects;
- Citizenship events and activities delivered off-timetable; for example, Human Rights Day, health week, school council election, mock elections;
- Citizenship as part of a pastoral or tutorial group activity in tutorial time;
- Citizenship learnt through pupils' participation in the life of the school and wider community.

Task 18.4

Take each of these modes of delivery and consider what the advantages and disadvantages of them might be.

Schools are free to decide how to implement citizenship and clearly no two schools will operate exactly the same model. Figure 18.2 summarizes the advantages and disadvantages of each approach and you may wish to compare it with your own response to the task above. Most importantly, it is not intended that schools should adopt a single mode of delivery but rather that they will *combine* a number of approaches according to their own particular needs. For example, a school may adopt a model that looks something like this at KS3:

- two blocks of PSHE lessons, totalling 14 lessons, in Years 8 and 9 devoted to specific citizenship elements;
- responsibility for delivering aspects of the citizenship curriculum located within the history, geography, RE and English departments in Years 7, 8 and 9;
- a whole-day event for each year group, for example Human Rights Day in Year 9;
- extended tutorial time every Friday in Years 8 and 9 to discuss and debate current affairs;
- increased status and influence of school council; pupils allowed to stand for election to join the school's governing body;
- community projects including fund-raising by individual tutor groups and involvement in local recycling schemes.

As you can see, this model combines several of the modes of delivery contained in Figure 18.2 opposite.

One of the biggest decisions a school must make with regard to implementing the citizenship curriculum is whether to deliver much of the content through separate citizenship lessons or through PSHE, or whether to integrate it into other subject areas. History was mentioned in the Crick Report as having particular relevance, as were geography and English, but in fact, citizenship can inform the teaching of *all* subject areas. This was recognized in the QCA Official Schemes of Work which include advice about maximizing opportunities for the delivery of citizenship in all the core and foundation subjects at KS3 (QCA 2001).

18.5 Understanding your subject's contribution to citizenship education

Much of the school curriculum is devoted to the study of particular subject disciplines. This is because it is felt that study of these disciplines offers a way for young people to make sense of, and thrive in the society they will be part of when they leave school. It is important for subject teachers to think about the full breadth of benefits which the study of their subject can bestow on the pupils they teach. In different ways, all subjects help to prepare pupils to be active, participating citizens, explore ethical and moral values, and help pupils towards a critical understanding of a part of their world. Effective teachers not only possess a sophisticated understanding of the benefits which can accrue from study of their subject, they are able to transmit an understanding of these benefits to their pupils. Several recent studies have shown however that many pupils have a very limited grasp of why they are studying

This chart is intended to help schools discuss and decide on ways of combining different modes of delivery for citizenship. *It is not intended that schools should select a single mode of delivery.*

Citizenship delivery	Advantages	Disadvantages	Implications
Discrete citizenship provision taught by a specialist in separate curriculum time	· Separate subject identity · Expert input · Aids progression · Effective monitoring and evaluation · Effective reporting to parents	· Citizenship seen as the responsibility of only one person · May discourage whole school approach · Timetable pressures · Lacks strength of team approach	· Training needed for specialists · Expertise invested in only one person · Need for senior management support · Communication · Timetabled slot
Citizenship taught as part of a timetabled PSHE course by a specialist team	· Expertise through team knowledge and experience · Team support · Specialist planning and development · Focused sessions on specific themes · Context of overall personal and social development	· Teachers may not know personal aspirations of pupils · Lessons may be seen as separate from other personal development activities · Competing timetable demands	· Timing of activities · Citizenship coordinator part of team · Time needed to do the subject justice · Range of specialist teachers needed
Citizenship taught within and through other subjects	· Context for citizenship learning within other areas of the curriculum · Integrated approach gives relevance for learning in the subject · Raises standards and enriches other subjects (see Key Stage 3 National Strategy)	· Different approach needed at Key Stage 4 · Danger of 'tokenism' · Possible lack of experience in active learning · Lack of consistency · Coordination across departments	· Training in knowledge and participatory approaches for all subject teachers · Liaison to provide informed support for subject specialists · Extra time needed to meet both citizenship and subject objectives
Citizenship events and activities delivered off-timetable, e.g. Human Rights Day, health week, school council election, mock elections	· Focus on a specific element · High status event for the school · Pupil enjoyment · May be planned and taught by experts · Attracts high-quality speakers/visitors	· Timetable disruption · Difficult to develop analytical and critical abilities · Pupils may be absent · Citizenship may be seen as a series of isolated events	· Advance planning · Cooperation of a wide staff/pupil group · Time needed to prepare and follow up · Incorporate into existing activity weeks or events
Citizenship as part of a pastoral or tutorial group activity in tutorial time	· Links to other areas of personal development · Opportunities for pupils to reflect on personal strengths and undertake target-setting · Builds relationship between tutor and pupils	· The tutor room may restrict teaching approaches · Teaching expertise likely to be limited for citizenship · Lack of time – possible dilution by other issues · Difficult to maintain consistency of teaching and learning	· Production of materials and delivery strategies · Training for NQTs · Ongoing training for tutors if they move through the Key Stage · Need to ensure consistent delivery
Citizenship learnt through pupils' participation in the life of the school and wider community	· Encourages whole school approach · Pupils learn from real-life activities · Pupils involved in decision making gives relevance to policies · Good links between school and community	· Need to cover all requirements of programme of study · Difficult to ensure progression · Time needed to set up mechanisms where they do not exist	· Time needed for pupils to reflect on participation · Community links need to be identified · Need to encourage all pupils to participate

Figure 18.2 Different modes of delivery for citizenship
(Appendix 2: combining modes of delivery from *Citizenship Scheme of Work for KS3 Teacher's Guide* QCA 2001)

particular school subjects (Adey and Biddulph 2001; NASC 2002). It can be helpful for teachers to be explicit about *why* pupils are studying their subject, as well as possessing conceptual clarity in their own minds about the full range of benefits it offers, and the ways in which it will contribute to their ability to become fulfilled and successful citizens in their lives after school.

Task 18.5

What contribution do you think your own subject area could make to citizenship educa-tion at KS3, KS4 or both? Look at the programmes of study again (www.nc.uk.net). Does your subject lend itself to the development of any aspects of the three elements? Remember, it may be the case that you are well placed to develop the *skills* of citizen-ship more than the *knowledge* and *understanding*.

    Note down some of the ways your subject area might make a relevant contribution. You may wish to compare your thoughts with the advice provided by QCA/DFES (www.standards.DfES.gov.uk/schemes3/).

18.6 Modelling citizenship in your classroom

As well as considering the contribution that your subject can make to citizenship education, you should remember that pupils will also be influenced simply by spend-ing time (in many cases, hundreds of hours) in your classroom. The classroom in itself is a community of citizens, albeit 'embryo' ones. What happens in your class-room, how things operate, how people are treated, what rules and conventions apply, will have an impact on the values, attributes and dispositions which pupils acquire, and will influence pupils' interactions with others as 'social human beings'. Even something as apparently trivial as the practice of leaving the classroom reasonably tidy for the next teaching group sends messages to pupils about respect and consider-ation for others. Cultivating and sustaining a classroom climate where aggressive and intimidating anti-social behaviour does not occur is another (and perhaps more important) aspect of modelling the sort of 'society' which pupils will learn to respect and appreciate. Research has indicated that pupils prefer teachers who are able to create a relaxed and cooperative working atmosphere in the classroom, and who are able to prevent some pupils interfering with the learning of others, in a calm, reason-able and understated way, rather than by stridency and threats – a democratic but ordered classroom as opposed to an autocratic or anarchic one (see, for example, Rogers 1998; NASC 2002).

    One of the most graphic descriptions of the qualities which pupils should acquire in order to prepare them for citizenship and adult life can be found in the section of the NC which defines its values, aims and purposes (DfEE/QCA 1999: 10–13). This can be a comparatively neglected component of the NC amongst trainee teachers, and yet it provides clear guidance, and a powerful mandate, for how teachers might run their classrooms in order to help develop 'the good citizen'.

    Task 18.6 asks you to consider the extent to which your classroom provides opportunities for pupils to develop some of the qualities and attributes described in this section of the NC which will prepare them for adult life and make them 'good citizens'.

Task 18.6

In your classroom, to what extent do pupils get the opportunity to develop the following qualities and attributes? (These are some, but not all, of the opportunities mentioned).

- to learn and work independently and collaboratively;
- to think creatively and critically;
- to solve problems and make a difference for the better;
- to become enterprising and capable of leadership;
- to develop integrity and autonomy;
- to challenge discrimination and stereotyping;
- to make informed judgements and independent decisions;
- to understand their rights and responsibilities;
- to form and maintain worthwhile and satisfying relationships based on respect for themselves and others;
- to develop the ability to relate to others and work for the common good.

Education is not a value free zone. This section of the NC also states that education should 'reaffirm our commitment to the virtues of truth, justice, honesty, trust and a sense of duty' (DfEE/QCA 1999: 10). All the qualities and attributes described above can either flourish or wither in secondary classrooms, and the individual classroom teacher is one of the key factors in determining the extent to which these attributes and values will be developed.

18.7 Citizenship and school ethos

Citizenship education is not just about delivering the curriculum, however. In principle, at least, it should also have an impact on the whole *ethos* of a school. This was highlighted in the Crick Report:

> There is increasing recognition that the ethos, organisation, structures and daily practices of schools, including whole-school activities and assemblies have a significant impact on the effectiveness of citizenship education. Through such climate and practices schools provide implicit and explicit messages which can have a considerable influence, both positive and negative, on pupils' learning and development. Schools need to consider how far their ethos, organisation and daily practices are consistent with this aim and purpose of citizenship education and affirm and extend the development of pupils into active citizens. In particular, schools should make every effort to engage pupils in discussion and consultation about all aspects of school life on which pupils might reasonably be expected to have a view, and wherever possible to give pupils responsibility and experience in helping to run parts of the school. This might include school facilities, organisation, rules, relationships and matters relating to teaching and learning. Such engagement can be through both formal structures such as school and class councils and informal channels in pupils' daily encounters with aspects

of school life. To create a feeling that it is 'our school' can increase pupil motivation to learn in all subjects.

(QCA 1998: 36)

Some people argue that schools as institutions are antithetical to true citizenship. This is because they tend to be largely non-participatory in terms of structures and rules and are characterized by pupils being told what to do rather than being invited to debate and negotiate. There are signs, however, that this is starting to change. School councils are now well-established in most schools. In some schools they are to a degree cosmetic, and exert little influence on the running of the school; in others, they have a significant role in interviews for staff, on decisions relating to uniform and rewards and sanctions, and on a range of issues which make a difference to how the school is run.

18.8 Teaching approaches to citizenship education

We have already explored how citizenship can be modelled through day-to-day teaching and also how it can be integrated into your own subject teaching. But there may also be times when you teach citizenship more explicitly. Teaching elements of citizenship well – and in particular, controversial issues – requires particular approaches. The Programme of Study for citizenship states that: 'Teaching should ensure that knowledge and understanding about becoming informed citizens are acquired and applied when developing skills of enquiry and communication and participation and responsible action.' An essentially didactic, one-way style of teaching is clearly not appropriate here. Instead, a more active, participatory style which invites pupils to take responsibility for their own learning, to discuss and debate and to reach informed, independent judgements is encouraged. For many teachers, this is a style with which they are already familiar and, indeed, it may already characterize their typical teaching strategies. For others, however, it represents a departure from the norm and from strategies with which they feel comfortable. Certainly, the teaching of controversial and sensitive issues is an area with which many feel uncomfortable. How can they avoid accusations of bias? How can they avoid conflict breaking out in the classroom? How can issues be handled sensitively enough by both teachers and pupils? Teachers trained in the humanities are probably the most at ease with such topics, but there are certain questions that are very helpful prompts in exploring such issues. For instance, the following questions, taken from QCA guidance, encourage pupils to think around citizenship issues:

- What are the rights and responsibilities in this situation? How might they conflict?
- Do you think that situation (or rule, behaviour, etc.) is fair? Why, or why not?
- How could it be made more fair?
- How does this relate to your experience?
- What are the issues here (including the rights and wrongs of the situation)?
- Which moral or legal rules are relevant here?
- What do you think would be the best (or fair) outcome for all concerned?
- Who do you empathize with (or feel sorry for)? How do you think they feel?

- What might be the consequences of that (for individuals or the group)?
- What should happen to the people who did that and why?
- What would happen if everyone behaved like that?
- What could you say to X to persuade them differently?
- Who had power and/or authority? How did they use it? Fairly? Wisely?
- Who should make that decision? An individual? The whole group?
- How far should these people be treated as equal or different and on what grounds?
- What personal qualities are needed for this role or task?
- What beliefs or ideas are commonly held about this type of situation?
- What kind of society do you want to live in?

Task 18.7

Imagine you have been asked to teach your tutor group about *either* fertility treatment for women who have passed the menopause *or* about the wearing of religious symbols like the cross or the veil. Which of these questions might help you to tease out the key ideas?

18.9 Assessing citizenship

The assessment procedure for existing NC subjects, using an eight-level scale, was deemed inappropriate for citizenship. Instead, there are end-of-Key-Stage descriptions for KS3 and KS4. These descriptions summarize what pupils will know/be able to do. Teachers are required to decide whether a pupil is achieving the expectation, working towards it or exceeding it. Ofsted reports suggest that the assessment of pupils' progress in citizenship is still one of the weaker elements of citizenship teaching, with many teachers having 'only a very tentative understanding of standards and progression in citizenship' (Ofsted 2006a: 39). However, both Ofsted and the Citizenship Foundation (citizenshipfoundation.org.uk) have suggested ways of assessing pupils' progress effectively, derived from visits to schools where they have encountered 'good practice' in citizenship assessment. The QCA site, *Assessing Citizenship*, provides guidance on assessment and examples of pupils' work (www.qca.org.uk/14653.html).

One of the underpinning principles behind more successful approaches to assessment is the acknowledgement that it should be broad and balanced, across the three main strands of citizenship, avoiding a narrow focus on what pupils know and understand, and taking account of the active and 'social' nature of the aims of the citizenship curriculum:

> The assessment of skills and application and participation are continuous and formative, often based on teachers' observation of process, as well as discussion with individuals and groups of pupils about success criteria and how far these

have been met. But there is also sufficient emphasis on knowledge and under-standing through assignments, the assessment of formal presentations, written tests and examinations and other evaluations.

(Ofsted 2006a: 40)

In some schools, teachers have successfully used group, peer and self-assessment, with an emphasis on process as much as outcome. Assessment needs to take account of the full breadth of the citizenship curriculum, and encompass pupils' knowledge and understanding, skills and dispositions and willingness to participate and 'make a positive contribution'. It is important to note that some schools were criticized for setting *too little* written work in citizenship – as with other subjects, there is a body of knowledge that pupils need to acquire, and written work is one way of testing for knowledge and understanding in this area.

The following list gives examples of aspects of pupils' performance where judgements might be made on pupil progress:

- How good is their substantive knowledge of the factual content of the course? (knowledge and understanding)

- How sophisticated is their understanding of key concepts and issues? (knowledge and understanding)

- How good are they at expressing and justifying a personal opinion, orally and in writing? (skills)

- How appropriately do they respond to the opinions of others? (social interaction/dispositions)

- To what extent do they contribute appropriately to whole class and small group discussions? (participation)

- To what extent do they demonstrate an interest in social, moral and political issues? (dispositions/commitment)

- How well do they work cooperatively with others? (skills/dispositions)

- To what extent do they get involved in school or community affairs? (participation)

It should be added that the extent to which pupils involve themselves in school activities or groups outside school is to some extent a personal issue, and needs to be handled sensitively. There are pupils who are not 'joiner-inners' but who have an intelligent personal interest in and understanding of citizenship issues, and who are developing as mature and responsible citizens.

Pupils can also take citizenship as an examination subject. At KS4, there are a number of short course GCSEs available in Citizenship Studies which deliver the KS4 citizenship curriculum and recognize the work completed by pupils by awarding a grade. Schools are not obliged to follow this route but it is interesting to note that there has been a rapid increase in the number of pupils taking GCSE short course citizenship, up from 38,000 in 2005, to 53,607 in 2006 (Ofsted 2006a).

18.10 Evaluation: challenges and opportunities

What can we learn from the first years of compulsory citizenship education in the UK? Ofsted reports emphasize that citizenship education places particular demands on teachers, especially if they are not subject specialists, 'many working far from their comfort zone both in subject knowledge and teaching approaches' (Ofsted 2006a: 1).

Commitment

Ofsted report wide variations in the quality of citizenship education, with some schools providing inspirational and high quality experiences for pupils, but over a quarter of provision being deemed 'inadequate'. Much of the variation is attributed to differing levels of commitment which schools, departments and teachers bring to citizenship education. Ofsted talk of some teachers being almost in denial about citizenship education, hoping that 'it will go away', (Ofsted 2006a: 1), and 'reluctance, resistance, scepticism' (Ofsted 2005b: 6). Recent reports express the view that citizenship education is most effective when it has a discrete and definite place on the curriculum, rather than a 'we do it already' (in a vague, general and unspecified sort of way) approach.

The importance of active learning and pupil talk

Citizenship is in some ways distinct from other subjects in its overall objectives, with greater emphasis on process issues. This requires teachers to develop skills in facilitating high quality pupil talk, discussion and argument. Discussion needs to be 'well planned and sequenced, with due attention to inclusion, and with pupils required to justify opinions, sustain their argument and make informed judgements on the issues being discussed. Additionally, there should be opportunities for reflection on their conclusions or the reasons for differences of opinion to reinforce learning and achievement' (Ofsted 2005b: 5).

The importance of initiative with resources

Another criticism of citizenship provision in some schools was poor preparation, and the lack of high quality resources which would have an impact on pupil engagement in the subject. There can sometimes be a temptation for teachers teaching 'out of field' to spend less time preparing lessons rather than more, or to be over-reliant on resources provided by others, without reading through materials carefully, and refining and adapting them so that they are used effectively. Given the development of citizenship resources which are freely available in the internet over the past few years, there is no excuse for overdependence on low grade worksheets and tatty, dull handouts. As long as pupils are not left to browse purposelessly on the internet, ICT can be a way of building up what Walsh (2003) terms 'powerful learning packages'. The internet can be useful in finding 'impact' resources, which can be vividly imprinted on pupils' memories long after the lesson has ended. (See the webliography for some examples of citizenship portals.)

Making citizenship relevant to the lives of young people

Ofsted (2005b: 4) reports that 'achievement is high where pupils understand the relevance of what they are studying'. Citizenship lends itself to use of modern media, news, newspapers and the internet. Many schools adopt a flexible approach to the topics which will be dealt with in order to maximize topicality and relevance, by incorporating 'stories of the day', and emphasis on 'the issues of the day and how we read them'. It can also be helpful to be explicit about the relevance of such issues to the lives pupils will lead when they leave school.

The challenges and opportunities for citizenship education are therefore manifold. It is clear from surveys conducted with pupils (e.g. Kerr et al. 2003; Kerr 2005) that their political and civic knowledge is extremely variable and is strongly linked with parental educational background. Pupils also appear to place significantly greater trust in their families and friends than they do in politicians and government-related institutions and, whilst most say they intend to vote in national and local elections, very few express a desire to join a political party or become involved in local politics. If one of the key (though not uncontested) aims of citizenship education in this country is to encourage greater participation in public life, then these findings suggest that there is a long way to go. Nevertheless, the very fact that citizenship education now has a statutory presence in the secondary school curriculum is a far cry from the rather more token gestures of previous years. Taking it further – ensuring that all pupils have access to high quality citizenship education – will depend on the commitment and enthusiasm of well informed and inspirational teachers who believe that citizenship education is an important entitlement for all young people.

18.11 What citizenship education means for you

It is very likely that at some point, you will be involved in citizenship education in some form or another. Whilst there are now a small number of teachers who are trained specifically to teach citizenship, its delivery in schools is likely to affect all teachers, whether in their capacity as form tutors, subject teachers or simply as members of the school community. The *Every Child Matters* agenda (see Chapter 20), and the values, aims and purposes of the NC (DfEE/QCA 1999) make it clear that all teachers have a part to play in education for democratic citizenship. If – as recommended by the Advisory Group – the implementation of citizenship education involves a re-examination of a school's ethos, organization and structures, then at the very least, you will be part of this. It is easy, perhaps, to dismiss citizenship education as yet another initiative on top of many others: something else to reference in a SoW so you can tick a box. But think again about the reasons you want to become a teacher. For most, the answer lies in making some kind of a difference. As a subject teacher, that difference mainly lies at an individual level – helping pupils achieve their best. As a teacher of citizenship, the difference can be about individuals *and* society as a whole. The Crick Report acknowledges that teachers are only one influence on young people: 'we must not ask too little of teachers, but equally we must not ask too much'. But schools – and the teachers in them – are one of the best places to start.

18.12 Recommendations for further reading and webliography

Huddlestone, T. and Kerr, D. (2006) *Making Sense of Citizenship: A Continuing Professional Development Handbook*. London: Hodder Murray.

QCA (1998) *Education for Citizenship and the Teaching of Democracy in Schools: Final Report of the Advisory Group on Citizenship*. London: QCA.

QCA/DfES (2001) *Citizenship: A Scheme of Work for Key Stage 3*. London: QCA.

Ofsted (2006) *Towards Consensus? Citizenship in Secondary Schools*. London: Ofsted.

Citizenship Foundation website: www.citizenshipfoundation.org.uk

National Curriculum Online: www.nc.uk.net

Nuffield Education for Citizenship: www.citizenship.org.uk

QCA schemes of work: www.standards.dfes.gov.uk/schemes3/

19

14–19 curriculum reform

Ian Abbott and Prue Huddleston

19.1 Introduction

Since the early 1980s there have been several attempts to reform and re-structure the 14–19 curriculum in England in an effort to address some long-standing and inter-related problems. First, the 14–19 curriculum was dominated by a narrow range of academic qualifications which were perceived to be insufficiently applied or practical. Furthermore, pupils were encouraged to specialise in a small number of subjects, often in related areas, at an early stage in their education. Vocational awards, on the other hand, were held in low esteem. This problem was compounded by the fact that vocational qualifications were developed on an ad hoc basis by different awarding bodies leading to a proliferation of awards and no coherent framework to show how these different awards might relate to one another or to academic qualifications. Academic and vocational pathways remained separate, making it difficult for learners to combine elements from each or to change pathways. Perhaps the most serious consequence of these failings was that too many young people left education or training prematurely because available provision failed to meet their needs and aspirations.

Over the years, different reform initiatives have attempted to:

- achieve parity of esteem between academic and vocational qualifications;
- develop a flexible system which allows pupils to combine vocational and academic elements or switch pathways;
- develop a framework which incorporates the three pathways – general (academic), vocationally-related and occupational – and shows how they relate to one another;
- treat 14–19 as a unified phase rather than two separate phases thereby opening up opportunities for pupils to progress at variable rates or to skip certain qualifications altogether;
- encourage more young people to stay in education and training for longer.

By the end of this chapter you should have developed:

- an understanding of the policy debate taking place within 14–19 education;
- an understanding of the proposed 14–19 curriculum reforms;
- an awareness of the range of new 14–19 qualifications;
- an awareness of the new organizational structures being developed for 14–19 education.

The current Government has been committed to significant reform of the education system with the initial focus being on the primary sector and, more recently, on KS3. However, 14–19 education has now become more of a policy focus and the pace of change has accelerated. A number of key policy initiatives illustrate the major changes that have taken place. For instance, Curriculum 2000 (QCA 1999c) introduced the first major reform of A level since its inception in 1951 in an attempt to broaden the post-16 curriculum and raise the status of equivalent vocational programmes. This has had a significant impact on post-16 teaching and learning strategies in all subject areas with, for example, revised subject content and much greater use of coursework. In September 2002, a range of applied GCSE courses was introduced in eight curriculum areas. Work-related learning has grown in importance and, in recent years, a large number of pupils in Years 10 and 11 have had aspects of the NC disapplied to allow them to spend part of their week studying vocational programmes at local FE colleges. Partly as a consequence of this type of development, different partnerships and collaborations have been developed between schools, colleges and other agencies. Many schools, especially in urban areas, have developed close links with FE colleges to broaden the curriculum available to their pupils across the full range of 14–19 provision. Funding arrangements for post-16 education have also changed with the transfer of responsibility from the LA to the Learning and Skills Council (LSC).

There is a growing acceptance that the school system should move away from a focus on the age 16, with the completion of GCSEs, as a cut-off point. Instead, 14–19 provision should become more flexible and responsive to individual pupil needs with increased emphasis on personalised learning. A number of alternative, but equal, pathways could then be developed. Diversity of provision is a key feature of Government policy as schools specialise in certain areas, for example business and enterprise, sport, languages and technology. Greater diversity could lead to increased use of individualized learning programmes. Pupils would study a variety of programmes in different institutions with different learning outcomes. Whatever the future may bring, there is no doubt that the pattern of provision for 14–19 education has altered significantly since 2000, and further change is certain.

As a consequence of this debate and the various policy initiatives implemented by the Government, there is an opportunity for significant reform of 14–19 education. All the major components of the system are likely to undergo further scrutiny and review, even A level which was previously viewed as an educational 'gold standard' with which successive governments were reluctant to tamper. Radical changes to the organization of schooling, patterns of provision, teaching, learning and assessment strategies are almost certain to happen during the early part of your career. As you enter the teaching profession, you need to keep abreast of the broader policy debate taking place within 14–19 education and how this is affecting your subject.

Task 19.1

What are the strengths and weaknesses of the existing 14–19 curriculum?
    For your subject area, list the changes you would like to see introduced to the 14–19 curriculum.

19.2 14–19: the current policy agenda

The Government has professed a desire to design a 14–19 curriculum and qualifications system which meets the aspirations of all and encourages as many young people as possible to participate in education and training post-16. In comparison with our major competitors, the post-16 staying on rates have continued to lag behind, with substantial regional variations, from 55% in some areas to over 75% in others. The target for post-16 participation in education and training has been set at 90%, a target comparable with the participation rate in the best performing countries, whilst the target for participation in higher education has been set at 50 per cent (currently about 42% participate in higher education). This implies that the staying on rate post-16 will have to increase significantly if the higher education participation figure is to be achieved. There are similarly ambitious targets for apprenticeships. The Leitch Report (2006) has recommended a target of 500,000 a year by 2020. Taken together, these targets for post-16 participation, in whatever form, place a significant demand upon the system at KS4 to provide a curriculum which is challenging and engaging, which allows breadth and flexibility of opportunity sufficient to encourage young people to commit themselves to continued learning.

The Government has set out an agenda to achieve this vision (DfES 2003b), undertaken a review of the post-16 qualifications system (DfES 2004b) and published its policy and an implementation plan (DfES 2005c) to roll-out its curriculum and qualification reforms for 14–19 education and training. The key drivers for reform continue to be the need to build a system which meets the needs of a diverse range of learners, which permits a wide choice of courses and qualifications and which allows for flexibility across and between learning pathways, for example, schools, colleges and workplaces. Central to the vision is the desire to ensure that programmes of learning lead to clear destinations for learners, rather than the current 'snakes and ladders' arrangement whereby learners are often prevented from pursuing different pathways once they have embarked on a particular route.

At the same time the Government is committed to ensure that the 'basics' are in place for all young people. Although school standards have improved since the mid-1990s, more than one in six young people leave school without being able to read and write, and add up properly (Leitch 2006). Thus, a target of level 2 achievement in functional skills (English, mathematics and ICT) has been set as part of any learning pathway. For example, no young person will be able to achieve a GCSE grade C in these subjects unless the functional skills have been achieved. Similarly, functional skills are incorporated within the proposed Specialised Diploma design (see below) and within apprenticeships frameworks. In addition to the renewed emphasis placed on the achievement of basic skills, as part of the reform programme, the so-called 'soft skills', much lauded by employers, have been re-packaged as personal, learning and thinking skills. These include skills aimed at developing 'independent enquirers', 'creative thinkers', 'reflective learners', 'team workers', 'self managers' and 'effective participators'.

Although Curriculum 2000 was intended to broaden the range of academic and vocational qualifications which could be accessed by young people post-16, in reality this has not happened to any significant extent. Young people have tended to take additional qualifications within the same subject group and to continue to pursue a vocational or academic pathway, rather than a mixed diet.

The current renewed emphasis on work-related learning at KS4 was further strengthened by recommendations set out in the Davies Review (Davies 2002) that all young people should have an entitlement to the equivalent of five days' enterprise education at this Key Stage. To this end, every secondary school, including special schools, received funding for three years from September 2005 to provide enterprise education to every pupil at KS4. Set alongside this development is the expectation that employers will be willing and able to engage more extensively with the education system. Such engagement might include the provision of more extended work experience placements, acting as pupil mentors, even involvement in curriculum design and qualifications, as in the case of the GCSEs in vocational subjects and the Specialised Diplomas. Whether business has the capacity to deliver on such a wide agenda remains to be seen.

These proposed changes are supported by a statutory framework for careers education 11–19, through Connexions, as well as the provision of citizenship education. Underpinning the whole area of 14–19 reform is the recognition that any change needs to build on secure foundations at KS3. The current reform of 14–19 education and training is intended to bring about long-term change throughout the whole system rather than attempt to tackle reforms in a piecemeal fashion. The key features of the reforms include:

- 'getting the basics right': ensuring that all young people reach a functional skills threshold and develop the personal, learning and thinking skills necessary for employment and for participation in the wider society;
- developing an increasingly personalised approach to learning by creating flexibility in the ways and contexts in which young people learn and the pace at which they learn;
- qualification and curriculum reform, particularly within the structure and content of full-time vocational programmes, in order to motivate young people, meet the needs of employers, and to encourage greater post-16 participation;
- strengthening and developing greater coherence across different learning programmes and facilitating progression across and between pathways;
- the creation of manageable assessment arrangements that are appropriate to different course types and teaching and learning styles;
- the development of a framework of qualifications, which sufficiently 'stretches' and challenges and that enables all learners to reach their full potential and encourages continued participation in education and training;

- creating an infrastructure of providers (schools, colleges, training providers and work-based provision) to deliver the new curriculum and qualifications;
- tackling disengagement.

The development of a 14–19 continuum of learning, rather than a system punctuated by a clear end-point at 16, as in the present arrangements, opens up the possibility for increased flexibility in the place, pace and progression of learning. It has been argued that 16 is an arbitrary end-point for many young people. For instance, it might be appropriate for some pupils to skip GCSEs in certain subjects and progress immediately to AS level. Alternatively, significant numbers might benefit from rather more extended programmes which allow them to reach the 'Holy Grail' of five A★–C GCSE grades, or their equivalent, in three rather than two years (Huddleston 2002). Many of these pupils choose to continue their studies in FE colleges, often as a result of poor prior learning experiences. The courses that they select are often vocational in orientation.

19.3 The qualifications framework

During recent years, QCA has developed a National Qualifications Framework (NQF) which has attempted to locate qualifications within a common framework with an indication of equivalences across three pathways: occupational, vocationally-related and general (academic). All accredited qualifications are awarded an NQF level. If a qualification shares the same level as another qualification, for example NVQ2 and GCSE A★ –C, it means that the demands on learners are roughly equivalent although the content and duration of the two qualifications may differ. There has been an attempt to bring the majority of qualifications within the National Qualifications Framework, although a significant number, particularly vocational qualifications, still remain outside it. Figure 19.1 illustrates the way in which the current structure is classified. You should note that at 14–19 the main focus is upon qualifications at entry to level III. Qualifications at Level IV and above are broadly comparable to those within the Framework for Higher Education (FHEQ), including Higher National Diplomas, undergraduate and postgraduate degrees and professional qualifications.

You will probably recognize immediately that attempts to corral all qualifications within a rigid framework and to assign equivalences across different pathways is something of a cosmetic exercise. These qualifications are so different in their content, structure and purposes that it is like trying to compare chalk and cheese. Nevertheless, this reform sought at least to ensure that, although qualifications may differ, there would be opportunities to move across and between them.

The current reform of 14–19 provision is considering ways in which vocational pathways and qualifications might be streamlined. Also under trial, at the time of writing, is a Qualifications and Credit Framework (QCF) which allows credits to be built up in small steps, according to the needs of learners. A unit is the smallest element of learning for which credit can be awarded and credits for individual units can be accumulated to provide full qualifications. The trialling of these proposals will be completed by July 2008. It will also consider whether other learning experiences,

Level	Occupational	Vocationally-related	General
IV–VIII	NVQ IV–V	Undergraduate degrees, Higher National Diplomas, postgraduate and professional qualifications	
III	NVQ III	BTEC National Diploma; Specialised Diploma Level III (from 2008)	A levels, International Baccalaureate
II	NVQ II	OCR National Certificate; Specialised Diploma, Level II (from 2008)	GCSEs Grades A*–C
I	NVQ I	BTEC Introductory; Specialised Diploma Level I (from 2008)	GCSEs Grades D–G
Entry		3 2 1	

Figure 19.1 The National Qualifications Framework

for example part-time employment or voluntary activities, might be accredited. In order to support young people who would experience financial difficulty if they remained in full-time education beyond 16, Educational Maintenance Allowances (EMAs) have been made available to those whose parental income falls below a specified level. Nevertheless, many young people in full-time education post-16 experience financial hardship and depend upon income from a steady stream of part-time jobs. The retail, hospitality and catering sectors are highly dependent upon student labour to sustain their operations. The reform is exploring ways in which this type of informal learning might be recognized within the proposed new structures. Whether or not young people would wish to have this type of experience recorded is another matter. The development of young people's employability skills has become a higher priority for the DfES both as part of the social inclusion agenda for getting young people into training and employment and as part of the drive to high skills and economic competitiveness (DfES 2001a, 2002a; Leitch 2006).

Proponents of such a Framework argue that there will be benefits for learners, learning providers and employers in these arrangements in that they will provide, amongst other things, flexibility, choice, opportunities to vary the pace of learning, and to build increasingly personalised programmes of study to meet individual learner and employer needs. Clearly, the infrastructure required to support the implementation of such a complex system, which will include unique learner numbers and electronic learner achievement records, will be significant, not to mention the professional development needs of those who are to deliver such programmes. For further information, and to keep abreast of developments concerning the 'tests' and 'trials', visit (www.qca.org.uk).

19.4 GCSEs in vocational subjects

A significant development which has impacted on the 14–16 curriculum is the introduction, since September 2002, of a new range of GCSE programmes, now referred to as GCSEs in vocational subjects. Eight such awards are available at the time of writing. They are double awards that are equivalent to two 'standard' GCSEs and have been designed to replace the previous GNVQ Part One qualifications. They are currently available in the following areas:

- applied art and design;
- applied business;
- engineering;
- health and social care;
- applied ICT;
- leisure and tourism;
- manufacturing;
- applied science.

The implementation of the GCSEs in vocational subjects illustrates some of the wider issues and the practicalities of reform of the 14–19 sector, in particular the involvement of other organizations. The delivery of these courses allows pupils to spend part of their time in different learning environments, for example, within an FE college or workplace. Successful implementation often requires partnerships between schools, colleges and employers. In some cases, such partnerships are between schools and local training centres or LA centres. These partnerships aim to support the applied GCSE qualifications, provide opportunities for courses that combine applied GCSE qualifications and other vocational awards, for example NVQ, and enable the formation of training and work experience placements linked to qualifications. According to the QCA schools are employing a number of different models for the delivery of GCSEs in vocational subjects:

- in school with support from business and industry partners;
- in school with support from a partner college;
- shared delivery with a partner college;
- specific topics or units delivered by a college or other provider;
- wholly delivered by a college of further education;
- using e-learning packages;
- or combinations of the above.

Schools are developing a range of strategies to allow pupils access to college provision and off-site visits to industry. These include:

- timetabling vocational subjects in half-day blocks;
- liasing with colleges to agree a common day, or half-day, for vocational subjects on the timetable;
- timetabling double or long lessons in vocational subjects;

- placing GCSEs in vocational subjects in an option box with other subjects that need or prefer longer lessons;

- timetabling GCSEs in vocational subjects against option blocks and core subjects. (QCA 2006 www.qca.org.uk/14–19/6th-form-schools/68_264htm)

For more information, consult the following website: www.qca.org.uk/qualifications.

These qualifications are designed to provide a vocational context for the study of a subject as well as much of its content. Links with business are expected and project work has to draw upon real and relevant business scenarios. It is also anticipated that pupils should be able to use extended work experience placements to gain an in-depth understanding of the vocational context in a practical way. The engineering sector, for example, sees this as a potential means of attracting young people into the sector and has been encouraged by positive take-up of the qualification. Again, the notion of a 14–19 learning continuum is helpful. Young people embarking on a GCSE in vocational subjects should be able to continue on that vocational pathway post-16, either through one of the new Specialised Diplomas (see below), an Applied GCE in a related area, or through an apprenticeship, or on to other forms of occupational training, or by pursuing the A level route.

As we mentioned in 19.1, some colleges already had good links with local schools and similar programmes had existed previously. In such cases, the school has been able to build on existing practice with FE staff already experienced in delivering to a younger clientele. However, for others it is a new and challenging experience.

CASE STUDY 19.1

Sunnymead College is a medium-sized general FE college situated in a market town serving a dispersed rural area. The town is a focus for tourism and there are many leisure and tourism facilities in the area; the College has therefore become a centre for hospitality, catering, leisure and tourism and business. It became involved in the delivery of GCSE and is part of a partnership involving five nearby schools. The College had been involved in school link programmes in a variety of areas; this has been instrumental in developing its rationale for school link work. A college lecturer is responsible for coordinating the programme in college and liaising with schools.

Pupils attend College one day a week and are working towards a food hygiene qualification in addition to GCSE leisure and tourism. They gain experience of working in the College, serving real customers and working in a service environ-ment. Pupils work to industry standards and there are high expectations in terms of dress, attendance, punctuality, working practice, time management and professionalism. The lecturer in charge of the programme reports that:

'At first they [the schools], when we started working with them, used to send us anybody they could, people they did not want in the classroom. It was a nightmare. The behaviour was dreadful, we simply cannot have that sort of thing in a working environment, there's too many opportunities for

> flashpoints, when they are working with members of the general public. Now it is much better. We interview students before they come, we pick the ones we really want and who have an interest in the area. We liaise very closely with schools and we involve the parents. Most of these young people want to carry on to a level II qualification and attend College full-time after they have finished at school.'
>
> In what ways can pupils, schools and FE colleges benefit from this type of programme? Are there any problems associated with this type of development?

You may wish to reflect upon these developing relationships between schools and colleges. To some extent, schools and colleges have always been in competition for post-16 pupils. Now, they are being encouraged to work together in a spirit of cooperation and in the interests of providing a more flexible and 'fit for purpose' curriculum, not just for post-16 pupils but for 14–16-year-olds as well. However, unless funding mechanisms are compatible with such flexibility of provision, and unless young people have a clear view of the possible transition opportunities at 14, the idea of a 14–19 continuum of learning will fail to materialize.

Perhaps for this reason attention is being given to the whole range of qualifications on offer post-16, including National Certificates and Diplomas and other types of awards. There are currently over 3000 certificates at levels I, II and III, which cover 700 qualifications; many of them lead to a dead end with no further opportunities for progression. The QCA is charged with rationalizing the range of qualifications on offer, ensuring that they are fit for purpose and that they meet the needs of students, employers, FE and higher education. Part of this rationalization has been the trialing of a QCF as discussed in 19.3 above. It has to ensure that assessment is carried out rigorously and fairly and that assessment processes are transparent; above all, that confidence in the examinations system is restored following the A level debacle in the summer of 2002, the first occasion on which the revised qualification was awarded. The move to the new A Level led to a questioning of standards, tarnishing the reputation of an award that had hitherto been regarded as an academic 'gold standard': 'it is vital that all the changes are communicated effectively and speedily to all relevant groups; if nothing else, this inquiry has revealed the need for far better communication of changes to our qualification system' (Tomlinson 2002: 2).

19.5 Specialized Diplomas

A central feature of the 14–19 reforms is the proposed introduction of a new suite of Specialised Diplomas covering 14 lines of learning, corresponding to the main economic sectors, the first five of which will be available for teaching from September 2008. Specialised Diplomas are intended to provide opportunities for applied learning which are clearly related to a vocational area and which reflect the demands and standards of the sector which they represent. The design and content of the Diplomas have been developed by Diploma Development Partnerships (DDPs), led by Sector

Skills Councils (SSCs), and have involved employers, learning providers, awarding bodies and higher education.

The Diplomas will be available at levels I, II and III across the 14–19 age range. They will be composite qualifications including, at all levels and across all lines of learning, the following key components:

- principal learning (this is sector related and gives the Diploma its title, for example, Specialised Diploma in Engineering);
- additional/specialist learning (as approved by the DDP; this may be complementary to the principal learning, for example additional mathematics within an engineering diploma, or additional free choice units);
- generic learning (including functional skills and personal, learning and thinking skills);
- an extended project;
- integrated work experience.

The proposed model is represented in Figure 19.2.

The timetable for the introduction of the Diplomas will be phased as in Table 19.1. Successful delivery of the new Specialised Diplomas will be dependent upon partnerships between schools, colleges, training providers and employers; some of which was presaged in the arrangements in the existing links that have been developed between schools and colleges. In order to meet the entitlement for all 14–19-year-olds to be able to access all 14 Diploma lines at all three levels by 2013, it is clear that

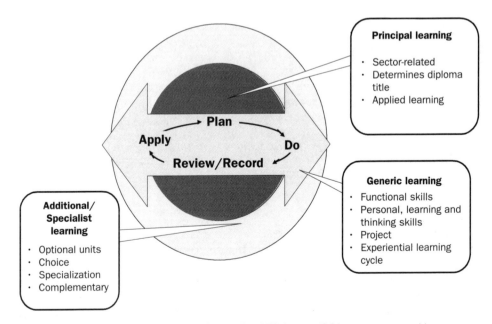

Figure 19.2 The proposed model for Specialised Diplomas (QCA www.qca.org.uk)

Table 19.1 Timetable for the introduction of Specialised Diplomas

Phase	Diploma area	Availability
Phase 1	ICT Health and Social Care Creative and Media Construction and the built environment Engineering	September 2008
Phase 2	Land-based and environmental studies Manufacturing Hair and beauty Business administration and finance Hospitality and catering	September 2009
Phase 3	Public services Sport and leisure Retail Travel and tourism	September 2010

(Source: QCA www.qca.org.uk)

much will need to be achieved in terms of building the appropriate infrastructure, resources, facilities and professional expertise to deliver such an ambitious programme.

Task 19.2

The key messages outlined in the DfES (2005c) *14–19 Education and Skills White Paper* are designed to:

- place a greater focus on the basics;
- offer learners a better curriculum choice;
- provide learners with more challenging options and activities;
- provide new ways to tackle disengagement.

How far do you feel that some of these reforms have already been set in train by the changes outlined above? What are the barriers to the full implementation of such reforms? What are the drivers for reform?

19.6 Conclusion

As you begin to teach, you can be certain that the profession you enter will change rapidly as your career unfolds. It seems that this is even more likely to be the case for those of you who spend most of your time teaching the 14–19 curriculum. The Tomlinson Report (DfES 2004b) suggested that the timescale for change should be ten years.

The drivers for reform are multiple, inter-related and complex. They reflect wider changes at a societal and, increasingly, global level. The reforms are being driven by the twin agendas of high standards and inclusion. These include the economic imperative to develop a highly qualified, skilled and flexible workforce to maintain the country's competitiveness in increasingly global markets and the need to ensure that opportunities are available for all irrespective of the route they choose to follow. Earlier attempts to reform 14–19 education have resulted in a range of schemes and interventions, the majority of which failed to fulfil their early promise and did not achieve the hoped for parity of esteem between different pathways.

A key obstacle has been a market, funding and qualification-led reform process. Another has been a sectoral approach which has separated off various forms of provision, some of them overlapping, including school, FE, higher education and work-based learning. However, the current reforms include a renewed emphasis on collaboration and cooperation between institutions, providers, government agencies and employers. The vision is one of facilitating learning through a seamless web of academic, vocational and work experiences that challenges old sectoral divisions, including the academic/vocational divide. This shift, backed by different partnerships and collaborations between schools, colleges, training providers, higher education and employers, supported by greater cooperation between the DfES, LSC, QCA, Connexions (formerly the Careers Service), LAs and other agencies, promises to deliver a policy coalition to meet local and regional needs. The extent to which it offers a genuine ladder of opportunity to every young person, rather than a series of hurdles to weed people out of education and training, remains to be seen.

19.7 Recommendations for further reading and webliography

Department for Education and Skills (DfES) (2003) *14–19 Opportunity and Excellence*. London: DfES.
Department for Education and Skills (DfES) (2003) *Working Group on 14–19 Reform. Principles for Reform of 14–19 Learning Programmes and Qualifications*. London: DfES.
Department for Education and Skills (DfES) (2004) *Curriculum and Qualifications Reform: Interim Report of the Working Group on 14–19 Reform*. London: DfES.
Department for Education and Skills (DfES) (2005) *14–19 Education and Skills*. London: DfES.
Leitch, A. (2006) *Prosperity for All in the Global Economy – World Class Skills*, Final Report. London: HM Treasury.

www.dfes.gov.uk/14–19
www.qca.org.uk/ages14–19
www.vocationallearning.org.uk

SECTION 4

Making schooling work for all:
Every Child Matters and the
inclusion agenda

20

Does every child matter? Education, social care and the new agenda for children's services

Chris Husbands

20.1 Introduction: the Laming report and *Every Child Matters*

Victoria Climbié was 8 years old when she died. She had been sent by her parents, in west Africa, to be looked after by her great aunt, who lived in the London Borough of Haringey. In 2001, after months of physical and mental abuse, Victoria was murdered by her great aunt and her great aunt's lover. The government established an inquiry into the circumstances of Victoria's death under the chairmanship of Lord Laming, a former chief inspector of social services. Laming's report, published in January 2003, was devastating; he concluded that at every stage child protection arrangements had failed Victoria. Professionals were not sufficiently informed about what was happening to her; those who had information had not shared what they knew; when they shared information, they did not realize its significance. In one dreadful conclusion, he observed: 'sadly, many of those from social services who gave evidence seemed to spend a lot of time and energy devising ways of limiting access to services, and adopting mechanisms designed to reduce service demand' (DOH 2003: para 1.52). His report called for a fundamental reconfiguration of care for children, integrating child protection with health, education and children's services more generally. The government response was swift. On 28 January, 2003, the Health Secretary, Alan Milburn, outlined legislative plans for the biggest reform of child welfare services in England for 30 years, including the establishment of Children's Trusts in all 150 local authorities. Children's Trusts would aim to improve services for children through coordinated management of education, health and social services, establishing greater strategic coherence, better integration of services and improved access to services. Less than six months later, the Government went further, appointing, for the first time, a Minister for Children with overall responsibility for children's welfare and well-being. Nationally, the administration of children's services was brought under the control of a single ministry – the Department for Education and Skills – and in Autumn 2003 the DfES published a wide-ranging green paper under the title *Every Child Matters*.

Every Child Matters outlined an ambitious vision for the reform of children's services: 'The vision we have is a shared one. Every child having an opportunity to fulfil their potential. And no child slipping through the net' (DfES 2003e: 5). Central to the reform agenda are aspirations that child policy should be framed around all children, so that no child is missed, and that children's well-being should be at the core of the planning, commissioning and delivery of services. *Every Child Matters* set in place two underlying concepts to deliver the Government's vision. First, children's services should be reconfigured around the *needs of the child*, rather than around the way teachers, or social workers, paediatricians or health visitors worked and were trained. Second, these reconfigured children's services should be organized to deliver *five outcomes* for children. These five outcomes – equally weighted in *Every Child Matters*, and covering children's education, health and well-being – should form shared objectives for all children's professionals. The resulting programme has been described as the most ambitious cross-government agenda of change for children anywhere in the world, and it is rapidly re-shaping the professional world of schools and teachers (House of Commons Education and Skills Committee 2005).

It was clear from the moment of its publication that *Every Child Matters* commanded widespread professional support and commitment. The inspirational vision at its core – a re-configuration of children's services around children's needs and the construction of arrangements which allowed all children to thrive – spoke powerfully to the motivation of all those who worked with children. What was also clear was the sheer scale of the reform programme needed to address children's needs. Children's services – schools, hospitals, community paediatrics, social services – provide for the needs of 11 million children in England. Of these 11 million, one and a half million live in poverty. Each week, some 400,000 encounter social services, including children experiencing acute stress, disabled children, children and adolescents with mental health needs, children whose parents are ill or disabled, children whose parents regularly abuse drugs, young people who offend or are at risk of offending, children who are at risk of abuse or neglect and children and young people who the local authority looks after. These 400,000 children are the equivalent of one child in every classroom. Fifty-nine thousand children, or about four in every school, are 'looked after' by the local authority. At any one time, 32,000 children are on the child protection register – again, that means about two children in every school (DfES 2003e: 15). Meeting the needs of all children involves the management of a large and complex workforce including teachers, special needs coordinators, social workers, nurses, health visitors, doctors, psychologists, police officers and family support workers, each group with a different professional culture, training, accountability framework and preoccupations. The challenge is enormous.

By the end of this chapter, you should:

- have a general understanding of the principles and content of *Every Child Matters*;
- have considered the implications of *Every Child Matters* for schools and teachers.

20.2 *Every Child Matters*: the five outcomes

Every Child Matters sought to provide a unifying vision for children's services by setting out five outcomes which should underpin the work of all those working with children. The five outcomes, based on work with children undertaken for the Government by the National Children's Bureau, were deliberately aspirational. They are that all children, whatever their background, origin, dispositions, attributes or difficulties should:

- enjoy and achieve;
- achieve economic well-being;
- stay safe;
- be healthy;
- make a positive contribution.

Children's professionals were to put the five outcomes at the core of their planning and thinking. Local authorities were given statutory responsibilities in the Children Act of 2004 to cooperate with other professionals to achieve the five outcomes. In some ways curiously, the statutory duty to cooperate was not placed on schools despite their centrality to the *Every Child Matters* agenda.

Along with the five outcomes, *Every Child Matters* outlined a series of principles which were to underpin the development of children's services, and began to construct a new architecture for the delivery of the outcomes. The first principle was that there should be a long-term shift from *intervention* in children's lives after difficulties had been encountered to *prevention* of difficulties at an earlier stage. It was argued that early preventative work – either early in children's lives or at the early stages of difficulty – would prevent later difficulties and – in the long-term – lower the overall cost of intervention spending. This principle involved a series of complex administrative issues. LAs would need to articulate with some precision the relationship between universal services for all children, such as mainstream schooling, vaccination programmes, routine health monitoring, and targeted services for some children, such as special schools, additional in- or out-of-school provision and adolescent mental health services. They would need to identify how and by whom these services were to be provided and ensure seamless provision. They would need to develop effective information and assessment frameworks which meant that children at risk or in need were identified early and effectively. The second principle was that there should be a movement away from structures in which separate services met individual needs towards a *coherent framework which would meet the holistic needs of children*: children should be treated as individuals, and their needs assessed and met as a whole by teams or groups of professionals working together. The third principle was that children and young people themselves should play an *active part* in the identification of their needs and in the design, delivery and evaluation of services which were established to meet them. Services for children – including those provided by schools – should not be 'done to' children but designed, wherever possible, in consultation with them. A fourth, and final, principle was that of *information sharing*. Laming had argued that many of the warning signs which should have triggered interventions in Victoria Climbié's case were missed because although different professional groups often completed reports assiduously, the information was not routinely shared on a systematic basis. In the post-*Every Child Matters* world, professionals working with children would need to develop common approaches to assessment and protocols for information storage and sharing which achieved two ends: first, children and their parents should not be required to repeat information they had already provided to other professionals and second, professionals would need to ensure that case records provided the range of information needed to ensure that needs were identified and strategies for prevention and intervention devised.

20.3 Developing the children's workforce

Taking these principles together, it is easy to see just how huge a challenge *Every Child Matters* poses for children's professionals. Its bold vision of coherent children's services arrangements integrating the work of teachers, social workers and health professionals around a common framework for assessment and action, involving children actively at all stages in their interaction with professionals is compelling, but the challenge should not be underestimated. We have already seen that the sheer numbers of children involved are enormous – nearly half a million in contact with social services in any one week. To add to this complexity, many children present profound and complex needs, for instance, the multiply disabled adolescent on the autistic spectrum; the speech and hearing impaired girl suffering emotional neglect; the sibling children of a drug-abusing mother who has been arrested on serious charges; the teenager with severe mental health difficulties from an earlier history of abuse. Added to this the children's workforce is itself huge and diverse: in addition to the 440,000 teachers and 250,000 teaching assistants, there are 83,000 early years workers, 30,000 play workers, 40,000 social workers working with children and families, about 10,000 workers in Youth Offending Teams, 6,000 speech and language therapists, 2500 school nurses, some 50,000 other health professionals including health visitors, paediatricians and community nurses (DfES 2003e: 84).

Every Child Matters seeks to bring coherence to this diverse workforce. None-the-less, there are demanding challenges. Particular difficulties relate to a common assessment and information framework. The detailed information needed by, say, a community paediatrician to diagnose difficulties and support a case for action, is different from the detailed information needed by a school SENCo, and different again from the information needed by a family support worker. A common assessment framework which tries to meet the needs of all groups might not, in the end, meet the needs of any one of them. There are particular difficulties – often powerfully articulated by parents – about confidentiality and access to such information: although most professionals will subscribe to the idea that information sharing is essential, in practice there might be strong arguments why some information should remain confidential to the family and the professional group meeting the child's needs. As a result, there are difficult decisions to be made about what is recorded, by whom and for what purpose, and complex decisions about where information should be stored and accessed, and who has 'lead' professional responsibility for maintaining the information base.

20.4 *Every Child Matters* and the work of schools

It may be tempting to see *Every Child Matters* as being largely about 'complex needs', about special needs or special schools. It may be tempting to see that its implementation relates to the work of highly skilled professionals in social work or child health, or is chiefly about the challenging issues of child protection and intervention. It may then be tempting to see it as being of limited direct relevance to classroom teaching and learning. These suppositions are wrong. It is certainly the case that many children with particularly complex, multiple needs will need the intensive support of specialist professionals, and that many may be educated outside mainstream schools. It would obviously be unwise, and almost certainly counterproductive or dangerous, for any teacher – however well-meaning – to believe that uninformed intervention in case work with a child who is receiving support from social services for complex needs could be justified solely on the grounds of wanting to 'do good'. However, *Every Child Matters* is of huge relevance to classroom teachers. There are a number of reasons for this. The first two are to do with issues of underlying principle. *Every Child Matters* outlines a coherent vision for all children based around the five interlocking outcomes: every child should enjoy and achieve, make a positive contribution, be safe, be healthy and enjoy economic well-being. The Green Paper was not written to suggest that children in difficulty should achieve these five outcomes – but that *every* child should. In the striking words of one children's service professional, this is a reminder that the 'quality of what we offer to the minority in difficulty needs to be judged by the standards we apply to the many' (Dessent 2006: 18). *Every Child Matters* has strong, direct messages for teachers and schools: teachers have a responsibility not just to ensure that children achieve, but that they *enjoy* and achieve: children should enjoy their schooling. Schools need to think hard about how they help children to stay safe: this means how they promote safety not simply in the classroom, but also in the corridor and the playground, and beyond this, on pupils' way to and from school. Schools need to consider how in the curriculum they are preparing children to enjoy economic well-being and to be healthy. Finally, they need to consider how far their internal systems and structures provide opportunities and models for young people to make a positive contribution – to the school through participation in decision making, or to the community more generally. The boldness of the *Every Child Matters* vision is a compelling one precisely because it is an aspiration for *all* children.

Task 20.1

Choose one of the five outcomes *other* than 'enjoy and achieve'.
Think about how i) teachers individually and ii) schools as institutions can work to achieve the outcome you have chosen.

The second issue of principle relates to how schools help children to achieve the five outcomes. In the discussion above, a distinction was drawn between 'universal' services and 'targeted' services. Schools, of course, are the universal service *par excellence*: almost every child goes to school, and schools have historically been used by other services which aspire to universality to try to ensure full population coverage – you can probably remember queuing in a school hall to receive vaccinations. Schools were used for this purpose *because* they allowed health workers to reach almost all children. One of the major preoccupations for schools has always been to maximize children's cognitive attainment in tests and examinations, a preoccupation that has intensified since the mid-1980s as targets for pupil achievement have been extended to all schools. Increasingly, schools have realized that the barriers to learning, and the barriers, therefore, to attainment, do not necessarily lie within the school. Whilst it is imperative that teachers plan properly, teach well, meet individual needs in the classroom and make use of assessment to support learning, the barriers to learning for many pupils lie outside the school. They may be to do with pupils' material circumstances at home: one and a half million children – or one in ten of the school population – still live in poverty. The difficulties may be to do with the consequences of family breakdown – almost one in every two marriages ends in divorce. The difficulties may be to do with pupils' mental health, with their emotional well-being, and so on. Schools alone cannot overcome the barriers to learning for children. All schools – and thus all teachers – need to be able to work in partnership with external agencies.

One of the most influential frameworks for thinking about the ways in which schools and other agencies can work together to meet children's needs was developed by Hardiker et al. (1991), and adopted by the Children and Young People's Unit (CYPU) within the DfES in its early thinking around intervention and prevention (CYPU 2000). Hardiker outlined a tiered model of provision according to the acuteness of need (see Figure 20.1). You may be familiar with a version of this model in phrases such as 'School Action' or 'School Action Plus' in thinking about SEN. The overall intention of *Every Child Matters* is to reduce the need for interventions at levels 3 and 4 by strengthening the focus and effectiveness of preventative interventions at levels 1 and 2 – in other words, to support schools in dealing with the behavioural and learning manifestations of problems before they escalate out of control. The Hardiker/CYPU framework helps to set *Every Child Matters* into a reasonably clear framework for action, but it is also a reminder that a significant number of children will need additional support and intervention at various stages of their school career and for different purposes: for example, a self-harming 15-year-old girl needing support from the Child and Adolescent Mental Health Service to respond to serious emotional issues or a 14-year-old boy who has become involved in petty theft after serious domestic turmoil needing support from a Youth Offending Team. *Every Child Matters* is about developing a framework to provide these young people with effective support from a variety of agencies.

20.5 The changing role of schools

Beyond these issues of principle, the significance of *Every Child Matters* in schools has been enhanced by a series of policy and practice developments since 2003. One of the

Level 1: Diversionary Here the focus is before problems can be seen – thus prevention strategies are likely to focus on whole populations.	Children at level 1 are likely to be in school and the subject of monitoring by class teachers, teaching assistants and learning support.
Level 2: Early prevention This implies that problems are already beginning to manifest themselves and action is needed to prevent them becoming serious or worse.	Children at level 2 will also be in school, with some supplementary support commissioned from outside the school.
Level 3: Intensive prevention/intervention Intensive prevention would focus on where there are multiple, complex and long-standing difficulties that will require a customization of services to meet the needs of the individual concerned.	Children at level 3 may not be in school. However, children may move between levels 2 and 3 at various points in their school career.
Level 4: Restorative intervention Restorative prevention focuses on reducing the impact of an intrusive intervention. This is the level of provision that would apply to, for example, those permanently excluded from school or in youth offender institutions and/or those receiving assistance within the child protection framework.	Children at level 4 will not be in school, though, again there may be long-term aspirations to reintegrate.

Figure 20.1 Tiered model of provision according to acuteness of need (Based on Hardiker et al. 1991)

most significant was the decision made by Ofsted in 2005 to require schools to report on their work across the five *Every Child Matters* outcomes in the 'Self Evaluation Form' which provides the basis for Ofsted inspection. The decision, which was associated with the Government's own decision to extend Ofsted's remit from the inspection of schools to the inspection of children's services provision more generally, effectively forced schools to consider the ways in which their provision equipped them to deliver the given outcomes. As a long-term impact on the way in which schools think about their work – for example, about the relationship between 'enjoyment' and 'achievement', or about the relationship between 'making a positive contribution' and the school's provision for involving children in decision making – this may be of huge significance, as well, incidentally, as demonstrating the way in which an assessment regime (in this case inspection) can bring about changes in behaviour. It may, along with other developments, be shaping the way we think about the role and function of schools in our society. Although it is obviously to be welcomed, since it shows schools thinking hard about their wider role and their wider impact on young people's lives, there are some early negative consequences.

The first is that because school inspection is focused on the individual school, schools have been inclined in their early drafts to consider how they individually work to meet the five outcomes rather than to reflect on the ways in which they construct relationships with other agencies to integrate provision and work together. The second, equally well meaning but equally unhelpful, consequence has been a tendency to ask teachers to link lesson plans to the five outcomes, which has been a feature of some schools and some advice. Although teachers need to reflect the five outcomes in their thinking, it would be wrong to force a lesson into service for one of the five outcomes where that was inappropriate. It's also the case that when teachers plan lessons they are translating the school's *curriculum* vision into practice; the curriculum (see Chapter 13) is only one of the tools which a school uses to address its aims and objectives, and much of a school's five outcomes work will be outside the scope of the formal taught curriculum.

Task 20.2

Consider the *Every Child Matters* outcome 'enjoy and achieve'. Think about i) the ways in which you can help children *both* to achieve *and* to enjoy and ii) the ways in which you might embed children's participation in your planning for the outcome.

The second significant development in the implementation of *Every Child Matters* has been the rapid development of 'extended schools'. Extended schools, developed since 2003, are schools which are funded to provide a 'core offer' of extended activities. At root this means that they are to be open from 8 a.m. to 6 p.m., with the timetabled school day providing only the central part of their work. Wrapped around the school day will be a variety of other activities, including breakfast clubs, after-school clubs, community work and sport activities. Because these activities, although provided on the school site and under the executive responsibility of the headteacher, will not be provided by the teaching staff, they inevitably involve the school in close working relationships with other professionals. Extended schools have also extended their offer in other ways, including the provision of adult learning, and in many cases, in partnership with local authorities they have become co-locations for the delivery of other social services. The remit of extended schools has been focused on making provision in areas of disadvantage, and the early evaluations have been very positive, with evidence that activities could have an impact on attainment, behaviour and attendance (Dyson et al. 2004). For families, there is evidence that activities have had an impact on their involvement in children's learning and on parental perceptions of what schools can achieve. At the time of writing, there are 3,800 extended schools, with a complex extended offer.

The third significant development has been the rapid pace of workforce development in schools. Originally conceived as a set of devices to allow teachers to focus on their core responsibilities for teaching and learning, workforce development has led schools to remodel their workforces, in some cases very extensively. Many schools now have a non-teaching staff which is as large as the teaching staff. The most obvious developments have been in the areas of TAs and learning mentors. Both groups typically work with individual pupils or small groups, to remove barriers to achievement – barriers which may be cognitive, behavioural or emotional – and to allow pupils to maximize their learning in school. Inevitably, this involves such adults in dealing with what Hardiker would label 'level 1' activity, perhaps involving liaison with a teacher or with parents, but again, very much in the spirit of the assessment and integrated solution which underlies *Every Child Matters*. Some schools have gone further, appointing family support staff, or liaison officers, who have a specific brief to work with families and other agencies to broker solutions at level 2 or 3 for individual learners, which keep them in school and address early and emerging difficulties. Many of these schools report quantifiable indicators of success in reduced exclusions and lower absence rates, as well as a less quantifiable sense that behaviour has improved, and that the small minority of young people who absorb vast amounts of school time and effort in responding to their learning difficulties and emotional and behavioural needs are more effectively supported.

Every Child Matters grew out of a horrific murder, and a catastrophic failure of children's support services. It put in place a bold vision for a holistic children's service with the child at the centre and a shared focus on children's success broadly conceived. It saw child protection as one strand in the way in which society provides for the welfare of all, and established the principle that the welfare of the vulnerable minority is indivisible from the welfare of the many. It has spawned a huge programme of change and development affecting everyone who works with children. This programme is far from complete. The evidence we have is that the vision commands almost universal support from those who work with children. In the process of implementation, *Every Child Matters* appears to be doing something else too. It has changed our sense of what outcomes we should focus on. It is changing the way teachers work with others, broadening the commitment to collaborative and interprofessional working. As a result, it may be changing, in fundamental ways, the way we think about what schools are for in their work with children, young people and the wider community.

20.6 Recommendations for further reading and webliography

Department for Education and Skills (DfES) (2003) *Every Child Matters*. London: DfES. (www.everychildmatters.gov.uk/publications/)

Horner, N. and Krawczyk, S. (2006) *Social Work in Education and Children's Services*. London: Learning Matters (Chapters 2 and 5).

www.everychildmatters.gov.uk

21

Special educational needs and inclusive schooling

Dimitra Hartas

21.1 Introduction

Special educational needs (SEN) is an all-encompassing term that reflects diversity in children's learning and developmental profiles. Specifically, it refers to pupils' characteristics that can be grouped into the following four domains: cognitive and learning difficulties; emotional, behavioural and social difficulties; communication and interaction difficulties; and sensory and/or physical difficulties (DfES 2001b). These domains do not form homogeneous groups in that there is a great deal of diversity within each group. There is also a great deal of overlapping with boundaries that are 'cross-cutting, fluid and shifting' (Thomas 1997: 103).

By the end of this chapter, you should be able to:

- understand the main principles and concepts in SEN;
- explain the central differences between SEN and special needs;
- track the evolution in our thinking regarding SEN over time;
- outline the key legislative requirements with respect to assessment and provision for pupils with SEN;
- engage in the 'rights vs evidence' debate regarding inclusion.

21.2 Principles and concepts in SEN

As society becomes more heterogeneous, understanding multiple facets of diversity becomes a challenge in itself. This is true not only for concepts that refer to visible markers of diversity – that is race, ethnicity – but also for those that are less quantifiable, that is people's understandings of disability and individual difference. In the field of education, there has always been a distinction between visible and invisible disability or forms of SEN. Specifically, areas of need such as sensory impairments or Down's syndrome are identified by using 'objective' criteria, whereas the diagnosis of emotional and behavioural difficulties or specific learning difficulties involves 'relativistic' judgement (Frederickson and Cline 2002). Areas of need are becoming increasingly heterogeneous, each involving many sub-groupings, and thus applying either objective or relativistic criteria may not be sufficient in mapping their diverse nature. In this context, approaching SEN as another aspect of diversity has important implications. For example, some children with SEN are likely to experience institutionalized racism, manifested in terms of an over-representation of children from minority ethnic backgrounds in SEN registers because their linguistic and social-cultural differences are perceived as difficulties or disabilities (Tomlinson 1984).

Models of disability

Understanding issues regarding identification, assessment and provision for heterogeneous SEN groupings requires us to reflect on different models of disability and their influence on our perception of individual difference. The 'medical' model of disability was dominant for most of the twentieth century. Its main premise is that the cause of the difficulty/disability is located within the child. The 1944 Education Act reflects the principles that underlie the medical model with its focus on the 'disability of body or mind' and its limited consideration of other factors external to the individual (for example, the quality of teaching, socio-economic background or learning environment). The medical model shaped views of disability as being an individual's property resulting in fatalistic views with respect to provision (Frederickson and Cline 2002). Indeed, the underlying assumption of the medical model is that individual difficulties are fixed characteristics, and thus environmental intervention is less likely to be effective.

On the other hand, the 'social' model of disability considers external factors in terms of the social/political/ideological mechanisms and systems likely to trigger and perpetuate disability (Apple 2001). For example, poor teaching, social disadvantage, limited tolerance of individual differences, stereotypical views of disability, curriculum structures and demands and, finally, a disabling environment all play a significant role in shaping views of disability. Both the medical and social models have shaped public views and understandings of disability to a great extent. The medical model has encouraged the medicalization of individual difference, whereas the social model has been very influential in setting policies on children's rights, and supporting inclusive educational practices.

The dualism of disability as a pathology and disability as a social construction has dominated disability studies for a long time. Shakespeare and Watson (2002: 19) stated that '[disability] sits at the intersection of biology and society and of agency and structure. Disability cannot be reduced to a singular identity: it is a multiplicity, a plurality.' Robinson and Jones Diaz argue that the 'cultural binary opposition of us/them', typically expressed when encountering persons with disabilities, reinforces the fear of the 'Other' (2006: 2). Within current discourses of disability, the notion of 'otherness' is either feared or forced to become 'sameness'. Acceptance of human differences requires us to reposition the 'other' by focusing more on a discourse of respect, care and citizenship, and by moving towards an inclusive social theory of disability and transforming educational institutions into 'loci of ethical practices' (Dahlberg and Moss 2005: 86).

Frederickson and Cline (2002) argue that the learner, the learning situation, teacher–pupil interactions and the task all influence individual children's competencies and needs, pointing to the importance of adopting an interactive model to understand individual difference. This is a more comprehensive model in that it considers both external and internal factors that are likely to shape children's abilities and areas of need. As already mentioned, seeing disability as an individual's fixed trait is less likely to result in environmental changes to meet pupils' needs. Likewise, a focus on environmental demands only takes into consideration the features of a situation and ignores the child's characteristics, strengths and weaknesses that can be particularly helpful in explaining why a child underperforms academically. It is potentially problematic, for example, to consider poor teaching as the only reason why a child cannot read in that by understanding the nature of their difficulties we can tailor the teaching of reading in a way that is relevant and appropriate for the child's ability and prior reading skills. Thus, taking an interactional approach by focusing on the learner and the learning situation enables us to understand how children interact with tasks and situations and explain variability in their responses. It allow us to reflect on the resilience displayed by some children who learn despite reduced educational opportunities, and the persistence of other children who have difficulties learning despite good teaching.

Concepts in SEN

The 1944 Education Act set the stage for the creation of a categorization system for disabled pupils. The Warnock Report in 1973 recommended that the statutory categories should be abolished and, instead, the needs of children should be identified following an assessment, with the necessary arrangement for educational provision being made based on their profile of needs. By abolishing a system of categorization, SEN were placed on a continuum, along with assessment and provision. The latter was emphasized in the revised Code of Practice (DfES 2001b) by adopting a graduated approach to educational provision (discussed in detail later in the chapter).

SEN was introduced as a legally defined term by the 1981 Education Act following advice from the Warnock committee (DES 1978). Prior to 1981, the focus was on identifying and providing for handicapped individuals. Also, the term 'special needs' has been used to describe children whose educational requirements differ from those of their peers. Of particular relevance at this point is to stress the conceptual differences between the terms SEN and special needs. SEN refers to learning difficulties experienced by children in an educational setting which make them eligible for educational provision. Special needs, on the other hand, is not a legally defined term. It refers to needs displayed by children whose cultural, linguistic and social backgrounds and experiences are different from those of the majority of children in a school.

There is a tendency to use 'SEN' and 'special needs' interchangeably, and this is likely to have ethical and practical implications. Children who experience special needs may not necessarily have special educational needs. Special needs tend to refer to social phenomena that may be shared by children from similar social/cultural and linguistic backgrounds and, thus, they are distinct from individual experiences of learning difficulties which underlie the concept of SEN (Frederickson and Cline 2002). There is a legislative framework to support this distinction. For example, 'a child must not be regarded as having a learning difficulty solely because the language or medium of communication of the home is different from the language in which he or she is or will be taught' (DfEE 1996: section 312). Confusion of the concepts 'SEN' and 'special needs' may result in perceiving children from ethnic and linguistic minority backgrounds as having learning and/or language difficulties and, as a result, the planning and delivery of educational support that is not relevant or developmentally appropriate for these children.

CASE STUDY 21.1

Consider the following pupils. Each has a variety of needs from their school's point of view. List as many of the pupils' needs as you can.

Case Study A: A 6-year-old girl from an Urdu-speaking family without any pre-school education has just recently entered the English education system and has learned little English thus far. She is exposed to English only at school because all family members speak Urdu at home. Her school attendance is good but she never completes homework nor does she participate in classroom discussions and activities.

Case Study B: A 12-year-old boy and his mother arrived in England as asylum seekers. The boy has missed a great deal of education due to war and social upheaval in his own country. He was admitted to a school in the area where he and his mother temporarily reside and he has been displaying difficulties settling down and following classroom routines. He is making very slow progress in acquiring English, literacy and numeracy.

Case Study C: An 8-year-old boy from a literary-rich environment with both parents in the teaching profession experiences difficulties with literacy. Specifically, he still displays problems with phonics: blending and segmenting sounds; making letter-sound correspondences and confusing simple words when reading. His spelling is poor with many letter reversals taking place and his copying is slow and inaccurate. He is capable of contributing orally but has difficulties transferring his thoughts to paper. Overall, his academic progress is slow and he has started experiencing frustration and low self-esteem.

Once you have listed as many of the pupils' needs as you can, decide which of them should be described as special needs and which should be described as SEN.

Using the case studies as examples, consider the possible consequences of confusing the concepts of special needs and SEN. How might such confusion lead to low expectations, inappropriate attributions for academic success and failure, discrimination or, potentially, racism?

21.3 Inclusion

Recently, there has been increasing interest in exploring educational policy and practice in the context of social justice and human rights, and striving for inclusive educational practices. This has stimulated paradigm shifts which challenge prevailing concepts of knowledge, children's rights and entitlement to education, and propose new and diverse ways of describing and analyzing educational experience especially for individuals with diverse learning profiles and SEN. An important question remains: whether placing SEN in the context of children's rights, inclusion and our rapidly changing understandings of disability would allow us to capture fully its heterogeneity and diversity.

A brief history of inclusion

The concept of inclusion is not new in the UK. It can be traced back to the Wood Committee (1927) when the first discussions about integration took place. In 1978, the Warnock committee (DES 1978) raised the need for a major reconceptualization of special education, and set the stage for the integration of pupils with SEN but with certain conditions attached (for instance, children to be educated according to their parents' wishes; provision of appropriate support services; the education of other children must not be compromised and appropriate resources and expertise should be available). It is interesting to note that even today, in the revised Code of Practice (DfES 2001b), two of these conditions remain when inclusive education is considered (i.e. the wishes of the parents and the provision of efficient education for other children).

The Warnock committee shifted the focus from separate or special provision to one that was supplementary to that normally provided in mainstream schools by introducing a continuum from non-segregation to segregation, distinguishing between locational, social and functional integration. Locational integration refers to physical integration in terms of special classes located in a mainstream school, or a special school that is located on the premises of a mainstream school. Social integration refers to social interactions between children with SEN and their peers in terms of engaging in extra-curricular activities (e.g. play, sport clubs). Finally, functional integration refers to participation in educational programmes that are planned in such a way that all children can benefit (Frederickson and Cline 2002).

At this point, it is necessary to discuss the distinction between integration and inclusion. Ainscow (1995) argues that integration refers to making a number of additional arrangements for individual pupils with SEN in schools without expecting schools to make any major changes themselves. On the contrary, inclusion implies that schools engage in changes by restructuring themselves so they can provide good education for all. Frederickson and Cline (2002) describe integration and inclusion in terms of assimilation and adaptation. Integration refers to assimilating individual children with SEN or special needs to enable them to fit into existing school structures. By contrast, inclusion involves adapting to/accommodating the needs of an individual child by radically changing school organization and curricular focus and adapting materials and procedures accordingly. Despite the important differences between integration and inclusion, they are often used as though synonymous.

The notion of inclusion as adaptation is also stressed by Flem, Moen and Gumusdottir (2004) who view inclusion as a process of fitting the school to meet the needs of the pupils through changing the values and beliefs of those involved. Fitting the school to meet pupils' needs, according to Booth (1996), can be achieved through increasing the participation of pupils in the cultures and curricula of mainstream schools and communities. In other words, inclusion is a process of reducing exclusion of pupils from mainstream cultures and communities.

Ainscow, Booth and Dyson (2004) understood inclusion as a concept that applies not only to education but also society. Inclusion is, thus, defined as a social mechanism reflecting in its process the make-up of the society. It is about ensuring that society does not exclude pupils as a result of their diverse needs, for example, emotional, cultural, linguistic, medical, neurological, physical and/or social. Inclusion is understood as a matter of school policy, a policy that needs to address issues of diversity and marginalization.

The concept of inclusion is not easy to define and reach a consensus upon. As Peters argues, 'inclusive education appears to mean different things to different planners and developers and is translated to yet more varied concepts and practices by practitioners at school levels' (2006: 2).

Inclusion as a children's right

The idea that children have rights first appeared in 1924 when the League of Nations drafted the first Declaration of the Rights of the Child. However, it was much later that the rights of the child were incorporated into UK law in the form of the Children Act 1989 (Curtis and O'Hagan 2003). The Convention on the Rights of the Child was adopted by the United Nations general assembly and came into force as an international law in 1990. Enabling children to exercise their rights by ascertaining their views and ensuring participation in decision making on issues that affect their lives is more complex than it appears. Saraga (1998) states that 'rights' like 'needs' are highly contested when applied to children in that children rely on their carers to assert their rights, and this dependency is thought to limit their rights.

A worldwide movement towards inclusive education as a right has been supported by many international developments, including the Salamanca Statement and Framework for Action (UNESCO 1994), the European Convention for Human Rights and the UK Human Rights Act (1998). Notions of inclusion are embodied in the Salamanca Statement, for example, which states that: 'inclusion and participation are essential to human dignity and to the enjoyment and exercise of human rights. Within the field of education this is reflected in the development of strategies that seek to bring about a genuine equalisation of opportunity' (UNESCO 1994: 34).

In the UK, the Special Educational Needs and Disability Act (2001) strengthens the right to a mainstream education for children with SEN. The Act has amended the 1996 Education Act and transformed the statutory framework for inclusion into a positive endorsement of inclusion. The Act seeks to enable more pupils who have SEN to be included successfully within mainstream education. Inclusive educational policies are expected to support and protect the rights of pupils (for instance, pupils with SEN, pupils with special needs and disadvantaged pupils), extending the idea of inclusion from a concept relevant to special needs education to one that permeates all educational experiences in schools.

In both the developed and developing world, children with SEN in particular are likely to experience discrimination and to receive stereotypical responses to their needs. Slee (2001: 174) states that some current school practices are likely to: 'deny human rights and exclude students on the basis of race, ethnicity, disability and class', stressing that inclusive education should be: 'a project of educational reconceptual-isation and radical reconstruction'. As part of an educational reconceptualization, schools are expected to engage in an exploration of disability and its social outcomes (for example, social exclusion or marginalization) particularly for pupils with SEN. When schools provide support for pupils with SEN, they allocate resources to pupils whose academic performance is likely to remain low and may have no impact on measures of the school's academic success. As a result, these schools are open to being criticized as ineffective (Frederickson and Cline 2002). This form of measurement of success in a market-driven environment causes a series of dilemmas regarding the feasibility of inclusive practices.

Inclusive educational policies are expected to support and protect the rights of all pupils, extending the notion of inclusion from a concept relevant to special education to one that will permeate all educational experiences in schools. In general, schools seem to 'be caught in a tension between the inclusion agenda and the education reform agenda' (Frederickson and Cline 2002: 72). With respect to the latter, NC testing, inspection, competition and pressure to raise standards are likely to impact negatively on inclusive education. Likewise, the emphasis on market forces and con-sumer choice have created another disadvantage for those who are likely to be seen as 'undesirable customers' based on 'social class, race and ethnicity, special educational needs and behaviour problems' (Tomlinson 2000: 28), again creating obstacles to inclusion.

Inclusion as an effective educational practice

According to the DfES, inclusion is a process by which schools, LAs and others develop their cultures, policies and practices to include pupils. With the right training, strategies and support, nearly all children with SEN can be successfully included in mainstream education. The rationale for supporting inclusive practices is as follows:

- An inclusive education service offers excellence and choice and incorporates the views of parents and children;
- The interests of all pupils must be safeguarded;
- Schools, LEAs and others should actively seek to remove barriers to learning and participation;
- All children should have access to an appropriate education that affords them the opportunity to achieve their personal potential.

(DfES 2001d: 2)

The revised Code of Practice for SEN (DfES 2001b) has established inclusive educational practice as its main imperative. Inclusion is a complex and contested concept and, thus, we need to take into consideration practical and conceptual issues and the tensions between and within areas of need (Lindsay 2003). According to the Salamanca Statement: 'every child has unique characteristics, interests, abilities and learning needs' and thus 'education systems should be designed and educational programmes implemented to take into account the wide diversity of these character-istics and needs'. The Salamanca Statement also states that children with SEN: 'must have access to regular schools which should accommodate them within a child-centred pedagogy capable of meeting these needs' (UNESCO 1994: viii). However, it is also important to ask whether 'regular schools' are always the most effective in accommodating children's diverse characteristics and needs.

This question highlights a key distinction between rights and effectiveness with regard to inclusive educational policy and practice. Is inclusion a moral imperative and a children's right or an effective educational practice? There is an ongoing debate as to whether we need evidence to support the effectiveness of inclusive education. Some theorists argue that inclusion is an issue of rights not evidence, rendering the need for evidence unimportant (Gallagher 2001). Inclusion as a human right, accord-ing to Clarke et al. (1997: 93), is not 'something which has to wait upon the ability of professional educators to resolve questions of feasibility, effectiveness and efficiency, or which is bounded by the capacity of mainstream schools to respond to children with marked impairments. On the contrary, the development of truly inclusive schools constitutes a moral imperative which professionals are obliged to find ways of obeying.' However, if we accept inclusion as a human right and a moral imperative regardless of its effectiveness, then it is possible that different views on social justice and human rights are likely to create conflict, both in policy and in practice (Lindsay 2003).

There is a need for research to monitor the outcomes of inclusive education. A number of studies in the USA have examined the effectiveness of inclusive and non-inclusive education, looking at measures of educational attainment, social adjustment and self-confidence (e.g. Baker et al. 1994). However, there are serious method-ological concerns about some of these studies rendering their findings inconclusive (Madden and Slavin 1983; Frederickson and Cline 2002). Many factors need to be controlled (for example, type of programme, curriculum objectives, definitions of integration/inclusion, children's characteristics and the nature of the intervention) in order to tease out the effects of inclusion from other types of influence.

Reviewing a body of international research on the effectiveness of inclusion, Hegarty (1993) reported that the results were inconclusive. However, he argued that this does not necessarily mean the opposite – that is to say that non-inclusive educa-tion is effective. Zigmond and Baker (1995) provided descriptions of inclusive classrooms in five different states in the USA and found a number of practices that are likely to facilitate inclusion: using instruction that is matched to pupils' needs and skills; providing opportunities for pupils to progress at their own pace; allowing pupils to function as independent learners; engaging pupils in collaborative peer learning; and good home–school relationships. These findings suggest that some inclusive practices are more effective than others and that judging the effectiveness of inclusion is not an easy undertaking in that multiple and complex factors need to be taken into consideration.

Although there is a lot of discussion of inclusion as a human rights issue, the political and ideological nature of the systems that are there to support individuals with disabilities or SEN is rarely debated (Apple 2001). There are ongoing discussions about competition, markets and choice, on the one hand, and accountability, performance objectives and the NC, on the other, leaving inclusive educational practices suspended between them. The question remains: 'Does inclusive education benefit all children with SEN all of the time?' The answer is that inclusive education may not always be right for every child all of the time. Equally, just because education in an inclusive setting may not be right at a particular stage, it does not prevent the child from being included successfully at a later stage.

Every Child Matters (DfES 2003e) (see Chapter 20) places considerable emphasis on developing services around the needs of the child. In this context, inclusion should not be about moral, political or rights agendas, but about processes towards the development of children's services that are inclusive and responsive to their needs. According to the five outcomes of *Every Child Matters*, all children, regardless of their social, cultural and linguistic background or difficulties, should enjoy and achieve, stay safe and be healthy, as well as make a positive contribution and achieve economic well-being. If inclusion is to be given the best opportunity to be effective in supporting children to achieve these five outcomes, schools and other educational institutions need to take a careful look at how they cater for children's individual needs. Ainscow (1995) identified a number of characteristics of schools that are likely to facilitate provision of high quality education for all:

- leadership which establishes a clear vision for the school and builds consensus without sacrificing individuality and innovative thinking;
- involvement of parents, pupils and the community;
- an ethos of collaboration and information sharing;
- a climate of enquiry and reflection and the use of evidence to inform decision making;
- staff development focused on opportunities to engage in professional learning and take a lead in developing schools as learning environments.

Task 21.1

To which of these characteristics could a classroom teacher contribute? In what ways?

21.4 SEN policy and practice

The SEN Code of Practice

The Code of Practice (DfES 2001b) provides practical advice on meeting children's SEN. It defines SEN as the result of a child having learning difficulties. Although the

Code is a non-statutory document, it states that school inspections will look for evidence of effective SEN provision. The 1996 Act defines children with learning difficulties as those who:

- have a significantly greater difficulty in learning than the majority of children of the same age; or
- have a disability which prevents or hinders them from making use of educational facilities of a kind generally provided for children of the same age in schools within the area of the LEA; or
- are under compulsory school age and fall within the two definitions above or would do so if special educational provision was not made for them.

According to the Code of Practice (DfES 2001b: para 1.3), special educational provision means:

- for children of 2 or over, educational provision which is additional to, or otherwise different from, the educational provision made generally for children of their age in schools maintained by the LEA, other than special schools, in the area;
- for children under 2, educational provision of any kind.

The revised Code of Practice (DfES 2001b) sets out a number of principles. These include:

Inclusion:
An emphasis on meeting pupil needs in the mainstream with the recognition that alternative provision may be required, establishing a continuum of provision. Issues related to definitions of inclusion, children's rights and the effectiveness of inclusive educational practices were discussed earlier in this chapter.

Graduated approach:
This approach places pupils' needs and provision on a continuum, tackling learning difficulties at different levels: School Action, School Action Plus and a Statement of SEN. The higher the level, the greater the resources and expertise devoted to it. The School Action phase addresses concerns triggered by parents and teachers mainly regarding children's educational progress. It is the initial phase of intervention aimed at raising awareness about pupils' academic difficulties and taking the first steps to support their learning through interventions that are specified in an IEP. At this phase, the school's SENCo may become involved, especially with the formulation of the IEP and the collection of evidence through assessments and meetings with teachers and parents.

The School Action Plus phase is characterized by the involvement of external support services which will advise on assessment procedures and reformulation of an IEP. This takes place when an evaluation of the School Action phase suggests that existing support is inadequate to meet a child's needs.

There is an expectation that most children's SEN will be met effectively at the

School Action or School Action Plus phases. However, a minority of children present educational difficulties that cannot be accommodated by the support available at either of these phases. These children require a detailed evaluation of their needs through a statutory assessment, and this may lead to the provision of a Statement of SEN. It is important to note that not all statutory assessments result in a Statement of SEN, but when a Statement is obtained, more resources and services are made available.

Pupils' voice:
The revised Code of Practice stresses the importance of ascertaining the views and wishes of children with SEN, where they are able to express a point of view. This is consistent with Article 12 of the United Nations Convention on the rights of the child. Furthermore, one of the principles of *Every Child Matters* stresses the need for children to play an active role in articulating and identifying areas of need, and participating in the design, delivery and evaluation of services that target their needs.

Parental involvement:
Parents and carers should play a crucial role throughout SEN processes because they are able to provide first-hand information about their children's needs, development and educational progress. They are able to fulfil multiple roles by:

- providing information about their children;
- expressing their own wishes and convictions;
- engaging in decision making;
- providing consistency in the intervention strategies adopted in the home;
- providing feedback on the effectiveness of intervention for use during reviews.

SEN assessment

After the implementation of the 1981 Act, the purpose of SEN assessment changed from diagnosing disability to identifying SEN. 'Need' is conceptualized as an interaction between the learner's strengths and weaknesses and the learning situation (appropriateness of teaching methods and learning styles, educational provision). Research on school effectiveness has found that schools with successful initiatives for inclusion respond flexibly to pupils with diverse needs in terms of assessment and provision. Assessment and identification have become particularly important to allow children's services to carry out early preventative work, as it is stressed in *Every Child Matters* (DfES 2003e).

An interactional approach to assessment takes into consideration not just the characteristics of the learner but also the learning environment. According to the Code of Practice: 'the assessment should always be fourfold: it should focus on the child's learning characteristics, the learning environment that the school is providing for the child, the task and the teaching style' (DfES 2001b: para. 5.6). This involves taking four distinct approaches to assessment (Cline 1992), namely, focus on the learner, focus on the teaching programme, focus on the ZPD (Vygotsky 1962; see Chapter 4), and focus on the learning environment. The focus on the learner assumes that the difficulties are located within the child and are permanent or fixed characteristics (the main premise of the medical model). Thus, assessment should be very similar to a medical diagnosis where the 'cause' of the problem is identified and treatment is prescribed. This approach often compares children's performances to norms for their age group by using standardized assessment devices with external factors not being considered as influencing children's strengths and weaknesses.

The 2001 Code incorporates a shift towards focusing on the external environment within which children operate, for instance, the social setting, teaching styles and tasks. This shift is associated with national and international movements towards inclusive education. Here, the underlying assumption is that aspects of the curriculum, tasks set and the overall learning environment are not conducive to supporting children's learning needs. Thus, the assessment should focus on analyzing situational factors and the tasks presented in terms of their developmental and pedagogical appropriateness and ways of acquiring new skills, transferring them to new contexts and adapting them to respond to different challenges. A third approach assesses children in the ZPD while their performance is being supported by an adult. This type of assessment is not static but enables us to see the progress a child can make when supported by an adult.

Task 21.2: Evaluating possible hypotheses for a child who experiences specific learning difficulties

The list below gives five hypotheses that have been put forward as possible explanations of the difficulties being experienced by a child with specific learning difficulties. Having made a hypothesis, it is necessary to evaluate it – that is, to investigate how well it is supported by evidence and how well it explains the concerns observed. For this activity, you need to think about the four approaches to assessment, namely, focusing on the learner, the learning environment, teaching styles and tasks and the ZPD. For each hypothesis you should choose which of the four approaches to assessment is/are most appropriate for use in its evaluation.

1. The child is learning more slowly than others because the curriculum and the environment of the school are not conducive to learning.
2. The child is not learning because her good oral language skills have masked her difficulties with written work.
3. The child has not attained good phonological skills for segmenting and blending sounds and making letter-sound correspondences because she was taught using a 'whole language' approach.
4. The child experiences learning difficulties due to stress, socio-economic disadvantage and the social isolation affecting her family.
5. The child experiences difficulties with short-term memory and her speed of writing and information processing is very slow.

Differentiation

Although differentiation is seen as an important aspect of the NC, it is less clear to the majority of teachers what it entails. Many in education understand differentiation as a process of teaching the same curriculum to all pupils and tailoring teaching methods in order to match curriculum requirements to the children's ability, prior skills and needs. Others have conceptualized differentiation as a way of teaching different aspects of the curriculum to meet children's diverse needs. The latter notion of differentiation, however, is less likely to support inclusive education.

Hart (1996) argues that differentiation for pupils with SEN should involve 'differential thinking' which takes a three-stage approach. First, teachers should engage in what is called 'diagnostic thinking' in order to identify children's needs. Second, through the process of differential thinking, teachers should explore ways to match provision closely to pupils' needs. Third, and most importantly, Hart refers to 'innovative thinking' which includes ways of examining concerns, analyzing current understandings and engaging in a teacher–pupil interaction.

CASE STUDY 21.2

Differentiation for a pupil with dyslexia

Simon is a 13-year-old son of professional parents with high educational aspirations. He attends a school characterized by excellent home–school relationships and the attainment of high academic standards. As a pre-schooler, Simon displayed a degree of speech and language difficulties for which he received speech therapy. Now, his oral language skills are very good and he always participates in classroom discussions, is lively and interacts with his peers successfully. His understanding of mathematical concepts is very good and he has a strong interest in the sciences. However, he experiences difficulties with reading in terms of word recognition and fluency and also transferring his thoughts to paper.

As a young child he enjoyed being read to and always displayed a good comprehension of texts. He seems to have difficulties applying strategies to decipher unknown words when reading and this impacts on his reading fluency and comprehension. He cannot retain a list of instructions in his memory, particularly multi-step instructions. His word recognition and spelling patterns are inconsistent, usually confusing frequently used words. His writing is very slow for his age and this undermines his academic performance, especially completing timed examinations. These difficulties make him very self-conscious and frustrated, lowering his self-esteem and self-confidence considerably. He tends to be criticized by his teachers with respect to the amount, accuracy and presentation of his written work.

This is a profile of a child with dyslexia. He is able intellectually, with good educational opportunities, and has been raised in a literary-rich environment. He seems to experience difficulties in specific areas such as working memory, speed of processing information (as reflected in his copying and writing) and phonological strategies to decipher unfamiliar words. In order to support this pupil in the classroom through the process of differentiation, teachers need to think in terms of setting clear goals, matching teaching styles and tasks to his ability and skills and removing obstacles to learning. Specifically, they may modify teaching by introducing multi-sensory approaches to learning, using handouts and repetition to support working memory, engage him in phonological training and encourage him to use computers (word processor programs) to alleviate difficulties with the speed and accuracy of his handwriting.

Can you think of any other strategies likely to support learning for a child with this learning profile?

21.5 Conclusion

In this chapter, I have introduced principles and concepts of SEN, approaching SEN as another aspect of diversity. I have drawn a distinction between SEN and special needs due to linguistic, ethnic or cultural factors and provided examples to illustrate their central differences. Changes over time regarding our understandings of disability were tracked through a discussion of models of disability, stating the value of taking an interactional approach to understanding SEN. I have also presented different definitions of inclusion, and discussed inclusion as a right and as an effective educational practice by citing research findings from the UK and the USA. Finally, I summarized current legislation, that is the Code of Practice on identifying and assessing children's educational and other needs and making appropriate provision.

21.6 Recommendations for further reading and webliography

Booth, T. and Ainscow, M. (1998) *From Them To Us: An International Study of Inclusion in Education*. London: Routledge.

British Psychological Society (1999) *Dyslexia, Literacy and Psychological Assessment*. Leicester: British Psychological Society.

Clark, C., Dyson, A., Millward, A. and Robson, S. (1999) Theories of inclusion, theories of schools: deconstructing and reconstructing the inclusive school, *British Educational Research Journal*, 25(2): 157–77.

Cline, T. (1998) The assessment of special educational needs for bilingual children, *British Journal of Special Education*, 25(4): 159–63.

Lewis, A. and Lindsay, G. (eds) (2000) *Researching Children's Perspectives*. Buckingham: Open University Press.

www.bdadyslexia.org.uk (the website for the British Dyslexia Association offering information and advice on issues regarding assessment and identification of dyslexia, as well as teaching methods and strategies targeting dyslexia-associated difficulties)

www.nasen.org.uk (the website for the National Association for Special Educational Needs)

22

Schooling, ethnicity and English as an additional language

Sandra Howard

22.1 Introduction and background to the issues

By the end of this chapter you should:

- know about legislation and other initiatives aimed at raising the achievement of minority ethnic pupils;
- have an understanding of the range of issues impacting on pupils of minority ethnic backgrounds;
- have an awareness of the needs of pupils with English as an additional language including newly arrived pupils;
- be familiar with appropriate strategies to support pupils with English as an additional language in the classroom.

The publication of the Stephen Lawrence Inquiry Report (Macpherson Report 1999) following the murder of the black teenager in 1993 was a significant event in race relations in this country. It demonstrated that there had been a time lag between the experiences of minority ethnic communities in Britain and recognition of those experiences by the state and its institutions. In the words of Doreen Lawrence, Stephen's mother, 'The time is right for change, don't let this opportunity pass you by, cling to it with both hands' (Richardson and Wood 1999: v).

People from minority ethnic heritage have been present in Britain for a very long time. However, their numbers were relatively small until the period of reconstruction after the Second World War when people migrated from the New Commonwealth in response to the 'Mother Country's' call for labour. Post-war industrial expansion had created a need for cheap labour and effective recruitment campaigns in the 'colonies' lured people from the Caribbean, India and Pakistan to take up work in badly paid jobs that the indigenous population did not want. Few of these workers intended to stay in Britain for long and the aim of most was to improve their status so that they could return home assured of a better standard of living for themselves and their families. However, for many this was not to be the case until they reached the age of

retirement and, gradually, as minority ethnic families settled initially in the poor hous-
ing of Britain's large cities, their children entered the education system. The colonial
experience had not prepared Britain to cope with a multiracial society. However,
from 1960 some schools had an increasingly multiracial population. Whilst official
policies acknowledged the need for teachers to be aware of the backgrounds of minority ethnic pupils, and the Bullock Report (1975) promoted the importance of language across the curriculum, the educational needs of minority ethnic pupils were
not a priority and the state hoped to assimilate these 'immigrant' pupils with as little
disruption as possible to the school system.

Section 11 of the Local Government Act in 1966 provided additional funding to
LEAs with 2 per cent or more of Commonwealth immigrant pupils and this funding
was used predominantly for the teaching of English. Initially this took place in language centres where pupils were withdrawn from the mainstream. Gradually, the
language centres were phased out and pupils with English language needs first were
supported in schools in withdrawal groups and then more inclusively within mainstream classrooms. This additional funding continued until 1999 when the DfES
introduced the EMAG and placed responsibility for the achievement of minority
ethnic pupils on schools. In the same year, the Stephen Lawrence Inquiry Report
(1999) made a number of recommendations for education and emphasized the need
to address institutionalized racism. It stated that LEAs and school governors had a
duty to create and implement strategies in their schools to prevent and address racism.
The report also stated that consideration should be given to amending the NC, in
order to better reflect the needs of a diverse society and prevent racism. The following
year saw the publication of Curriculum 2000 which made statutory the duty to ensure
that teaching is inclusive. Also in 2000 the Race Relations Act of 1976 was amended
to place both general and specific duties upon schools. The general duty required
schools to be proactive in eliminating racial discrimination and in the promotion of
equality of opportunity and good relations between people of different racial groups.
For example, if patterns of racial inequality exist within a school then it is not enough
just to identify them – action must be taken to remove them. The specific duties
required English schools to prepare and publish a race equality policy and monitor
and assess how their policies affect ethnic minority pupils, staff and parents; the
emphasis here is on pupils' achievements.

22.2 Analyzing achievement

As attention focused on raising levels of achievement of all pupils during the 1990s,
reports by Ofsted in 1996 and 1999 indicated that whilst the achievement of minority
ethnic pupils as a whole was improving, the gap between the highest and lowest
achieving ethnic groups was growing. Particular concerns about the performance of
Caribbean, Bangladeshi and Pakistani pupils were raised, as well as the level of exclusions of Black Caribbean boys. Ofsted in their report on *Raising the Attainment of
Minority Ethnic Pupils* (1999) recommended that schools should monitor pupil
achievement and behaviour, including attendance and exclusions, by ethnic group.
This data should then be used to set targets for raising the attainment and improving
the attendance and behaviour of underachieving groups.

1966	Section 11 of Local Government Act
1975/6	Race Relations Act Bullock Report *A Language for Life*
1981	Rampton Report *West Indian Children in our Schools*
1985	Swann Report *Education for All*
1996	*Recent Research on the Achievements of Ethnic Minority Pupils* Ofsted *Teaching EAL: A Framework for Policy* SCAA
1998	*Teaching and Learning Strategies in Successful Multi-ethnic Schools* DfEE/OU
1999	*Raising the Attainment of Minority Ethnic Pupils – School and LEA Responses* Ofsted Macpherson Report Home Office Introduction of Ethnic Minority Achievement Grant (EMAG)
2000	*Removing the Barriers* DfEE Race Relations Amendment Act Curriculum 2000 *Learning For All Standards for Racial Equality in Schools* CRE *A Language in Common* QCA
2001	*Managing Support for the Attainment of Pupils from Minority Ethnic Groups* HMI *Evaluating Educational Inclusion* Ofsted
2002	*Achievement of Black Caribbean Pupils* HMI
2003	*Aiming High: Raising the Achievement of Minority Ethnic Pupils* DfES
2004	*Minority Ethnic Pupils in Mainly White Schools* DfES
2006	*Ethnicity and Education: the Evidence on Minority Ethnic Pupils aged 5–16* DfES

Figure 22.1 Summary of influential official publications

In March 2003 the Government released statistics showing the percentage of pupils with five or more A★–C grades at GCSE level across ethnic groups. This was the first time such data had been placed in the public domain and it served to illustrate the concerns expressed by Ofsted four years previously. Only 30 per cent of Black Caribbean pupils achieved five or more good GCSE passes in contrast to more than half of White pupils and 64 per cent of Indian pupils. In 2002 the highest achieving ethnic group was the 12,000 Chinese pupils. The release of this data coincided with the launch of a consultation document entitled *Aiming High* (DfES 2003d) which set out specific proposals for:

- a national framework to support bilingual pupils;
- raising achievement and reducing exclusions of African Caribbean pupils;
- meeting the needs of highly mobile pupils.

In the Foreword to the document schools minister, Stephen Twigg, made it clear that the 'long tail of underachievement for many Black and Pakistani pupils in particular' was unacceptable. He continued:

> The best schools already show us the way to deliver high standards for their minority ethnic pupils. They employ several complementary strategies. High expectations are matched by strong parental and community support. Data is monitored and used to improve teaching and learning. There is a clear whole school approach with a consistent approach to racism, bullying and bad behaviour.
>
> (DfES 2003d: 1)

In 2005 whilst the achievement of Black pupils overall improved, Black Caribbean boys and Black Other boys continued to be two of the lowest attaining groups (see Figure 22.2, overleaf). In schools that had been part of the *Aiming High* programme, Black pupils who received extra support had shown improvement. Some of the additional support provided included work with parents, residential study camps and Saturday classes.

22.3 Cultural and religious issues

Pupils in schools, even predominantly white schools, come from a range of cultural backgrounds. For some, there may be conflict between the culture of home or 'the street' and the culture of school. For pupils from minority ethnic groups, there may be other potential areas of tension connected with their cultural, religious or linguistic identity: 'Inclusive schools respect the identities of their pupils and students and their experiences, histories and concerns. They know where their pupils are coming from, and the tensions, difficulties and struggles in which they are engaged' (Richardson and Wood 1999: 17).

In their research into the characteristics of successful multi-ethnic schools Blair and Bourne develop the concept of 'the listening school', claiming that effective

Ethnic Group	%
White British	78.0
Irish	81.0
Traveller of Irish Heritage	92.0
Gypsy/Roma	61.9
Any White other background	78.4
White and Black Caribbean	69.2
White and Black African	73.5
White and Asian	84
Any other mixed background	78.7
Indian	81.9
Pakistani	67.1
Bangladeshi	65.5
Any other Asian background	79.6
Black Caribbean	65
Black African	72.5
Any other Black background	65.9
Chinese	84.9
Any other ethnic group	74.6
All pupils	**77.4**

Figure 22.2 2005 GCSE results – percentage of pupils in the 5+ A*–C group including A*–C passes in English and Maths

schools listen to and learn from pupils and their parents. They refer to interviews with secondary pupils where, 'all young people interviewed stressed the importance of being treated with respect by teachers' (Blair and Bourne 1998: 54). Being treated with respect is a powerful message that also comes out of specific research by Her Majesty's Inspectors into secondary schools that had been successful in raising the achievement of Black Caribbean pupils: 'What the pupils interviewed for the study appreciated most about their schools was being listened to, valued and supported. They saw the response to Black people in wider society as often marked by negativity and discrimination and the notion of "respect" in school was of critical importance to m' (HMI 2002: 4).

Racism has a powerful impact on the lives of those pupils who experience it as the Black Year 10 pupil in Case Study 22.1 illustrates.

CASE STUDY 22.1

'It makes me feel angry, really mad inside like nothing else does.' Michael talks about the name calling and comments on his skin colour that he has experienced ever since starting school. He describes how this kind of abuse continues. He talks about the 'new kids' who are refugees. 'They call everyone who's a refugee – Kosovan. It's like we used to get called Paki even though we weren't.' Michael talks about his concerns regarding one particular teacher who he feels is treating him in a racist way. He feels that he gets into trouble for doing exactly the same things that white boys in his group do and don't get into trouble for. He is the only black boy in this group. He feels that there is no one in the school he can talk to about this and that his new year head won't take his perspective seriously. He used to enjoy this subject and thought he was quite good at it. Now he is worried that he's going to get 'chucked out' as he's always on report.

The Commission for Racial Equality (CRE) has developed a set of standards to help schools address race issues and develop a socially inclusive ethos and environment. They advise that schools should have 'clear procedures in place to ensure that racist incidents, racial discrimination and racial harassment are dealt with promptly, firmly and consistently' (CRE 2000: 41). This section of the standards continues by listing a number of ways this can be achieved by schools, amongst which is that a named teacher has overall responsibility for dealing with such incidents and that this teacher's role is widely publicized. Clearly whoever has this role must be able to demonstrate that they are prepared to listen to and learn from pupils.

The curriculum provides an opportunity to show respect for pupils' cultural, religious and linguistic heritage by drawing on the backgrounds of all pupils. Resources in all curriculum areas should be inclusive with positive images of people from different ethnic groups and different religious backgrounds. The choice of content in subject areas and the teaching methods used should encourage positive attitudes to cultural diversity and race equality. Schools quite often forget to tap into the human resource that their parents and local minority ethnic communities provide. Some secondary schools have made good use of positive role models from their minority ethnic communities particularly in terms of mentoring older pupils. Schools with pupils from backgrounds where a language other than English is spoken at home have made arrangements for those pupils to study their first language to GCSE and A level standard. In the best of practice these languages are timetabled as modern foreign language options rather than extra-curricular activities. Some schools have liaised with their local Mosque regarding test and exam timetables and have set aside an appropriate space for Muslim pupils to use for prayer, particularly during the period of Ramadan (the Muslim month of fasting). Further good practice involves the monitoring of pupils' optional subject choices by ethnicity and the allocation of pupils to sets, bands and streams.

Task 22.1

Consider how well the schools you've worked in have reflected ethnic diversity in curricular or pastoral policies and practice. What would you do if a group of pupils started to make fun of an image of a person from a minority ethnic background during one of your lessons?

22.4 Meeting the needs of pupils with English as an additional language

Pupils learning EAL are by no means a homogenous group and, whilst they share some characteristics with pupils whose first or only language is English, their needs are very different. The process of learning a second or other language is intertwined with the pupil's cultural, social and first language development. You are likely to come across two main categories of pupils learning EAL:

- those who were born in Britain and who have progressed through the education system. Some of these pupils may have entered school with little or no English;
- those who have recently arrived in this country either because their families are seeking asylum or because one or both of their parents is studying or working in the United Kingdom.

Clearly, pupils' cultural and social experiences will influence their learning experiences in school. The acquisition of EAL is also dependent on the pupil's proficiency in their first language. It is vital that teachers find out as much information as possible about the individual pupils they teach rather than make assumptions based on stereotypes. Student teachers will need to take account of this broad range of factors when planning lessons.

The length of time it takes for a pupil learning EAL to acquire English to an academic level comparable to their peers will vary. Research has shown that it can take between five and seven years (Collier 1989; Wong Fillmore 1991). However, a range of factors will contribute to this and for some pupils, particularly those who have a lack of appropriate support at school and at home, it may take a lot longer. It is important not to confuse pupils' ability to converse socially with their ability in using academic language. Cummins (1984) distinguishes between Basic Interpersonal Communication Skills (BICS) and Cognitive Academic Language Proficiency (CALP). He explains that fluent use of English in social situations, for example, the playground and corridor conversations, does not necessarily equip pupils to use the academic language of the curriculum. As pupils move through school, the language of the curriculum becomes increasingly complex. By the time pupils reach KS3, they are expected to make sense of texts which are both cognitively and linguistically demanding and use this kind of language in an accurate way in their own writing. Many pupils, not just those with EAL, will require support to do this. Student teachers often feel overwhelmed by the amount of curriculum content they need to cover with their pupils. However, it is important that you also consider the language demands of your lessons, ask what pupils are expected to do with language during the course of the lesson and structure tasks appropriately so that language is used to aid pupils' learning.

Task 22.2

Choose a lesson that you have taught recently and consider what oral, written and reading tasks your pupils have needed to engage in. How did you support any pupils with EAL to complete these tasks effectively? Would they have benefited from any additional support?

Checklist

You may have asked your pupils to:

- give or justify an opinion;
- agree or disagree with something;
- pronounce words in a way that could be understood by others;
- challenge another view;
- understand both general and subject-specific vocabulary and use it appropriately;
- make notes;
- write grammatically correct sentences;
- form paragraphs and order them logically; and
- use an appropriate style.

Pupils for whom English is an additional language are likely to need support with some or all of these tasks depending on their level of English language development. It is also important to remember that pupils who appear to be quite fluent English speakers will need continuing support with understanding more abstract concepts and completing linguistically demanding tasks such as the kind of extended writing activities generated by exam questions.

In the absence of a nationally recognized framework for assessing EAL, most LEAs created their own individual systems. This not only meant that it was impossible to monitor the progress of pupils nationally but it also presented difficulties for teachers in understanding pupils' progress should a pupil move from one part of the country to another. In 2000 the QCA published *A Language in Common* which stated that the: 'assessment of English as an additional language should follow the same principles of effective assessment of all pupils' (QCA 2000a: 7). QCA recommended the use of a common scale of assessment for pupils learning EAL which is based on NC levels of attainment in English. Additional assessment criteria have been developed at two steps before NC level 1, and level 1 has been divided into 'threshold' and 'secure'.

The following case studies provide an opportunity for you to consider two EAL learner profiles.

CASE STUDY 22.2

Atif, who is in Year 9, was born in Britain and is of Pakistani heritage and speaks Urdu as his first language. Speaking Urdu is an important part of Atif's life and he can switch easily between Urdu and English. He uses both languages when talking with his siblings, his father and other Pakistani heritage pupils at school but always speaks in Urdu to his mother and grandparents. Atif's family is Muslim and after school he attends a class at the local Mosque from 4.30 p.m. to 7.30 p.m. Here he studies the Arabic text of the Quran. When Atif began Nursery in his local primary school, he knew very little English. He received specialist language support and made good progress. He obtained level 4 in his end-of-KS2 tests in maths and level 3 in science and English. This language sample is taken from a piece of written work Atif did in history on the effects of the agricultural revolution. The whole class were asked to complete a written answer to two questions written on the board. This is part of the answer.

William Read probably liked[2] the agricultural revolution and enclosure because he was always[1] well off anyway. He could use machinery which would make[1] farming easier and faster. He would make more money from crop[3] because he has[1] an estate which is big enough for machinery. It would be[1] more efficient and would benefit[1] him.

The agricultural revolution and enclosure wouldn't do much for Thomas Goddard because he was poor so he would probably be more[4] less[5] off than he was even though he was hard working[1] all his life. A landless labourer wouldn't be benefited by the agricultural revolution because they would be[1] moved out of their huts and become poor labourers working[6] hard.

While it would be inappropriate to consider only one sample of written work when making a judgement on a pupil, this individual piece of work does give us an indication of some problems Atif has. This piece of writing was considered to be at NC level 3. Atif's writing conveys meaning in non-narrative form, using some appropriate vocabulary. Ideas are developed in a sequence of sentences, demarcated by capital letters and full stops. However, the confusion over tense and the grammatical construction of some of his sentences indicates that he is not secure at level 3.

The following errors were noted:

1   Tense

2   Colloquial register

3   Plural

4   Inappropriate use of comparative

5   Word omission

6   Sentence order

It appears that Atif has made little progress in his written work since KS2. This often happens to pupils at this stage of linguistic development who may appear to be doing well orally and 'surviving' in the classroom. Also, additional support from EMAG funded teachers (see page 95) may not have been available for Atif. However, if Atif is going to cope with the more complex writing tasks expected of him as he enters KS4, and embarks on examination coursework, he will need significant support.

Atif would benefit from:

- support with understanding questions used for writing tasks, for example elucidation of terms like compare, explain, describe, summarize;
- modelling of paragraphs and sentence patterns;
- highlighting contextualized phrases and vocabulary;
- support in using grammatical structures accurately which could be done by oral rehearsal before writing or individual/paired re-drafting;
- support in writing different forms using writing frames;
- support in developing a greater range of language by the use of synonym and antonym word banks.

CASE STUDY 22.3

Maria arrived in Britain three weeks after the start of the Autumn Term when she was 12 years old. Her family is from Brazil and they are planning to stay in Britain for three or four years whilst her father completes his PhD. Maria speaks, reads and writes Portuguese and has attended school for five years in Brazil where, according to her parents, she was doing well. Maria has had very limited experience of hearing and/or using English and is having difficulty in 'tuning in' to British English.

This language sample was taken from Maria's geography notebook. The class were answering a question on the water cycle having seen a diagram with key words in their textbook.

The average Britain consume[1] use[2] each day of water is 200 litre[4]. 4,400 litre[3] of water people in our class use[3]. After you use water it is use[5] again to be[6] treated first than goes to been clean[5].

Maria has tried hard to explain a process without receiving any support. This piece of writing was considered to be at NC level 1 secure. She has attempted to use phrases to convey her ideas with some use of full stops and capital letters. However, the amount she has been able to write is limited and she has problems with word order and grammar. Maria has tried to use key vocabulary taken from the diagram but without support in structuring, her writing has run into difficulties.

The following errors were noted:

1 subject/verb agreement
2 additional verb
3 sentence structure
4 plural omission
5 tense
6 sentence structure/verb choice.

Maria would benefit from:

- using a Portuguese/English dictionary;
- bilingual teaching assistant support if available;
- the opportunity to participate in paired or small group talk in order to clarify her ideas and hear good role models and rehearse in preparation for written work;
- oral and written modelling of sentence structures;
- the use of writing frames;
- the use of cloze procedures (text with deleted words which the pupil fills in. These can be key vocabulary or structured words. To help the pupil you can initially list the missing words at the side).

It is important that teachers and pupils have high expectations of pupils and that 'commonly perceived setbacks such as poor command of English are regarded as challenges to be met rather than excuses for underachievement' (DfEE 2000: 8). Given appropriate support, both Atif and Maria have the potential to achieve so much more.

22.5 Supporting newly arrived pupils

Whilst the majority of pupils from minority ethnic backgrounds will have been born in this country, you may find yourself in the situation of teaching a pupil or pupils who are newly arrived in Britain. Their families may be seeking asylum in this country, they may be economic migrants particularly from other countries in the EU or they may be studying here. Entering schooling in a new country where you are unfamiliar with the system, teaching and learning styles and language, and, in addition, have no friends, is a challenge for all youngsters regardless of their reasons for being here. For children of families seeking asylum (applying for refugee status) their experiences prior to arriving in Britain, and whilst waiting for a decision on their application, which could take over a year, are likely to make schooling an even greater challenge.

The Refugee Council Information Service estimates that there were around 82,000 refugee or asylum-seeking children in UK schools in 2001. Although many asylum-seeker and refugee families are living in London and the South East, the system of dispersal introduced under the 2002 Nationality, Immigration and Asylum Act means that families are housed all over the country, sometimes in areas that are hostile to their presence. Children who may have experienced trauma due to their experiences of persecution, of possibly seeing a parent or family members killed, of leaving relatives behind as well as their home, possessions and friends are not necessarily able to feel safe once in Britain. For some, the experience of victimization will continue both at home, on the way to and from school and at school. For these children, it is hard to know who they can trust and teachers can help to give children some security.

Case Study 22.4 features Ornelo who shared her story when she was in Year 11.

CASE STUDY 22.4

My name is Ornelo and I came from Gjakova in Kosovo. My family and I are Muslims. I will share with you that I have a sister and two brothers. I now live in Coventry with my brothers and my mum. At this point I don't live with my dad and one of my brothers because they went missing during the war in Kosovo. When the war started my family was still together. It was the war that split my family apart and it's the worst thing that could happen to anyone. There wasn't a second without a bullet on the sky, there wasn't an hour without a bomb exploding. It was truly horrifying for me. My family and I ran away from this to a camp in Macedonia. This is the point where my family was destroyed.

Ornelo describes her traumatic journey to 'somewhere safe' and being found somewhere to live and attend school in London before being moved to the Midlands and another house and another school. She continues:

I'm doing my very best in school and teachers tell me that I'm doing well with the amount of English that I know. I think the people back home were kinder and nicer – they helped you when you needed help and it didn't matter what gender or colour you were. That was the best thing about school at home. It helped you to be more confident. But here in England the students bully each other. Me! I'm fine. I can't wait for weekends to be over just to go to school to be with my friends but mostly to learn. I really want a good future, not just for myself but for my family – especially after what they've been through. Today there is still no sign of my dad or my brother. Sometimes people do tell me that I am brave and clever. Brave because I always tell my story to people without a tear on my eye. I don't like people to see me cry. And clever because I have learnt English in just three years now. When I came to England I didn't know one word of English. Now I'm here writing my story for you to read.

Ornelo's story illustrates how important being successful at school is for asylum-seeking and refugee children and their families. It also demonstrates the progress that

Ornelo has made in terms of her English language acquisition. Like Ornelo, some newly arrived pupils will have no previous knowledge of English, whilst some may have had the opportunity to learn to read and write English in their home country. Some children may have had limited or disrupted experiences of schooling and for a few no experience of schooling at all. These pupils will need a great deal of support to settle into the school environment but, once settled, are likely to make rapid progress. When working with newly arrived pupils, it is important to remember that, whilst they may be limited in their use of English, they may in fact be very able pupils who are likely to be experiencing frustration on a daily basis as they struggle with the linguistic and cultural demands of the curriculum.

Task 22.5

The following checklist provides some suggestions for creating a learning environment that is supportive to the needs of pupils who are newly arrived in this country. When you have read it, consider how you might adapt your teaching style to incorporate some of the points.

Checklist for supporting newly arrived pupils

- ensure that you pronounce and spell their name correctly;
- establish a buddy system which is supervised and monitored and is the focus of classroom work;
- make use of any additional support from specialist/bilingual staff;
- if the pupil is literate in their first language, provide a bilingual dictionary;
- show you value the pupil's first language skills by giving them the chance to write in their preferred language;
- maximize the use of ICT including on-line translation sites;
- respect the pupils' right to a 'silent period' which could last for a number of months whilst they 'tune-in' to the language of the classroom and gain confidence;
- continue to communicate with pupils even if they do not speak and provide a range of opportunities for speaking and listening in pairs or small groups;
- prioritize activities which encourage collaboration between pupils and help to speed up the acquisition of English;
- consider how you group pupils for particular activities:
  i) with same language speaking pupils; and/or
  ii) with positive role models for behaviour and/or language.
- use 'key visuals', for example diagrams, tables, timelines and so on whenever possible;
- identify areas of strength and give praise to pupils' strengths and successes;
- remember pupils need cognitive challenge with structured language support – don't just ask them to copy paragraphs of text.

22.6 Conclusion

As in the previous chapter on SEN, the underlying principles that should inform provision for children from different ethnic backgrounds are enshrined in the ideal of inclusive schooling. Inclusion insists that whatever children's ethnic backgrounds or educational needs, they should be recognized as individuals, their rights should be respected, their potential should be harnessed and their needs should be met. Inclusion also dictates that all pupils should be prepared for life in an inclusive, pluralist society and the challenge is for schools to reflect that inclusivity.

22.7 Recommendations for further reading and webliography

Gravelle, M. (2000) *Planning for Bilingual Learners: An Inclusive Curriculum*. Stoke-on-Trent: Trentham Books.

National Key Stage 3 Strategy (2002) *Access and Engagement in: Science; Maths; English; Information Communication Technology; History; Geography; Physical Education; and Design Technology*. London: DfES.

Richardson, R. and Wood, A. (1999) *Inclusive Schools, Inclusive Society: Race and Identity on the Agenda*. Stoke-on-Trent: Trentham Books.

Rutter, J. (2003) *Supporting Refugee Children in 21st Century Britain*. Stoke-on-Trent: Trentham Books.

Travers, P. and Klein, G. (2004) *Equal Measures*. Stoke-on-Trent: Trentham Books.

www.babel.sh.com/translations.shtml (translation site)

www.becta.org.uk/info-sheets/english-eal.html (EAL information)

www.cre.gov.uk/ (Commission for Racial Equality)

www.flight.racism.org/solidar (information about languages, music, food, cultural and linguistic minorities)

www.qca.org.uk/inclusion/respect_for_all/examples.asp (Respect for all)

www.travlang.com/ (basic language in a wide range of languages)

23

Schooling and gender

Kate Shilvock

23.1 Background

Any reader of the national press during recent years could not fail to be aware of the concern being expressed about the educational underachievement of boys. Each summer, when GCSE and AS/A2 results are announced, attention is paid to the differences in relative performance between boys and girls. Girls, it is said, are in the ascendancy.

A generation ago it was a very different story. Underachievement by girls was highlighted as a national concern. Research published in the 1970s suggested that girls were marginalized in the classroom resulting in their low representation in higher education. Measures were taken to address girls' perception of themselves as achievers, to increase girls' interest in traditionally 'male' subjects such as maths and science and to ensure equal opportunities within, and access to, the school curriculum. Additionally, schools began to adopt teaching strategies designed to suit girls' learning styles and examination boards adapted assessment methods to shift the emphasis from terminal examinations towards the inclusion of more continuous assessment. The inclusion of coursework at GCSE was part of this.

At the same time, changes in society resulted in more women entering the workforce and changes in law resulted in equal access to some jobs which had hitherto remained male preserves.

In the 1990s, the Government of the day focused on raising standards of achievement by making schools more explicitly accountable. Also, the introduction of the NC prescribed what should be studied and obliged girls to continue with science subjects which in earlier years many had dropped at KS4. Against this background, girls have steadily improved their performance in areas of the curriculum once thought to be 'male' preserves, matching boys' performance in maths and science at GCSE for the first time in 1995. By 2001, girls outperformed boys at GCSE in all subjects except physics (Ofsted 2003a). It remains the case, however, that women earn less than men at all levels, even when compared to those who have the same qualifications and work in the same industries. At the end of 2006 just 10 per cent of non-executive directors of the UK's top 100 plc companies were female.

In this chapter you will:

- be introduced to the debate surrounding academic achievement and gender;
- learn about the current patterns of achievement and choice for boys and girls;
- consider the likely reasons for differences in achievement between the sexes;
- consider the research evidence for differences in achievement between the sexes;
- consider the current strategies for addressing underachievement related to gender;
- reflect upon the implications for your practice as a classroom teacher.

23.2 The world picture

Britain is not alone in its concern about male underachievement. *Literacy Skills for the World of Tomorrow* (2003), a report by the Organisation for Economic Co-operation and Development (OECD) and UNESCO, noted that at age 15 girls had higher reading scores than boys in every one of the 43 countries surveyed. The survey tested three forms of literacy – reading, mathematical and scientific – to assess how well pupils apply knowledge and skills to tasks that are relevant to their future lives. The executive summary of the report notes that 'reading is an increasingly essential pre-requisite for success in today's societies' (OECD/UNESCO 2003: 6). The report links reading underperformance by boys to 'lack of engagement' with more than half of boys saying they read only to obtain information. Given the importance attached to reading, and its relevance to examination performance, underperformance in reading by boys is likely to have a major impact on their overall achievement. On the positive side, Britain performs significantly above the OECD average in all three areas covered – reading, maths and science. British pupils rate the support they receive from their teachers more highly than in any other country included in the survey.

23.3 Patterns of achievement

'When boys enter secondary school they are already well behind girls in English, although they achieve marginally better than girls in mathematics. Except in a small number of schools, the gap does not close during the secondary years' (Ofsted 2003a: 3).

Differences in achievement are evident very early in a child's schooling. By the end of KS1, a higher proportion of girls than boys achieve level 2 in reading, writing and mathematics (Figure 23.1). By the end of KS2, girls continue to score more highly than boys in English (reading and writing), the sexes achieve roughly equally in science but boys achieve more highly than girls in mathematics (Figure 23.2). At the end of KS3, girls' lead over boys in English is maintained and the gap is significant, whilst in maths and science similar proportions of boys and girls achieve levels 5 and 6 (Figure 23.3).

At GCSE, girls gain more A*–C grades than boys in nearly all subjects, physics being the only exception amongst mainstream subjects. The difference between the sexes is greatest in language-based and creative subjects. Subject choices at A Level also reflect gender preferences and stereotypes with girls predominating in language

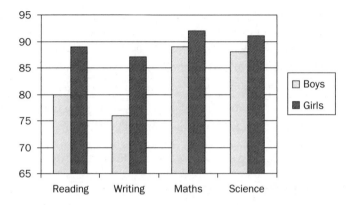

Figure 23.1 Key Stage 1. Percentage of pupils achieving level 2 or better, 2006

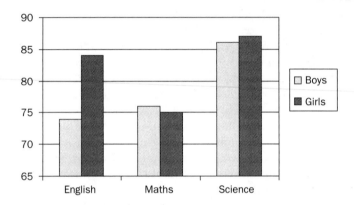

Figure 23.2 Key Stage 2. Percentage of pupils achieving level 4 or better, 2006

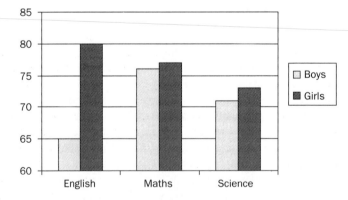

Figure 23.3 Key Stage 3. Percentage of pupils achieving level 5 or better, 2006

and creative subjects like English, history and modern foreign languages whilst boys opt in greater numbers for maths, physics and chemistry. Biological sciences, traditionally the 'soft science', are selected by girls.

It is important to stress that boys' achievement is not getting worse in absolute terms. Boys are improving their performance, as are girls. The difficulty lies in the fact that girls are improving at a faster rate than boys. Younger and Warrington (2005: 8) reporting on the findings of a four-year research project, *Raising Boys' Achievement* commented:

> Achievement levels in primary and secondary schools, as measured by national tests at the end of each key stage, are rising through time. In some schools and LEAs, this has widened the 'gender gap', at least in the short term, as girls' performances have 'taken off' at a more dramatic level than those of boys. Overall, however, evidence suggests that the gap has stabilised, against a background of a rising trajectory of achievement for both girls *and* boys.

It should also be noted that differences in achievement by gender are not as pronounced as differences associated with ethnic origin or social class.

Some groups of boys are particularly vulnerable. These include African Caribbean and white, working-class boys. Of course, not all boys are underachieving just as not all girls are achieving to their potential.

Task 23.1

Look at the data analyzed by gender in the *National Achievement Data* (see Chapter 10) to see trends in achievement over recent years.

www.teachernet.gov.uk/management/ims/datadiss/nadata/

23.4 Reasons for differing levels of achievement

It is difficult to isolate any one reason or area which could be responsible for the underachievement of boys. 'The overwhelming message from research is that there are no simple explanations for the gender gap in performance nor any simple solutions' (Arnot et al. 1998: 90).

Some attempts at explaining the gender gap focus on biological factors. When pupils enter school at age 5, girls are already more competent users of language than boys. Psychologists have suggested differences in the way the two sexes think (Kohn 1995; Gurian 2001) and research by neurologists has found that areas of the brain associated with language are more highly developed in females which may contribute to their better aptitude for language and social skills (Marrin 1997). Bleach (1998), however, cautions against assuming that differences are innate and so nothing can be done. The 'nature versus nurture' debate is recognized as being too simplistic to be of any real help in understanding the causes for gender differences in achievement. The situation is far more complex.

By the time children enter playgroup, they already have clear ideas about what girls and boys do. Observers note that boys tend towards physical activity, rushing around, whilst girls play quieter games and involve themselves more in discussion-based talk. By the age of 7, different attitudes to school are evident:

> Girls are more conscientious and concerned about presentation, they listen and pay attention . . . They tend to play without supervision, establishing their own rules and roles for each other in a way that mimics adult behaviour. Boys, by contrast, are more noisy and attention-seeking; they find it difficult to sit still and pay attention.
>
> (Bleach 1998: 4)

Other explanations focus more on social factors. Younger and Warrington (2005) point to the importance for boys of conforming to group norms, which are often in conflict with the expectations of the school. There is a narrower range of behaviour acceptable to the peer group for boys than for girls. Avoidance of the feminine and of the stigma of homosexuality are major concerns for boys. Whether this pattern of behaviour is innate or learned is open to question. It is likely to be the result of a mix of these factors.

Task 23.2

These are some commonly expressed views about the differences between boys' and girls' aptitudes and preferences.
    Consider your own reaction to them. Note your responses for later reference.

- Boys are loud and demanding in the classroom and get more attention from the teacher;
- Boys do not like writing;
- Girls prefer to work in groups;
- Girls find it difficult to think logically;
- Boys find it difficult to express themselves;
- Girls do not perform well under pressure of timed exams;
- Boys prefer physical activity to academic work.

At the start of their secondary school career, girls are more mature than boys. They are more likely to remain on task and to set themselves high standards. Bleach (1998), referring to an article by Lightfoot (1997), comments that the concentration span of a typical 13–14-year-old boy is 4–5 minutes, compared to 13 minutes for girls. Boys' need for frequent interaction with the teacher if they are to remain on-task has relevance for you as a teacher when planning tasks.

Teachers often comment that girls are more compliant, seeking to please by getting on with tasks, endeavouring to do their best and prepared to stick at tasks in order to complete them while boys rush to do things quickly and prefer short-term tasks. A survey of schools in Wales undertaken by HMI found that boys are less tolerant of poor or lacklustre teaching, quickly becoming off-task, indifferent and sometimes disruptive when they are bored or do not see the point of the activity

(Ofsted 2003b). This reinforces the point that boys' learning is more teacher-dependent than girls'.

In the home, it is often the mother who reads and engages in literacy activities with the children whilst the father engages in outdoor activities or playing computer games with his sons or helps with ICT and maths schoolwork. This reinforces the gender perception of literacy as 'female' and ICT or maths as 'male'. Adolescent girls are likely to spend their leisure time reading, doing homework and chatting to their friends whilst boys' activities have an emphasis on doing rather than talking. Thus boys, having a learning style which is experiential, fail to develop the reflective abilities of analyzing, discussing and expressing feelings. Whilst these are stereotypical statements and will not be the experience of all pupils, indeed may not be your experience, research has shown it to be broadly the case.

Society's attitudes towards males are also cited as a cause for boys' under-achievement. Traditional patterns of male employment have undergone radical change in recent decades, leading to uncertainty about what it is to be male. The decline of manufacturing industries with the loss of unskilled and semi-skilled jobs and their replacement by new technologies and service industries leads at once to a need for a better qualified workforce and to the replacement of traditional 'male' jobs with 'female' jobs. Additionally, an increase in family breakdown leaves many boys without a strong positive male role model in their everyday lives. This is compounded by a decline in the number of male teachers in primary schools and, increasingly, in secondary schools, especially in subjects which are 'language-based'.

In response to these changes and to the male image as portrayed in the media, many boys have a 'macho' peer culture which affects, often negatively, their attitude to school and to academic achievement. Shipman and Hicks (1998) found that the peer group culture was identified by both pupils and teachers as having the greatest negative influence on the motivation of boys. Teachers need to be aware of, and able to counter this peer culture, making academic success and being seen to work in class acceptable.

23.5 Approaches to raising achievement

The very first thing to emphasize is that, as the heading suggests, measures that a school could consider are about raising achievement for *ALL* pupils, male and female. Girls should not be disadvantaged by actions taken to raise the standards of boys. Indeed, there is the possibility that girls' achievement will be raised and the gender gap will not be decreased by any measures that a school adopts. Second, it is important for schools to adopt a strategy which suits their circumstances.

23.6 Building an achievement culture

Building a culture where achievement in all forms is valued and celebrated is crucial to raising standards. On a whole school level, this includes ensuring that a positive learning and achievement culture is developed amongst both pupils and staff. As regards gender, it is important that staff understand the issues surrounding boys' and girls' achievement and that school and departmental policies pay explicit attention to gender issues. This includes analysis of data relating to pupil performance by gender, including gender issues in departmental action plans and taking account of gender in lesson planning and delivery. Staff need to ensure that gender stereotypes and stereo-typical attitudes do not enter their classroom or teaching. The physical environment, including displays highlighting pupils' achievements, should encourage achievement, reflect work of both sexes and give positive signals about the subject's value to both sexes. Enabling pupils to use ICT to present work may help ensure that work is viewed as high quality and be of benefit to boys whose presentational skills may be weak.

Task 23.3

Does your subject have a gender stereotype or an achievement difference? What strategies can be used within your subject to address this?

Reflect upon how you can enable both sexes to access learning in your subject area.

Reward and sanction systems, where rewards are given for progress and effort in addition to attainment, and where sanctions are perceived to be fairly applied to both sexes, are important. Rewards, however, need to be of a type that boys value. Teachers know that praise is an important motivational tool but many adolescents, and particularly boys, prefer praise to be given privately rather than publicly.

School assemblies can be used to celebrate achievement, both academic and sporting. Research suggests that schools which place equal emphasis on celebrating academic or non-sporting achievement as on sporting achievement are effective in promoting a climate where standards are raised. In this way boys learn to value academic success equally with sporting prowess. Speakers who provide positive role models and challenge gender stereotypes are also used effectively.

Schools' pastoral structures offer many opportunities to support the academic curriculum and build a culture of achievement. PSHE lessons offer opportunities to deal with gender issues, presenting opportunities to examine the role of male and female in today's society, to look at career choices and stereotypes. Within a support-ive environment, the macho culture can be countered and strategies for resisting peer pressure developed. Many schools use PSHE to prepare pupils for subject choices at GCSE and post-16 levels giving further opportunities to counter gender stereotypes in subjects, for both girls and boys. Additionally PSHE can be used to teach study skills and organizational skills, benefiting all pupils.

The pastoral system provides opportunities to support pupils. Increasingly, tutors are involved in target-setting with pupils and have an overview of the individual pupil's development and learning. Target-setting is seen as an important tool in rais-ing standards and has been discussed in Chapters 9 and 10. An important point in addressing boys' underachievement is the active involvement of the pupil throughout the process and the regular reviews of progress, which are felt to be of particular benefit to boys. The tutor is often the secondary school equivalent of the class teacher in the primary school: the teacher who, because of their detailed knowledge of and daily involvement with the pupil, has most frequent contact and is well placed to pick up early signs of disaffection and provide individual support and encouragement. The role of the tutor and the relationships the tutor develops with tutees is crucial here. Pupils value being seen as individuals with individual needs. Tutors are also well placed to mediate between home and school, bringing an awareness of the pupil's home circumstances which may affect learning and able, through the use of pupil diaries, to communicate with parents or carers to promote pupils' achievement. Many teachers are involved in delivering the PSHE curriculum and so this has relevance for your classroom practice. Commenting on schools which are achieving success in closing the gender gap in achievement, Younger says, 'Where it's working is where the pastoral system in the school has as its aim the fulfillment of academic objectives' (in the *Independent* 2002). More is said about the role of the tutor and the PSHE curriculum in Chapters 24 and 25.

A further strategy for raising standards through developing pupils' self-esteem and awareness of learning potential has been the use of mentors. Mentors are used to target and support pupils who are identified as underachieving. Younger and Warrington (2005) report how targeting mentoring on pupils who were seen as 'key leaders', or particularly influential in their peer group, proved especially effective when combined with other strategies for building an achievement culture. Although mentors can be used with either sex, the disproportionate number of male under-achievers results in more boys than girls taking part. Two main forms of mentoring exist – both have at their heart the objective of building the pupil's confidence as a learner and enhancing self-esteem.

1   *Mentors taken from the business or commerce community.* Underachieving pupils, who may be of any ability level, are paired with an individual mentor. These volunteers meet with their pupil partner on a regular basis. Their remit is to act as a role model and sounding board, to encourage the young person to consider the value of learning and to raise aspirations. On a practical level, they might also provide advice on career choices or discuss strategies to resolve barriers to learn-ing the young person might have (for example, organizational skills or countering the 'anti-swot' culture). Meetings may take place off the school site. The mentor does not have a duty to assess the pupil or report back on the meetings.

2   *Mentors taken from the school staff.* Again, individual pupils who are felt to be underachieving are selected for the scheme. Each is assigned a member of staff – frequently a member of senior management. The mentor's role is to meet with the pupil regularly to review achievement in subject areas, to encourage and give positive reinforcement, to help the pupil set targets and to discuss strategies for resolving difficulties. The aim is to raise aspirations and expectations. This is a heavy commitment on staff time, so in some schools pupils are mentored in small groups.

A final point to consider in building a culture of success is that opportunities to succeed outside the classroom by taking part in extra-curricular activities can be beneficial in building self-esteem and in developing a less hostile view of school for some pupils. Extra-curricular activities help to build a school ethos, promote good relationships between teachers and pupils and encourage a feeling of belonging to an achieving community.

23.7 Groupings

A quick perusal of the league tables published following GCSE results would show that single-sex schools are highly placed. Many of these schools have a selective intake and a history and tradition of achievement. Research shows that it is difficult to separate the effects of single-sex teaching from other factors. The picture that emerges is very mixed and the proportion of pupils in single-sex schools is relatively small so that results should be treated with caution.

There is some evidence that girls' schools have a positive effect in encouraging girls to study subjects considered to be 'male' and in challenging stereotypical views, and girls in single-sex comprehensives achieve more highly than those in mixed-sex comprehensives. Boys in single-sex grammar schools perform better than those in mixed-sex grammar schools. Boys of low attainment perform better in single-sex comprehensives but for boys of middle or higher attainment whether the school is single or mixed sex does not appear to make a significant difference. The school's size, pupils' social class, prior attainment levels, history and tradition of achievement may all impact upon the achievement: league tables are far too crude to give a picture that a school could use to make decisions. Additionally, one needs to be aware that schools are concerned to develop pupils' social skills in addition to their academic skills and there are disadvantages in single-sex schooling. Consider, for example, the consequence of having the views of only one sex represented in discussion, or drama, and there is often a negative behavioural effect on all-boys low attaining groups.

However, some mixed schools have experimented with single-sex teaching, often in a few subject areas such as English and science. Single-sex teaching in a subject which has a large gender achievement gap and which sets by ability may avoid the problem of sets which are dominated by one sex. For example, many schools find that in English, higher ability sets are predominantly female whilst low ability sets are predominantly male. Such a situation can have negative effects upon the self-esteem of boys and lead to reinforcement of the idea that subjects are 'male' or 'female'. Frater (1997) reports that setting is the most common form of grouping in comprehensive schools and that heads and teachers caution that 'with the strictest forms of setting – on the basis of previous achievement alone – top sets would be nearly all female, the lower sets all male and *demotivated*' (1997: 15, original emphasis). Younger and Warrington (2005) report on an evaluation of examples of single-sex grouping in three mixed comprehensive schools. Results on the effects on pupils' achievements on the whole looked to be positive, but it was very difficult to isolate the effect of the intervention. Their work, though, gave strong evidence that pupils felt more relaxed about contributing to lessons without the pressure of having members of the opposite sex in the class and that they felt able to concentrate better. They conclude that the success of single-sex grouping depends on the teacher developing a relationship with the class which provides a basis for collaborative effort. They found no evidence that particular teaching styles were more appropriate for boys or for girls, but that a climate of collaboration and achievement was beneficial for both sexes.

Task 23.4

What has been your experience, if any, of single-sex teaching? Reflect upon the classroom situation and the advantages and disadvantages of the grouping adopted.

If you have no experience of single-sex teaching, consider your own schooldays and the way the two sexes behaved and learnt in the classroom. What differences can you discern?

What is your experience of the distribution of the sexes in ability sets and what impact did this have on the classroom environment?

A relatively new, and as yet infrequent, grouping strategy is to opt for gender-based seating in the classroom: boys sit next to girls. Group work is also constructed such that groups contain both sexes. Although evidence is scant, and more research in this area is needed, initial impressions are that attitudes to learning, particularly amongst boys, are improved. Many boys acknowledge that they work better when not allowed to sit with friends. Girls may benefit from the risk-taking, competitive attitude of the boys whilst boys benefit from the on-task, cooperative and communicative skills of girls. This is, of course, to generalize but early results are promising.

You will want to think carefully about grouping in the classroom and to ensure that grouping is selected to enable both sexes to achieve. It is not uncommon for teachers to seat pupils with a view to behaviour management but as Bleach (1998: 33) comments, 'the teacher should take the initiative in deciding where individuals should sit, based not on their behaviour but on optimising their learning'.

23.8 Teaching and learning

You may have read about learning styles and positive approaches to behaviour management in earlier chapters. Many schools are focusing their attentions on a whole school approach to raising the quality of teaching and learning with a consequent effect for all pupils but particularly for those who are underachieving, many of whom will be boys.

There have been some suggestions that boys are more likely to prefer more kinaesthetic, active, fast-paced and competitive teaching and learning styles. However, the picture is complex. In the interim report of their four-year research project referred to earlier in this chapter, Younger and Warrington found little overall difference in the learning styles favoured by boys and girls. They report that:

- girls are more likely than boys to have a good grasp of effective learning strategies;
- there is a marked preference for visual-kinaesthetic modes of learning amongst boys identified as potential underachievers or potentially disruptive;
- underachieving boys showed a predominance of interpersonal, mathematical/logical and musical intelligences.

(Younger and Warrington 2003: 5)

The final project report (Younger and Warrington 2005) found that teaching styles targeted both at preferred learning styles and at areas of weakness (for example, working explicitly on collaboration with groups of 'competitive' boys) can enhance learning opportunities for pupils. There was also evidence that simplistic approaches to learning styles were ineffective and genuine change in teaching practices difficult to achieve.

23.9 Assessment

It is often said that terminal examinations favour boys' learning styles emphasizing flair, risk-taking and short-burst effort, whilst continuous assessment and coursework which demands reflection and sustained effort over a considerable length of time favours girls. There may be some truth in this. However, when the proportion of coursework at GCSE was lowered, in the case of English from 100 per cent to 40 per cent, the gap between the genders did not decrease. Girls currently outperform boys in both coursework and examination components. Differences may reflect the type of questions asked: questions which demand discussion and reflection and require high-level language skills favouring girls; multiple choice and questions which do not require written English favouring boys, for example. It has also been shown that boys believe that a last minute burst of revision will suffice whilst girls work more conscientiously over a longer period. Encouraging self-assessment may help boys to develop a more realistic assessment of their learning and potential.

This has relevance for teachers. You have learned about formative assessment and the benefits it has for pupils' learning in Chapter 9. Assessment which provides quick feedback and targeted advice is helpful for all pupils but particularly for under-achieving boys who need close monitoring and to feel that their efforts are rewarded. It is important that the relevance of homework tasks is evident to pupils: whilst girls may conscientiously complete the work whether it appears relevant or not, boys are less likely to adopt this attitude.

Underachieving boys are helped by being given structures which enable them to succeed in tasks. This might include essay plans, mind maps and writing frames or being given short tasks which build towards creating an extended piece of work. They also benefit from being taught organizational skills.

23.10 Literacy

Literacy is one area to which many schools are paying particular attention in order to raise standards. Pupils entering secondary school face heavy new demands on their literacy skills. Reading competence is particularly important. The quantity of reading they are expected to do increases whilst the time devoted to teaching literacy skills decreases. Most pupils will already be aware of their difficulties with literacy and the effect of this on their achievement and many of these pupils will be boys. When a pupil whose literacy skills are insecure begins secondary school, the demands on their ability to read and write can be overwhelming and decrease motivation. Many pupils fail to progress in Year 7 and teachers note that demotivation and resultant disaffection often begins in Year 8 (Barber 1994). The KS3 Literacy Framework, which promotes the teaching of literacy across the curriculum, aims to address this. Boys in particular are helped by the structured approach, explicit teaching of reading and writing features of texts used in a range of subject areas, use of writing frames, modelling and scaffolding. You would find it useful to remind yourself of the teaching strategies advocated by the KS3 Framework (see Chapters 15 and 16).

Boys do not dislike learning, rather it is the style of teaching and learning that is important in addressing their underachievement. When you are in school, observe boys and girls in the classroom. How do they react to different types of tasks? What appears to aid their learning? What attitude to learning is displayed? What strategies do teachers use to keep boys motivated and enable their learning?

23.11 Conclusion

In this chapter you have learnt about the patterns of achievement shown by boys and girls and examined some of the reasons for the differences. Research evidence for the underachievement of boys has been discussed. Strategies for addressing underachievement have been outlined and related to the features of effective teaching examined elsewhere in this book.

Underachievement by boys in recent decades is a complex matter involving changes in society's attitudes and understanding of the male role, economic and workplace change and changes in schooling and assessment procedures. Those schools which have set out to raise the standards achieved by all pupils and tackle underachievement in general are most successful in narrowing the gender gap. Girls' learning should not be jeopardized by strategies to address underachievement by boys.

23.12 Recommendations for further reading and webliography

Epstein, D., Elwood, J., Hey, V. and Maw, J. (1998) *Failing Boys? Issues in Gender and Achievement*. Milton Keynes: Open University Press.
Francis, B. (2001) *Boys, Girls and Achievement: Addressing the Classroom Issues*. London: RoutledgeFalmer.
Howe, C. (1997) *Gender and Classroom Interaction*. Edinburgh: SCRE.
Sukhnandan, L., Lee, B. and Kelleher, S. (2000) *An Investigation into Gender Differences in Achievement*. Slough: NFER.
Younger, M. and Warrington, M. (2005) *Raising Boys' Achievement*, DfES Research Report No.636. London: HMSO.

www.ofsted.gov.uk/publications (for text of *Boys' Achievement in Secondary Schools*)
www.rba.educ.cam.ac.uk/ (the home page for the *Raising Boys' Achievement* research project)
www.standards.dfes.gov.uk/genderandachievement/ (the gender and achievement section of the government's standards website, including a lot of background data and links to research reports and development projects)

24

Pastoral care and the role of the tutor

Peter Lang

24.1 Introduction

The concept of pastoral care, in something similar to its current form, has existed in English secondary schools for over 30 years, yet its aims and practice remain among the less examined areas of secondary school activity. Indeed, the term 'pastoral care' only entered general use in schools in the late 1960s. Like so much else in pastoral care, the how and why of this remains undocumented. Nevertheless, pastoral care is a vital and pervasive part of teachers' work. By the end of this chapter you should:

- have some understanding of the nature of pastoral care and the way it has developed;
- be aware of the different dimensions of your pastoral role;
- have an awareness of the relationship between pastoral care and related areas, in particular PSHE;
- be able to think critically about pastoral care.

> **Task 24.1**
>
> Pastoral care is concerned with the well-being and development of pupils in ways beyond the purely academic. What aspects of school life would come under this heading? Write down three things that you think are important features of pastoral care. When you have done this, read the following definition. Are your ideas reflected in the definition?

The following definition provides a clear picture of much of the nature and scope of pastoral care:

> Pastoral care is essentially the commitment of schools (and teachers) to the all-round well-being and development of the child as a person (not just as a pupil).

This commitment operates through a number of different but related activities.

> **Reactive pastoral casework** undertaken on a one-to-one basis in response to the needs of children with problems of a social, emotional, physical, behavioural, moral or spiritual nature;
>
> **Proactive, preventative pastoral care**, often in the form of presentations or activities undertaken in tutor or form periods and assemblies, which anticipate 'critical incidents' in children's lives and are aimed at pre-empting the need for reactive casework;
>
> **Development of pastoral curricula**, aimed at promoting the personal, social, moral, spiritual and cultural development and well-being of children through distinctive programmes of PSHE, tutorial work and cross-curricular activities;
>
> **The promotion and maintenance of an orderly and supportive environment** by building community within the school, through extra-curricular activities, the 'hidden curriculum' of supportive systems and positive relations between all members, and the promotion of a pervasive ethos of mutual care and concern;
>
> **The management and administration of pastoral care** in the form of planning, motivating, resourcing, monitoring, supporting, evaluating, encouraging and otherwise facilitating all of the above.
>
> (Best 1999: 4–5)

As well as the above, the provision of support for pupils' academic work and achievement, sometimes known as academic tutoring, is an increasingly important feature of the pastoral care system in many schools.

For teachers at every stage of their careers, there are several ways in which they are likely to engage with their school's pastoral system:

- through their work as classroom teachers, teaching a subject and responsible to their department;
- through their work as form tutors, a role that NQTs are often expected to take from the very start of their first appointment;
- as members of the wider school community.

Task 24.2

Think about the definition of pastoral care given above in relation to your roles as subject teacher and form tutor. What expectations will pupils and other staff have of you in relation to pastoral care in each of these roles? Make two short lists, one for each role, of what you think are the most likely expectations. Make notes also of the expectations you are likely to have of them. You may find it interesting to look at these lists again at the end of the chapter and consider if there is anything you would want to change.

A brief history of the way in which pastoral care has developed will help you to understand current provision. Though understanding the way pastoral care has developed is not essential to fulfilling your pastoral roles effectively, it can provide a deeper understanding of pastoral care today and an appreciation that encourages a more reflective approach.

24.2 The development of pastoral care

The beginnings of what is now called pastoral care in England can be found in the public schools of the first half of the nineteenth century. In the first decade of that century, the most historic and prestigious public schools, which had during the eighteenth century been sordid and brutal institutions, began to change for the better. These changes were at least in part due to the influence of a number of reforming headmasters of whom Thomas Arnold of Rugby School is the best known. However, even in the case of the most famous of the reforming headmasters, achievements were limited:

> Arnold was not the first headmaster to attempt to end this warfare between masters and boys and to stifle the power of the mob, nor did he have the satisfaction of seeing his aims fulfilled. Thomas Hughes gives ample evidence of bullying and savagery and organised cribbing; and his testimony is corroborated by other Rugbians who were at school under Arnold.
>
> (Newsome 1961: 73)

Nevertheless, what Arnold sought to do was informed by ideals that he outlined to his prefects as follows: 'And what I have often said before I repeat now: what we must look for here is first, religious and moral principles, second gentlemanly conduct, and third intellectual ability' (Newsome 1961: 79).

Thus, almost two hundred years ago, we find a perception of education which goes well beyond the purely academic to encompass morality and principled behaviour. By the middle of the nineteenth century, it seems that these perceptions had been developed further to include consideration of how the structure of the school might respond to these needs. In 1860, the Clarendon Commission was established to examine the nine most prestigious public schools of the day and it collected evidence from staff working in the schools:

> The problem of numbers has been partly solved by putting each boy under a tutor whose connection with him remains unbroken during his whole stay in the school and whose duty it is to bestow that attention on him and undertake that responsibility for him that cannot be expected of the class teacher.
>
> (an Eton tutor) (quoted in evidence to the Clarendon Commission)

I think that besides any amount of class instruction the boy wants something else, something to tell upon his own personal needs, to make known to himself his personal deficiencies and to suggest that means of filling them up that class instruction must generally fail to give.

(Dr Moberley, Headmaster of Winchester) (as above)

The second of these quotations hints at the tension which has always existed in pastoral care between its caring and controlling aspects, and this can again be traced back to the nineteenth century. On the one hand, pastoral systems are designed to provide every pupil with a link to an adult who is responsible for their overall welfare in school, and on the other, it offers a structure for referring discipline issues.

The spread of comprehensive schooling from the late 1940s created fresh challenges for pastoral care. For instance, these schools tended to be much larger than existing secondary schools. The Chief Education Officer in Coventry, one of the first LEAs to introduce comprehensive schools, recognized some potential problems:

In a small school the loyalty of the pupil to the school and head teacher is comparatively easy to develop. The problem is to devise a system whereby the individual pupil is made to feel that he belongs (even in a large school of 1500) and in which careful supervision of progress of the individual is the responsibility of someone who has under his care a manageable number of pupils. . . . Such a system would not operate effectively unless each house had the opportunity of functioning as an entity at some period during each day. This can be achieved by providing the requisite number of physical 'houses' . . . the housemaster would act as a director of studies for the pupils of his house.

(Chinn 1949: quoted in Firth 1977: 80)

As a result, Coventry comprehensive schools were established with house systems within them. House systems were, of course, an important feature of the way public schools were organized. It is interesting to note the similarities in this quotation with what those reporting to the Clarendon Commission had said nearly one hundred years earlier.

In the post-war years four key concerns were discernible which shaped the development of pastoral care systems. These concerns were:

- the size of the new comprehensive schools and the potential for pupils to become alienated;
- the need for each pupil to be able to identify with somebody and something;
- recognition that each pupil should be well known by at least one member of the school staff;
- the need for an organizational structure should be able to respond to pupils' problems.

By the early 1970s, comprehensive schools had been established in many LEAs.

In the vast majority of comprehensive schools, the term pastoral care was being used and applied to the house systems which many had set up following the Coventry model.

A major issue for all schools was that whilst schools always described the primary task of their pastoral systems as the care of pupils, it was almost always the control of pupils and administration that were the main functions. According to Power (1996), another key issue was the pastoral/academic divide. Heads of house or heads of year and heads of academic departments operated completely independent systems, each under a deputy head teacher with responsibility for the area. It was quite common for the middle managers responsible for pastoral care and those responsible for the academic curriculum to have separate meetings and never to be involved in meetings of both groups. In some cases, the two parallel systems effectively worked in opposition to each other. The position of pastoral care in the early days of comprehensive schooling can be summed up as being vague on detailed aims, strong on structure and weak on process (what you actually do).

Task 24.3

In most schools today, thinking about and practice in pastoral care have moved on significantly from the situation described above. Investigate the situation in a school with which you are involved. Look at policy and guidance documentation that exists in relation to pastoral care and talk to some members of staff.
    You might seek answers to the following points:

- What are the aims for pastoral care and how high a profile are they given?
- Do the teachers you talk to have clear ideas about the aims of pastoral care in their school, and how do these compare with each other and with the school aims?
- Do the pastoral and academic systems in the school work mainly in separate or in integrated ways?
- How much guidance is given about the actual processes through which pastoral care should be provided? For example, on what basis do tutors decide how they should use their tutorial time?

24.3 Pastoral care's relationship with other areas

Pastoral care can be seen as having two kinds of relationship with other aspects of the school's work. The first is its relationship with the academic curriculum and the academic structure of the school. Pastoral care supports the work of subject departments and the school as a whole and, in reverse, it relies on support from subject departments and senior management to work effectively.

The other kind of relationship involves affective education. Pastoral care can be seen as one manifestation of a broader concern with pupils' affective education. Thus, pastoral care is part of a broader concept. Affective education is not confined to pastoral care and there are a number of other areas which, explicitly or implicitly, have an affective dimension. PSHE, citizenship and spiritual, moral, social and cultural education can all be seen as having an explicit affective dimension, whilst drama and RE, for example, have a strong implicit affective dimension. The form the relationship takes in a particular school will depend on two factors: organization and understanding. In the case of organization, the way tutors are involved in affective education gives the clearest example. Along with the pastoral middle manager, the tutorial role is the other major specifically pastoral one. In some schools, it is tutors who deliver the PSHE programme, whilst in others this is done by a semi-specialist team. The school's understanding of the nature of affective education is very import-ant, and the relationship between the pastoral and other manifestations of affective education within the school may be very close or relatively distanced. This is most significantly the case in relation to PSHE. In some schools, PSHE is seen as contain-ing a significant affective element and thus closely related to pastoral care, in others the programme is content driven, involves a large amount of worksheet completion and is not perceived as having a significant affective dimension, and thus little rela-tionship with pastoral care.

24.4 The organization of pastoral care

My review of the origins of pastoral care explained how its first form of organization was the house system. These systems are normally described as 'vertical' in that pupils entering a house remain in it until they leave the school, with the house head and tutorial team also working in that house on a permanent basis. This system has some key advantages:

- All the siblings from a particular family will join the house and thus a stronger relationship with the family will be formed;
- The house is an all-age grouping and it is easier to introduce both collaborative activities between year groups within the house and competitive activities between houses.

Over the years, there has been a move away from house systems to year group or 'horizontal' systems. The arguments for year group systems are partly administra-tive, but also pastoral. If all the pupils in a pastoral grouping are at the same stage, both administrative and personal issues are likely to be similar. Hamblin (1978) pre-sented the idea of 'critical incidents' and suggested that a key task for pastoral care was to support pupils in addressing these incidents. For example, the transition from primary to secondary school is a critical incident for the vast majority of pupils. At a later stage in a pupil's school career, the choice of subjects and working for GCSEs is another. More recently, however, there has been a renewed interest in mixed age tutor groups and the value they can have in providing cohesion within the school and a sense of responsibility amongst older pupils towards their younger class mates (Ireson 1999).

There are other important dimensions to the way pastoral care is organized. For example, the degree of continuity in staff–pupil relationships is significant. How important does a school think it is that pupils remain with a tutor and pastoral man-ager over a long period of time, and how effective is their organization in achieving what they feel is appropriate?

Task 24.4

Generally it is felt that it is most valuable if pupils remain with the same tutor and pastoral manager for as long as possible, but some argue that regular change is beneficial.
  Make a list of what you see as the pros and cons of each approach.

Another dimension of the organization of pastoral care concerns the key pastoral role you are likely to take – that of tutor. Marland (1974) wrote about the way the tutorial role varied from school to school. At one end of a continuum was what he described as the 'tutor subordinate'. Here the tutor undertakes mundane administrative tasks but has little or no responsibility. At the other extreme, a tutor has the key pastoral role, taking full responsibility for their tutees. Organizational differences which reflect this continuum still exist in schools and it is one of the most important factors in determining the pastoral teacher you can be. For example, at the most basic level there is a lot of variation in the amount of time made available to tutors to meet with their group. You may want to take this kind of difference into account when thinking about the school you would prefer to work in for your first post.

There has always been a tendency for pastoral care to be problem orientated, dealing with pupils' problems or, of course, dealing with the problems pupils create for schools. Recently, however, there has been an increasing emphasis on the support of achievement as a key justification for pastoral care (Megahy 1998). A 2002 report on the achievement of boys states: 'Where it's working is where the pastoral system in the school has as its aim the fulfillment of academic objectives' (Younger 2002, quoted in *The Independent*). Key factors in achieving this are the requirement for one person to act as academic tutor, that is to have an overview of the pupil's all-round progress, and to be able to provide the pupil with both feedback (how they are doing) and feedforward (what they can do to improve). It is normally the form tutor who takes the key role and, of course, to do this effectively they will need relevant, up-to-date information and also an appropriate amount of time.

Schools take various approaches to the need to provide time to talk to each pupil individually. Many set one or two whole days aside in the year when an individual tutor undertakes tutee interviews (parents may also be involved in this). Alternatively, tutees are withdrawn from classes for their individual interviews. Typically this will take place three times a year. Such approaches provide an opportunity to develop your tutorial role to the full. Though a key task of the interviews is likely to be target-setting and review, with thought and planning you can gain a much fuller understanding of your tutees and strengthen the quality of your relationship with them. If you are in a school that does not provide time for working with pupils individually, it is still important to find time for this activity. This may provide opportunities to identify pupils who are in particular need of your support in one way or another.

24.5 Pastoral aspects of your role as a subject teacher

Your timetable will in part determine the degree to which you can operate as a pastoral teacher. If you see a class for only one or two periods, as opposed to five or six a week, this is bound to influence what is possible. Current approaches to effective teaching stress the need to limit teacher talk, to praise, to be consistent and fair and to ensure that pupils understand what they should be doing and why. There is also emphasis on developing positive relationships. All of this, if achieved, will contribute to your quality as a pastoral teacher.

Schools have various ways of transmitting significant pastoral information to those who teach the pupils concerned. There is significant variation in the sensitivity with which this is done. Information about personal issues concerning a pupil (bereavement, parental divorce and so on) should be given to those who are likely to come into contact with the pupil concerned, but this should not enter the public domain, for example, on the staffroom noticeboard. As a class teacher, you should ensure that you are aware of any issues of this kind, possibly noting them discreetly as an aide-memoire when you are teaching the pupil concerned so that you can make any adjustments to your approach you feel appropriate. Equally, you should endeavour to maintain a sensitive watch for any signs of personal problems displayed by pupils you teach. You may feel able to follow this up yourself initially (if you have a good relationship with the pupil) or communicate directly with the relevant tutor or pastoral middle manager. If possible, provide opportunities for pupils to talk to you. Finally, it is important to pass on praise not just criticism to the staff with pastoral responsibility for pupils, and if possible not just for academic work. Thus, if a pupil has been particularly helpful, letting the tutor know this can lead to a positive acknowledgement.

24.6 The role of the tutor

There are many aspects to a tutor's role, including at least

- advocacy – speaking and acting on behalf of individual pupils or groups of pupils;
- academic tutoring – supporting the academic progress of individual pupils;
- discipline – enforcing the school rules;
- administration/communication – acting as a link between central school administration and your tutor group and between other staff and members of your tutor group.

Advocacy is an underemphasized aspect of the tutor's role. Many schools now have school councils and some also have peer mentoring schemes, but these provide a fairly limited way for individual pupils to express their views or seek support. There are situations where pupils will benefit from the support of a neutral adult who knows them well and can speak on their behalf. Taking the role of a neutral adult demands care and judgement. Pupils who come to you for help need to have their concerns recognized and not dismissed; they need to be listened to. They may also have needs for reassurance or for space to deal with their anger. Don't be tempted, though, to promise to sort out the problem for them, as this is likely to be beyond your powers. Make use of your more experienced colleagues if you are in any doubt how to respond.

Academic tutoring has become a much bigger part of the form tutor's role since the mid-1990s. This is partly as a result of the increased availability of assessment data which gives schools and pupils a way of benchmarking performance and making reasonable predictions. You will find more information about the sort of data that is available and its uses in Chapter 10. As a form tutor you are likely to be involved in setting and reviewing targets with pupils and, most importantly, in helping them to see how they can improve their results. Improving results is not all there is to academic tutoring, however, and you will also be called on to talk to pupils about important curriculum decisions (particularly at the end of KS3 and KS4). You will need a thorough understanding of the qualifications framework for 14–19 (see Chapter 19) and a knowledge of the sources of careers advice available to young people. You will also need to have some of the skill required to help young people to make informed decisions.

Both of these first two aspects of the tutor's role demand that you know your pupils well enough to offer them advice and support and to notice when they have a difficulty of some sort. They also demand that the pupils know you well enough to trust you with confidences and to rely on your guidance. Many of the activities that tutor groups and tutors undertake are essentially designed with this purpose in mind. You can get to know your pupils through working with them on collecting money for charity, organizing the form assembly, running a stall for the school Christmas fayre, tutor group outings, and so on. It is also important to provide regular situations where there is no formal agenda and where individual pupils can raise issues if they want to.

Many schools look to form tutors to enforce school rules on matters like dress and equipment, seeing it as a pastoral responsibility rather than a subject teacher's role to make sure that pupils are, in this sense, fit to start the school day. You will not be viewed favourably by your colleagues, or earn your pupils' respect, if you ignore this aspect of your role. However, blending this role with those of advocate and academic adviser needs some skill and sensitivity. A confrontation over make-up or trainers is not the best way to start a conversation about option choices.

As form tutor you will also be responsible for recording and monitoring attendance and punctuality. School attendance is a legal issue as parents or carers are legally responsible for ensuring that their children attend school. It is also a key political issue as government promises to cut down on truancy translate into targets for school attendance for LAs and individual schools. The school you work in will have strict procedures for recording and following up absence and you need to make sure that you understand and follow these procedures. Many schools will also have robust policies for reducing truancy in the form of rewards for good attendance, quick follow-up on absences and coordinated response to individuals who develop patterns of absence.

In order to fulfill the administrative aspects of your role effectively you will need to be very well organized as a tutor. Good organization will not only enable you to help your pupils understand and engage in school life, it will also help you to minimize the time and effort spent on administrative tasks so that more time can be spent on the more interesting aspects of your pastoral responsibility. Every school is different in terms of the administrative demands made of tutors, but it is well worth your while to get some tips on organization from the most efficient tutors in the school. The pastoral managers (year heads or heads of house) will be able to tell you who these people are!

24.7 Working with parents

All aspects of your pastoral role will bring you into contact with parents, but it is in your role as tutor that this is particularly important. Part of your role involves interpreting the school to your tutor group and this extends to parents. Schools will have different approaches to how and to what extent tutors should try to get to know parents. Whatever these are, it is always going to be worthwhile to make specific efforts to get to know your group's parents. In particular, where parents and tutors already know each other, confrontations over particular problems or issues are much less likely and can usually be dealt with in a more amicable fashion. You will find further guidance on contact with parents in Chapter 7.

24.8 Conclusion

The intention of this chapter has been to provide a thoughtful starting point for you as a pastoral tutor. The pastoral role is now central to the work of secondary schools, albeit this is partly in terms of the contribution it makes to supporting the academic performance of pupils.

Schools vary enormously in terms of the time and resources they allocate to pastoral care, the importance they attach to it, their interpretation of what it is and what it should entail. Though this chapter recognizes that not everyone will want the same degree of involvement in pastoral work, this is not to suggest that it is acceptable to work in an uncommitted and half-hearted way. Pastoral care is an important part of a school's work, and therefore of yours, and where it is effective all aspects of the pupils' development benefit.

24.9 Recommendations for further reading

Carnell, E. and Lodge, C. (2002) Support for students' learning: what the form tutor can do, *Pastoral Care in Education*, 20(4).

Carnell, E. and Lodge, C. (2002) *Supporting Effective Learning*. London: Paul Chapman.

Lodge, C. (2002) Tutors Talking, *Pastoral Care in Education*, 20(4).

Marland, M. and Rogers, R. (2004) *How to be a Successful Form Tutor*. London: Continuum.

Rosenblatt, M. (2002) Effective tutoring and school improvement, *Pastoral Care in Education*, 20(4).

Watson-Davies, R. (2005) *Form Tutor's Pocket Book*. Alresford: Teachers' Pocketbooks.

25

Personal, social and health education

Peter Lang and Chris Husbands

25.1 Introduction

There is an old saying, which suggests that the most important things we learn are learnt in nursery school, where we learn to line up, to take turns, and, most important of all, always to flush the toilet. It's a reminder that schools are not simply concerned with the formal, academic curriculum of subjects, but also with pupils' wider development – with their personal, social and health education (PSHE). We expect schools to play a leading role in the socialization of pupils, preparing them in the most general terms for the demands of adult and social life, and this involves learning to work effectively with others as well as to negotiate a path through the intricacies of life in a diverse and rapidly changing society. More than this, we understand that whilst pupils' academic attainments may be powerfully influenced by their cognitive skills and dispositions and the quality of teaching they receive, it is also the case that pupils' educational success is affected by their self-esteem, and their abilities to negotiate their way through the emotional and psychological complexities of childhood and adolescence. These considerations surround schools' work in PSHE. Since the review of the NC in 2000, PSHE has been a required part of the secondary curriculum, underpinned by non-mandatory national guidance, and it has replaced the narrower terms 'Tutorial Work' or 'Personal and Social Education', which schools previously used. The publication of *Every Child Matters* (DfES 2003e; see Chapter 20) has prompted a shift in the way schools think about their roles which might place PSHE at the centre of the curriculum.

By the end of this chapter you should:

- understand the aims and content of PSHE programmes;
- know the main methods of and issues in the organization of PSHE in schools;
- be aware of pedagogic issues in the teaching of PSHE.

Task 25.1

Note now what you think PSHE should involve and how it differs from pastoral care.

25.2 The aims and content of PSHE

The school curriculum, as you have seen in Chapter 13, is one of the main ways in which schools set out to provide opportunities for all pupils to learn and to achieve. The 1988 Education Reform Act saw the overarching aim of the school curriculum as being to promote pupils' spiritual, moral, social and cultural development and to prepare pupils for the opportunities, responsibilities and experiences of adult life. These are ambitious aims which go to the heart of the purposes of schooling in a modern, complex society. If schools are to succeed in achieving these aims, they need to suffuse the whole academic curriculum. This is a challenging task, and one way of thinking about PSHE is that it provides the framework which draws together the full range of schools' curriculum work: dealing with issues of pupils' confidence and motivation; supporting them in making the most of their abilities and preparing them for the demands of adult social and emotional life. In this context, schools' curricula for PSHE have wide-ranging aims and objectives, but they can normally be grouped into three main areas:

- aims in respect of supporting pupils' social and emotional development, includ-ing addressing issues of collaboration, prejudice reduction, team work and group work, and emotional literacy;
- aims in respect of supporting pupils' social and health education, including addressing areas of content such as developing a healthy lifestyle, making appropriate sexual decisions and understanding and evaluating risk in personal life in relation to issues of, for example, diet and sexual activity;
- aims in respect of pupils' abilities to take advantage of learning opportunities across the school, addressing issues of study approaches, learning and target-setting across the curriculum, thinking skills (McGuiness 1998) and 'learning how to learn', as well as careers guidance.

Task 25.2

Consider how these aims relate to the five outcomes set out in *Every Child Matters*, that children should:

- enjoy and achieve;
- achieve economic well-being;
- stay safe;
- be healthy;
- make a positive contribution.

It is apparent from this range of aims that the potential scope of PSHE programmes in schools is enormous. The non-mandatory programme of study for PSHE acknowledges this, identifying three strands for the teaching of PSHE: developing confidence and responsibility and making the most of their abilities; developing a healthier, safer lifestyle; developing good relationships and respecting the differences between people (QCA 2000b: 3). It invites each school to develop its own approach to PSHE, setting priorities within the broad framework which relate to pupils' own needs given the community the school serves. In some schools, the task of building a coherent and well-structured PSHE curriculum in what is often very limited time has proved very challenging and PSHE programmes can often appear to be made up of loosely related tasks each with their own implicit mini-objective. In a crowded curriculum, it is impossible to cover everything and attempts to synthesize mini-objectives into broad, holistic aims which themselves serve as the basis for robust curriculum planning remain rare (Ofsted 2002a). In many schools a taken-for-granted approach to the way PSHE is planned and delivered exists, with more concern for timetabling and fitting in all the topics that have become traditionally associated with PSHE, than evidence of an agreed set of overarching aims.

Pring (1984: 43) has tried to provide a systematic approach to thinking about the place of teaching and schools in relation to PSHE. He began by noting some of the difficulties teachers face:

> Too often teachers react to the consequences of the essentially controversial nature of PSE either by reducing it to trivia, or by saying that it is what they are doing all the time in helping each individual to realise his or her potential. There is rarely any systematic reflection upon the values which should be promoted in the school or in each classroom, or detailed analysis of what is defensible as personal development. Education or the process whereby individuals are helped to grow as persons, requires a clear idea of what counts as being a person. It is difficult to see how anyone can claim to be an educator (as opposed to trainer) unless he or she has addressed him or herself to such an examination.

Pring went on to suggest four underlying philosophical issues for PSHE curricula, conceived in terms of education of the person:

> First one characteristic of being a person is the capacity to think, to reflect, to make sense of one's experience, to engage critically with the received values, beliefs, and assumptions that one is confronted with – the development in other words, of the powers of mind. A second characteristic of being a person is the capacity to recognise others as persons. Hence it is a peculiarity of being a person that one is able to relate to others in a person-like way, not using them as instruments of one's own ends, but as deserving of respect in their own right, worthy of being listened to, able to contribute a distinctive point of view. Third, it is a characteristic of being a person that one acts intentionally, deliberately, and thus can be held responsible for what one does. Finally, what is distinctive of person-hood is the consciousness not only of others as persons but of oneself – a sense of

one's own unity as a person, one's own values and dignity, one's own capacity to think through a problem etc.

(Pring 1984: 43–4)

PSHE was ignored in the first version of the NC in 1988 and attempts to develop 'cross-curricular themes' in the years immediately following the 1988 Act were largely stillborn as schools devoted energies to implementing the NC and its associated testing regimes. Since the early 1990s there has been a dramatic improvement in the status and position of PSHE in schools. There are a number of reasons for this. In the first place, a widespread view developed that the academic curriculum of the NC was insufficient as a framework for thinking about the curriculum as a whole and its relationship to pupils' wider development. These views were linked to general concerns about the place of values in society and the effectiveness of schools in developing young people's values (Haydon 1997). In 1994, Ofsted published general guidance on *Spiritual, Moral, Social and Cultural Education* (Ofsted 1994). Three years later, the Schools Curriculum and Assessment Authority (SCAA) – the forerunner of QCA – established a national forum on education and values in order to develop general guidance for schools on personal and values education (SCAA 1997). These developments fed into the review of the NC in 2000 and to the development of national frameworks for PSHE. At their most general, these sought to help schools steer a curriculum course through the multiple demands of delivering education for citizenship, health, sex and relationships alongside a concern to support young people's moral, emotional and personal development. These developments were supplemented by resurgent interest in schools in the nature of learning across the curriculum and, in particular, interest in ideas such as thinking skills (McGuiness 1998), emotional literacy (Goleman 1996) and, in some schools, the development of what the Campaign for Learning has called 'learnacy' (Rodd 2002). As a result, schools now are probably more aware of their responsibilities in PSHE than they have ever been.

Task 25.3

Draw up a list of topics, which you would include in a Year 9 PSHE course.

Looking at your list of topics, reflect on what influenced your choice, and consider the impact of the following factors: pupils' emotional development; pupils' physical development; the impact of pupils' social experience outside school and the issues pupils are dealing with in terms of the academic demands of Year 9.

Having done this, ask some teachers and pupils to do the same and compare the results. It is possible that the results may provide you with a basis for further reflection.

The following website links to Harrow Way Community School, a comprehensive school in Andover, and gives you an example of how one school structures its PSHE.
http://www.harrowway.hants.sch.uk/?cat=23

25.3 The organization of PSHE in schools

Schools vary enormously in terms of the time, resources and importance they attach to PSHE. In most schools, PSHE coordination has been improved by the identification of formal positions of responsibility, and school PSHE coordinators are supported in most LAs by PSHE Advisers. However, the allocation of time, resources and staffing to PSHE remains difficult in many schools. One obvious reason for this is that in most – though not all – schools, PSHE is taught by teachers who have not been formally trained to teach it and who are not organized into the sort of strong faculties which predominate in the academic curriculum; student teachers are not trained to teach PSHE and teaching PSHE is a part-time commitment for many teachers. Although some schools have, as a result of the increased national focus on PSHE, developed specialist or semi-specialist teams to teach PSHE, it remains the case that almost all teachers can expect to find themselves teaching PSHE at some point in their career – normally to the pupils for whom they also act as form tutors. This in itself makes PSHE interesting in terms of its relationship to pastoral care in schools. Given the complexity of the PSHE curriculum, the range of topics which may need to be covered, the need to relate those topics to the needs and expectations of demanding adolescents with complex lives, and the sensitivity of many issues in health and particularly sexual health education, this is a daunting prospect. Beverley Labbett famously described preparing to teach PSHE as, 'learning to handle your own ignorance in public'.

In many respects, the teaching of PSHE can seem to be quite different from the teaching of the academic curriculum in schools, and many teachers – perhaps especially new teachers – find it a daunting prospect. However, this difference can also be more apparent than real. Although PSHE has its own timetabled time and, now, its own curriculum guidance, it is also obvious that all subjects contribute to pupils' personal and social education. In all subjects, pupils need to learn to cooperate in groups, to manage their time effectively and to make effective connections between their cognitive and emotional or 'affective' development. This means that there should be strong links between the academic curriculum and the PSHE curriculum, not just in terms of content (for example, in the teaching of aspects of health education in science and PSHE) but also in terms of study skills and learning processes. Successful schools will have considered the ways in which learning demands are made on pupils across the curriculum and developed PSHE programmes which support learning across the curriculum – for example, timing work on homework skills, or making the most of revision time, in ways which are most effective for pupils. Schools which are the most successful in managing the relationship between the academic curriculum and PSHE will have gone further to explore the effectiveness of learning processes and styles across the curriculum and may have used PSHE time to support pupils in reflecting on their own approaches to learning and the ways in which these operate in different subjects. Paradoxically, the recent focus on target-setting and on maximizing academic attainment has strengthened rather than weakened the place of PSHE in schools, opening a new role for it in providing a framework in which teachers and pupils can work together on identifying barriers to pupil achievement and developing cross-curricular and integrated approaches to addressing and removing these. Schools which have successfully diagnosed this issue and developed plans to address it have established extremely robust relationships between their academic and social missions for their pupils. The concept of the 'affective school' has been elaborated to describe schools which have developed strong structures for supporting pupils' acquisition of 'emotional literacy', that is an understanding of how emotions affect our decisions and actions (Lang 1999).

25.4 Teaching PSHE

A further difficulty in relation to teaching PSHE for many teachers relates to pedagogy. The NC guidelines for PSHE refer to the knowledge, skills and understanding to be developed. Clearly these are not things that should be developed separately, because all are essential parts of effective personal, social and health education. Critically, though, these are not just things to learn but things that have to be internalized, and this is more likely to be possible as a result of active experience rather than passive assimilation. It doesn't require much thought to decide which would have greater impact of pupils: filling in a worksheet about the dangers of HIV/AIDS or teenage pregnancy or taking part in an active role play bringing to life the issues and pressures involved. It is equally clear that teaching pupils to work collaboratively and to make effective contributions to group work demands teaching methods which are themselves based on collaborative and group-based planning.

However, the difficulties are more deep-rooted than this. The outcomes of teaching history or mathematics are frequently clear in terms of pupils' understandings and ability to put into practice what has been taught. The outcomes of a teaching session on HIV/AIDS are more difficult to assess: pupils' understanding of the biology and epidemiology of HIV could be assessed but, in PSHE, the concern is more likely to be with pupils' ability to make informed decisions about their behaviour some years after the teaching session. More complex still, in many PSHE teaching sessions, teachers find themselves dealing with pupils' experiences of life situations which they have not experienced themselves and where they lack confidence – particularly in the light of the complex family and personal circumstances of many young people. Finally, the content of PSHE differs from much of the conventional academic curriculum in some important respects. First, it is frequently process-based: that is to say, the content of the curriculum is also its medium: concerns with group work, with learning how to learn and with personal decision making are both the vehicle and the purpose of the curriculum. Second, it is highly learner-dependent in ways which the content of the English or science or mathematics curriculum is not. Third, it is sensitive in many respects. This is obvious in the case of developing pupils' capacities to make appropriate decisions about their sexual behaviour, but less obvious in relation to issues about healthy eating, or ways of learning, where teachers' values may be in tension with those of pupils, parents or powerful social groups.

PSHE lessons are likely to feature specific techniques including thought showering, ranking, values-continuum, role play or hot-seating and trust exercises. Although these techniques are used in most subjects, they are likely to feature more strongly in PSHE than in other subjects because of their focus on values issues and, in particular, on what has been called values-clarification: the intended outcomes of exploring issues through these activities is not a class agreement on a best course of action, but a clearer sense of what is at stake. It follows that in PSHE, more than anywhere else in the curriculum, a teacher's role may be to ask pupils to clarify their thinking and refine ideas rather than to correct misconceptions and errors. In PSHE, it is a teacher's responsibility to allow diversity of views and to protect dissent. It is likely that given a debate in society over a particular issue, in PSHE the concern will be to explore the debate rather than to reach a particular outcome.

25.5 PSHE pedagogies

Thought showering

This can be undertaken as a whole class activity or with smaller groups who then pool their results. It involves making a list of related ideas without thinking carefully about what springs to mind. Everything that participants suggest is recorded without discussion. No ideas are rejected. A thought showering exercise should be spontaneous and brief. Some advantages of the technique are:

- Everybody is equal and has a contribution to make;
- All ideas are accepted;
- It is a quick way of gaining a lot of information;
- It can help a group leader to assess the level of understanding;
- It is cooperative and open minded;
- It can help with problem solving;
- It helps develop self-confidence.

Ranking

There are various methods of ranking and a wide range of topics/issues that can be addressed. Ranking entails listing a series of statements or pictures according to the demands of the task; for example, ranking a series of statements from agreement to disagreement or ranking a series of photographs from the most to the least stereo-typical images. It is important to have each statement or picture on a separate sheet so that they can be manoeuvred during discussion. Items can be ranked in order, or 'diamond ranked' using nine separate sheets. This is useful with, for example, value statements where it may not be possible to create a strict hierarchy. A variation of this is known as twos and fours where pairs of pupils are given a set of, perhaps six, statements/points. They then have to decide which four are the most important and discard two. They then form a group of four who have to agree on the four most important out of eight. This process can be continued with a group of eight after which the groups report back and discuss their choices.

Values continuum

Individuals consider where they stand on particular issues and then rank themselves physically, in a line. This can also be done using statements on pieces of paper but the act of taking a 'standpoint' may be more thought-provoking or committed, for instance, 'Strongly agree' through to 'Strongly disagree'. Having established their relative viewpoints, pupils can be moved into structured discussion groups.

Role play

This allows students to explore a situation (through the feelings and attitudes they might experience) by assuming the persona of a participant in a situation. Role play means presenting a set of attitudes rather than any physical change or characterization. It is a way in which teachers can give pupils quick access to a topic or generate more concern for an issue. This can take place in small groups possibly followed by a reporting back session, but it can also be an excellent medium for whole group activities where the outcome need not be anticipated in advance. Role play can help individuals to share emotions or concerns which they feel unable to express normally since it allows them to say how they feel and, at the same time, distance themselves from the emotions by putting themselves in a fictional situation. Role play can be part of an ongoing scenario.

Trust exercises

The most common of these is where pupils are in pairs and one is blindfolded. The one who can see takes the other on a trust walk around the classroom and possibly beyond. You will find further ideas at the website mentioned at the end of the chapter.

Circle time

Although there is no definitive PSHE pedagogy, it is nonetheless true that PSHE has been particularly influenced by 'circle time'. The participants work in a circle, usually seated on chairs, with the teacher acting as a facilitator. Activities usually start with a round where pupils pass an object and take it in turns to complete a statement such as 'I feel happy when' or 'something I find upsetting is', or make comments on a particular theme. Ground rules normally include 'only one person talks', 'everyone else listens', and 'no negative statements about other individuals in the circle are allowed'. From this basis a wide range of activities, pair work, games and small and larger group discussions are often developed. The process is normally seen as democratic and unthreatening, with no participant having to speak if they do not want to. However, there are considerable variations in what teachers perceive the outcomes to be, and therefore also in practice. Perceived outcomes range from the development of speaking and listening skills, through improved behaviour to increased self-esteem and emotional maturity. One important aspect of circle time is that ways are found of getting pupils to change places (which is much easier to organize if pupils are sitting on chairs) so that everyone is sitting next to someone other than the person they chose to sit next to. This means that pupils get to know and work with a wider group of classmates than might otherwise be the case.

Task 25.4

Think about the range of teaching strategies above. Using one of them, plan a micro-lesson for pupils in Year 9 on a theme in health or sex education, or designed to promote pupils' thinking skills. Consider how you will plan for a starter activity, active involvement and some sort of conclusion which protects divergence of view and pupils' self-esteem.

25.6 Conclusion

PSHE is one of a school's most important responsibilities. In this area more than in any other, perhaps, there is a strong connection between the subject matter and the way it is taught. In PSHE, teachers are required to work directly with pupils on issues which raise complex moral and values difficulties. They need to do so in ways which are structured and professional so that values can be clarified and principles pro-tected. PSHE is not just something teachers teach to other people; if it is given the commitment it deserves, it affects and possibly changes teachers as much as pupils. For many new teachers, this makes PSHE a challenging prospect. However, it also offers the opportunity to work directly with young people on the issues which they see as affecting their lives. As a result, engagement with both the content matter of PSHE and, perhaps as important, the pedagogic approaches with which it is associated, has the potential to contribute strongly to teachers' own personal and professional development.

25.7 Recommendations for further reading and webliography

Hornby, G. and Atkinson, M. (2003) A framework for promoting mental health in school, *Pastoral Care in Education*, 21(2): 3–9.

Lang, P. (1999) Counselling, counselling skills and encouraging pupils to talk: clarifying and addressing confusion, *British Journal of Guidance and Counselling*, 27(1): 23–33.

Radford, M. (2002) Educating the emotions: interior and exterior realities, *Pastoral Care in Education*, 20(2): 24–9.

Web resources
Personal and social education

www.aberdeen-education.org.uk/guidance/resources/G_PSE/gen.htm

This information and support service is part of the Aberdeen Grid for Learning. It provides information about PSE/ PSHE resources for teachers in all sectors of education.

www.teachernet.gov.uk/pshe/

This DfES website gives access to government guidance on PSHE.

Spiritual, moral, social and cultural education

www.smsc.org.uk

This is the website of a UK charity designed to give teachers access to resources for SMSC education. It is run by Christians, but gives access to appropriate resources from all perspectives.

Circle time

Further information about circle time can be found on the following websites:

www.antibullying.net/circletimeinfo.htm

A website offered by the Scottish Executive Forum. The information on circle time is part of a wider focus on anti-bullying.

www.sln.org.uk/pshe/p15f1.htm

This is part of the website of the Staffordshire Learning Net and also includes resources for PSHE generally.

Emotional literacy

www.antidote.org.uk/

Antidote is a London-based charity set up in 1997 to work towards an emotionally literate society.

eqi.org/elit.htm

EQI is a group of volunteers in several countries who are interested in emotions, emotional needs and emotional intelligence. The information on the site covers the academic and corporate definitions of emotional intelligence as well as articles on parenting, education, relationships, abuse and society's unmet emotional needs.

Trust

www.roch.edu/faculty/lhalverson/icebreakers.htm

This space is dedicated to creating a learning community within the Winona State University Communication Studies Basic Course.

Healthy schools

www.kenthealthyschools.org.uk/

A website of resources for all aspects of health promotion in school, offered by schools in Kent.

www.wiredforhealth.gov.uk

Wired for Health is a series of websites managed by the Health Development Agency on behalf of the Department of Health and the DfES. Health information is provided for a range of audiences that relates to the NC and the National Healthy School Standard. The site includes materials aimed directly at pupils at all Key Stages.

Sex and relationship education

www.dfes.gov.uk/sreguidance

The government's official guidance can be downloaded at this site.

www.brook.org.uk

This is the website for Brook, a charity offering sexual health advice for young people. It provides access to fact sheets and other publications aimed at under 25s.

www.tht.org.uk

The website of the Terence Higgins Trust, a charity set up to combat the spread of HIV/AIDS.

26

Government policy

Ian Abbott

26.1 Introduction

Task 26.1

Before you start to read this chapter, list five recent education issues that have been in the news. Why do you think education is so important to the Government?

As a student teacher you should be aware that the present Labour Government, elected in 1997, has devoted a great deal of time and effort to a major reform of the education system. Even if you attended secondary school as a pupil fairly recently, you will have noticed a great deal of change when you went back into school as a student teacher. Teachers are always complaining about the amount and pace of change they have to deal with. You've probably heard teachers make comments such as: 'Why did they have to change that?' or 'Not another government initiative!'

Alongside the reform of the National Health Service, education has been at the forefront of the policy agenda for the Government. Every part of the system, ranging from nursery education to adult education, has been subject to scrutiny and change. The secondary sector has been at the forefront of these changes with policy shifts in areas such as inspection, management, curriculum content, teaching methods and assessment. The pace of change has been so rapid that many teachers have felt unable to accommodate each initiative before the next arrived. Given this rate of change, there is a danger that a chapter about government initiatives will become dated very quickly as policy continues to be developed and implemented. However, it is important that you have an awareness of some of the most important changes and an understanding of the reasons for the Government's emphasis on education. Therefore, we need to analyze the reasons for the Government's approach to education, to use some recent policy initiatives as exemplars of government strategy and to consider whether the policies have been successful. By the end of this chapter you should have:

- an understanding of the rationale for the recent reform of the education system;
- an awareness of overall government policy for secondary education;
- an understanding of the specific pattern of reform;
- an awareness of the impact of recent reforms on secondary teachers' lives.

26.2 What's the problem with our education system?

According to the Government, the simple answer to this question has to be standards, which have been considered too low in this country. The first education White Paper published by the Labour Government identified raising standards in schools as 'the Government's top priority' (DfEE 1997a: 9). Since the publication of *Excellence in Schools* numerous policies have been introduced to raise standards for individual pupils and for schools. So, why has the Government placed this emphasis on standards?

Most commentators would agree that access to education is a basic human right and it is clearly important in a civilized democracy that opportunities for a high quality education are made available to all young people. Whilst the Government accepts this argument, it also believes that education has a key role in dealing with a range of social and economic issues. Reducing social exclusion is a key factor and the economic consequences of globalization and the technological developments of the last decade have increased the need for Britain to have a highly educated and skilled workforce. To compete with other industrialized and developing nations, Britain must have well-educated and adaptable workers who are able to respond to the demands of the twenty-first century. The economic argument for improving school standards can be viewed as straightforward:

1   In order for Britain to survive as a prosperous nation, we must be able to compete in world markets.

2   Success in this enterprise depends upon having a highly numerate and literate workforce.

3   However, standards in our schools are not rising fast enough, and in this respect England compares unfavourably with many countries, especially those in the Pacific Rim.

4   The Government must therefore raise expectations among teachers by setting challenging targets for pupils' achievement.

5   In order that these targets might be realized within a few years, the Government needs to shake up school pedagogy through initiatives that ensure everyday classroom practice is in line with the best methods available and that ineffective strategies are discarded.

(Docking 2000: 3)

The *Five year Strategy for Children and Learners: Maintaining the Excellent Progress* identifies five clear priorities for maintaining progress in education:

- closing the gap in educational attainment between those from low income and disadvantaged backgrounds and their peers . . .
- while at the same time continuing to raise standards for all across the education system;
- increasing the proportion of young people staying on in education or training beyond the age of 16;
- reducing the number of young people on a path to failure in adult life; and
- closing the skills gap at all levels – from basic numeracy to post graduate research – to keep pace with the challenge of globalization.

(DfES 2006b: 2)

In Chapter 20 you will have read about the introduction and the significance of *Every Child Matters* and the impact this has had on the system and on schools and teachers. *Every Child Matters* has altered the focus and placed the child at the centre of the system. In addition to this fundamental reform of the system the Government has introduced a range of specific policies to raise standards. You might disagree with the policies, but it is difficult to disagree with the Government's drive to raise standards in education. Earlier in this book, you will have read about strategies to raise standards in areas such as literacy and numeracy, to reduce truancy and combat social exclusion. Targets have been set for pupils and schools and performance indicators are used to gauge the success of policy. The results of these have been published in an attempt to drive up standards across the board. Probably the best examples of this are the annual publication of league tables for schools and the regular Ofsted inspection process. If you are undertaking a school placement, or are looking for a teaching job, you will almost certainly have consulted the school Ofsted report and looked at the various measures of school performance which are publicly available. An army of inspectors and statisticians is employed to collect this data. All of this effort will clearly result in better information and should enable clear identification of problem areas. As a consequence, remedial action can be taken to address particular issues. For example, as a response to perceived poor performance in reading and writing, the NLS was introduced. The collection and the publication of data by the Government is a valuable means of evaluating particular policy initiatives. However, what we need to do now is to consider in broad terms what policies have been implemented and how they are likely to impact on you as a new secondary school teacher.

26.3 Government policies

A central feature of the Government's commitment to education has been the increased level of resourcing made available to schools. The proportion of National Income spent on education has increased from 4.7% when the Labour Government came to power to an expected 5.6% in 2007–2008 (DfES 2006b). Average real terms expenditure per secondary pupil in England has increased from £3300 in 1997–98 to £4530 in 2005–06. There has been massive capital expenditure on education with a £45 billion building programme to rebuild or renew every one of England's 3500 secondary schools over a 15-year period (Partnership for Schools 2007). The composition of the workforce has changed as the overall size of the workforce has increased: 'Teacher numbers have grown by 36,200 since 1997. There are now 435,400 full time equivalent (FTE) teachers in the maintained schools sector in England, the highest level since 1981. Support staff numbers have also risen with 287,100 FTE support staff in schools, including 152,800 teaching assistants, an increase of 162,800 since 1997' (DfES 2006b: 11).

You are entering the teaching profession during an unprecedented period of rapid expansion and increased expenditure on education. However, in return for this significant investment, the Government is implementing continuing reform of the system and expects to see rising standards in all areas. The White Paper, *Higher Standards, Better Schools for All: More Choice for Parents and Pupils* (DfES 2005a), sets out plans to improve the system:

> by putting parents and the needs of their children at the heart of our school system, freeing up schools to innovate and succeed, bringing in new dynamism and new providers, ensuring that coasting – let alone failure – is not an option for any school. In this way we will ensure that every school delivers an excellent education, that every child achieves to their potential and that the system as a whole is increasingly driven by parents and by choice. To make that happen we need an education system that is designed around the needs of the individual – with education tailored to the needs of each child and parents having a real say in how schools are run. And to achieve that we need to reform schools so that they have the freedoms and flexibilities to deliver that tailored, choice-driven education.
>
> (DfES 2005a: 7–8)

In particular, the Government will aim to develop a radical new school system which is supported by improved choice and access for all. This will engage parents and pupils fully in improving standards. Education will become more tailored to the individual needs of pupils. The Government, through Ofsted, will take strong measures to tackle failure and under performance, but there will be lighter touch inspection for good schools. Better discipline will be fostered through use of learning mentors and on-site units in addition to greater use of off-site units. Parents will be expected to take greater responsibility for their children. All of this will be supported by a new role for LAs as part of their wider responsibilities for children. According to the Government, this will lead to irreversible change for the better in schools:

> We have pushed higher standards from the centre: for those standards to be maintained and built upon, they must become self-sustaining within schools, driven by teachers and parents.
>
> No longer will it be possible for any schools to hide its low or mediocre standards; or to argue that parents should not play a fundamental role in their child's education, having both rights and responsibilities to do so.
>
> No longer will it be acceptable for young people to be denied the opportunity

to achieve their full potential, whatever their abilities and talents; or for artificial barriers to prevent choice and diversity from playing its full part in delivering a good education for every child.

(DfES 2005a: 12)

It is difficult to disagree with the rhetoric of the White Paper about raising standards, improving choice and allowing children to fulfill their potential. However, these aspirations have to be turned into practical policies that make a difference to teaching and learning. So how might this national policy agenda impact on you as a classroom teacher? Let us take one small aspect of the reform process and see how it could impact on your work in school. In 2006, to meet the needs of individual children, the Government announced 'an additional £500 million this year to support the development of personalised learning, and which will be increased by a further £490 million next year bringing total resources for personalisation in schools to £990 million. The Primary and Secondary National Strategy will provide support for schools to personalise learning' (DfES 2006b: 12).

Task 26.2

During your school placement, find out what policies the school has in place for personalised learning. How successful are these policies?

You haven't misread the figures – that is a massive investment in this area of work of £990 million. As you enter the teaching profession, one of the policy priorities set by the Government will be the development of personalised learning (see also Chapter 6). The Teaching and Learning in 2020 Review Group (DfES 2006b: 14) recommended 'all schools should reflect a commitment to personalising learning and teaching in their policies and plans, indicating the particular strategies the school is exploring to fulfill the commitment to all children.' In order to develop personalised learning in schools we must begin by acknowledging that giving every single child the chance to be the best they can, whatever their talent or background, is not the betrayal of excellence, it is the fulfillment of it. Personalised learning means high quality teaching that is responsive to the different ways students achieve their best.

For pupils it means:

- having their individual needs addressed, both in school and extending beyond the classroom and into the family and community;
- coordinated support to enable them to succeed to the full, whatever their talent or background;
- a safe and secure environment in which to learn with problems effectively dealt with;
- a real say about their learning.

For teachers it means:

- high expectations of every learner, giving the confidence and skills to succeed;
- access to and use of data on each pupil to inform teaching and learning, with more time for assessment and lesson planning;
- opportunities to develop a wide repertoire of teaching strategies, including ICT;
- access to a comprehensive CPD programme (www.standards.dfes.gov.uk/personalisedlearning).

Task 26.3

Reflecting on your own teaching experience, how does your current approach to teaching reflect the expectations placed on teachers to develop personalised learning? What support, if any, would you require to develop personalised learning within your classroom?

26.4 Impact of government policies

The Government has placed a great deal of emphasis on the drive to raise standards in schools. Given the additional resources devoted to education since 1997 there is an expectation that there will be a significant improvement in standards in secondary schools. According to Ofsted:

> More than nine in 10 maintained schools inspected this year are at least satisfactory in their overall effectiveness, while almost six in 10 are good or outstanding . . . However the challenge of dealing with some persistent weaknesses remains. Too many schools are inadequate: about one in 12 of maintained schools inspected, and a higher proportion of secondary schools than primary schools.
>
> (Ofsted 2006b: 5)

A 2006 report by the House of Commons Education and Skills Committee on Public Expenditure provides evidence that public expenditure in this area has increased significantly in real terms with the school sector receiving the greatest share of this increase (House of Commons Education and Skills Committee 2006). Evidence was provided to the Committee by Sir David Normington that the increase in expenditure had led to an increase in standards: 'If you ask me what I am proudest of in terms of performance, I think that, despite all the qualifications we might want to make, school performance, both primary and secondary is dramatically up over the period and I think that has been money well spent because that is the investment in the future' (House of Commons Education and Skills Committee 2006: 8)

The DfES (2006b: 10) claim that 'since 1997 there have been dramatic and sustained improvements in attainment throughout the school system'. They go on to argue that at GCSE there are 'an extra 11 children in every 100 gaining 5 GCSEs at grade C or above (or their equivalent) than was the case in 1997 and an extra 9 gaining GCSEs at grade C or above or equivalent including English and Maths'.

However, significant differences also continue to exist in the levels of support provided to underachieving and deprived pupils from different areas:

The second issue is how to provide extra funding to pupils from deprived backgrounds. In the Schools White Paper the Government announced additional funding of £335 million by 2007–08 for those local authorities with the largest numbers of underachieving and deprived children. We agreed this was welcome investment but argued it would not reach children from similar backgrounds living in other communities, and so recommended that Government should develop with local authorities a system to deliver additional funding at individual pupils from disadvantaged backgrounds wherever they live using local funding formulae.

(House of Commons Education and Skills Committee 2006: 12)

Research by Ainscow et al. (2007) also identifies significant differences in levels of support for different pupils:

In recent years the Government has targeted funding at disadvantaged communities to help break patterns of inequity and improve all children's life chances. Whilst this has undeniably had many benefits, in 2006 there was also a growing sense that the ways in which funds were allocated was itself creating patterns of inequality. Children in inner cities were seen to be 'mattering' more to government than those in towns and rural communities who experience equally stark, if not starker, inequities.

(Ainscow et al. 2007: 10)

The sheer volume and variety of policy initiatives has also created some problems for schools and LAs:

Although the significant amounts of additional funding which had come into our inner city area had clear benefits, there was also a feeling of 'overload'. In some respects, the way in which interventions were formulated and introduced was felt to be undermining efforts to create a sustainable challenge to inequities as noted by one local authority officer:

'We tend to find that the Government throw a lot of funding into the city to tackle issues, so we do tend to get every project going which can be a strength or a barrier because all projects come separately and have their agenda – it's hard to coordinate them, and we don't always do it because of the way projects come in, and sometimes projects are just short-lived 12 months–3 years . . . That in itself is a barrier. It stops you thinking about how you do anything long term.'

The concern was expressed by one head teacher that the continual introduction of short term interventions could feed deficit views about learners in the area if gains in attainment were not made despite the additional funding.

There was also a feeling that schools needed to be given much more flexibility in the way they were allowed to use the additional resources provided by interventions. The very specific targets and conditions attached to Standards

Grants projects were not always felt to reflect learners' and schools' needs – as one headteacher put it, 'it's not possible for the Government to micro manage 25,000 schools in this way'.

(Ainscow et al. 2007: 11)

Task 26.4

During your school placement, find out what new initiatives the school has been involved in over the past five years. How were these initiatives evaluated and how successful have they been in improving standards?

It is important to remember that the notion of educational standards is open to more than one interpretation, an ambiguity which complicates any attempt to measure educational standards. Moreover, statistics are also open to interpretation and different groups will put a different spin on the same data. You need to be aware that there are conflicting agendas and messages in the daily output of government statistics and information relating to education.

For you as a beginning teacher, the significance of any government initiative is the impact it has on your school and your classroom teaching. Polices will directly impact on you in your subject area as you are compelled by the Government to adopt particular approaches, introduce new subject content or assessment procedures. In a wider school context, government initiatives will directly affect the amount of resource available, staffing levels and your conditions of service. If you are training or working in a specialist school or in an Academy School, there is a strong likelihood that you will have greater access to additional resources and more specialised equipment. If, however, you find yourself teaching in a rural school, you might have significantly fewer resources to deal with similar issues. However, the key significance of all education initiatives is the impact they have on the individual school pupil and your ability to operate effectively as a classroom teacher.

26.5 Conclusion

There is general agreement on the importance of education for the individual and for the wider community. All political parties recognize the need to improve educational standards and to create a more educated workforce to enable the creation of:

- a just society, where outcomes are determined by aptitude and ambition, not by circumstances of birth;
- a safe cohesive society, with young people entering adulthood able to make a positive contribution; and
- a prosperous society, successful in a globalized economy and able to support excellent public services.

(DfES 2006b: 3)

However, there is no general agreement about how these objectives can be achieved. In political terms, education remains a key battleground between the main parties. All governments will be keen to be seen to be improving education and it is very easy to confuse change with improvement. Whether or not they can be unambiguously viewed as improvements, changes in policy are set to continue. The policy debate taking place in Parliament and in the media might seem far removed from your day-to-day responsibilities as a classroom teacher. However, you cannot close your classroom door and ignore the latest policy initiatives. Ultimately, policy initiatives filter down to the classroom and affect the way you teach. You will be in the best position to make the changes effective in a positive way if you have taken the time to understand where they are coming from and why.

It is rather early to make a judgement about the success or failure of many recent government policies. Education policies often take a great deal of time to produce results and numerous questions about ongoing government reform remain unanswered. For instance:

- Even if standards are improving, are they rising at a fast enough rate or in the right areas?
- Should the emphasis be on developing skills for employment or on more general education?
- Are the changes being suggested for the secondary curriculum right?
- Should the Government develop a radical new school system?
- Is the pace of change right?

Imagine this scene. The year is 2015 and you are arriving at your newly built school, sponsored by a local software company, on a Monday morning. The first thing you do is to download the homework that has been emailed to you over the weekend, along with one or two excuse messages. You check over the slide presentation that has been put together for you from your notes by the department's ICT assistant and set off to greet your Year 10 tutor group who have been working on their personalised learning programme. Six of your group have registered remotely from the industrial unit where they are on a work-based learning placement on Mondays this year. The rest of the group are busy checking the e-conference notice-board whilst you talk to a few individuals about arrangements for the modular exams they will be sitting next month. At 9.00 you dismiss the group and go to deliver your presentation to the 85 pupils who are taking your subject at foundation diploma level. After the small group follow-up seminars you use the video phone to contact your colleague at the local college to discuss timetabling for next year.

This may seem far-fetched, but it is just as likely to be a very conservative assess-ment of the changes that will take place before 2015. Every aspect of this scenario is a foreseeable result of government policy initiatives current at the time of writing. Some of these changes will seem more desirable to you than others. More than ever, teachers, through their professional associations, the GTCE, subject associations and research networks, have the chance to influence the policies that impact on their work at local, regional and national level. In this sense, as well as others, the future of teaching is in your hands.

26.6 Recommendations for further reading and webliography

DfES (2005) *Higher Standards, Better Schools for All: More Choice for Parents and Pupils.* London: DfES.
DfES (2006b) *2020 Vision: Report of the Teaching and Learning in 2020 Review Group.* London: DfES.

www.standards.dfes.gov.uk (contains details of major government policy initiatives)
www.standards.dfes.gov.uk/personalisedlearning/ (provides guidance on current practice and information about personalised learning)
www.tlrp.org/documents/ESRCPerson.pdf (this report contains details of the TLRP work on personalised learning in schools)

References

Adey, K. and Biddulph, M. (2001) The influence of pupil perceptions on subject choice at 14+ in geography and history, *Educational Studies*, 27(4): 439–47.

Ainscow, M. (1995) Education for all: making it happen, *Support for Learning*, 10(4): 147–54.

Ainscow, M., Booth, T., and Dyson, A. (2004) Understanding and developing inclusive practices in schools: a collaborative action research network, *International Journal of Inclusive Education*, 8(2): 125–39.

Ainscow, M., Crow, M., Dyson, A., et al. (2007) *Equity in Education: New Directions.* University of Manchester: Centre for Equity in Education.

Apple, M. (2001) *Educating the 'Right' Way: Markets, Standards, God and Inequality.* New York: Routledge.

Arnot, M., Gray, J., James, M., Ruddock, J. with Duveen, G. (1998) *Recent Research on Gender and Educational Performance.* HMSO: Ofsted.

Arthur, J., Davies, I., Wrenn, A., Haydn, H. and Kerr, D. (2001) *Citizenship Through Secondary History.* London: Routledge Falmer.

Ausubel, D. (1968) *Educational Psychology: A Cognitive View.* New York: Holt, Rinehart and Winston.

Ayers, H., Clarke, D. and Murray, A. (2000) *Perspectives on Behaviour: A Practical Guide to Effective Interventions for Teachers*, 2nd edn. London: David Fulton.

Baker, E.T., Wang, M.C. and Walberg, H.J. (1994) The effects of inclusion on learning, *Educational Leadership*, 52(4): 33–5.

Bandura, A. (1985) *Social Foundations of Thought and Action.* Englewood Cliffs, NJ: Prentice-Hall.

Barber, M. (1994) *Young People and Their Attitudes to School.* Keele: Keele University.

Barnes, D., Britton, J., Rosen, H. and the LATE (1969) *Language, the Learner and the School.* Harmondsworth: Pelican.

Basic Skills Agency (1997) *Does Numeracy Matter? Evidence from the National Child Development Study on the Impact of Poor Numeracy on Adult Life.* London: HMSO.

Bennett, N. and Carré, C. (1993) *Learning to Teach.* London: Routledge.

Best, R. (1999) The impact of a decade of educational change on pastoral care and PSE: A survey of teacher perceptions, *Pastoral Care in Education*, 17(2).

Bigger, S. and Brown E. (eds) (1999) *Spiritual, Moral, Social and Cultural Education: Exploring Values in the Curriculum.* London: David Fulton.

Bills, C.J. (2002) Mental mathematics, in L. Haggarty (ed.) *Aspects of Teaching Secondary Mathematics:Perspectives on Practice*. London: Routledge Falmer.

Black, P. (1998) *Testing: Friend or Foe? Theory and Practice of Assessment and Testing*. London: Falmer.

Black, P. and Wiliam, D. (1998a) Assessment and classroom learning, *Assessment in Education*, 5(1): 7–78.

Black, P. and Wiliam, D. (1998b) *Inside the Black Box: Raising Standards through Classroom Assessment*. London: King's College.

Black, P., Harrison, C., Lee, C., Marshall, B. and Wiliam, D. (2002) *Working Inside the Black Box:Assessment for Learning in the Classroom*. London: King's College.

Blair, M. and Bourne, J. (1998) *Making the Difference: Teaching and Learning Strategies in Successful Multi-ethnic Schools*. London: DfEE and Open University.

Bleach, K. (ed.) (1998) *Raising Boys' Achievement in Schools*. Staffordshire: Trentham Books.

Bloom, B.S. (ed.) (1956) *Taxonomy of Educational Objectives*, Longmans: New York.

Bloom, B.S., Ebgelhart, M., Furst, E., Hill, W. and Krathwohl, D. (1956) *Taxonomy of Educational Objectives: The Classification of Educational Goals, Handbook 1: Cognitive Domain*. New York: Longmans Green.

Blum, L. (1980) *Friendship, Altruism, and Morality*. Boston: Routledge & Kegan Paul.

Boaler, J. (1997) Setting, social class and survival of the quickest, *British Educational Research Journal*, 23(5): 575–95.

Booth, T. (1996) A perspective on inclusion from England, *Cambridge Journal of Education*, 26(1): 87–99.

Brown, M., Askew, M., Baker, D., Denvir, H. and Millett, A. (1998) Is the National Numeracy Strategy research-based? *British Journal of Educational Studies* 46(4): 362–85.

Brown, M. and Millett, A. (2003) Has the National Numeracy Strategy raised standards?, in I. Thompson (ed.) *Enhancing Primary Mathematics Teaching*. Maidenhead: Open University Press.

Chitty, C. (2002) *Understanding Schools and Society*. London: Routledge.

Clark, C. (1989) Asking the right questions about teacher education: contributions of research on teacher thinking, in J. Lowyck and C. Clark (eds) *Teacher Thinking and Professional Action*. Leuven: Leuven University Press.

Clark, C., Dyson, A., Millward, A.J. and Skidmore, D. (1997) *New Directions in Special Needs*. London: Cassell.

Claxton, G. (1984) The psychology of teacher training: inaccuracies and improvements, *Educational Psychology*, 4(2): 167–74.

Clegg, S. and McNulty, K. (2002) Partnership working in delivering social inclusion: organizational and gender dynamics, *Journal of Education Policy*, 17(5): 587–601.

Cline, T. (1992) Assessment of special educational needs: meeting reasonable expectations?, in T. Cline (ed.) *The Assessment of Special Educational Needs: International Perspectives*. London: Routledge.

Coffield, F.J., Moseley, D.V., Hall, E. and Ecclestone, K. (2004) *Should We be Using Learning Styles? What Research Has to Say to Practice*. London: Learning and Skills Research Centre/ University of Newcastle upon Tyne.

Collier, V. (1989) How long? A synthesis of research on academic achievement in a second language, *TESOL Quarterly*, 23(3).

Comber, C., Watling, R., Lawson, T., Cavendish, S., McEune, R. and Paterson, F. (2002) *ImpaCT2 – Learning at Home and School: Case Studies*. Coventry: Becta.

Cope, B. and Kalantzis, M. (2003) A multiliteracies pedagogy: a pedagogical Supplement, in B. Cope and M. Kalantzis (eds) *Multiliteracies*. London: Routledge.

Cowley, S. (2003) *Getting the Buggers to Behave 2*. London: Continuum.

Cox, B. (ed.) (1998) *Literacy is Not Enough. Manchester.* Manchester University Press.

CRE (Commission for Racial Equality) (2000) *Learning For All, Standards for Racial Equality in Schools.* London: CRE.

Cuban, L., Kirkpatrick, H. and Peck, C. (2001) High access and low use of technologies in high school classrooms, explaining an apparent paradox, *American Education Research Journal,* 38(4): 313–34.

Cummins, J. (1984) *Bilingualism and Special Education: Issues in Assessment and Pedagogy.* Clevedon: Multilingual Matters.

Curtis, A. and O'Hagan, M. (2003) *Care and Education in Early Childhood. A Student's Guide to Theory and Practice.* London: RoutledgeFalmer.

CYPU (Children and Young People's Unit) (2000) *Children's Fund Guidance.* London: DfES.

Dahlberg, G. and Moss, P. (2005) *Ethics and Politics in Early Childhood Education.* London: RoutledgeFalmer.

Dall'Alba, G. (2006). Learning strategies and the learner's approach to a problem solving task, *Research in Science Education,* 16(1): 11–20.

Daloz, L. (1986) *Effective Teaching and Mentoring.* San Francisco, CA: Jossey-Bass.

Davies, H. (2002) *Review of Enterprise and the Economy in Education.* London: HMSO.

Dawkins, R. (1989) *The Selfish Gene.* Oxford: Oxford University Press.

Day, C. (1994) Quality assurance and professional development, *British Journal of In-Service Education,* 17(3): 189–95.

Day, C. (1999) *Developing Teachers The Challenges of Lifelong Learning.* London: Falmer Press.

Department for Education and Employment (DfEE) (1996) *Education Act.* London: DfEE Publications.

Department for Education and Employment (DfEE) (1997a) *Excellence in Schools.* London: HMSO.

Department for Education and Employment (DfEE) (1997b) *From Targets to Action: Guidance to Support Effective Target-setting in Schools.* London: DfEE.

Department for Education and Employment (DfEE) (1997c) *Literary Task Force: The Implementation of the National Literary Strategy.* London: DfEE.

Department for Education and Employment (DfEE) (1999) *The National Numeracy Strategy: Framework for Teaching Mathematics from Reception to Year 6.* Cambridge: Cambridge University Press. (Download at www.standards.dfes.gov.uk/numeracy/publications).

Department for Education and Employment (DfEE) (2000a) *Removing the Barriers.* London: DfEE.

Department for Education and Employment (DfEE) (2000b) *SEN Code of Practice on the Identification and Assessment of Pupils with Special Educational Needs and SEN Thresholds Good Practice Guidelines on Identification and Provision for Pupils with Special Educational Needs.* London: DfEE Publications.

Department for Education and Employment (DfEE) (2001a) *Key Stage 3 National Strategy. Framework for Teaching Mathematics: Years 7, 8 and 9.* London: DfEE Publications. (Download at www.standards.dfes.gov.uk/keystage3/publications).

Department for Education and Employment (DfEE)/Qualifications and Curriculum Authority (QCA) (1999) *The National Curriculum: Values, Aims and Purposes.* London: DfEE/QCA. Online at www.nc.uk.net/nc_resources/html/valuesAimsPurposes.shtml.

Department for Education and Employment (DfEE)/Qualifications and Curriculum Authority (QCA) (2000) *The National Curriculum Handbook for Secondary Teachers in England: Key Stage 3 and 4.* London: DFEE/QCA.

Department for Education and Skills (DfES) (2001a) *Schools: Achieving Success.* London: DfES.

Department for Education and Skills (DfES) (2001b) *Special Education Needs Code of Practice.* London: DfES.

Department for Education and Skills (DfES) (2001c) *Key Stage 3 National Strategy. Numeracy Across the Curriculum: Notes for School-based Training.* London: DfES Publications. (Download at www.standards.dfes.gov.uk/keystage3/publications).

Department for Education and Skills (DfES) (2001d) *Inclusive Schooling: Children with Special Educational Needs.* London: DfES.

Department for Education and Skills (DfES) (2002a) *Extending Opportunities: Raising Standards.* London: DfES.

Department for Education and Skills DfES (2002b) *Developing the Role of School Support Staff.* London: HMSO.

Department for Education and Skills (DfES) (2002c) *National Strategy for Key Stage 3: Managing the Second Year.* London: DfES.

Department for Education and Skills (DfES) (2003a) *14–19 Opportunity and Excellence.* London: DfES.

Department for Education and Skills (DfES) (2003b) *Working Group on 14–19 Reform. Principles for Reform of 14–19 Learning Programmes and Qualifications.* London: DfES.

Department for Education and Skills (DfES) (2003c) *Effective Teaching and Learning in Science.* London: DfES.

Department for Education and Skills (DfES) (2003d) *Aiming High: Raising the Achievement of Minority Ethnic Pupils.* London: DfES.

Department for Education and Skills (DfES) (2003e) *Every Child Matters.* London: DfES.

Department for Education and Skills (DfES) (2003f) *The Learning Challenge.* London: DfES.

Department for Education and Skills (DfES) (2004a) *A National Conversation about Personalised Learning.* London: DfES.

Department for Education and Skills (DfES) (2004b) *Working Group on 14–19 Reform: Interim Report.* London: DfES.

Department for Education and Skills (DfES) (2004c) *Strengthening Teaching and Learning in Science through Using Different Pedagogies Unit 1: Using Group Talk and Argument.* London: DfES.

Department for Education and Skills (DfES) (2005a) *Higher Standards, Better Schools for All.* London: HMSO.

Department for Education and Skills (DfES) (2005b) *Leading in Learning: Developing Thinking Skills at Key Stage Three.* London: DfES

Department for Education and Skills (DfES) (2005c) *Education and Skills.* London: HMSO.

Department for Education and Skills (DfES) (2006a) *The Offer to Schools for 2006.* London: DfES.

Department for Education and Skills (2006b) *The Five Year Strategy for Children and Learners: Maintaining the Excellent Progress.* London: DfES.

Department for Education and Skills (DfES) (2006c) *A Guide to the Law for School Governors.* London: DfES.

Department for Education and Skills (DfES) (2007) *2020 Vision: Report of the Teaching and Learning in 2020 Review Group.* London: DfES.

Department for Education and Skills (DfES)/Teacher Training Agency (TTA) (2002) *Qualifying to Teach: Professional Standards for Qualified Teacher Status and Requirements for Initial Teacher Training.* London: DFES/TTA.

Department for Education and Skills (DfES), Younger, M. and Warrington, M. (2003) *Raising Boys' Achievement* Interim Report. London, DfES.

Department of Education and Science (DES) (1978) *Special Educational Need* (Report of the Warnock Committee). London: HMSO.

Department of Education and Science (DES) (1975) *A Language for Life* (Bullock Report). London: HMSO.

Department of Education and Science (DES) (1988) *The Education Reform Act.* London: HMSO.

Department of Education and Science (DES) (1989) *Discipline in Schools: Report of the Committee of Enquiry chaired by Lord Elton.* London: HMSO.

Department of Health (DoH)(2003) *The Victoria Climbié Inquiry: Report Of An Inquiry By Lord Laming.* Presented to Parliament By the Secretary of State for Health and the Secretary of State for the Home Department by Command of Her Majesty. Cm 5730.

Dessent, T. (2006) Will Mrs Thatcher have her way? Future options for children's services, in B. Norwich (ed.) *Taking Stock: Integrated Children's Services, Improvement and Inclusion.* SEN Policy Options Group, Policy paper 1, 6th Series, accessible at www. Nasen.org.uk.

Docking, J. (ed.) (2000) *New Labour's Policies for Schools: Raising the Standard.* London: David Fulton.

Doyle, W. (1986) Classroom management and organisation, in M.C. Wittrock (ed.) *Handbook of Research on Teaching.* New York: Macmillan.

Dyson, A., Cummings, C. and Todd, C. (2004) *Evaluation of the Extended Schools Pathfinder Projects.* London: DfES.

Earl, E., Watson, N., Levin, B., Leithwood, K., Fullan, M. and Torrance, N. (2003) *Watching and Learning 3: Final Report of the External Evaluation of England's National Literacy and Numeracy Strategies.* London: DfES.

Dunn, R. (1990) Understanding the Dunn and Dunn learning styles model and the need for individual diagnosis and prescription, *Reading: Writing and Learning Disabilities,* 6: 223–47.

Elliott, B. and Calderhead, J. (1993) Mentoring for teacher development: possibilities and caveats, in D. Mcintyre, H. Hagger and M. Wilkinson (eds) (1994) *Mentoring: Perspectives on School-based Teacher Education.* London: Kogan Page.

Elliott, J. (1997) *The Curriculum Experiment: Meeting the Challenge of Social Change.* Buckingham: Open University Press.

Ellis, V., Butler, R. and Simpson, D. (2002) Planning for learning, in V. Ellis (ed.) *Learning and Teaching in Secondary Schools.* Exeter: Learning Matters.

Firth, D. C. (1977) *Coventry: 75 years of Service in Education. The Story of Coventry Education Committee.* Coventry: Coventry LEA.

Flem, A. Moen, T., and Gumusdottir, S. (2004) *Inclusive Practice: A Biographical Perspective.* Norwegian University of Science and Technology.

Flynn, J. R. (1994) IQ gains over time, in R.J. Sternberg (ed.) *Encyclopaedia of Human Intelligence.* New York: Macmillan.

Fones, D. (2001) Blocking them in to free them to act, *English in Education,* 36(3): 21–31.

Frater, G. (1997) *Improving Boys' Literacy.* London: The Basic Skills Agency.

Frederickson, N. and Cline, T. (2002) *Special Educational Needs, Inclusion and Diversity: A Textbook.* Buckingham: Open University Press.

Freeman, R. and Lewis, R. (1998) *Planning and Implementing Assessment.* London: Kogan Page.

Fullan, M. (2001) *The New Meaning of Educational Change.* London: Continuum.

Furlong, J. and Maynard, T. (1995) *Mentoring Student Teachers: The Growth of Professional Knowledge.* London: Routledge.

Gallagher, D.J. (2001) Neutrality as a moral standpoint, conceptual confusion and the full inclusion debate, *Disability and Society,* 16(5): 637–54.

Galloway, S. (2000) Issues and challenges in continuing professional development, in S. Galloway (ed.) *Continuous Professional Development: Looking Ahead.* Proceedings of a symposium by the Centre on Skills, Knowledge and Organisational Performance, Oxford, May 2000.

Gardner, H. (1983) *Frames of Mind*. New York: Basic Books.

Gardner, H. (1993) *Multiple Intelligences: The Theory in Practice*. New York: Basic Books.

Gardner, H. (1995) Reflections on the multiple intelligences: myths and messages, *Phi-Delta Kappan*, 77(3): 200–9.

Gardner, H. (2003) *Multiple Intelligences After 20 Years*. Presentation delivered at the Annual Meeting of the American Educational Research Association, Chicago, Ill, 21 April.

Gipps, C. (1994) *Beyond Testing: Towards a Theory of Educational Assessment*. London: Falmer.

Gipps, C. and Murphy, P. (1994) *A Fair Test? Assessment, Achievement and Equity*. Buckingham: Open University Press.

Goleman, D. (1996) *Emotional Intelligence: Why It Can Matter More Than IQ*. London: Bloomsbury.

Gould, J. (1983) *The Mismeasure of Man*. New York: Norton.

Graham, D. (1993) *A Lesson for All of Us? Making the National Curriculum*. London: Routledge.

Guild, P. (1994) The culture/learning style connection, *Education Leadership*, 51(8): 16–21.

Guppy, P. and Hughes, M. (1999) *The Development of Independent Reading*. Buckingham: Open University Press.

Gurian, M. (2001) *Boys and Girls Learn Differently!* San Francisco, CA: Jossey-Bass.

Hamblin, D. (1978) *The Teacher and Pastoral Care*. Oxford: Basil Blackwell.

Hardiker, P., Exton, K. and Barker, M. (1991) *Policies and Practices in Preventive Child Care*. Aldershot: Avebury.

Hargreaves, D.H. (2003) From improvement to transformation. Keynote address to the 16th International Congress for School Effectiveness and Improvement, Sydney, January 2003.

Hargreaves, D.H., Hestor, S. and Mellor, F. (1975) *Deviance in Classrooms*. London: Routledge & Kegan Paul.

Harlen, W. and Deakin Crick, R. (2002) A systematic review of the impact of summative assessment and tests on students' motivation for learning (EPPI-Centre Review, version 1.1*), in *Research Evidence in Education Library*. London: EPPI-Centre, Social Science Research Unit, Institute of Education.

Harris, A. (1998) Effective teaching: a review of the literature, *School Leadership and Management*, 18(2): 169–83.

Harris, A. (2002) *School Improvement: What's in it for Schools?* London: Routledge.

Harrison, C., Comber, C., Fisher, T. et al. (2002) *ImpaCT2 – The Impact of Information and Communication Technologies on Pupil Learning and Attainment*. Coventry: Becta.

Hart, S. (1996) *Beyond Special Needs: Enhancing Children's Learning Through Innovative Thinking*. London: Paul Chapman.

Haydon, G. (1997) *Teaching About Values: A New Approach*. London: Cassell.

Head, J. (1995) *Gender Identity and Cognitive Style*. Paper presented at the UNESCO colloquium: *Is there a pedagogy for girls?* London.

Heater, D. (2001) The history of citizenship education, *The Curriculum Journal*, 12(1): 103–24.

Hegarty, S. (1993) Reviewing the literature on integration, *European Journal of Special Needs Education*, 8(3): 194–200.

Hilgard, E. (1995) *Theories of Learning*. New York: Appleton.

HMI (2002) *Achievement of Black Caribbean Pupils: Good Practice in Secondary Schools*. London: HMSO.

HMSO (1999) *Highly Able Children. Third Report form the Education and Employment Committee 1998–99*. London: HMSO.

HMSO (2002) *Education Act*. London: HMSO.

Hopkins, D. (2003) Transforming schools. Keynote address to DfES 'Transforming Schools Conference', London, September.

House of Commons Education and Skills Committee (2005) *Every Child Matters: House of Commons Select Committee Report*. www.publications.parliament.uk/pa/cm200405/cmselect/cmeduski/40/4002.htm

House of Commons Education and Skills Committee (2006) *Public Expenditure on Education and Skills*. London: The Stationery Office Limited.

Howe, M.J.A. (1997) *IQ in Question: The Truth about Intelligence*. London: Sage.

Huddleston, P. (2002) Uncertain destinies: student recruitment and retention on GNVQ intermediate programmes, *SKOPE Research Paper*, 37, Winter.

Ireson, J. (1999) *Innovative Grouping Practices in Secondary Schools*. London: DfEE.

Jordan, J. (1974) The organisation of perspectives in teacher–pupil relations: an interactionist approach. MEd thesis, University of Manchester, cited by B. Joyce, E. Calhoun and D. Hopkins (1998) *Models of Teaching: Tools for Learning*. Buckingham: Open University Press.

Joyce, B., Calhoun, E. and Hopkins, D. (1998) *Models of Teaching: Tools for Learning*. Buckingham: Open University Press.

Kerr, D. (1999) *Re-examining Citizenship Education: The Case of England*. Slough: NFER.

Kerr. D. (2005) 'England's teenagers fail the patriotic test': the lessons from England's participation in the IEA Civic Education Study, in S. Wilde (ed.) *Political and Citizenship Education: International Perspectives*. London: Symposium.

Kerr, D., Cleaver, E., Ireland, E. and Blenkinsop, S. (2003) *Citizenship Education Longitudinal Study: First Cross-sectional Survey 2001–2002*. London: DFES.

Kinder, K., Wakefield, A. and Wilkin, A. (1996) *Talking Back: Pupil Views on Disaffection*. Slough: NFER.

Klein, P.D. (1997) Multiplying the problems of intelligence by eight: a critique of Gardner's theory, *Canadian Journal of Education*, 22(4): 377–94.

Kohn, M. (1995) In two minds, *Guardian Weekend*, 5 August.

Kotulak, R. (1996) *Inside the Brain*. Kansas City: Universal Press Syndicate.

Kyriacou, C. (2005) The impact of daily mathematics lessons in England on pupil confidence and competence in early mathematics: a systematic review, *British Journal of Educational Studies*, 53 (2): 168–86.

Kress, G. (2003) *Literacy in the New Media Age*. London: Routledge.

Lackney, J.A. (1999) Twelve design principles for schools derived from brain-based learning research, *Schoolhouse Journal*, 2(2): 1–12.

Lang, P. (1999) Counselling, counselling skills and encouraging pupils to talk: clarifying and addressing confusion, *British Journal of Guidance and Counselling*, 27(1): 23–33.

Leitch, A. (2006) *Prosperity for All in the Global Economy – World Class Skills*, Final Report. London: HM Treasury.

Leask, M. (ed.) (2001) *Issues in Teaching Using ICT*. London: RoutledgeFalmer.

Lewis, M. and Wray, D. (1998) *Writing Across the Curriculum*. Reading: Reading Language Information Centre.

Lewis, M., and Wray, D. (eds) (2000) *Literacy in the Secondary School*. London: David Fulton Publishers.

Lightfoot, L. (1997) Attention span of boys' only five minutes, *Daily Telegraph*, 26 April.

Lindsay, G. (2003) Inclusive education: a critical perspective, *British Journal of Special Education*, 30(1): 3–12.

Little, J. W. (1993) Teachers' professional development in a climate of educational reform, *Educational Evaluation and Policy Analysis*, 15(2): 129–51.

MacGrath, M. (1998) *The Art of Teaching Peacefully*. London: David Fulton.

McGuiness, C. (1998) *From thinking Skills to Thinking Classrooms*. London: DfEE.

Macpherson Report (1999) *The Stephen Lawrence Inquiry: Report of an Inquiry by Sir William Macpherson*. London: HMSO.

McWilliam, N. (1998) *What's in a World?* Trentham Books: London

Madden, N.A. and Slavin, R.E. (1983) Mainstreaming students with mild handicaps: academic and social outcomes, *Review of Educational Research*, 52(4): 519–69.

Margo, J. and Dixon, M. (2006) *Freedom's Orphans: Raising Youth in a Changing World*. London: Institute for Public Policy Research.

Marland, M. (1974) *Pastoral Care*. London: Heinemann.

Marrin, M. (1997) Mr Evans is right about women MPs, *Sunday Telegraph*, 9 March.

Marshall, T. H. (1950) *Citizenship and Social Class, and Other Essays*. Cambridge: Cambridge University Press.

Megahy, T. (1998) Managing the curriculum: pastoral care as a vehicle for raising student achievement, in M. Calvert and J. Henderson (eds) *Managing Pastoral Care*. London: Cassell.

Midgley, P., Beskeen, L., Egginton, N. et al. (1999) *Promoting Students' Spiritual, Moral, Social and Cultural Development through Specific Learning Strategies across the Curriculum*. (www.becal.net/toolkit/smrtvalues/documents/values_interventions_summary_report.pdf)

Milbourne, L., Macrae, S. and Maguire, M. (2003) Collaborative solutions or new policy problems: exploring multi-agency partnerships in education and health work, *Journal of Education Policy*, 18(1): 19–35.

Moll, L. (1992) Literacy research in community and classrooms: a sociocultural approach, in R. Beach, J. Green, M. Kamil and T. Shanahan (eds) *Multidisciplinary Perspectives on Literacy Research*. Urbana, IL: National Council of Teachers of English.

Morgan, H (1996). An analysis of Gardner's Theory of Multiple Intelligence, *Roeper Review*, 18: 263–9.

Muijs, R. D. (1997) *Self, School and Media: A Longitudinal Study of Media Use, Self-concept, School Achievement and Peer Relations Among Primary School Children*. Leuven: Catholic University of Leuven, Department of Communication Science.

Muijs, R.D. (2004) *Doing Quantitative Research in Education*. London: Sage.

Muijs, R.D. and Reynolds, D. (2002) Teachers' beliefs and behaviors: what matters, *Journal of Classroom Interaction*, 37(2): 3–15.

Muijs, D., Day, C., Harris, A. and Lindsay, G. (2004) Evaluating CPD: an overview, in C. Day and J. Sachs (eds) *International Handbook on the Continuing Professional Development of Teachers*. Maidenhead: Open University Press.

Muijs, R.D. and Reynolds, D. (2003) Student background and teacher effects on achievement and attainment in mathematics, *Educational Review and Evaluation*, 9(1): 289–313.

National Advisory Committee on Creative and Cultural Education (1999) *All our Futures: Creativity, Culture and Education*. London: DfEE and DCMS.

National Curriculum: www.nc.uk.net/index.html

National Curriculum Council (1990) *Curriculum Guidance Eight: Education for Citizenship*. York: National Curriculum Council.

Neill, S. and Caswell, C. (1993) *Body Language for Competent Teachers*. London: Routledge.

Nesta (2004) *The Good Guide to Interactive Whiteboards*. Hull: University of Hull.

Newsome, D. (1961) *Godliness and Good Learning*. London: John Murray.

Newton, L. and Rogers, L. (2001) *Teaching Science with ICT*. London: Continuum.

Nolan Committee (1996) *Second Report to the Committee on Standards in Public Life*. London: HMSO.

Norman, K. (ed.) (1992) *Thinking Voices: The Work of the National Oracy Project*. London: Hodder & Stoughton.

Norwich Area Schools Consortium (NASC) (2002) *Pupil Perceptions of School Subjects.* Online at www.uea.ac.uk/~m242/nasc/cross/cman/leasteffort.htm

O'Donohue, W. and Ferguson, K. (2001) *The Psychology of B.F. Skinner.* Thousand Oaks: Sage.

O'Neill, O. (2002) Reith Lectures available online www.bbc.co.uk/radio4/reith2002.

OECD/UNESCO (2003) *Literacy Skills for the World of Tomorrow.* www.oecd.org

Office for Standards in Education (Ofsted) (1993) *Access and Achievement in Urban Education.* London: Ofsted.

Office for Standards in Education (Ofsted) (1994) *Spiritual, Moral, Social and Cultural Education: A Discussion Paper.* London: Ofsted.

Office for Standards in Education (Ofsted) (1996a) *The Annual Report of Her Majesty's Chief Inspector of Schools.* London: HMSO.

Office for Standards in Education (Ofsted) (1996b) *Recent Research on the Achievements of Minority Ethnic Pupils.* London: HMI.

Office for Standards in Education (Ofsted) (1998) *Secondary Education 1993–1997: A Review of Secondary Schools in England.* London: HMSO.

Office for Standards in Education (Ofsted) (1999) *Raising the Attainment of Minority Ethnic Pupils.* London: HMI.

Office for Standards in Education (Ofsted) (2002a) *Inspecting Spiritual, Moral, Social and Cultural Education: Guidance for Inspectors.* London: Ofsted.

Office for Standards in Education (Ofsted) (2003a) *Boys' Achievement in Secondary Schools.* London: HMSO.

Office for Standards in Education (Ofsted) (2003b) *Quality and Standards in Secondary Initial Teacher Training.* London: Ofsted.

Office for Standards in Education (Ofsted) (2004) *Promoting and Evaluating Pupils' Spiritual, Moral, Social and Cultural Development.* London: Ofsted.

Office for Standards in Education (Ofsted) (2005a) *Framework for the Inspection of Schools from September 2005.* London: Ofsted.

Office for Standards in Education (Ofsted) (2005b) *Annual Report of Her Majesty's Chief Inspector for Schools.* London: Ofsted.

Office for Standards in Education (Ofsted) (2006a) *Towards Consensus? Citizenship in Secondary Schools.* London: Ofsted.

Office for Standards in Education (Ofsted) (2006b) *Annual Report of Her Majesty's Chief Inspector of Schools.* London: Ofsted.

Partnership for Schools (2007) *Partnerships for Schools.* Available on-line at www.p4s.org.uk/

Piaget, J. (2001) *The Child's Conception of Physical Causality.* New Brunswick, NJ: Transaction Publishers.

Peters (2006) *Inclusion Imperative.* Paper presented at the two-day National Conference Honoring Diversity. New York, Syracuse University Hotel.

Pollard, A. and James, M. (2004) Personalised Learning: A Commentary by the Teaching and Learning Research Programme. London: DfES (available at www.tlrp.org/documents/ESRCPerson.pdf).

Porter, L. (2000) *Behaviour in Schools: Theory and Practice for Teachers.* Buckingham: Open University Press.

Power, S. (1996) *The Pastoral and the Academic: Conflict and Contradiction in the Curriculum.* London: Cassell.

Pring, R. (1984) Personal and social education in the primary school, in P. Lang (ed.) *Thinking about ... Personal and Social Education in the Primary School.* Oxford: Blackwell.

Qualifications and Curriculum Authority (QCA) (1998) *Education for Citizenship and the*

Teaching of Democracy in Schools: Final Report of the Advisory Group on Citizenship. London: QCA.

Qualifications and Curriculum Authority (QCA) (1999a) *The National Numeracy Strategy: Teaching Mental Calculation Strategies: Guidance for Teachers at Key Stages 1 and 2.* London: QCA.

Qualifications and Curriculum Authority (QCA) (1999b) *The National Numeracy Strategy: Teaching Written Calculations: Guidance for Teachers at Key Stages 1 and 2.* London: QCA.

Qualifications and Curriculum Authority (QCA) (1999c) *Qualifications 16–19: A Guide to the Changes Resulting from the Qualifying for Success Consultation.* London: QCA.

Qualifications and Curriculum Authority (QCA) (2000a) *A Language in Common: Assessing English as an Additional Language.* London: QCA.

Qualifications and Curriculum Authority (QCA) (2000b) *Personal, Social and Health Education at Key Stages 3 and 4: Initial Guidance for Schools.* London: QCA.

Qualifications and Curriculum Authority (QCA) (2001) *Citizenship: A Scheme of Work for Key Stage 3: Teacher's Guide.* London: QCA.

Qualifications and Curriculum Authority (QCA) (2003) *Non Statutory Guidelines for PSHE at Key Stages 3 and 4.* London: QCA.

QCA: http://www.standards.DfES.gov.uk/schemes3/

Qualifications and Curriculum Authority (QCA)/Department for Education and Employment (DfEE) (1999) *The National Curriculum.* London: HMSO.

Qualifications and Curriculum Authority (QCA) NFER (2003) *Consultation on Proposed Changes to the Key Stage 4 Curriculum.* Slough: NFER.

Race Relation (Amendment) Act (2000) *New Laws for a Successful Multi-racial Britain.* London: Home Office.

Reynolds, D. Treharne, D., and Tripp, H. (2003) ICT – the hopes and the reality, *British Journal of Educational Technology*, 34(2): 151–67.

Richardson, R. and Wood, A. (1999) *Inclusive Schools, Inclusive Society.* Stoke-on-Trent: Trentham Books.

Riding, R. and Cheema, I. (1991) Cognitive style – an overview and integration, *Educational Psychology*, 65: 113–24.

Robinson, K. and Jones-Diaz, C. (2006) *Diversity and Difference in Early Childhood Education: Issues for Theory and Practice.* Maidenhead: Open University Press.

Rodd, J. (2002) *Learning to Learn in Schools.* Crediton: Campaign for Learning.

Rogers, B. (1998) *You Know the Fair Rule: Strategies for Making the Hard Job of Discipline in School Easier.* London: Pitman.

Rogers, B. (2006) *Classroom Behaviour: A Practical Guide to Effective Teaching, Behaviour Management and Colleague Support*, 2nd edn. London: Paul Chapman.

Rose, D. and Meyer, A. (2002) *Teaching in the Digital Age.* Alexandria, VA: ASCD.

Sammons, P., Hillman, J. and Mortimore, P. (1995) *Key Characteristics of Effective Schools: A Review of School Effectiveness Research.* Ringwood: MBC Distribution Services.

Saraga, E. (1998) Children's needs: who decides? in M. Langan (ed.) *Welfare: Needs, Rights and Risks*, London: Routledge/Open University.

Schön, D. (1983) *The Reflective Practitioner.* New York: Basic Books.

Schools Curriculum and Assessment Authority (SCAA) (1995) *Spiritual and Moral Development.* London: SCAA.

Schools Curriculum and Assessment Authority (SCAA) (1997) *Consultation on Values in Education and the Community.* London: SCAA.

Selwyn, N. (2001) Why the computer is not dominating schools: a failure of policy or a failure of practice?, *Cambridge Journal of Education*, 29(1): 77–92.

Shakespeare, T. and Watson, N. (2002) The social model of disability: an outmoded ideology? *Research in Social Science and Disability*, 2: 9–28.

Shipman, K. and Hicks, K. (1998) *How Can Teachers Motivate Less Able Boys?* London: TTA.

Shulman, L. S. (1986) Those who understand: knowledge growth in teaching, *Educational Researcher*, 15: 4–14.

Skinner, B.F. (1974) *About Behaviorism*. New York: Random House.

Slee, R. (2001) *The Inclusive School*. London: Falmer.

Smith, R. and Alred, G. (1994) The impersonation of wisdom, in D. McIntyre, H. Hagger and M. Wilkin (eds) *Mentoring: Perspectives on School-based Teacher Education*. London: Kogan Page.

Somekh, B., Underwood, J., Convery, A. et al. (2006) *Evaluation of the ICT Test Bed Project, Annual Report*. Coventry: Becta.

Somekh, B., Lewin, C., Mavers, D. et al. (2002) *ImpaCT2 – Pupils' and Teachers' Perceptions of ICT in the Home, School and Community*. Coventry: Becta.

Sousa, D. (1998) Brain research can help principals reform secondary schools, *NASSP Bulletin*, 82(598): 21–8.

Tett, T., Crowther, J. and O'Hara, P. (2003) Collaborative Partnerships in community education, *Journal of Education Policy*, 18(1) 37–51.

Thomas, G. (1997) Inclusive schools for an inclusive society, *British Journal of Special Education*, 24(3): 103–7.

Tomlinson, J.B. (1984) *Studies in the Theory of Ideology*. Berkeley, CA: University of California Press.

Tomlinson, M. (2002) *Inquiry into A Level Standards Final Report*. London: QCA.

Tomlinson, P. (1995) *Understanding Mentoring*. Buckingham: Open University Press.

Tomlinson, S. (2000) Ethnic minority and education: new disadvantages, in T. Cox (ed.) *Combating Educational Disadvantage: Meeting the Needs of Vulnerable Children*. London: Falmer Press.

Training and Development Agency for Schools (TDA) (2007) *Professional Standards for Teachers*. London: TDA.

Tyler, K. and Jones, B.D. (2002) Teachers' responses to the ecosystemic approach to changing chronic problem behaviour in schools, *Pastoral Care in Education*, 20(2).

UNESCO (United Nations Educational, Scientific and Cultural Organization) (1994) *The Salamanca Statement and Framework for Action on Special Needs Education*. Paris: UNESCO.

Unsworth, L. (2001) *Teaching Multiliteracies Across the Curriculum*. Maidenhead: Open University Press.

Vygotsky, L.S. (1962) *Thought and Language*. Cambridge, MA: MIT Press.

Vygotsky, L.S. (1978) *Mind in Society: The Development of Higher Psychological Processes*. Cambridge, MA: Harvard University Press.

Vygotsky, L.S. (1986) *Thought and Language*. Cambridge, MA: The MIT Press.

Walsh, B. (2003) Building learning packages: integrating virtual resources with the real world of teaching and learning, in T. Haydn and C. Counsell (eds) *History, ICT and Learning*. London, RoutledgeFalmer.

Watkins, C. and Wagner, P. (2000) *Improving School Behaviour*. London: Paul Chapman.

Watson, D. (2001) Pedagogy before technology: re-thinking the relationship between ICT and teaching, *Education and Information Technologies*, 6(4): 251–66.

Wertsch, J. and Tulviste, P. (1992) L.S. Vygotsky and contemporary developmental psychology, *Developmental Psychology*, 28(4): 548–57.

White, J. (1998) *Do Howard Gardner's Multiple Intelligences Add Up?* London: Institute of Education, University of London.

Wiliam, D. and Black, P. (1996) Meanings and consequences: a basis for distinguishing formative and summative functions of assessment?, *British Educational Research Journal*, 22(5): 537–48.

Wintersgill, B. (2002) Spiritual development – what do teenagers think it is? Unpublished MA Field Study, University of Warwick.

Wong Fillmore, L. (1991) Second language learning in children, a model of language learning in social context, in E. Bialystock (ed.) *Language Processing in Bilingual Children*. Cambridge: Cambridge University Press.

Wubbels, T. (1992) Taking account of student teachers' preconceptions, *Teaching and Teacher Education*, 8: 47–58.

Younger, M. (2002) How should we teach boys? *Independent*, 12 September.

Younger, M. and Warrington, M. (2005) *Raising Boys' Achievement*, DfES Research Report No.636. London: HMSO.

Zigmond, N. and Baker, J.M. (1995) An exploration of the meaning and practice of special education in the context of full inclusion of students with learning disabilities, *Journal of Special Education*, 29(2): 1–25.

Index